CRITICAL RHYTHM

VERBAL ARTS: STUDIES IN POETICS

Lazar Fleishman and Haun Saussy, series editors

Critical Rhythm

The Poetics of a Literary Life Form

BEN GLASER AND
JONATHAN CULLER, EDITORS

Fordham University Press
NEW YORK   2019

Copyright © 2019 Fordham University Press

All rights reserved. No part of this publication may be reproduced, stored in a retrieval system, or transmitted in any form or by any means—electronic, mechanical, photocopy, recording, or any other—except for brief quotations in printed reviews, without the prior permission of the publisher.

Fordham University Press has no responsibility for the persistence or accuracy of URLs for external or third-party Internet websites referred to in this publication and does not guarantee that any content on such websites is, or will remain, accurate or appropriate.

Fordham University Press also publishes its books in a variety of electronic formats. Some content that appears in print may not be available in electronic books.

Visit us online at www.fordhampress.com.

Library of Congress Cataloging-in-Publication Data

Names: Glaser, Ben, editor. | Culler, Jonathan D., editor.
Title: Critical rhythm : the poetics of a literary life form / Ben Glaser and Jonathan Culler, editors.
Description: New York : Fordham University Press, 2019. | Series: Verbal arts: studies in poetics | Includes bibliographical references and index.
Identifiers: LCCN 2018028222| ISBN 9780823282043 (cloth : alk. paper) | ISBN 9780823282036 (pbk. : alk. paper)
Subjects: LCSH: Rhythm in literature. | Poetics—History—19th century. | Poetics—History—20th century.
Classification: LCC PN1059.R53 C75 2019 | DDC 808.1—dc23
LC record available at https://lccn.loc.gov/2018028222

Printed in the United States of America

21 20 19   5 4 3 2 1

First edition

Contents

Introduction
Ben Glaser — 1

Rhythm's Critiques

Why Rhythm?
Jonathan Culler — 21

What Is Called Rhythm?
David Nowell Smith — 40

Sordello's Pristine Pulpiness
Simon Jarvis — 60

Body, Throng, Race

The Cadence of Consent: Francis Barton Gummere,
Lyric Rhythm, and White Poetics
Virginia Jackson — 87

Contagious Rhythm: Verse as a Technique of the Body
Haun Saussy — 106

Constructing Walt Whitman: Literary History
and Histories of Rhythm
Erin Kappeler — 128

Beat and Count

The Rhythms of the English Dolnik
Derek Attridge — 153

How to Find Rhythm on a Piece of Paper
Thomas Cable — 174

Picturing Rhythm
Meredith Martin — 197

Fictions of Rhythm

Beyond Meaning: Differing Fates of Some Modernist Poets' Investments of Belief in Sounds
Natalie Gerber — 223

Sapphic Stanzas: How Can We Read the Rhythm?
Yopie Prins — 247

Rhythm and Affect in "Christabel"
Ewan Jones — 274

Acknowledgments — 297
List of Contributors — 299
Index — 303

Critical Rhythm

Introduction

Ben Glaser

Winter, writes W. H. Auden, is a "time for the trying-out / Of new meters and new recipes, proper time / To reflect on events noted in warmer months."[1] Those months follow a natural and unconscious rhythm:

> Spring-time, summer and fall: days to behold a world
> Antecedent to our knowing, where flowers think
> Theirs concretely in scent-colors and beasts, the same
> Age all over, pursue dumb horizontal lives
> On one level of conduct and so cannot be
> Secretary to man's plot to become divine.
> Lodged in all is a set metronome: thus, in May
> Bird-babes still in the egg click to each other *Hatch!*
>
> (1–8)

This metronomic clicking echoes the term famously chosen by Ezra Pound to forbid what he took to be the unnatural thud of overly metrical iambic rhythm: "As regarding rhythm: to compose in the sequence of the musical phrase, not in sequence of a metronome."[2] Auden revisits the dictum and asks how poetic meter defies the potentially limited rhythms of lived experience. His poem does more than imagine a different, metrical temporality. The careful enjambment of "proper time" yokes "new meters" with winter, translating the syntactical yoking of cooking and meter—of life and art—into a metrical experience in its own right. That experience requires in turn another round of wintry reflection; the poem is written in asclepiads, an Aeolic Greek meter built around a choriambic nucleus

(–˘ ˘–). Auden refers to his poem as "accentual Asclepiadeans," replacing the classical quantities of long and short with stress and unstress: / x / x x / / x x / x /.³ This import is out of joint not just with English's more-or-less native iambics but with the usual stories about how meter's abstracted pattern emerges from the welter of linguistic (and other) rhythm as natural artifice, as a sensitive abstraction from the feel of an accentual tongue. To "reflect" in such a meter is not to seamlessly or properly engage the native or collective rhythms of a linguistic and cultural heritage. It is to encounter rhythm (through meter) as a defamiliarized and defamiliarizing force.

In an earlier and more sanguine moment, however, when Auden is editing an anthology to convince a suburban, commuting British public that they already like poetry and should do more of what they like, he depends upon a very broad sense of rhythm as both a social and aesthetic form:

> All speech has rhythm, which is the result of the combination of the alternating periods of effort and rest necessary to all living things, and the laying of emphasis on what we consider important; and in all poetry there is a tension between the rhythm due to the poet's personal values, and those due to the experiences of generations crystallised into habits of language such as the English tendency to alternate weak and accented syllables, and conventional verse forms like the hexameter, the heroic pentameter . . .⁴

Here "rhythm" means linguistic rhythm, physical or physiological rhythm, the idiolect or subjective stressing of "the poet's personal values," and finally something closer to meter. I quote this in part to show the messiness and power of rhythm as it is called up by criticism. The passage manifests rhythm's scalar power in the critical imagination and its tendency to paradoxically transcend the boundaries of the literary (or the poetic or lyric) in order to establish new aesthetic domains. That rhythm cannot always sustain this boundary game is, in my reading, one subject of "In Due Season." There, even the commonplace "tension" between two *rhythms*—the idiosyncratic rhythm of the poet's tongue and the rhythms of traditional meters—becomes a largely abstract tension between devalued conventional meter and a meter with largely "personal value." As the prosodist Paul Fussell reminds us in *Poetic Meter and Poetic Form* (1965), Auden's self-described "dream reader" is one who "keeps a look out for curious prosodic fauna like bacchics and choriambs."⁵ Are we such readers? What does it mean to discover innovative rhythms not by experience and intuition but through recognition of marked metrical idiosyncrasy? How does poetry fare as a genre when poems leave the formalist pathways that happily accept meter as a reflection of and on linguistic rhythm? What happens when, as with most theories of post-metrical and free verse, criticism makes a sharp turn to rhythm?

In the following pages I will suggest that a critical concept of rhythm more attentive to its genesis and present function will substantially aid present debates over formalism and its objects. I will suggest some paths forward from several tricky moments in twentieth- and twenty-first-century efforts to corral rhythm in order to articulate conceptions of form, poetry, and the literary. I pay special attention to pivots between meter and rhythm, such as Auden's. My readings, and the essays in this volume, reveal in rhythm a term at once suspicious and essential to the discipline of literary study. My co-editor notes, in his recent *Theory of the Lyric*, how "seductive" rhythm can be.[6] Readers will find an extensive survey of "statements about the foundational character of rhythm" for poetry in the opening pages of his chapter on "Rhythm and Repetition." These make clear that the attraction of rhythm as sound device tends to become the attraction of the concept of rhythm, especially as it offers escapes from interpretation or from what some see as a too hermetic concept of formalism.

Critical Rhythm asks where the attraction of rhythm comes from, and how it operates (secretly or openly) in the history and present practice of criticism. A blunt but telling measure of that attraction might be the institutional prominence of Derek Attridge's treatise *The Rhythms of English Poetry* and the eight reprints of his shorter handbook *Poetic Rhythm: An Introduction* between 1995 and 2008. When and why is it the case that rhythm, as Attridge puts it, arrives "not as one of a number of features that make up the poetic experience, but the heart of the experience"?[7] Like "In Due Season," which interrogates an idea of rhythm that Auden articulated more than three decades earlier but also entices us carefully back to the rhythms of "the poet's personal values," *Critical Rhythm* continues to reimagine rhythm as the potential nucleus of our engagement with poetry. In his contribution here, Attridge defines a widespread foundation of rhythmic play in what he calls the "English Dolnik," but also attests to the variations and variable difficulties of its poetic executions. Thus if rhythm is still an apt synecdoche for poetic experience, that experience will not appear as unitary or given as the beating of a heart. As these essays worry our rhythmic inheritance, they consistently warn against taking rhythm to be a given, preexisting formal element later sorted out through scansion, description, and taxonomy. They press beyond isolated descriptions of technique, in the style of the prosody and poetics handbook, or inductive declarations of what rhythm "is," and towards genealogical and methodological inquiry. In doing so they develop new critical models for understanding how rhythm, in light of its historicity and generic functions, permeates poetry's composition, formal objectivity, circulation, performance, and present critical horizons.

In large part the following essays center on literary and specifically poetic concepts of rhythm, though they engage with cognitive linguistics, anthropology, musicology and scientific acoustics, and continental philosophy. The collection is largely but not exclusively focused on English language poetry and criticism, primarily post-1800, for reasons detailed in this essay and several others. Attridge, in his entry on "Rhythm" for the *Princeton Encyclopedia of Poetry and Poetics*, provides a straightforward rationale for this periodization: "by the eighteenth century [rhythm] was being consistently employed to refer to the durational qualities of poetry and music, and soon extended to analogous properties of the visual arts. In the nineteenth century it was generalized to movement of a regular kind—most often the alternation of strong and weak elements—in any sphere, and appropriated by the physical sciences for periodicities and patterns in a wide range of natural phenomenon."[8] This narrative makes clear that there is much to be said about rhythm not covered here; a different set of essays could treat rhythm in cinema, visual arts, music, works of prose, and literature of many languages and time periods. But it also makes a clear case for scholars interested in rhythm outside this domain to reckon with its genesis in literary discourse of the past quarter-millennium.

Why is rhythm so portable or, less generously, labile? How do we account for the returns of such a peripatetic concept to literary discourse? Should we play along when poets and critics construct categories and genres around rhythm, often through genitive and adjectival constructions such as the "rhythm of verse" or the "rhythmic experience" of novelistic form? The latter example comes from Caroline Levine's recent *Forms: Whole, Rhythm, Hierarchy, Network*. Levine explicitly adopts rhythm as a "term," "category," and "organizing concept" for her project because of its portability: "The term *rhythm* moves easily back and forth between aesthetic and non-aesthetic uses."[9] I would argue that the critical license to count rhythm as a form, or to define form through rhythm, derives from the history Attridge begins to trace in his entry and which this collection helps flesh out. This history, especially the late nineteenth-century reframing of poetic meter as a matter of the human pulse, supplies excellent material for the embodied, anti-hermetic, "political" formalism Levine pursues. She begins her chapter on "Rhythm" with an observation about this history: "Unlike the constraints of artful unities and rigid boundaries, rhythmic forms have often seemed natural, arising from the lived time of the human body."[10] This limited appeal to organicism becomes "conventional" and "traditional" as we arrive at Levine's own formalist practice:

> It is conventional to say that there are work rhythms and social rhythms. The traditional claim that poetic and musical rhythms arise in the body suggests an easy crossover between artistic and nonartistic realms. Rhythm is therefore a category that always already refuses the distinction between aesthetic form and other forms of lived experience.[11]

Between the nineteenth century and the present, following the demands and desires of formalism at its "millennial reboot,"[12] rhythm grows into the expansive, analogic role most exemplified by the genitive form "rhythm of." This suggests that we might alter "always already" to "has come to," and then explore both the slippery notions of the aesthetic or literary hiding behind rhythm and the sometimes awkward necessity of rhythm to conceptions of form and formalist practice.

David Nowell Smith suggests one such approach in his essay's wide-ranging survey of philosophical and literary conceptions of rhythm. Rhythm is central, he argues, in laying the ground for the post-Kantian critical subject's appearance in language and poetry. But it is also a proleptic figure, always doing explanatory work in advance of labors of definition. For Philippe Lacoue-Labarthe and others it is a "legend" in a double sense: both key and myth. The double view of rhythm as key and myth for definitions of literary and poetic language resonates across the diverse contexts of these essays. For example, rhythm is a key to understanding twentieth-century African-American poetry as it participates in and builds from musical traditions like the spirituals or blues. But it also evokes the myth of the "naturally musical black," and a much longer tradition of racializing subjects and peoples through theories of rhythmic aptitude and development.

Rhythm is the key, in several essays in this collection, to understanding the critical force through which poems rupture dominant logical, representational, or conceptual views of language. This has special importance for lyric theory, an important area of debate in essays by Virginia Jackson and others.[13] Even as rhythm offers criticism an opportunity to reassert textual musicality, the potential for alternate voicing, and the development of new kinds of sympathetic awareness, it remains as a myth unfolding logics of expressive form and voice that threaten to submerge technical play. As Yopie Prins' essay shows, for instance, poets have long sought "a primal rhythm" and Sappho herself at the "heart" of the Sapphic stanza.

Perhaps the foremost rhythmic "legend" involves this claim to embodiment and experience, especially in the (prosodic) phonology of spoken language. This was the case well before structural and generative linguistics began articulating increasingly more refined theories of exactly how rhythm manifests in language (for instance, the "English Rhythm Rule").[14] Rhythm, unlike meter, rarely gets described without some claim that it can be heard, felt, and shared because it has physical effects on bodies or tympanums. Valéry, in a passage cited by Culler, claimed that it is "via rhythm and the sensory properties of language that literature can reach the organic being of a reader with any confidence in the conformity between intention and the results." Yet it can be odd, if not unfortunate, to use the same word to describe both linguistic and poetic rhythm. That the latter has been most commonly understood as an abstraction from linguistic properties and assigned the name "meter" suggests we must pause and consider rhythm's complex relation to meter.

Meter and Rhythm

An argument could be made that "critical meter" might more safely retain the historicity of versification, and indeed several of the essays below gain traction from studying the techniques of traditions best called metrical. There has been excellent and diverse work on meter in historical prosody, a field that at its best puts formalist and cultural studies methodologies in conversation with help from archival work and digital projects. Recent debates within and about historical poetics also focus on meter.[15] So in a sense we are already benefiting from a newly critical sense of meter, one that reveals both the centrality and eccentricity of rhythm within a prosodic discourse whose focal term was, until the twentieth century, meter.

There continues to be a strong and useful tendency within Anglo-American criticism to think primarily in terms of meter, and to limit rhythm to what Isobel Armstrong has helpfully called the "binary account of meter": its normative metrical pattern and rhythmic departures.[16] For instance, John Hollander's *Rhyme's Reason*, which playfully enacts a range of meters and forms with emphasis on local effects, defines rhythm in the limited sense of a "particular rhythm which depart[s] from the metrical pattern slightly."[17] Like *Rhyme's Reason*, Timothy Steele's 1999 *All the Fun's in How You Say a Thing: An Explanation of Meter and Versification* prefers the term "meter." This is to be expected from the author of *Missing Measures* and two books of poetry in Sapphics. At less generous moments meter has been understood as a prescription, as merely one rigid and codified rhythmic possibility. Attridge, in the encyclopedia entry on "Rhythm" noted earlier, feels no such prescription yet argues that "meter can be . . . understood as a particular form of rhythm" and that meter is perceived when regularities in "language's natural rhythm" become "marked."[18]

Modernism in particular structured its ideas of prosody around the realignment of meter as a species of rhythm rather than a meaningful aesthetic process defined by the abstraction and patterning of linguistic material. As tracked here in Natalie Gerber's study of modernism's particular extremities of belief in alternate terminologies, twentieth-century invocations of rhythm frequently harbor a desire to escape the merely "technical." Rhythm's importance to modernist and then twentieth-century poetics helps explains why the first word of Fussell's aforementioned handbook is "rhythm." It begins a quotation of Ezra Pound—"Rhythm *must* have meaning"—an idea Fussell immediately restates in terms of meter: "Meter is a prime physical and emotional constituent of poetic meaning."[19] That Fussell doesn't intend to equate meter and rhythm bespeaks the slippery relation between the two terms; elsewhere he frames rhythm in the binary sense, as the opposition between a "'sense' pattern of the language" and the "normal or 'base' abstract rhythm of the metrical scheme."[20] Moreover, Fussell emphasizes how poems often "reveal an excitement with meter almost as an object of fundamental meaning itself." Why start with Pound's comment—in its epistolary context a screed against meter's tendency to produce cliché[21]—only to revert to technical formulations of rhythm as a property of language that both generates and works in tension with meter? It is, I think, because Pound's (often exorbitant) ideas about rhythm preclude a hermeneutic approach to meter as anything more than a prop to poetic meaning. Rhythm, via Pound, helps Fussell channel a theory of poetry in which a too prosaic sense of "poetic meaning" is destabilized by the primacy of prosodic organization. Pound and later theorists ranging from Henri Meschonnic to Mutlu Blasing have taken rhythm as the locus of intention, of (as Culler puts it) "higher level functions that mark language as embodying the intention to mean." It is not that meter does not do this. Its formal (rather than authorial) intentionality is central to Wordsworth's theory of meter as "co-presence" in the *Preface to the Lyrical Ballads*.[22] Rather, meter appears now to require the supplement of rhythm to preserve the salience of sound-form within theories of the aesthetic or literary.

Rhythm has a similarly ephemeral but critical role in John Thompson's seminal *Founding of English Metre* (1961). It may be that Thompson overcame the "prevailing confused rivalry of metrical theories," as W. K. Wimsatt put it in his book review, by almost entirely avoiding the term rhythm.[23] As John Hollander notes in his preface to the book's 1989 reprint, the modernist desire for a return to speech "cadences" (a common synonym for rhythm) and the confusion of terms across mid-century criticism necessitated Thompson's "housecleaning of formal discourse."[24] His central term is meter, yet this housecleaning and an engagement with new work in structural linguistics mandates a striking encounter with rhythm. Thompson, in line with Wordsworth and Fussell, views meter as having a "kind of independent existence." It exemplifies poetic form as "imitative" of its linguistic material in the sense of being an abstraction from it. At the central moment where Thompson defines meter and, much more broadly, poetry as formal mimesis, "rhythm" and especially "the rhythm of verse" appear eight times in one paragraph before disappearing for the remainder of the book:

> The rhythms of verse are . . . an imitation of speech. When we hear the sounds that are our language, it is the rhythmic pattern of stresses and junctures that gives us our understanding of the grouping and ordering of these sounds. There is even in English a tendency for the rhythm to become regular, for the stresses to occur at 'isochronic' intervals. This tendency of our speech, abstracted and simplified into a pattern, becomes the rhythms of our verse. It is not rhythm itself which distinguishes verse from other kinds of language; it is the fact that the rhythm of verse is the result of the process of art. The elements of rhythm have been abstracted from their source in the language and then ordered into patterns; the patterns imitate in a simplified form the patterns that occur naturally in the language. In altering the natural speech rhythms of the language in verse, these patterns of course alter the meaning of the language . . . . If there is one meaning which the metrical pattern enforces on all language submitted to its influence, it is this: *Whatever else I may be talking about, I am talking also about language itself.*[25]

Thompson carefully manages the relation between rhythm as the natural province of speech ("the rhythmic pattern of stresses," "natural speech rhythms") and "the rhythm of verse," or rhythm as poetic effect or abstraction. "Rhythm itself" exists in language prior to poetry, as a phonological fact that may tend towards equal units (whether or not those units are temporally equal, i.e. "isochronic"); this is not controversial or surprising and corresponds to both more recent work in prosodic phonology and the nineteenth-century philological understanding of English (and other Germanic languages) as stress-based. Thompson recognizes, however, that rhythm gets much thornier when linguistic observations become claims about literary forms and traditions; this is especially evident in the not-yet-banished nineteenth-century understanding of Old and Middle English poetry through an "accentual paradigm."[26] It is because of this potential for slippage that Thompson so carefully constructs the genitive "rhythm of verse," which suspends a question endemic to his theory of art, and perhaps formalism today: whether and how the natural rhythms of speech become poetic meter.

Verse's mimesis of rhythm is especially interesting because it occurs, in the body of Thompson's treatise, at a much larger scale than that of individual lines or poems. Thompson's realization about the "founding" of early modern prosody from Wyatt to Sidney is that the abstractions of metrical rule variably align with the rhythms of natural language. When he (and the tradition) arrives at Sidney, he discovers a moment of "maximal tension" between colloquial language (i.e. speech, not disfigured by the requirements of meter) and the "abstract pattern of the metre" now settled into place. This is close-readable tension; even the term "tension" conforms to New Critical nomenclature. But without the story of "founding"—of the suboptimal moments where language is not quite language and meter is not yet meter—we lose sight of Thompson's deep investment in aesthetics as a process of formal imitation via abstraction. The triumph of "tension," which becomes the triumph of the binary model of meter and rhythm and the triumph of one kind of formalist reading, obscures the developmental moment where both terms are in states of suspense. Even Hollander, in his preface, locates the life of verse in "rhythmic incident . . . occasioned by the complex relation between meter . . . and the actual phonological *rhythm* of any utterance."[27] This is why the "rhythm of verse" is so important a concept for Thompson, and for the study of poetic and metrical form now. It can be distinguished from the objective guise of rhythm that Erin Kappeler's essay locates in Amy Lowell and others' attempts to "scientifically" measure poetic rhythm. They do so to feel less alienated from spoken language, the rhythms of which, Gerber notes, get treated as de facto aesthetic material by modernism's utopian prosodic theory.

Thompson, like many of the contributors here, turns to rhythm to understand the tricky ontological (or generic) position of aesthetic objects that obey their own formal laws but depend as well on the shared qualities of the language they imitate. His suspension of "rhythm" between natural and aesthetic language can only exist ephemerally, however, within this foundational work on meter. A very different, entirely negative role falls to rhythm in an important article published while Thompson developed his dissertation into a book. W.K. Wimsatt and Monroe Beardsley's *PMLA* article "The Concept of Meter: An Exercise in Abstraction" avoids the term rhythm and focuses on meter as an aesthetic law that poetry gives unto itself (in a more thorough and achieved "abstraction" from properties of language).[28] Meter is objective but not in an empirical sense (they attack pseudoscientific "timers and linguistic recorders").[29] Yet avoiding rhythm does not eliminate the ontological questions it frames for Thompson. Tom Cable's essay notes Wimsatt and Beardsley's oddly visual construction of what must at some level be a temporal form. A *PMLA* rebuttal from 1962 attacked their "intellectualist" removal of the reader, turning predictably to the reader's "experience of rhythm" and taking issue with a supposedly erroneous equation of meter and rhythm.[30] Wimsatt and Beardsley responded that temporal aspects are subjective and therefore (as they had previously argued) "beyond verifiable public discussion."[31]

As in "The Affective Fallacy," the authors here foreclose an exploration of how poetry does or does not circulate publicly. But, as will be obvious from the essays in this collection, rhythm is all about public discussion even if its "observable phenomena" have eluded ultimate verification. Consenting to meter as "verifiable" would have raised few eyebrows in 1960. Thompson's work, in line with earlier figures like George Saintsbury, discovers in meter something like a teleological "iambicisation" to which generations of poets and readers ultimately consent.[32] Wordsworth felt this to be the case by 1802: "Metre obeys certain laws, to which the Poet and Reader both willingly submit because they are certain."[33] Consent to *rhythm*, however, turns out to be a very different matter. For Wimsatt and Beardsley it is impossible; for nineteenth-century thought about poetry it was essential. For Francis Gummere, a nineteenth-century theorist of balladry discussed at length in Jackson's contribution, the notional power of poetry to develop and represent a public depended upon a shared rhythmic capacity that seemed attenuated in modern societies (but present in racial others, especially the African-American "folk"); Wimsatt and Beardsley erase the doubt about rhythmic consent (though likely unaware of it) through an improvised canon and a set of underlying assumptions about what a poem is and what qualities it has. "We are concerned," they respond, "with such observable facts as that when two poems have the same meter, they have a common quality which can be heard in both . . . ."[34] For theorists of folk and oral poetry in previous intellectual generations this "common quality" would have been spoken of with nostalgic desire for a community of "hearers" entranced by common qualities of rhythm. Wimsatt and Beardsley are correct exactly to the degree that they make possible such hearing through pedagogy: their essay, like Whitman's grand claims to unify the nation through his new poetic forms (studied in Kappeler's contribution), would need to be a self-fulfilling prophecy. Yet there is, simply, not a great deal of common training in prosody, nor has there been since the *fin de siècle* ascendency in English national culture and schooling of what Meredith Martin terms the "military-metrical complex."[35] The subsequent "Fall of Meter" and the emergence of what one critic has called the twentieth century's "prosodic pluralism" return us to "rhythm" as the crucial term for exploring poetry's generic and aesthetic instability.[36]

There is no possibility of fully articulating here a disciplinary history of rhythm as a keyword for the study of poetics and prosody, but these episodes show its place at the root of debates over literariness, the nature of poetic language, techniques of reading and listening, and the circulation of poetic sound. The essays in this collection all deal in various ways with the problematic inheritance of "rhythm" as a disciplinary term, debating and demonstrating its value.

Description of Essays

The first grouping of essays, *Rhythm's Critiques*, opens the collection by sketching rhythm's insubordination with respect to language and especially poetic language's conceptual, representational, and semantic order. Rhythm is an event, for Jonathan Culler, not only in the experience of passions or affects, but in its dense system of references to other poetic rhythms and in its mnemonic potency. His essay cites a wide range of nineteenth and twentieth-century poets and critics "seized" by rhythm and for whom rhythm is foundational to any intention to produce meaning. David Nowell Smith explores this same foundational status as a crucial component of post-Kantian critical philosophy, and specifically as an exploratory, provisional name for the subject's emergence into language and literature. His essay invites us to return to both critical theory and contemporary poetics for rhythms of absence and presence not restricted to stress and unstress. Simon Jarvis' contribution provides a rich description of the endeavors of rhythm and other verse technique in Browning's *Sordello* as they push against the "syntactic day job" of lines. Through a compelling reading of the role of prosody as necessary constraint in Kant's *Critique of Judgment*, Jarvis invites us to "read irresponsibly," attentive to the endeavors of rhythm as a mode of verse thinking antagonistic towards meaning and content (whether propositional, expressive, historical, etc.).

The second grouping of essays, *Body, Throng, Race*, explores claims of rhythm's embodiment and the stakes thereof, especially concerning logics of race. Each denaturalizes rhythm by situating it within histories of science, anthropology, ethnography, and the nascent enterprise of literary criticism. Across these essays one discovers an unexpectedly intense belief in or nostalgia for a rhythmic "throng" which emerged in nineteenth and then twentieth-century literary discourse from Herder's theories of the *Volksgeist*. Virginia Jackson's essay attends to the racialized reading of rhythm, past and present, which manifests the desire to recover through rhythm an "imagined community"—a term first used, she notes, by Gummere. Jackson extends her previous work on the disembodied and dehistoricized subject of lyric and lyric reading by arguing that such imagined communities of rhythm render poetry "racial in origin and post-racial in effect." Haun Saussy's essay expands the history of conceiving and testing rhythmic bodies to the Anglophone and Francophone natural sciences, for instance Herbert Spencer's theories of rhythm as it evolves from a "homogenized" presence in the music-speech-dance of the primitive throng to the increasingly specialized faculties of complex civilization. Leveraging Marcel Mauss' theory of bodily techniques as cultural processes "mounted" in bodies (rather than organically present, as rhythms are often imagined to be), he encourages a comparatist critical practice focused on moments where rhythms are exposed as they interact and break down. Erin Kappeler's essay picks up on rhythm's theoretical harmonizing of the potentially disparate aspects of complex national culture. Studying Whitman's critical legacy across the late nineteenth and early twentieth centuries, she explores anxieties about the lack of "social consent," aesthetic and otherwise, in the industrial era, and resulting efforts to claim "ancestral cadences" flowing through Whitman and his free verse.

The third grouping of essays, *Beat and Count*, explores the embodiment and phenomenology of rhythm from the alternate perspective of our experience of phonology and especially verse's uncertain temporality. The question, answered differently in each essay, is what "counts" as poetic rhythm and what constitutes a rhythmic verse form cognitively and historically. Derek Attridge's essay makes a strong case for an extended tradition in poetry and song of a four-beat stanza form called "dolnik," in which readers without specific training or efforts of scansion perceive rhythmic patterning in either double or triple time. What makes that tradition interesting, however, are the "psycho-physical" boundary conditions engaged by complex verse as it sets up and contravenes the stanza's powerful expectations. Tom Cable's essay studies these boundary conditions through neglected but promising work in cognitive science. Bringing this field into conversation with theories of phenomenology and recent work in musicology, Cable shows how our expectations of rhythm can be shaped pre-consciously. This does not imply that poems have a definite or given rhythm, however, as the written form of poetry gives way to variations in performance dependent in turn on culturally determined reading practices. Neither Attridge nor Cable would expect much potential for rhythmic expectation or play in "recherché" meters such as Auden's, mentioned previously, or the syllabics studied in Meredith Martin's contribution. Yet syllabics occupy a fascinating and neglected place in the history of versification as a form at once aesthetic and scientific. Depending on the recent formalization of the "syllable" as a linguistic object, the efforts of Adelaide Crapsey, Robert Bridges, and others eschewed the new kinds of scientific measurement explored by Saussy and Cable. While syllabics are among the least "rhythmic" forms we might conceive in an accentual language like English (Romance languages are a separate matter), Martin shows how dynamically modern poets invested in a rhythmic experience at a tangent from the prosodic phonology of the language. This returns us to rhythm's critique of poetry's aspiration to the status of natural language or oral form.

The final section, *Fictions of Rhythm*, embraces the divide between spoken and poetic rhythm and between subjective expression and its various metrical incarnations. Natalie Gerber articulates and compares often radically divergent treatments of speech rhythm by modernist poets. Frost engaged with rhythm at the phrasal or intonational level, while Stevens placed words to enjoy disjointing effects of their stress, and Williams divided his verse into syntactic units. The latter approach might have encouraged the appearance of simulated speech (such has been claimed), and yet Williams himself later found many of his efforts as "overdone, artificial, archaic" as Spenser's alexandrine. Obscuring the imbrications of voice and speech in meter leads, Yopie Prins shows, to the discovery of Sappho's voice and rhythm in what became known, across time and language, as *her* stanza. Prins reads Sappho as an allegorical figure for rhythm rather than its lyrical origin. The many excited historical reinventions of her stanza from the nineteenth century to the present reveal changing theories of meter and meter's materialization as rhythm. The collection closes with what might be rhythm's Ur-invention in its "critical" post-Kantian form: Coleridge's "Christabel" meter. Ewan Jones interrogates rhythm's association, via that poem, with a free, impassioned human will. In Jones's rereading, "Christabel" is a poem that confuses rhythm, and whose rhythm confuses, and in which we often do not know who speaks, much less which passion or emotion the rhythm compels. As it "engenders drama and character" rather than reflecting or illuminating existing voices, rhythm compels attention to the philosophical problem (felt across Coleridge's works, and many other poets and theorists discussed in these essays) of how texts mediate intersubjective passions, affects, and voices.

This point returns us to a central lesson of the collection as a whole: rhythm may constitute the most substantial part of encounters with (many) poems, and may appear prior to hermeneutic efforts, but actual definitions of rhythm seem to be playing catch-up across the critical landscape. The ontology of rhythm need not be secure, however, to be critical, and these essays repeatedly show how many of the lacunae of literary studies, especially in its Anglophone, post-Romantic incarnation, revolve around ideas and experiences of rhythm. It has been, for instance, a focal point in African-American and Caribbean poetics since the New Negro Renaissance and Negritude movements. Even as rhythm stands for the possibility of new orality, nationality, embodiment, and tradition, scholars have cautioned against the continued invention of "African" rhythm and reminded us of the mediation and transformation of musical or natural rhythms in literary practice. As Tsitsi Jaji notes, Senegalese president and poet Leopold Senghor's "elastic use of rhythm . . . render[s] the notion that 'le Nègre était un être rythmique' so broad that it becomes virtually meaningless."[37] It is telling that Kamau Brathwaite's *History of the Voice*, effectively a manifesto of post-colonial rhythm, spells the word "riddim": a nod to orality built on orthographic play and deeply conscious of dialect traditions.[38] Braithwaite's contemporary John Figueroa, a Jamaican poet known for classical allusion and form, spells the word "rydhm" in his ironic appeal to Derek Walcott to listen to a white critic and be "Full of rydhm like all true spades."[39] The divergent spelling of the word in this Afro-Caribbean context neatly reflects both the potency and instability of investments in rhythm across the relatively brief history of its preeminence in literary criticism. Figueroa's pun on "spade" as both slur and as the laborer's rhythmic object returns us to rhythm's mercurial relation to embodiment, race, and will; but his orthographic and lexical sleight also recalls rhythm's creative destabilization of language in the poem and beyond. He suggests, as do each of the essays in this collection, that it is impossible to imagine a poetics or literary history inattentive to rhythm's decisive role in how we conceive aesthetic objects, literary genres, subjectivity, nation, language, and culture.

Notes

1. "In Due Season," W. H. Auden, *Collected Poems: Auden* (New York: Vintage, 1991), 801–2.
2. "A Retrospect," in *Poetry in Theory: An Anthology, 1900-2000*, ed. Jon Cook (Malden, Mass.: Blackwell, 2004), 84.
3. Possible variations include an opening spondee. See Edward Hirsch, *A Poet's Glossary* (New York: Houghton Mifflin Harcourt, 2014), 41.
4. W. H. Auden and John Garrett, *The Poet's Tongue* (London: G. Bell & sons ltd, 1935), v.
5. Paul Fussell, *Poetic Meter and Poetic Form* (New York: McGraw-Hill, 1965), 3.
6. Jonathan Culler, *Theory of the Lyric* (Cambridge, Mass.: Harvard University Press, 2015), 134.
7. Derek Attridge, *The Rhythms of English Poetry* (London; New York: Longman, 1982), 1.
8. Derek Attridge, "Rhythm," in *Princeton Encyclopedia of Poetry and Poetics*, ed. Roland Greene and Stephen Cushman, 4th ed. (Princeton, N.J.: Princeton University Press, 2012), 1195.
9. Caroline Levine, *Forms: Whole, Rhythm, Hierarchy, Network* (Princeton, N.J.: Princeton University Press, 2015), 53.
10. Ibid., 49.
11. Ibid., 53. For the trope of rhythm as heartbeat see especially Oliver Wendell Holmes' 1875 essay "The Physiology of Versification," where he argues for a more general "unconscious adaptation of voluntary life to the organic rhythm." "The Physiology of Versification," in *Pages from an Old Volume of Life*, vol. 8, The Works of Oliver Wendell Holmes (Boston: Houghton, Mifflin and Company, 1892), 319. More recently Alfred Corn grounds rhythm in early infant perception of a range of embodied and intuitive experiences: the mother's heartbeat and walk, the infant's own heartbeat and breathing, and then "visual equivalents of rhythm" from diurnal cycles to wallpaper patterns. *The Poem's Heartbeat: A Manual of Prosody* (Port Townsend, Wash.: Copper Canyon Press, 2008), xix. Recent work on the historical prosody of the nineteenth century has detailed a broad investment in such theories of embodied rhythm. Catherine Robson has shown, for instance, how the figure of memorizing poetry "by heart" with help from the beats of meter gives way, at times, to literal pedagogical beating. *Heart Beats: Everyday Life and the Memorized Poem* (Princeton: Princeton University Press, 2012). See also Jason Rudy, *Electric Meters: Victorian Physiological Poetics* (Athens: Ohio University Press, 2009).
12. Jonathan Kramnick and Anahid Nersessian, "Form and Explanation," *Critical Inquiry* 43 (Spring 2017): 652. The authors characterize Levine's as a kind of "fundamentalist formalism" for its belief that "one ought to be able to analyze form without making reference to its various predicates: this genre, that historical example, and so on" (656).
13. Culler worries, for instance, that "the model of lyric as dramatic monologue ... deprives rhythm and sound patterning of any constitutive role." "Theories and Methodologies: Why Lyric?," *PMLA* 123, no. 1 (2008): 202. D. W. Harding warns specifically against "attributing to rhythm an expressive significance that stems in reality from other features of language." *Words into Rhythm: English Speech Rhythm in Verse and Prose*, The Clark Lectures 1971–1972 (Cambridge: Cambridge University Press, 1976), 153. Such scenes of production and reading leave little room for non-expressive,

non-mimetic prosodic functions. Relevant here is Jackson's theory of "lyricization" as the displacement of subgenres and accompanying modes of reading and circulation into the master genre of the "expressive romantic lyric"; this model of lyric occurs in an "idealized moment of reading progressively identified with an idealized moment of expression." *Dickinson's Misery: A Theory of Lyric Reading* (Princeton, N.J.: Princeton University Press, 2005), 7. One outcome of lyricization would be a formalism that obsessively reads prosodic form as expressive form.

14. I.e., the tendency toward alternation that shifts stress from "fourtéen" to "fòurteen wómen." See Bruce Hayes, "The Phonology of Rhythm in English," *Linguistic Inquiry* 15, no. 1 (1984): 33.

15. The field has been dominated by work in the nineteenth century. Especially important here are the 2008 Exeter conference "Metre Matters" and subsequent collection with that title edited by Jason David Hall (2011); a special 2011 issue of *Victorian Poetry* dedicated to prosody (ed. Meredith Martin and Yisrael Levin); a 2014 conference at the University of Chicago on "Poetic Genre" dedicated to questions of historical poetics and with keynotes by two prosodists also present in this collection, Yopie Prins and Simon Jarvis. Their dialogue has resulted in several important essays concerning the definition of "historical poetics"; these pivot in large part on the question of our "cognition" or "recognition" of versification. Simon Jarvis, "What Is Historical Poetics?," in *Theory Aside*, ed. Jason Potts and Daniel Stout (Durham, N.C.: Duke University Press, 2014), 97–116; Yopie Prins, "'What Is Historical Poetics?,'" *Modern Language Quarterly: A Journal of Literary History* 77, no. 1 (2016): 13–40. Although "historical prosody" needs no absolute origin story, Prins' *Victorian Sappho* (1999) contained a landmark analysis of the aesthetics of Victorian meter in their broader discursive context, a research project more directly and broadly defined by Meredith Martin's *Rise and Fall of Meter*. Martin's forthcoming online *Princeton Prosody Archive* will support that program and enable a range of digital projects.

16. Armstrong notes that a largely nineteenth-century conception of meter included both the abstract or ideal form (now often called "meter") and the corresponding or non-corresponding embodiment (now often called "rhythm") (28). "A residual form of this belief," she observes, "is the common distinction between rhythm and meter" (29). "Meter and Meaning," in *Meter Matters: Verse Cultures of the Long Nineteenth Century*, ed. Jason David Hall (Athens: Ohio University Press, 2011), 26–52.

17. *Rhyme's Reason: A Guide to English Verse*, 4th ed. (New Haven, Conn.: Yale University Press, 2014), 6.

18. *Princeton Encyclopedia of Poetry and Poetics*, 1197. Prins' essay in this collection provocatively inverts such formulations, arguing that the phenomenology of rhythm "depends on readings of meter generated by a wide range of metrical theories at different moments in history."

19. Fussell, *Poetic Meter and Poetic Form*, 3.

20. Ibid., 14.

21. Fussell is citing a 1915 letter to Harriet Monroe in which Pound, as is often the case, defines rhythm negatively against the "inebriety of metre," the "careless dash off . . . a tumty tum tumty tum tum ta." *The Selected Letters of Ezra Pound, 1907-1941*, ed. D. D. Paige (New York: New Directions Publishing Corporation, 1971), 48–49.

22. In particular, his claim that meter not only "temper[s] and restrain[s] the passion" but is a kind of "co-presence" that "divest[s] language in a certain degree of its reality, and thus . . . throw[s] a sort of half-consciousness of unsubstantial existence

over the whole composition." William Wordsworth, *The Major Works*, ed. Stephen Gill (New York: Oxford University Press, 2008), 609-10.

23. "Review of The Founding of English Meter," *Renaissance News* 16, no. 2 (July 1, 1963): 131.

24. John Hollander, "Preface," in *The Founding of English Metre*, by John Thompson (New York: Columbia University Press, 1989), x.

25. Thompson, *The Founding of English Metre*, 13.

26. As Ian Cornelius notes, it was Edwin Guest's *History of English Rhythms* (1838) (and later W. W. Skeat in his revised edition) who "made accentual rhythm the uniform organizing principle of English poetry, from Caedmon to the present." *Reconstructing Alliterative Verse: The Pursuit of a Medieval Meter* (Cambridge: Cambridge University Press, 2017), 54. It is telling that Guest turns to "rhythm" to conflate two metrical traditions now known to be radically different: the alliterative corpus of Old, Middle, and Late Middle English (roughly up to the court of James VI of Scotland), and the accentual-syllabic tradition whose fitful beginnings Thompson traces. See also Thomas Cable, *The English Alliterative Tradition*, Middle Ages Series (Philadelphia: University of Pennsylvania Press, 1991); Eric Weiskott, "Alliterative Meter and English Literary History, 1700–2000," *ELH* 84, no. 1 (Spring 2017): 268-69.

27. "Preface," xi.

28. "The Concept of Meter: An Exercise in Abstraction," *PMLA* 74, no. 5 (December 1959): 585-98.

29. Ibid., 587.

30. Elias Schwartz, W. K. Wimsatt Jr., and Monroe C. Beardsley, "Rhythm and 'Exercises in Abstraction,'" *PMLA* 77, no. 5 (December 1, 1962): 668.

31. Ibid., 674.

32. George Saintsbury, *Historical Manual of English Prosody* (London: Macmillan and Co. Limited, 1910), 38.

33. Wordsworth, *Major Works*, 608.

34. "Rhythm and 'Exercises in Abstraction,'" 674.

35. Meredith Martin, *The Rise and Fall of Meter: Poetry and English National Culture, 1860-1930* (Princeton, N.J.: Princeton University Press, 2012), 130, 182.

36. Enikő Bollobás, *Tradition and Innovation in American Free Verse: Whitman to Duncan* (Budapest: Akadémiai Kiadó, 1986).

37. Tsitsi Jaji, *Africa in Stereo: Modernism, Music, and Pan-African Solidarity* (New York: Oxford University Press, 2014), 78.

38. Kamau Braithwaite, *History of the Voice: The Development of Nation Language in Anglophone Caribbean Poetry* (London: New Beacon Books, 1984), 30.

39. John Figueroa, "Problems of a Writer Who Does Not Quite . . . ," *Caribbean Quarterly* 49, no. 1/2 (2003): 54.

Rhythm's Critiques

Why Rhythm?

Jonathan Culler

Le vers—trait incantatoire

—MALLARMÉ

"We know poetry is rhythm," writes W. B. Yeats, contrasting the rhythms that pick up and spectrally convey a tradition with the mechanistic cadences of music hall verse: "It is the rhythm of a poem that is the principal part of the art."[1] Other poets attribute the genesis of a poem to a rhythm that enters their head obsessionally, and won't let them go until they have found words for it. And for readers rhythm is often what makes a poem especially memorable. Many of us have a good deal of verse stuck in our minds, lodged there not by any wisdom it conveys, but by rhythms that have refused to desert us, as if they led a life independent of our will.

> One, two,
> Buckle my shoe.
> Three, four;
> Shut the door.

Counting rhymes and nursery rhymes are perhaps the least of it, since they bear the association of childhood days. The lines we recall from the verse of great poets, encountered later when we could practice more mature judgment, may owe their persistence to their rhythm more than to any insight they might have granted us:

> Break, Break, Break,
> On thy cold gray stones, o sea.

or

> How to kéep —is there ány any , is there none such, nowhere known
> some, bow or brooch or braid or brace, láce or latch or catch or key to
> keep
> Back beauty, keep it, beauty, beauty, beauty, . . . from vanishing
> away?

The psychoanalyst Nicolas Abraham maintains that "rhythm produces in the reader the fundamental affect of the entire poem."[2] Although it is hard to imagine how to demonstrate this (what about other aspects of sound patterning, not to mention the well-documented effect of meaning in generating the impression that a particular sound-pattern is in some way mimetic?), Abraham's claim at least calls us to focus on rhythm more than criticism has been generally inclined to do.

I have argued elsewhere that lyric aims not to be a representation of an event but to be itself an event, so an account of lyric needs to grant primacy to what happens in and through lyric, the distinctive events of lyric discourse, which make rhythm and repetition central.[3] Quite apart from the historical link of lyric to chanted recitation and the modern usage that emphasizes the close connection with rhythm by calling the words of songs "lyrics," is it not rhythm above all that makes lyrics attractive, seductive, and memorable? If lyric is pleasurable language, language that gives pleasure, its rhythms and sound patterning may be largely responsible. If lyric is memorable language—language that asks to be learned by heart and repeated, recited—is this not also because of its rhythms? Rhythm gives lyric a somatic quality that novels and other extended forms lack—the visceral experience of rhythm linking it to the body and, often rather dubiously, to the rhythms of various natural processes—and thus contributes to a different sort of pleasure from those promoted by novels and a sense of otherness. Lyrics are language, but language shaped in other ways, as if from elsewhere, which is how Valéry writes about rhythm: "I was suddenly *seized* by a rhythm that imposed itself on me and soon gave me the impression of a foreign process. As if someone was making use of my *machine for living.*"[4] Although our body has its own rhythms, of breathing and of heartbeats, our rhythmic competence most often responds to rhythm as something exterior which nonetheless engages us, draws us to beat in time with it, finding or sensing a pattern, in noises, movements, action in the world. When we find rhythm in language, it enlists us in a process in ways that other texts do not. Rhythms make us want to repeat them, generating a different effect from that of novels, for instance, where we recall characters, incidents, and an occasional telling phrase, but seldom desire to recite passages.

Rhythm is one of the major forces through which poems haunt us, just as poems themselves are haunted by rhythms of other poems. The tenacity with which rhythms can lodge in our memory, as the tune of a song might, encourages thoughts of occult forces, as if potent effects must have mysterious absent causes.

If rhythm is fundamental to the appeal of lyric, it is largely neglected by criticism, in part because traditional foot scansion offers only limited access to rhythms. As Derek Attridge has argued, in a devastating discussion that should be conclusive, the traditional account of meter in the *Norton Anthology of Poetry* (an essay by John Stallworthy that has been reprinted from one edition to another and is indeed typical of introductions to meter) makes it difficult to describe many of the poems in the anthology, beginning with the first of the "Anonymous Lyrics of the Thirteenth and Fourteenth Centuries, "the section where we first are offered English rather than Anglo-Saxon poems."

This poem has a clear four-beat rhythm:

Nou goth sonne under wode—
B   B   B   B
Me reweth, Marie, thi faire rode.
    B   B   B   B
Nou goth sonne under tre—
 B   B   B   B
Me reweth, Marie, thi sone and the.[5]
    B   B   B   B   B

As Attridge notes, "Although this metrical form is highly familiar to any reader familiar with the tradition of English verse (and, indeed, many other verse traditions), it is not mentioned in Stallworthy's essay. The student is left to struggle with the Procrustean task of mapping feet with Greek names onto resistant lines of verse, or manhandling sequences of elementary rhythms" into the iambs and trochees, anapests, dactyls and spondees demanded by foot prosody. How is this rhythm to be described, he asks? "As freely varying iambic meter? As free trochaic meter? As shifting between iambic and trochaic?"[6] The difficulties of fitting the lyric to the patterns of foot prosody imply that it is rhythmically highly complex and full of uncertainties. But in fact it has an immediately recognizable rhythm that foot scansion obscures: stanzas of four four-beat lines, with some freedom in the disposition of unstressed syllables (in particular, lines can begin or end on an off-beat). This is the rhythm of much song and popular verse and also highly rhythmic moments of literary verse. In an amusing survey of other introductions to poetry, Attridge notes how often discussions break down or become excessively elaborate when confronted with poems of this kind, with a pronounced rhythm that is easy for readers to grasp. Take Robert Frost's "The Need of Being Versed in Country Things":

> The house had gone to bring again
> To the midnight sky a sunset glow.
> Now the chimney was all of the house that stood,
> Like a pistil after the petals go.

Here we have a strong four-beat rhythm with a variable number of unstressed syllables between stressed syllables. As the final stanza illustrates, lines may begin with either a stressed or unstressed syllable, without causing any difficulties for readers:

> For them there was really nothing sad.
> But though they rejoiced in the nest they kept,
> One had to be versed in country things
> **Not** to believe the phoebes wept.

What Frost called "loose iambics" Attridge proposes we call by the established Russian term, *dolnik,* and he notes that a considerable range of important poems in English use this meter. For instance, Milton's "L'Allegro" and "Il Penseroso," whose meter gives foot-prosodists great difficulty, comes easily to readers:

> But, hail, thou Goddess, sage and holy,
> Hail divinest Melancholy,
> Whose Saintly visage is too bright
> To hit the Sense of human sight;
> And therefore to our weaker view,
> Ore laid with black staid Wisdoms hue.
> Black, but such as in esteem,
> Prince *Memnons* sister might beseem,
> Or that starr'd *Ethiope* Queen that strove
> To set her beautys praise above
> The Sea Nymphs, and their powers offended,
> Yet thou art higher far descended.

More strikingly, Blake's "The Tyger," where readers cannot escape the driving four-beat rhythm is taken to be complicated and anomalous by foot-prosodists.

Tyger! Tyger! burning bright
In the forests of the night,
What immortal hand or eye
Could frame thy fearful symmetry?

In what distant deeps or skies
Burnt the fire of thine eyes?
On what wings dare he aspire?
What the hand dare seize the fire?

And what shoulder, & what art.
Could twist the sinews of thy heart?
And when thy heart began to beat,
What dread hand? & what dread feet?

What the hammer? what the chain?
In what furnace was thy brain?
What the anvil? what dread grasp
Dare its deadly terrors clasp?

When the stars threw down their spears,
And watered heaven with their tears,
Did he smile his work to see?
Did he who made the Lamb make thee?

Tyger! Tyger! burning bright
In the forests of the night,
What immortal hand or eye
Dare frame thy fearful symmetry?

In his refreshingly down-to-earth introduction to writing poetry, *The Ode Less Travelled*, Stephen Fry asks, "Are the odd lines out really iambic, or are they trochees with an extra weak syllable at the beginning?"[7] Since every line ends in a stressed syllable, foot-prosodists are tempted to treat the poem's meter as iambic tetrameter (with a truncated [catalytic] initial foot in most cases), although only five lines begin with an unstressed syllable, but this would obscure the vigorous dominant rhythm of initially-stressed lines. Hence, the inclination to call the rhythm trochaic is strong. Such hesitations, whether conducted publically or privately, suggest that the rhythm is complicated, requiring analysis and reflection, but it is so only for critics seeking feet. For readers the rhythm is entirely clear—indeed inescapable.

Blake's is a lyric that has generated a substantial literature of interpretation, most of which passes by its rhythmic structure, but what is most salient, what makes it a striking poem, rather than a prose reflection on the power of creation, or on the threat of the French revolution, or anything else, is its rhythm: the four-beat rhythm, with strong initial stress in all but five lines, the rhythm of nursery rhymes and counting songs. "It is the rhythm of song-verse," Andrew Welsh writes, "in which the one-two-three-four of the steady beat is far more important in determining the movement of the language than the consistently repeated patterns and counted syllables of foot-prosody."[8] Accompanying this steady beat of the song-rhythm is the patterning of the syntax, with short questions contrasting with those verse lines that are not broken up syntactically. Other rhythmical effects—taking this larger view of rhythm—are created by repeated sounds: the alliterations, assonances, rhymes, and other sound echoes woven through "The Tyger." Along with **bur**ning **br**ight, T**y**ger **br**ight, and **fr**ame **f**earful, we have the hammering repetition of the twelve *what*s. This is a charm-rhythm, the language of incantation, invocation. In addition to the meter, Welsh writes, "we also hear in it the questioning of the rhythms of speech-*melos* and the sound echoes of charm-*melos* caught up and carried along on the steady beats of a children's song. And in such songs the deeper powers of this old rhythm persist."[9]

This rhythm is the dominant aspect of the poem. What we make of the poem when we apply interpretive pressure, place it in one or another thematic or mythic or historical context in order to derive a meaning, is relevant, certainly, but one might wonder whether these interpretive efforts are not in some measure the product of a desire to justify the hold that such strange, yet deeply familiar rhythmic sequences have on us. Such verses have a power to insert themselves in mechanical memory independently of any attempt to remember them, and rather than consider ourselves victims of some jejeune susceptibility to rhythm independent of meaning, victims of its "fearful symmetry," we devote ourselves to intricate thematic explorations, which count for us as a response to the poem but in fact leave the rhythmical power unexplained.

Most discussions of rhythm in fact focus on meter, and that may well seem the place to start, since the most salient feature of this rhythm is the vigorous four-beat line of these quatrains. The problem of the relation between rhythm and meter is long standing: among the Greeks there was already a division between the *rhythmikoi* and the *metrikoi*; the former saw poetic rhythm as related to music, a temporal art, and the latter treated it as a structure of types of syllable. But the vast body of work on the verse line focuses on meter, which has long been seen as the basis of rhythm, and for most of the history of lyric, poems were written in relation to particular metrical frames, specific patterns of syllables of particular types. Metrics, or the study of prosody,[10] has been an extremely contentious field, with different systems of notation and conceptions of meter and vigorous struggle between the proponents of different approaches. T. V. F. Brogan concludes the 1993 *Princeton Encyclopedia*'s article on *Prosody* by noting,

> Over the past century there has been a general perception that prosody is a desiccated subject, a stony little patch of ground frequented only by eccentrics, fanatics, and pedants. The indictments are easy to finger: verse theory took nearly two millennia to free itself from the detritus of Classical prosody; it has never been able to give even an adequate theory of meter; it has been unable to agree on not merely concepts and terms but underlying assumptions about the nature of poetry itself (text, performance, experience).... It has been too willing to base theory on whatever versions of linguistics have been current; it has too often failed to distinguish linguistic processes from artistic conventions.... Yet the failure to give final answers is not proof that the questions are trivial; quite the contrary ... verse structure lies at the very core of our understanding of poetry.[11]

Put most simply, traditional prosody describes English meters, in terms taken from Greek, by the dominant type of foot (iambic, trochaic, anapestic, dactylic) and by the number of feet per line, but the artifact of the foot does not correspond to units of modern languages, and analysts must multiply variations, in endless small-scale tinkering, to capture the actual pattern of stresses in accentual-syllabic verse. Traditional descriptions of English stress meters analyze rhythms as involving the substitution of classical feet, such as trochees, spondees, or anapests, for the expected iamb, and, as Natalie Gerber notes in a compelling article exploring the strengths and weaknesses of foot prosody and generative metrics, lines with more substitutions are said to be more complex than lines with fewer substitutions.[12] Critics who scan the lines try to explain the semantic or thematic appropriateness of such substitutions.[13] Although it is scarcely clear that these alleged substitutions are the rhythmical features that require attention (they certainly do not in Blake's "Tyger," where the salient feature is the vital energy of that relentless four beat rhythm), the strategies for thematically recuperating metrical structures are in any case fairly limited—speeding up, slowing down and emphasis are the most common effects cited by interpreters—and since these are not particularly compelling, this induces a neglect of rhythm. As Gerber writes, when documenting such feeble interpretive sallies, "the potential for rhythm as compositional energy is largely overlooked, as well as the possibility that rhythm—among other sonic features of a text, can be contradistinctive to, or prioritized independent of meaning."[14]

The ad hoc attempts to justify foot substitutions distract from more fundamental questions about what sort of principles actually govern the rhythmic practices of English verse. Gerber notes that one problem with the traditional metrical approach to rhythm is its assumption that English verse should be treated as a succession of syllables, bracketing off other features of the language that affect rhythms and metricality. She pairs a line from Shakespeare's Sonnet 19 with a variant displaying the same succession of stressed and unstressed syllables but which clearly differs from it both rhythmically and metrically:

```
   /   _   /   /    _   _   /    /  _   /
Pluck the / keen teeth / from the / fierce ti / ger's jaws
   /   _   /   /    _   _   /    /  _   /
Pluck im / mense teeth / from en / raged ti / gers' jaws
```

Traditional foot prosody assigns both lines the same description, with the same series of foot substitutions: iambs replaced by a trochee in the first foot, a spondee in the second and fourth, and a pyrrhic in the third. This apparatus offers no resources to explain why the first is deemed metrically well-formed and is regularly attested in practice, and why the second is much less so.[15] Generative metrics, Gerber argues, is better able to do so, since it looks at word and phrase boundaries in theorizing rhythmic phrasing.[16] The description in terms of feet creates problems and points away from needed insights about principles governing rhythmic organization.

"Rhythm and meter actualize two completely different principles, which should never be confused," writes Clive Scott. "Crudely put, meter is linguistic, objective, quantitative, mono-dimensional, and repeatable/discontinuous; rhythm, on the other hand, is paralinguistic, subjective, heterogeneous, qualitative multi-dimensional, and irreversible/non-repeatable."[17] This is indeed crude for often the most noticeable, most palpable aspects of rhythm come from a metrical frame, as in "The Tyger." But study of rhythm is especially difficult because, on the one hand, rhythm is something as utterly familiar as our tapping a foot in time to the music or as the regular strides with which we walk most comfortably. It is near to hand yet a phenomenon observed throughout nature, wherever there is periodicity. It appears to be a property of systems yet it is above all an experience: dependent upon the frames and expectations with which we approach phenomena (as we make the ticking of a clock into a duple rhythm, *tick, tock*). And the notion of rhythm encompasses both the regularity of a musical beat or higher-level forms of symmetry and various forms of irregularity, from the syncopation that is tied in with beats it answers, to higher-level asymmetrical structures where prominences diversely signaled create differing temporal periodicities, as phrases become rhythmic units.

While it would be very desirable to find a successful way of describing rhythm, a crucial first step is to recognize its centrality to the lyric: to the construction of the lyric and the experience of lyric. Focusing on rhythm rather than meter allows us to give weight to other sorts of patterning—phonological and syntactic above all—that contribute to the experience of verse as rhythmical. Rhythm is more than variation upon the norm of meter.

An alternative to foot-scansion, championed above all by Derek Attridge, maintains that the foundation of English verse is four-beat line. Even young children who may have trouble with the pronunciation of words can easily get the rhythm right for nursery rhymes. "There is nothing remarkable, therefore, about a two-year-old chanting the following rhyme with perfect metrical placing of the syllables,"[18]

> Star light star bright,
> The first star I see tonight,
> I wish I may, I wish I might,
> Have the wish I wish tonight.

This is despite the fact it requires "knowing"—I put the word in quotation marks—that each word in the first line takes a stress, whereas in the third line only every second word is stressed. It is upon this edifice of shared ability, a rhythmic competence, that is built the whole English poetic tradition, he argues. The four-by-four formation, four groups of four beats, "is the basis of most modern popular music, including rock and rap, of most folk, broadside, and industrial ballads from the middle ages to the 20th century, of most hymns, most nursery rhymes, and a great deal of printed poetry."[19]

In fact, lyrics that seem to use other meters may actually have the underlying rhythmical structure of the 4x4 stanza. Attridge notes that various popular stanza forms include a silent or virtual beat at the end of a line, making a three-beat line in effect a four-beat line, where the last beat is realized as a pause in reading or reciting.[20] Notoriously, limericks, which are printed in five-line stanzas, have three four-beat lines, each with a virtual (silent) beat at the end, and two short lines which add up to a four-beat line with internal rhyme, so they are a version of the fundamental 4x4 form, the version sometimes called "short meter":

A **can**ner, excee**ding**ly **can**ny [beat],
One **mor**ning re**marked** to his **gran**ny, [beat],
"A **can**ner can **can** / Any**thing** that he **can**;
But a **can**ner can't **can** a can, **can** he?" [beat].

Many of Emily Dickinson's poems are written in common measure, frequent in hymns, which is described as a stanza of alternating four and three-beat lines but is actually a stanza of four four-beat lines in which the final beat of the second and fourth lines is virtual, expressed as a pause:

I heard a Fly buzz—when I died—
The Stillness in the Room [beat]
Was like the Stillness in the Air—
Between the Heaves of Storm—[beat]

So far I have considered cases where the metrical pattern does much to generate the rhythm, but in many cases rhythmically salient effects are not at all accounted for by the meter: similar meters can have quite different rhythmic effects, depending on other factors. Richard Cureton notes that Blake's "The Sick Rose" has a meter similar to that of many nursery rhymes, with two four-line stanzas, two strong beats per line, alternating with one or two unstressed syllables, and a rhyme scheme of abcb, but rhythmically it is very different from something like "Rock-a-bye Baby":

Rock-a-bye baby,
On the treetop,
When the wind blows,
The cradle will rock.

Like this nursery rhyme, which attributes to nature a catastrophic possibility that the rhythm renders benign, Blake's poem has an engaging rhythmic pulse and regular rhyme scheme, but, writes Cureton, "the real rhythmic action in the poem is something that develops more against and within this controlled [metrical] structure than because of its presence."[21] That is to say, the very different syntactic organization of Blake's poem gives it quite a different rhythm from the metrically-similar nursery rhyme.

O Rose, thou art sick!
Th' invisible worm,
That flies in the night,
In the howling storm,

Has found out thy bed
Of crimson joy;

And his dark secret love
Does thy life destroy.

The first line, a complete sentence, becomes one complete rhythmic unit, set against the other sentence that comprises the rest of the poem, where the predicate is postponed into the second stanza. Cureton offers a detailed analysis of the way in which the complex second sentence begins with unimpeded duple units in lines 2-4 (invisible / worm, flies / night, howling / storm), accelerates rhythmically, riding over the stanza break, to its "dramatic structural arrival and extension in lines 5 and 6, and a muted, concentrated climax in lines 7 and 8."[22] The syntactic relations and intonational contours produce a highly effective rhythm, and "a rhythmic theory that overlooks this other rhythmic patterning," Cureton concludes, "overlooks the better part of verse rhythm."[23]

If foot-substitution scansion often fails to capture dimensions of verse that are relevant to the rhythm, one could make a case for attempting to bypass the quarrels of *metrici*, old and new, and turn to the work of those modern *rhythmici* who have attempted to theorize rhythm directly. Although Henri Meschonnic has, in numerous books, developed an account of rhythm that is said to encompass everything, from meaning to history, his theory is notoriously difficult for others to deploy, though it has the virtue of instructing us to consider other kinds of sound patterning as essential to the rhythm.[24] The boldest account of rhythm that I have encountered is Amittai Aviram's *Telling Rhythms: Body and Meaning in Poetry*. He claims that there are three possible relations between rhythm and meaning: (1) rhythm is a rhetorical device subordinated to meaning, to which it can contribute, the most common view; (2) there is no significant relation between rhythm and meaning; and (3) meaning is subordinate to and refers to rhythm.[25] Bravely opting for number 3, he argues that seeing content as a representation of the form is the only way of relating the two without reducing form to content. He views meaning in poetry as representing, allegorically, "aspects of the power of the poem's own rhythm to bring about a physical response, to engage the readers or listener's body and thus to disrupt the orderly process of meaning."[26] Thus, for example, in "Tyger! Tyger! burning bright/ In the forests of the night,"

> Much of the power and thrill of the poem comes from the insistent repetitiveness and parallelism that gives the poem a strong, relentless beat. It makes sense, then, to see the Tyger himself as a local habitation and a name for the powerful rhythm that comes into existence at the same moment as the language and images but with which the

language of the poem is also trying to come to terms—and failing in the effort. The result is a feeling of the awesome ineffability of reality itself—of God's creation.[27]

In fact, most poems come to be about what he calls the sublime power of their rhythm—sublime in that it resists or lies beyond efforts of representation and can only be experienced, not comprehended. If the term "sublime" seems excessive for what one might also call the "catchiness" of poetic rhythms, it certainly is not exorbitant to think of rhythm as a force that works on us but lies beyond our immediate comprehension. The poem tells, allegorically, about how its rhythm escapes representation.

This is not very satisfactory hermeneutically, as Aviram recognizes, because poems end up with much the same meaning. In fact, it becomes a matter of definition, of stipulation, that the poem's meaning is an allegory of the sublime power of rhythm: either the thematic material can be construed as an allegory of the power of rhythm, or, the meaning's failure to represent the rhythm itself makes the poem mean that the sublime power of rhythm escapes representation. But Aviram has created difficulties for himself. By emphasizing the idea that the meaning of a poem is an allegory of its rhythm he effectively accepts the hermeneutical presumption: that the task of literary study is the production of interpretations and that the test of a theory is whether it can generate new and plausible interpretations. By leading readers to imagine that attending to the rhythm will allow them to come up with an interesting new interpretation as a result of taking the meaning of the poem to be an allegory of its rhythm, he sets them up for disappointment, which may, unfortunately, lead them to stop attending to rhythm.[28]

The test of the theory should be, rather, the vision it gives us of the lyric. Its virtue is to direct attention to the problem of grasping the action of the rhythm, a problem we have neglected, though it is a mystery of the first order. What makes a rhythm work on us? What do these lyric rhythms accomplish? Experientially, it is often the case that meaning is subordinate to rhythm: what attracts us to a poem is its rhythm, not its meaning, which may be rather banal. Poems have the power to make us remember bits of language that concern us not at all. Why do I remember "Little boy blue, come blow your horn"? It is certainly not because it makes sense or even because it was drummed into me as a child. Or why has "Les sanglots long / Des violons / De l'automne / Blessent mon coeur /D'une langeur/ Monotone," inscribed itself in mechanical memory, when this meaning is of no possible consequence to me? This power of rhythm, whether we choose to call it "sublime" or not, is certainly something we should acknowledge and try to factor into our dealings with poetry. I have suggested that critics conceal this power of rhythm to seduce by undertaking complex interpretative operations for poems that attract us. Such efforts cannot be satisfied with the idea that this poem allegorizes the sublime power of its rhythm to attract and enthrall us. They require a deeper distinctive meaning to compensate for our being easily seduced by a haunting rhythm.

I maintain that, as Natalie Gerber suggests, we can and should think of rhythm as functioning quite independently of the meaning, but in the case of Blake's "Tyger" it seems not inappropriate to say that the image of the tiger and the questions about what forces brought it into being reinforce the effect of the powerful rhythm of this tetrameter verse, which engages readers but which we don't know how to account for, whether we want to link this mysterious power to that of God or not. Still, rather than stipulate that the poem's meaning is an allegory of its rhythm, it might be better to allow that rhythm functions independently of meaning, though of course from time to time the very independence of that mysterious power becomes a meaning that can be integrated in an interpretation of the poem.

The independence of rhythm is a possibility also asserted by Mutlu Blasing in her account of the lyric: a lyric, "far from being a text where sound and sense, form and meaning, are indissolubly one, is a text where we witness the *distinct* operation of the two systems. We can always yield to the seductive call to 'stop making sense' and attend to the patterning of the non-sense. Or we can choose to switch to the symbolic and make sense. We cannot do both at once."[29] For her, rhythm is especially important as the crux of language acquisition: children learn by imitating speech rhythms: "Training in vocal rhythmization, in the prosody of human speech, . . . precedes speech, which could not happen without it."[30] While biological and environmental rhythms may be given, social rhythms are learned, and verbal rhythm is social, part of what she calls the "intentionalization" of language. "Rhythm has no symbolic value, and is distinct from meter, insofar as meter is an abstract representation of the sound shape of a language and can be represented as an abstract scheme. Rhythm is experienced in and as time, as a persuasive movement of the voice. It does not represent and is not representable."[31]

While she agrees with Aviram in seeing rhythm as neither representational nor representable, she accuses him of conflating rhythm and meter, which she sees as a formal system, a norm, against which the rhythm of the poem marks the intending of the subject. Much of what Aviram calls the pulsational rhythm of Blake's Tyger would for Blasing be meter, against which the syntactic contours of English embody a social, signifying subject.[32]

It is tempting to pick up on Blasing's contention as the basis of a distinction; on the one hand, there would be poems where metrical beating dominates and which characteristically do not project a speaker, such as limericks, nursery rhymes, and a range of other poems, from "The Tyger" to Hopkins' "Spelt from Sibyl's Leaves." On the other hand, there would be poems where the rhythmic movement of phrasing, working against the pulse of meter, produces the image of voice, the idea of a speaking subject. Anthony Easthope, notoriously, links iambic pentameter with hearing a "voice," and thus the representation of the speaking subject as individual, and associates tetrameter with a position of enunciation not marked as that of an individual subject and thus impersonal or potentially collective.[33] Four-stress popular meters make available a collective subject position, and one joins that position as one chants or repeats: "Pease porridge hot, / Pease porridge cold, / Pease porridge in the pot, / Nine days old," or even "A gentleman dining at Crewe / Found a rather large mouse in his stew." We are not inclined to ask who is speaking here or to try to posit a person from the image of voice, and much of the pleasure comes from participating in that implicitly collective position. The same is arguably true of "Tyger, Tyger, burning bright, / In the forests of the night," but not of the pentameter "That time of year thou mayest in me behold . . ." Certainly four-stress meter can impose an impersonality, even in a poem like Auden's "Lullaby," ("Lay your sleeping head, my love / Human, on my faithless arm,") where a personal situation is thematically invoked but qualified by the ritualistic aura of the meter, as in popular songs. The role of meter and especially rhythm in promoting the impersonality of poetry seems to me incontrovertible.

But Blasing seems to be operating at a level above or prior to distinctions between types of poems or different meters. Rhythm "belongs neither to the systems of meter and rhyme nor to the discursive organization of figure and meaning, but it *intentionalizes* both systems. The indexical function of rhythm renders both language and speech meaningful and sounds a metaphysically groundless, and historically grounding, intention to mean." Rhythm "both renders language sensible and reveals the experienced temporality of an intending 'I' to be a necessary condition of meaningful language."[34] That is, it is rhythm that makes language utterance that can mean, makes it more than phonemes or words. If one sort of poem projects an "I," offers the image of a voice, and another does not, that is a subsequent discrimination within the general poetic system she is describing.

Aviram's metrical rhythm is linked to the body and seen as disruptive of meaning, whereas for Blasing rhythm belongs to a social body:

> The rhythmic body is the "socially-constructed body"; rhythmization *is* socialization, and it secures meaning. And it is difficult to tell apart bodily responses to poetic rhythm from our total memory of verbal rhythm. Our sensory experience of the materials of words is already emotionally and historically charged, and we cannot experience verbal rhythm in a way that is distinguishable from a mental experience.[35]

It is the metrical segmentation of the sonic flow that opposes or resists meaning, not a rhythmical engagement. And she firmly denies that poetry presents an irrational resistance to linguistic meaning, or a primal irrationality, since to do so would be to accept a rational norm for language. On the contrary, lyric deploys formal, non-rational orders as the ground against which the complex thought processes and figurative logic of lyric can play out. She might thus regard appeals to tapping in time to music or swaying to a beat as marginal to questions of poetic rhythm, for it is through rhythm that the inhuman orders of language are intentionalized as meaningful.

Such disagreements are difficult to adjudicate and might seem to confirm Brogan's claim that rhythm is the vaguest term in criticism. But the disagreements are quite understandable. On the one hand, given the link of the notion of rhythm to bodily response, it is tempting to associate rhythm with forces that counteract the usual movement of language and enforce a different order. On the other hand, if one takes *meter* as the name for non-meaningful pulsation, the sort of sound pattern associated with reading a line of pentameter without intonation contours, stressing each beat equally—

The **quálitý** of **mércy ís** not **strained**

then one could associate *rhythm* in turn—as theorists such as Meschonnic and Cureton are inclined to do—with higher level functions that mark language as embodying the intention to mean.

Young children generally like poetry: they are engaged by its rhythms, entranced by its repetitions, and perhaps at some level deeply pleased by a regime of adult language so full of nonsensical rhyming and chiming. By the time they leave school, they have generally come to avoid it, perhaps because it has been linked to a practice of interpretation, even though their attraction to rhythmic language has not diminished. Their attention has shifted to music but, strikingly, songs with lyrics are vastly more popular among the young than music without lyrics—testimony to the enduring attraction of rhythmic language, even when its formulations are banal.

Historically, of course, lyric is linked to singing, dancing, chanting, though classicists disagree about the importance of instrumental music to the Greek lyric and about what sort of vocalization—singing, chanting, reciting—was most common for early lyric genres. It seems very plausible that the frequent references in Latin lyrics to singing and to lyres mark an affinity for rhythm rather than for melody.[36] In its rhythmical character, however, lyric is in touch with fundamental bodily rhythms: the timing of heartbeats, of breathing, of walking, of marching, of dancing. And the bodily, experiential dimension of rhythm itself—our bodily participation in rhythm—seems to achieve two distinguishable though closely-related effects. Paul Valéry writes, "it is almost only via rhythm and the sensory properties of language that literature can reach the organic being of a reader with any confidence in the conformity between intention and the results."[37] At a basic level rhythm seems not so much a matter of interpretation as a direct experience, the result of a rhythmic competence, though mediated by culture; it thus offers a somatic experience that seems to have a different status than the comprehension of a poem. Bringing someone to hear or feel a rhythm is procedurally different from trying to explain the meaning of a poem, though people's ability to hear some rhythms is highly dependent on past experience. Even though we know that rhythms are constructed (we hear the ticking of a clock as a two beat rhythm, *tick, tock*, even though the two sounds are identical), this visceral experience seems to give rhythms an exteriority to the mind, as if they were an external force. The words of the poem may be signs for which we have to supply the signifieds, but the rhythm seems independent of us.[38] "The pleasure of the text," Roland Barthes writes, "is the moment when my body begins to follow its own ideas, for my body does not have the same ideas as I do."[39] Rhythm appeals to the body's own ideas.

This brings us to the second effect: in its somatic dimensions, rhythm is a source of pleasure—a topic not much discussed in the critical literature, but not easily deniable. Barthes was not a lover of poetry, except haiku, and does not write of pleasure in verse rhythms, but in *Le Plaisir du texte*, he offers an observation that seems promisingly pertinent: when he tries to analyze a text that has given him pleasure, he reports, what he finds is not his subjectivity: "It is my bliss-body that I encounter. And this bliss-body is also my historical subject, for it is as the product of a very subtle combination of biographical, historical, sociological, neurotic etc.

elements that I organize the contradictory play of pleasure (cultural) and bliss (non-cultural)."[40] The body and its history, which is also of course cultural, is entrammeled in scenarios of pleasure.

The unexpected rise of rap, a form of heavily rhythmical language that relies on rhythm and wordplay, and its enormous persisting popularity among the young of all social strata, suggests a hunger for rhythmic language that might find some satisfaction in lyric. In the case of pop music our sense of the success, of the catchiness, the memorability of a song, (we need a theory of *catchiness*) is at least as much dependent on rhythm as on meaning, since words of songs we repeat and those we love (not necessarily the same—such is the seduction of rhythm) can be wholly banal or even unintelligible. The words are often misheard but they invariably have the correct rhythm when they are repeated. People grasp and repeat the rhythm even when words and meaning escape them. A greater foregrounding of rhythm as central to lyric might enable the teaching of poetry to regain some of the ground lost in recent years and also might lead to a different sort of poetics. One could imagine an approach more connected with evaluation, which has not been central to literary studies recently: what works and what doesn't? What engages our attention, our *corps de jouissance*—to use Barthes' term—and what does not? For such a poetics, an important part of the teaching of poetry would be accustoming students to hearing and experiencing the rhythms of traditional verse, so that these rhythms come to have some of the bodily appeal of the other forms of repetition that so manifestly work to structure their experience of the world.

Notes

1. W. B. Yeats, "Four Lectures by W. B. Yeats, 1902–4," *Yeats Annual* 8 (1991): 89. This is an historical moment when regularity may be deemed anti-poetic.

2. Nicolas Abraham, *Rhythms: On the Work, Translation, and Psychoanalysis*, trans. Nicholas Rand (Stanford, Calif.: Stanford University Press, 1995), 123.

3. See Jonathan Culler, *Theory of the Lyric* (Cambridge, Mass.: Harvard University Press, 2015), particularly chapter 4, "Rhythm and Repetition."

4. In the original, "je fus tout à coup *saisi* par un rythme qui s'imposait à moi et qui me donna bientôt l'impression d'un fonctionnement étranger. Comme si quelqu'un se servait de ma *machine à vivre*." Paul Valéry, "Poésie et pensée abstraite," *Oeuvres* (Paris: Gallimard, 1957), vol. 1, 1322. His italics.

5. Derek Attridge, "The Case for the English Dolnik, or How Not to Introduce Prosody," *Poetics Today* 33, vol. 1 (Spring 2012): 7. Reprinted with revisions in Attridge, *Moving Words: Forms of English Poetry* (Oxford: Oxford University Press, 2013), 147–87.

6. Ibid., 7, 5.

7. Stephen Fry, *The Ode Less Travelled* (London: Arrow Books, 2007), 69. Quoted in Attridge, "The Case for the English Dolnik."

8. Andrew Welsh, *Roots of Lyric* (Princeton, N.J.: Princeton University Press, 1978), 8.

9. Ibid., 196.

10. The term *prosody* has become a possible source of confusion. Long the name for the science of versification, including meter, sound-patterning, stanza forms, rhyme, etc., in twentieth century linguistics it has become the study of the rhythmic ordering of a language in general, including word and phrasal stress, intonation. The two uses are of course closely related, which only increases possibilities of confusion.

11. T. V. F. Brogan, "Prosody," *Princeton Encyclopedia of Poetry and Poetics* (Princeton, N.J.: Princeton University Press, 1993), 992.

12. Natalie Gerber, "Stress-Based Metrics Revisited," *Thinking Verse* 3 (2013), 135.

13. Part of the problem, of course, is that criticism tends to assume that the goal of literary study is to produce interpretations, which generates a disposition to discover thematic effects for features that are noted, and thus to take note only of such features as seem susceptible to being assigned thematic implications. But if what makes a poem attractive is its rhythm, then one risks passing over its particularly salient features.

14. Ibid., 137–38. Gerber generously concedes that in such an endeavor critics may achieve "interpretive elegance rarely equaled by proponents of generative metrics," but because of its *ad hoc* character, "it must be recognized as a skill of interpretation and not of analysis."

15. Ibid., 141–42. She does note that Donne allows lines with this sort of structure.

16. For discussion of Generative Metrics' approach to this question, too complex to attempt to summarize here, see ibid., 143–62.

17. Clive Scott, *Translating the Perception of Text: Literary Translation and Phenomenology* (London: Modern Humanities Research Association, 2012), 111.

18. Derek Attridge, *Poetic Rhythm: An Introduction* (Cambridge: Cambridge University Press, 1995), 43.

19. Ibid., 54–55.

20. Ibid., 58–61.

21. Richard Cureton, *Rhythmic Phrasing in English Verse* (London: Longman. 1992), 2.

22. Ibid., 5.

23. Ibid., 81. Paul Fussell, a distinguished prosodist, reads the same poem in terms of foot-substitution. He gives the poem "an iambic-anapestic base" and argues that "the whole poem depends on one crucial substitution." In line 7, "the cause that extinguishes hope is a spondaic substitution, the only one in the poem: 'And his dárk sécret lóve' . . . . The meter conducts the argument. The meter is the poem." *Poetic Meter and Poetic Form* (New York: Random House, 1979), 103–4. Of course, as Cureton rightly says, the meter is not the poem; the rhythm is the product of many other elements. But the strategy of trying to explain rhythmic effects by foot-substitution leads to a bizarre result, where Fussell distorts the fundamental two beat rhythm of the poem by scanning the line - - / ′ ′/ -′/ [And his / dárk sé / cret lóve], inventing a third foot for this two-beat line.

24. For an application, see Henri Meschonnic, "Un poème est lu: 'Chant d'automne' de Baudelaire," *Pour la poétique vol. III, Une parole écriture* (Paris: Gallimard, 1973), 277–336.

25. Amittai Aviram, *Telling Rhythm* (Ann Arbor: University of Michigan Press, 1994), 232–33.

26. Ibid., 5.

27. Ibid., 22.

28. As far as I know, Aviram's proposal has not really been taken up by anyone, and I think the reason is obvious: most criticism is hermeneutic in orientation. Critics want theories to help them discover hidden meanings and are rather less interested in theories that set out to account for how poems have the effects that they do.

29. Mutlu Konuk Blasing, *Lyric Poetry: The Pain and Pleasure of Words* (Princeton, N. J.: Princeton University Press, 2007), 14.

30. Ibid., 53.

31. Ibid., 55.

32. Ibid., 57.

33. Anthony Easthope, *Poetry as Discourse* (London: Methuen, 1983). I imagine that it is his treating iambic pentameter as a *bourgeois* form that has prompted criticism, for the general point seems to me eminently defensible.

34. Blasing, *Lyric Poetry*, 52–53.

35. Ibid., 58.

36. Michele Lowrie, in *Writing, Performance and Authority in Augustan Rome* (Oxford: Oxford University Press, 2009), surveys the use of terms such as *cano* and *carmen*.

37. Paul Valéry, *Vues* (Paris: La Table ronde, 1948), 291.

38. "Verse is that language in which the sonority and the linking of words, their signifying effect and their psychological responses, the rhythms, the syntactic arrangements are so tightly bound that our memory is necessarily cleansed of them, and the words form an object which appears as if it were *natural*, as if it were born out of real life." Paul Valéry, *Cahiers* (Paris: CNRS, 1958), vol. 8, 586.

39. "Le plaisir du texte c'est ce moment où mon corps va suivre ses propres idées, car mon corps n'a pas les mêmes idées que moi." Roland Barthes, *Le Plaisir du texte* (Paris: Seuil, 1973), 30.

40. "C'est mon corps de jouissance que je retrouve. Et ce corps de jouissance est aussi mon sujet historique; car c'est au terme d'une combinatoire très fine d'éléments biographiques, historiques, sociologiques, névrotiques, que je règle le jeu contradictoire du plaisir (culturel) et de la jouissance (inculturelle)." Ibid., 99.

What Is Called Rhythm?

David Nowell Smith

The current chapter concerns the definition of rhythm. Why should the definition of rhythm pose itself as a problem? Part of this reason lies in the expansiveness of its concept: "rhythm" extends beyond the domains of prosody and versification, and even of music and dance, to encompass the broader dynamics of sense-making. Today, rhythm is *intermedial* (involving music and dance especially, but also, increasingly throughout the century due to its explorations of color, of abstraction, its reflection back on the modalities of vision, an awareness of painterly dynamics, all brought together in Wagner's *Gesamtkunstwerk* and Pater's adoption of the term *Anders-streben*[1]), and even *cross-disciplinary*—or, better, it disregards the disciplinary boundaries of our own intellectual division of labor, with its institutional formations, its ideologies of expertise, etc. Hence "rhythm" will extend to include circadian rhythms,[2] corporeal rhythms (of the cardiovascular system, of the menstrual cycle, of sleep patterns), and through *ruthmos* invokes a metaphysical heritage reaching back to Democritus, Plato, and Aristotle, and in particular the question of how entities appear in time. Within the term "rhythm" thus crystallize so many heterogeneous movements, from which arises the question of poetic "rhythm" in particular: at once a point for the intersection of these broader rhythmic movements, and at the same time merely one set of movements amongst others. Rhythm becomes, to use Martin Heidegger's word, *fragwürdig*: both "questionable," and "worthy of question."

If "rhythm" today is marked by such expansiveness, this results from a historical expansion of the concept of rhythm. As many scholars have demonstrated in an Anglophone context (including several, notably Ben

Glaser, Ewan Jones, and Meredith Martin, who feature in the current volume), it is over the course of the nineteenth century that "rhythm" becomes one of the central terms through which to grasp the phenomenality of language and its relation to the material practices of historical subjectivity.[3] This is not a peculiarly Anglo-American phenomenon, though in continental Europe the transformation of the concept of rhythm becomes, if not a concept *for* philosophy, then a concept through which poetics sets itself in relation to philosophy, a concept through which philosophy tries to adopt a poetics. For instance, one might look to Friedrich Hölderlin's opening assertion to his "Notes on *Antigone*":

> Just as philosophy always treats only one faculty of the soul, so that the representation of this *one* faculty makes a whole, and the mere connection between the *parts* of this faculty is called logic: so poetry treats the various faculties of a human being, so that the representation of these different faculties makes a whole, and the connection between *the more independent parts* of the different faculties can be called the rhythm, taken in a higher sense, or the calculable law.[4]

Elsewhere, he is reported to have said that "All is rhythm; the entire destiny of man is one celestial rhythm, just as the work of art is a unique rhythm."[5] What distinguishes his notes on *Antigone*, however, is its avowed desire for art to supersede philosophy: the claim for a *rhythmic* totality superior to any totality that can be brought together by "logic." Yet in the "Preface" to Hegel's *Phenomenology of Spirit*, "rhythm" belongs to "logical necessity": the "rhythm of the organic whole" is the way in which the system holds together in differentiation. "This nature of scientific method, which consists partly in not being separate from the content, and partly in spontaneously determining the rhythm of its movement, has . . . its proper exposition in speculative philosophy"—a philosophy whose vocation is to attend to "the immanent rhythm of the Notion" without intruding upon it.[6] Or one might look to those thinkers—such as Schopenhauer or Wagner—who grasp rhythm as a "law" of harmonization. Thus for Schopenhauer: "Rhythm is in time what *symmetry* is in space."[7] And Wagner:

> The corporeal-man proclaims his sensations of weal and woe directly in and by those members of his body which feel the hurt or pleasure; his whole body's sense of weal or woe he expresses by means of correlated and complementary movements of all, or of the most expression-able of these members. From their relation with each other, then from the play of complementary and accenting motions, and finally

from the manifold interchange of these motions. [...] the law of this ordering is Rhythm.[8]

Or, at the far end of this century, lies another poet-philosopher, Stéphane Mallarmé, (whose own poetics does homage to Wagner above perhaps anyone else). Whilst he does not speak of rhythm as "Law," he has recourse to the "Idea," with music and rhythm his two preferred figures through which to see the Idea enter (provisional, aporetic) articulation. The "Book" he aspires to would by virtue of its "symmetry" constitute "a total rhythm."[9] The poet's task is to "provide an exact account of the pure rhythmic motifs of being," he writes, and they do so by "bringing human language back to its essential rhythm."[10]

Why should the expansion "rhythm" take place at this particular period in history? When Gilles Deleuze and Félix Guattari proclaim: "meter is dogmatic, but rhythm is critical," they might not be attempting to make a historical observation (they continue, echoing the now-customary opposition of rhythm to meter along the axes of flux and fixity, freedom and constraint, temporality and spatialization: "it ties together critical moments, or ties itself together in passing from one milieu to another. It does not operate in a homogeneous space-time, but by heterogeneous blocks. It changes direction").[11] And yet, they have unwittingly put their finger on a crucial moment in the historical constitution of rhythm as concept (term, constellation): Kant's awakening from his "dogmatic slumber" and foundation of a "critical" project which reframes the questions of (objective) ontology as questions of (subjective) conditions for the possibility of experience. Rhythm, as it were, becomes "critical" in the wake of philosophy reformulating itself as *critique*. If rhythm is "critical," it is not merely in the Kantian sense of establishing limits for thought/experience; rather, it is also in the attempt to exceed these limits, in the attempt to grasp precisely those harmonies that Kant had barred from the domain of philosophy. Perhaps it would be wiser to say that, for the poets and philosophers worked from out of the legacy bequeathed by Kant, rhythm is not so much "critical" as *speculative*.

When we look to the definition of rhythm, then, we first have to understand the historical singularity of this project. And while I have alluded to the elaboration of a "critical" philosophy, this is not sufficient as a response to the question of why the concept of rhythm should be subject to such expansion in the nineteenth century. To make sense of this to any satisfactory degree would further require the delicate work of understanding discourses on, and in, poetics in dynamic relation with the broader historical processes taking place: for instance, the various language politics arising with the growth of literacy, or with increased literary explorations of vernacular speech, be it in order to give voice to class/geographical experiences hitherto denied it (with all the attendant metaphysical baggage with which such invocations of "voice" are laden), or in shifting conceptions of linguistic diversity, where diversity is grasped as an integral feature of languages rather than an aberration to them; similarly, it would require tracing the development of technologies able to record and project sound, both for their effects on the way orality-aurality subsequently comes to be lived, and the scientific developments in phonetics and phonology they would facilitate, notably with regard to the significance of Helmholtz's experiments in acoustics for metrical study;[12] or transformations in everyday corporeal life, for instance through mass urbanization, the repetitive work practices of rationalized labor, be it industrial-proletarian or bureaucratic (such that they might seem "rhythmic" in some naturalized way that had not been apparent beforehand)—all those phenomena that led Walter Benjamin to see Charles Baudelaire's *Spleen de Paris* and *Tableaux parisiens* as constituted by the "shocks" which assail consciousness and atrophy experience in urban modernity: the crowd, mechanization, mass information.[13]

However, it is a second set of problems which will take up the large part of the chapter: namely if this expanded notion of rhythm becomes questionable—and worthy of question—at this period, then what questions are subsequently thrown up? This is where the work of *definition* becomes crucial. In the preliminary remarks to his "The Echo of the Subject," Philippe Lacoue-Labarthe cites some of those speculative propositions from Hölderlin and Mallarmé I have documented, to which he adds: "Such statements are a kind of emblematic formula. Or better, they are *legends*."[14] The French *légende* draws together two overarching meanings: a mythic tale (indeed, such statements are integral moments to the Hölderlin myth, the Mallarmé myth, the nineteenth century poet-philosopher myth); and the key to a map. So will definition function in the below: the creation of a *muthos* through which we can start to orient ourselves in conceptual space. Or, to see it another way: when Heidegger asks *Was heißt Denken?* (commonly translated as "What is called thinking?"), he plays on the indeterminacy of the German *heißen*, both "to call" and "to be called." The question "what is called thinking?" at the same time entails its reverse, namely: "what does thinking call?"[15] To "define" in this sense means to figure out which phenomena, which problems, can be designated and brought into focus by the concept, or term, or constellation, of "rhythm." It is not a question of determining that rhythm "is" *x*, but rather of formulating what it is that rhythm *calls*,

calls *for*, and calls *to*—what it allows us to think, what it demands that we think. My suggestion, in other words, is that "rhythm" functions not as *proper* name, but proleptically, pointing to this set of broader problematics, most notably regarding how we grasp the dynamic unfolding, and enfolding, of sense. But if the concept of "rhythm" thus brings into focus so many broader problematics, this raises a third set of questions, with which I will close. Namely—what is the relation between this expanded "rhythm" and individual poetic rhythms? How will this expanded rhythm affect our grasp of individual prosodic figures; and inversely, how might such figures open up the broader rhythmicity the various thinkers I discuss are trying to make sense of?

Order, Configuration, *Ruthmos*

One way to go about finding a definition for this expanded, expansive "rhythm," might be to return to the "original" meaning of the Greek *ruthmos*. Long taken to mean flux (derived from *rein*), both Emile Benveniste and Martin Heidegger, independently of one another and at more or less the same time, argued it should in fact be understood first and foremost as "structure," "configuration." This is not to say that *ruthmos* lacks a dynamic dimension: rather, we are being asked to reconceive of "structure" along dynamic lines. This immediately has broader repercussions: where the rhythm-meter distinction so often falls along those canonical axes already mentioned, of subjective-objective, temporal-spatial, individual-collective, flux-fixity, etc., the retrieval of *ruthmos* exacts a thinking that resists such a framework.

Heidegger's first discussion of *ruthmos* comes in his 1939 lecture on Aristotle's *Physics*, where he translates the Greek term as "articulating, impressing, structuring, and forming" [*Gliederung, Prägung, Fügung, und Verfassung*].[16] At this juncture in the *Physics*, Aristotle is responding to Antiphon's claim that the *proton arruthmiston,* that which is untouched by the temporality of appearance, is what is "most being" (even if, for precisely this reason, what is "most being" will never enter presence). Aristotle, Heidegger argues, inverts this: *ruthmos* does not describe entities that appear temporally, but rather indicates the temporal structure by which the entity remains within appearance. It is only in *ruthmos* that a being can disclose itself as "being." For Antiphon, what is "most being" cannot admit of a change of state, as this would amount to saying that its being is incomplete; the Aristotelian thematization of *ruthmos*, by contrast, entails that we conceive of being not as stable substance, but as dynamic "presencing." *Ruthmos*, on this account, names not flux, instability, but rather the temporal configuration through which beings come into presence.

At stake for Heidegger in the definition of *ruthmos* is nothing less than the conceptualization of being itself—in particular the decision as to whether we posit being as transcendent principle outside of time, or wish to argue that being "is" through its temporalization. Whilst Benveniste's observation does not frame itself with the same ontological focus, it nevertheless demands a similar line of questioning. Observing that *-mos* as a suffix for Greek abstract nouns "indicates, not the accomplishment of the notion, but the particular modality of its accomplishment as it is presented to the eyes,"[17] Benveniste continues:

> *ruthmos*, according to the contexts in which it is given, designates the form in the instant that it is assumed by what is moving, mobile and fluid, the form of that which does not have organic consistency; it fits the pattern of a fluid element, of a letter arbitrarily shaped, of a robe which one arranges at one's will, of a particular state of character or mood. It is the form as improvised, momentary, changeable.[18]

The transition from *ruthmos* to what we would today recognize as "rhythm" can only take place once the notion of form (*schema*) has been detemporalized, made static: the remaining temporal element—now grasped as flux, or flowing—gets named "rhythm." In Roland Barthes's gloss: *ruthmos* "is the pattern of a fluid element."[19] And at the same time, "rhythm" becomes the preserve of the arts: verse, dance, and song. As "rhythm," *ruthmos* is, as it were, doubly regulated: it now takes place within a circumscribed field only (a field, moreover, of imitation and non-truth—hence "less being"), and even within this field we find "the notion of a corporal *ruthmos* associated with *metron* and bound by a law of numbers."[20] This "law of numbers," presumably, is itself not temporally conditioned. Rhythm becomes the other to stasis only by being subject to static categories.

Given the thrust of his argument thus far, the conclusion Benveniste subsequently draws is perhaps surprising. He describes the overarching historical movement in the semantics of *ruthmos* as follows: "Starting from *ruthmos*, a spatial configuration defined by the distinctive arrangement and proportion of the elements, we arrive at 'rhythm,' a configuration of movements organized in time."[21] And yet, in his previous discussions of *ruthmos*, he had identified it not with "space" but with "mobility" and "provisionality"—both of which imply a temporal as much as (if not more than) a spatial plane. As Barthes puts it, *ruthmos* describes an arrangement or form that is "mobile, moving, fluid," and without "organic consistency."[22] Benveniste appears to remain within the framework of an either-or: he gives up on temporality at the very juncture where what is required is a rethinking of temporality, such that it is not reduced to "flow," but rather is grasped more broadly as dynamic configuration. This is the point at which Benveniste stops short; it is Heidegger's starting point. His account of *ruthmos* is inscribed within a broader attempt to grasp temporality not as a succession of "nows," or a subjectively experienced *durée*, but as the countermovements of presencing and absencing. In *Being and Time* this took place through his account of "ecstatic temporality": the three "temporal ecstases" of futurity, presence, and having-been (which correspond to the three existentials of projection [*Entwurf*], discourse, and thrownness [*Geworfenheit*]).[23] In the Aristotle lecture, and then in "Anaximander's Fragment" (1946), he appeals to cognates of the German *fügen*: *Fügung* (structure) and *Fuge* (jointure). Entities can come to presence, he argues, only by being "joined" [*gefügte*] together into a particular temporal configuration. He continues: "The jointure [*Fuge*] of the while confines and bounds what presences as such-and-such a thing."[24]

Why should Heidegger and Benveniste both return to the "original" meaning of *ruthmos*? One temptation is to portray this as a far broader search for an "origin": ontological, as well as historical, anteriority, where etymological speculation verges on myth-making. For Benveniste in particular this can seem unjust, given his meticulous philological analysis. And yet, perhaps we *should* see the work to be imbued with an irreducibly mythic dimension. Namely, it is counter-myth, drawing to our attention the historical contingencies of our own dominant conceptual categories, which are not without mythologies of their own, however naturalized they may have become. The point is that *ruthmos* has been thought otherwise, and hence can be again. Where Heidegger had turned to Anaximander, Benveniste notes the centrality of *ruthmos* as a term within Democritus' atomistic philosophy: the unraveling of the *episteme* which models the universe on static entities (be they Plato's forms, which as epistemological if not ontological constants remain foundational to Western thought, or Aristotle's law of the excluded middle) through the discoveries of particle physics, relativity, etc., coincides with a reappraisal of Greek atomism.[25]

Similarly, whilst so often criticized for positing an ontological origin by way of speculative (read: tendentious) accounts of etymological origins, Heidegger himself argued that he was not reconstructing an original usage, but rather tracing an "unthought." At the moment of the closure of the metaphysical tradition set into motion by Plato and Aristotle, he reads those early thinkers who might offer a *new inception*.[26] Such a reading, he reminds us, necessarily requires "violence:" it is not simply the reconstruction of what was lost, but takes up hints never articulated overtly. Again, the turn to etymology comes out of a thinking of one's own historicity: those concepts and assumptions that have become hardened over time but lead to an intellectual dead-end. The rethinking of *ruthmos*, then, arises from a very contemporary need to rethink structure in terms of movement.

Mobility, Oscillation, Relation

What draws both Heidegger and Benveniste to the question of rhythm, and *ruthmos*, is the attempt to think the dynamics (or, perhaps better, the *chronemics*) of language. This is integral to Benveniste's writing on pronouns, on tense, and on the sentence as "unit of discourse" irreducible to smaller phonological, semiotic, or syntactic units: "a complete unit that conveys both meaning and reference; meaning because it is informed by signification, and reference because it refers to a given situation."[27] To think the dynamism of language requires a pragmatics of discourse. For Heidegger, by contrast, this dynamism takes place within language's own capacity for making-appear. This capacity is double: language only makes other entities appear (through naming, referring, alluding, indicating) insofar as it itself appears as *language*; instead of the purported "transparency" of a linguistic token being the condition for successful reference, Heidegger suggests that reference is only possible by virtue of the phenomenality of words. These suggest two different levels at which Heidegger is grasping linguistic meaning through movement. First are the processes of naming, referring, alluding, indicating, and so forth: oscillations and modalities between word and thing, in which the thing both enters name and withdraws from naming. Second, he thematizes the ways in which language itself comes into appearance: its phonological-phonetic sounding, with its concomitant withdrawal from sounding into either noise or silence; its inscriptions, be it alphabetic script or other meaning-making signs; its performances and performatives of sense-making and opacity. Yet he also envisages a third level, subtending and linking these two, in what he calls language's "linguistic essence." In "The Way to Language" (1959), he describes *die Sprache* as *die Be-wëgung*, a "way-making movement" through which an originary saying (*das Sagen*) enters, and withdraws from, speech (*das Sprechen*).[28] At issue here is language's own oscillation between presence and absence, which in turn facilitates human self-articulation, our inhabiting the "open region" in which we are exposed to being. This implies an additional dynamic at work in rhythm: the countering movements of ecstasis and proprioception, opening up to exteriority and withdrawing to self.

What rhythm calls us to think, then, is not just the dynamics of *prosody*—the movements of linguistic sound—but the dynamics through which language enters appearance, and through which we open ourselves to, and in, language. But such entry into appearance also involves the rhythmicity of linguistic *absencing*, not just as countermovement to appearing, but also as it sets up the space in which appearance can take place. Such a thinking thus exacts a rhythmics of the inapparent. To see this, we can return to Mallarmé. In the *Crise de vers*, the "disappearance of the poet speaking, who yields the initiative to words" [*la disparition élocutoire du poëte, qui cède l'initiative aux mots*] is recast in terms of a "vibratory disappearance" [*disparition vibratoire*] effected by "the play of language" [*le jeu de la parole*].²⁹ Maurice Blanchot glosses this transition as follows: "Nature is transposed by language into the rhythmic movement that makes it disappear, endlessly and indefinitely; and the poet, by the fact that he speaks poetically, disappears into this language and becomes the very disappearance that is accomplished in language, the only initiator and principle: the source."³⁰ It is not just that, proffering its tokens in their place, language makes the entities it names disappear; rather, it is that language itself withdraws from sense, withdraws into itself. The poem not only makes manifest the disappearance of poet, and of what the poet describes, but the disappearance of language itself—makes this manifest *in language*. At this juncture, Blanchot's account, at first blushed diametrically opposed to Heidegger's, coincides with it: rhythm describes the oscillations of presence and absence, rendering manifest not merely absence, but the oscillations of this absencing movement.

When Jacques Derrida invokes these same passages from Mallarmé, this absencing movement becomes a "measure," as well as a rhythm. In "The Double Session" (1969-72), he homes in on Mallarmé's description of "a total rhythm, which would be the poem stilled, in the blanks,"³¹ and uses this to recast *ruthmos* as "the regular intervention of the blanks, the ordered turn of the white spaces, the measure and order of dissemination, the law of spacing."³² That Derrida should focus on "spacing" here is striking, given the problems that both Benveniste and Heidegger saw in the reduction of *ruthmos* to temporal flux. Whilst Derrida's most immediate allusion is to Mallarmé's tabular page, and his use of blanks as at once prosodic devices (as they regulate our voicing), and as resisting prosodic formulation (notably in their disjunction from the versified timing of speech), he is also signaling a train of thought initiated in *Voice and*

Phenomenon (1967). Here he had outlined a reciprocal movement: on the one hand, "*the temporalization of sense is from the beginning 'spacing'*"; on the other, "Space is 'in' time. It is the pure exiting of time to the outside of itself. It is outside-of-itself as the self-relation of time. The exteriority of space, exteriority as space, does not take time by surprise. Exteriority opens itself as the pure 'outside' 'in' the movement of temporalization."[33] Like Heidegger, Derrida intuits that the "opening" of meaning entails human exposedness to the *movement* of sense—a movement which encompasses the withdrawal of sense, and the withdrawal from sense. In *Voice and Phenomenon* he thematizes this as the movement of *différance*; in "The Double Session," this opening up of exteriority and inapparence is grasped overtly as *ruthmos*.

If rhythm comes to describe the oscillations of presencing and absencing, the opening up of exteriority and inapparence, then it cannot itself ever be wholly present, must show itself only through its disappearance—a frustratingly counterintuitive claim for any empirically minded prosodist. Derrida pursues this suggestion when, almost two decades later, in his introduction to the English translation of Lacoue-Labarthe's *Typography*, he perceives in Lacoue-Labarthe's treatments of rhythm a "rhythmo-typy" (drawing together *ruthmos* and *tupos*, rhythm and character) in which "the Same" falls into difference-with-itself through repetition: "Rhythm—the spaced repetition of a percussion, the inscriptive force of a spacing—belongs neither to the visible nor to the audible, neither to figuration nor to the verbal representation of music, even if it structures them *insensibly*. The structuration that a moment ago I called rhythmo-typical or typorhythmic must remain outside the order of the sensible. It belongs to no sense."[34] Rhythm becomes the dynamic articulation of sense while itself exceeding the order of sense—both as "meaning" and as the "sensible." This same logic is at work in Julia Kristeva's portrayal of a "semiotic materiality" which continually rises up into the symbolic realm, whose *kinesis*, "as rupture and articulations (rhythm), precedes evidence, verisimilitude, spatiality and temporality."[35] *Precedes* temporality, insofar as its *kinesis* belongs to the "drives," whereas temporality is a structure of conscious life; ruptures temporality insofar as temporality is one means through which the symbolic order is established as a *continuum*. "The semiotic is articulated by flow and marks: facilitation, energy transfers, the cutting up of the corporeal and social continuum as well as that of signifying material, the establishment of a distinctiveness and its ordering in a pulsating *chora*, in a rhythmic but nonexpressive totality."[36] The anteriority to sense is grasped as a resistance to sense.

Just as had Benveniste, Kristeva pits *kinesis* against temporality, rather than attempting to rethink temporality along the kinetic lines. It is for this, I would suggest, that she aligns rhythm's "articulation" with "rupture." But here there is an equivocation: is rhythmic articulation "essentially" negativity and rupture, or does it just appear so to the current constitution of the sensible? By modeling rhythm solely as negativity and rupture, the symbolic structure it negates remains strangely intact: if anything, these articulations remain dependent on "the symbolic."[37] And at the same time, the focus on what the symbolic realm leaves out, what exceeds the sensible, overlooks the question of how we account for the dynamism of appearance—the salient fact that things appear at all.

To which, I would like to propose an alternative reading of rhythm's "articulation," which does not reduce it to "rupture" and "cutting up," but also attends to Blanchot's suggestion that "rhythmic becoming [. . .] is the pure movement of relations."[38] Such setting-into-relation posits rhythm as fundamentally *medial*, a "between." In this respect it is not unlike Deleuze and Guattari's account of rhythm's "critical distance."[39] This is distance not simply as spatial relation, but rather as function of "a transcoded passage from one milieu to another, communication of milieus, coordination of heterogeneous space-times"; such rhythmic articulations would open up the difference through which repetition can return.[40] Or, one can think of Henri Meschonnic's insistence that rhythm should be understood first and foremost as the continuous [*le continu*], binding us to discourse and thereby to each other: again, a linkage of ec-stasis and proprioception.[41] It also reminds us that *Gliederung* (articulation) was one of Heidegger's proposed translations of *ruthmos* in the 1939 Aristotle lecture, along with *Fügung* (structure). Such "articulation" constitutes a setting-into-relation that incorporates countermovements of *jointure* as well as difference—indeed, becomes the jointure of difference. Thus conceived, articulation is necessarily multidimensional, gathering together differences that operate on heterogenous planes. This recalls the distinctions Heidegger made between the dynamism of language's naming, of its sounding, and of the "linguistic essence" through which "saying" enters speech. Here, we encounter one articulation of language qua "network of differences," where the differences between the various terms within the system are held in dynamic interrelation (so each signifier is differentiated from those contiguous with it), along with the relations of signifier to signified, sign to referent, etc. Yet there is another form of articulation at work—namely, in the self-relation of language itself. For language is simultaneously of the world and outside it; it is both embedded in matter, in sensuous life, and inheres in non-sensuous structures of meaning, such that it refers to entities within the world by virtue of its supervenience over them. Such an articulation would also set into relation those differences that Benveniste identifies within discourse and enunciation: between speaker [*énonciateur*] and utterance [*énoncé*], between speaker and interlocutor, between tenses, between pronouns, between subject positions. This is before we even consider the symbolic codes (also articulated around difference) through which ethical and epistemological categories become thinkable. Each of these articulations will have their "rhythms," insofar as they are continually unfolding, and enfolded, in time. And yet, what is "articulated" is not simply one single plane of differences, but the interrelations of these heterogeneous planes. "Rhythm" becomes a means of grasping how these different levels of articulation might themselves hold together in a dynamic whole.

What we thus encounter is a rhythmic opening-up of the horizon in which subjectivity becomes a position to be inhabited, something, which can be achieved. Of course, many of these thinkers would reject the term "subjectivity"; I use it on the proviso that we see it not as the structure of intentional consciousness, but from out of the opening of sense: a horizon in which subject positions become available. This horizon is "articulated" both in Meschonnic's sense of *le continu*, and Kristeva's sense of "rupture." And ultimately, this process is what is at stake in grasping the dynamic unfolding/enfolding of sense: a process of opening characterized by its oscillations, its countering movements—in short, its "rhythms."

The Oscillations of Poetic Rhythm

At this juncture, we might in fact advance a provisional definition of rhythm: that is, "rhythm" names the dynamic unfolding/enfolding of sense. And yet it names it not as a precise designation, but rather as the concept/term/constellation of rhythm demands that we *think* such unfolding and enfolding. All this, however, seems far removed from questions of prosody or versification. But I would suggest it raises two reciprocating questions: firstly, how might this expanded understanding of rhythm allow us to pay attention to oscillations and dynamics of verse that are not described by the technical repertoire of relative stress, figures of sound, or even higher level phonological/paralinguistic units such as intonation? and secondly, how might verse's deployment of these rhythms, its patterned temporality, provide a focus through which to grasp the broader rhythmic dynamics at work in such unfolding/enfolding?

To take the second question first: in each instance where a piece of verse attends to the latent rhythmicity of its verbal medium, it will necessarily be rendering manifest the dynamics of its own presencing: the appearances and disappearances of sense broadly conceived. In "Language in the Poem," Heidegger suggests that the poetry of Georg Trakl all arises from a single "site," which endows the individual poems with their animation: the effect is of a "wave" both rising up into the poems and yet "flow[ing] back to its ever more hidden source"—the poems offer momentary crystallization before withdrawing into hermeticism. And yet, this is not simply a question of sense-making: when he comes to grasp that movement, he concludes: "The site of the poem, as the source of the animating wave, holds within it the veiled essence of what—to metaphysical-aesthetic representation—can at best appear as rhythm."[42] "To metaphysical-aesthetic representation" can here mean two, intersecting things: either, that within the epoch of metaphysics, where poetic "form" is reduced to the "aesthetic," we can only grasp this "animating wave" as "rhythm;" or, that for these poems written in the epoch of metaphysics, it is as "rhythm" that they become able to trace and render manifest those animations for which in our present conjuncture we have no other means of grasping.

In Heidegger's account of Trakl, what is brought into appearance is a movement of withdrawal, described here as "rhythm" but concerned with the rhythms of sense-making as much as with prosodic movement. As we noted, Mallarmé sees the play of language to effect a *disparition vibratoire*, and elsewhere he describes words as the centre of a *suspens vibratoire*, with language remaining on the threshold of sense.[43] Blanchot depicts this as an "anterior point—the song anterior to the concept—where all art is language, and where language is undecided between the being it expresses by making it disappear and the appearance of being it gathers into itself so that in it, the invisibility of meaning acquires form and eloquent mobility. This moving indecision is the very reality of the space unique to language."[44] What distinguishes Blanchot from Heidegger is his attentiveness to the specific modes through which these individual poems actually appear, and render manifest their impulse towards disappearance. This is what permits him to argue that "[p]oetry then becomes what music would be were it reduced to its silent essence: an entrainment, a deployment of pure relations, that is, pure mobility."[45] Building on this one might say: if rhythm is the oscillation between presence and absence, then poetry's deployment of particular rhythmic figures renders manifest these oscillations and thus reflects back on its own dynamic presencing.

Blanchot's essay is modeled on Heidegger's "soundings-out" [*Erläuterungen*] of Hölderlin. As he clarifies in a footnote:

> Here we ought to remark that the attention brought to language by Heidegger, which is of an extremely probing nature, is attention to words considered in isolation, concentrated in themselves, to such words thought of as fundamental and tormented to the point that, in the history of their formation, the history of being is made to be understood—but never to the connections of words, and even less to the anterior space that these connections presuppose, and whose original movement alone makes possible language as unfolding. For Mallarmé, language is not made of even pure words: it is what words have always already disappeared into, the oscillating movement of appearance and disappearance.[46]

For Blanchot, Heidegger's problem is that he cannot actually *read* language as movement: he is not alone among critics in noting the contradiction between Heidegger's insistence on the dynamics of being, the fact that *Sein* is a verb, and irreducible to "essence," "substance," etc., and his tendency towards nominalization, towards positing so-called "foundational words" of being, which are anything but dynamic. Blanchot, by contrast, looks to the "connections of words," to their interrelations, for that anterior "space" whose movement-into-relation would constitute the originary temporalization of language.

The "mobility" of language is for Blanchot, as noted, made manifest as disappearance, as silence, as blank. And when Heidegger provides his gloss of *ruthmos* as structure, immediately he is drawn to a structuring stillness: "Rhythm, *ruthmos*, does not mean flux and flowing, but rather structure [*Fügung*]. Rhythm is what is at rest, what structures [*fügt*] the movement [*Be-wegung*] of dance and song, and thus lets it rest within itself. Rhythm bestows rest."[47] Within Heidegger's pattern of thought, such rest is far from being the *absence* of motion. In "The Origin of the Work of Art," he argues that what characterizes the artwork is its apparent self-subsistence, through which it advertises its facticity, the fact that it is rather than is not. In this instance, "rest . . . is an inner concentration of motion, hence a highest state of movedness."[48] In his reading of Trakl's "Ein Winterabend," he traces the poem's depiction of a threshold rent open, embarking on a broader reflection on the "dif-ference" [*Entscheidung*] within whose space entities appear. Heidegger reads the rending-open of the threshold in "Ein Winterabend" as a "rest" which brings entities into presence: "The dif-ference stills the thing, as thing, into the world."⁴⁹ What is most "still" is, for Heidegger, the entry into presence itself. He continues: "As the stilling of stillness, rest, conceived strictly, is always more in motion than all motion and always more restlessly active than any agitation." If this "insensible" rhythm becomes "sensed," it is precisely through attuning us to the thresholds of our sensing.

We might extrapolate from this two orders of stillness in rhythm. On the one hand, there are those crystallizations and intensifications of temporality that occur when the enfolded countermovements of the rhythmed work cohere in a singular configuration; on the other hand, there are those moments of dispersal, syncopation, rupture, points at which "silence" becomes a metonym for semantic and prosodic "noise" (itself a metonym). In both cases, what is being figured is (borrowing opportunistically, as Heidegger does, from the link between *Dichtung* and *Verdichtung*) a certain temporal thickening that is effected in art, a thickening of the art medium's own dynamics, its modes of appearance.⁵⁰ When Heidegger says that "*all art* [. . .], *is in essence, poetry*,"⁵¹ this is what he has in mind: every artwork draws its specific material support into openness, renders manifest the modalities of its own movement into presence. If at one level "rhythm" describes the dynamic unfolding/enfolding of sense as a whole, at another it describes the specific deployment of such unfolding/enfolding: a patterned temporality—and patterned out of the material support in question—through which these anterior rhythmic articulations take provisional form. In the case of poetry, this patterning of the art materials would not be restricted to phonological structure, but would concern the dynamics of sense-making more broadly: indeed, the "rhythm" Heidegger goes on to describe as "structure" is a sequence of images across Stefan George's poem "In stillste ruh": "Secure soul and sudden sight, stem and storm, sea and shell"—albeit a sequence characterized by its prosodic repetitions and alliterations as much as its shared metonymic palette: *Sichre Seele, jäher Blick, Stamm und Sturm, Meer and Muschel*. At stake is a broader rhythmic enfolding/unfolding, within whose jointures and disjunctions we orient ourselves in the poem.

When "rhythm" extends to this generalized movement into appearance, and ceases to belong solely to the domains of "lexical stress" and "musical beat," we start to attend to the rhythmicity of *discourse*, encompassing deictics, tense, aspect, and all that makes up the "situation" of enunciation. Verse rhythm in this instance will draw together configurations of temporality in segmented language—some of which might be considered "immanent" to the language (phonological and phonetic properties of the individual language), whereas others are channeled in verse but not evidently linguistic. However, it will comprehend not solely the segmentation of speech and paralanguage, but its broader segmenting and reconstituting of temporality, be it through address, complications in the intersections of narrated time, time of utterance, time of reading—all that makes up, in Jonathan Culler's phrase, "the anomalous lyric present," "lifted into a distinctive temporality without removing it from time."[52]

How, and where, might we see this rhythmicity taking place? In 1968, Gilles Deleuze, no doubt attentive to the programmatic/serial forms of recursion that accompanied late modernism, identified as his paradigm cases of difference-generating rhythm two modes of repetition, which he aligned to Raymond Roussel and Charles Péguy respectively:

> Roussel creates an after-language where, once everything has been resaid, everything is repeated and recommenced. Peguy's technique is very different: it substitutes repetition not for homonymity but for synonymity; it concerns what linguists call the function of contiguity rather than that of similarity; it forms a before-language, an auroral language in which the step-by-step creation of an internal space within words proceeds by tiny differences.[53]

To finish, then, let me extend such reflections to contemporary poetry. Remaining in an Anglophone context for now, one might think of the seriality through which motifs take on animation in the recent work of Lisa Robertson (*The Men* [2006], *Cinema of the Present* [2014]), where repetition effects a double movement of depersonalization and rearticulated personhood. As individual motifs attain an agency of their own (*disparition élocutoire* and *vibratoire*, as it were), we find open up a space in which subject positions emerge and articulate themselves. Or Claudia Rankine's *Citizen* (2015), whose accumulated reiterations of microviolences have the effect of grasping an experience that is simultaneously erasure and exposure, thereby redrawing the visible as political category, rendering visible what vision cannot see. Or of Juliana Spahr's *That Winter the Wolf Came* (2015), where recursions serve not just to ingest and rework arbitrary violence, but also to construct a polyphony and speculative time in the interstices of which lies the willed articulation of a political collective.

It is perhaps not for nothing that, in each of these instances, the work of rhythm is *political* work, probing the thresholds of a collective subjectivity. Perhaps, ultimately, this is where an expanded *ruthmos* would lead: attending to the dynamics around the thresholds of sense called for, and indeed called up, by the thickening of rhythm, what these different poetics open up is a revaluation of the sensorium: the distribution of bodies and languages. Here is the speculative work of rhythm that remains to come.

Notes

1. Pater defines this as an artwork's "partial alienation from its own limitations, through which the arts are able, not indeed to supply the place of each other, but reciprocally to lend each other new forces." Walter Pater, "The School of Giorgione," *The Renaissance* (Oxford: Oxford World's Classics, 1986), 85.

2. The term was coined by Franz Halberg in the early 1950s, with assistance from his colleague from the English Department at the University of Minnesota, Henry Nash Smith ("circadian" comes from "circa," because the period is *circa* twenty four hours). A nice example of how literary wordplay enters scientific terminology. cf. Halberg et al., "Transdisciplinary unifying implications of circadian findings in the 1950s." *Journal of Circadian Rhythms* 1 (2003): 9–10. The field of anatomical "rhythms" was well established by this time.

3. The term "material practice" comes from Marx, *The German Ideology*. On the notion of art arising out of not simply "materiality" but "material practice," see Henry Staten, "The Origin of the Work of Art in Material Practice." *New Literary History* 43, no. 1 (2012): 43–64.

4. Friedrich Hölderlin, "Notes on Antigone," *Essays and Letters*, trans. and ed. Jeremy Adler and Charlie Louth (Harmondsworth, U.K.: Penguin, 2009), 325.

5. Friedrich Hölderlin, cited in Philippe Lacoue-Labarthe , "The Echo of the Subject," trans. Christopher Fynsk, in *Typography* (Stanford, Calif.: Stanford University Press, 1989), 139–40.

6. G. W. F. Hegel, *Phenomenology of Spirit*, trans. A. V. Miller (Oxford: Oxford University Press, 1977), 34–36.

7. Arthur Schopenhauer, *The World as Will and Representation*, vol. 2, trans. E. F. J. Payne (New York: Dover, 1969), 453.

8. Richard Wagner, *The Art-work of the Future*, trans. William Ashton Ellis (1895), 100–1. One paragraph later he terms this a "law of reckoning." Translation available at http://users.belgacom.net/wagnerlibrary/prose/wagartfut.htm. Last accessed 18 April 2016.

9. Stéphane Mallarmé, "Crisis of Verse," in *Divagations*, trans. Barbara Johnson (Cambridge, Mass.: Belknap Press of Harvard University, 2007), 209. This total rhythm is to be opposed to both "the sublime incoherence of a romantic page," and "that artificial unity that adds up to a block-book."

10. Stéphane Mallarmé, *Oeuvres complètes* ed. Henri Mondor and G. Jean-Aubrey (Paris: Gallimard, 1992 repr.), vol. 1, 345; vol. 2, 266.

11. Gilles Deleuze and Félix Guattari, *A Thousand Plateaus*, trans. Brian Massumi (Minneapolis: University of Minnesota Press, 1987), 313. Deleuze had already anticipated this point in *Difference and Repetition*: "Cadence-repetition is a regular division of time, an isochronic recurrence of identical elements. However, a period exists only in so far as it is determined by a tonic accent, commanded by intensities. [. . .] On the contrary, tonic and intensive values act by creating inequalities or incommensurabilities between metrically equivalent periods or spaces. They create distinctive points, privileged instants which always indicate a poly-rhythm" (Deleuze, *Difference and Repetition*, trans. Paul Patton [London: Bloomsbury, 2014], 25). More recently, we find this opposition posited by some of the most advanced thinking currently taking place amongst "timers" (as opposed to "stressers"). See, for instance, Richard Cureton, "A Disciplinary Map for Verse Study," *Versification* 1 (1997). http://oregonstate.edu/versif/backissues/vol1/essays/

cureton.html (accessed 8 April 2016). Clive Scott makes a similar claim: "'Periodicity' I would define as the recurrence of linguistic units of the same length and the same structuring principle. Because it can only be ascertained in retrospect, at the end of the unit, periodicity belongs to the spatial rather than temporal, to units immobilized and juxtaposed. 'Rhythmicity,' on the other hand, is a principle of modulation in time, the way in which a sequence characterizes itself in movement, constructs a particular dynamic for itself." "Free Verse and the Translation of Rhythm," *Thinking Verse* 1 (2011): 71.

12. See, for instance, Cary Jacob, "On Tonality in English Verse," *Sewanee Review* 17, no. 4 (1909): 448–57.

13. Walter Benjamin, "Some Motifs in Baudelaire." *Illuminations*, trans. Harry Zohn (New York: Schocken Books, 2007), 159.

14. Lacoue-Labarthe, "The Echo of the Subject," 139–40. "L'Echo du sujet," *Le Sujet de la philosophie: Typographies I* (Paris: Flammarion, 1979), 220.

15. Martin Heidegger, *What is Called Thinking?*, trans. J. Glenn Gray (New York: Harper and Row, 1968), 21.

16. Martin Heidegger, "The Concept and Essence of *Phusis* in Aristotle's *Physics B, I*" trans. Thomas Sheehan in William McNeill, ed., *Pathmarks* (Cambridge: Cambridge University Press, 2001), 204, translation modified.

17. Émile Benveniste, "The Notion of 'Rhythm' in its Linguistic Expression," *Problems of General Linguistics*, trans. Mary Elizabeth Meek (Miami: University of Miami Press, 1971), 285.

18. Ibid., 285–86.

19. Roland Barthes, *How to Live Together: Novelistic Simulations of Some Everyday Perspectives*, trans. Kate Briggs (New York: Columbia University Press, 2013), 7.

20. Benveniste, "The Notion of 'Rhythm,'" 287.

21. Ibid. Michael Sheringham has suggested that Benveniste is here distinguishing between *rythmos* (the Platonic model as regularity) and *rhuthmos* (the fluid configuration of movement). See "Everyday Rhythms, Everyday Writing: Réda with Deleuze and Guattari," in *Rhythms: Essays in French Literature, Thought and Culture*, eds. Elizabeth Lindley and Laura McMahon (Bern: Peter Lang, 2008), 148. However, Benveniste in his essay never makes this etymological distinction explicit. In fact, Roland Barthes reads Benveniste to be saying that whilst the derivation of *ruthmos* from *rein* is "morphologically accurate," the "semantic shortcut" it suggests is "inadmissible." *Comment vivre ensemble: Simulations romanesques de quelques espaces quotidiens,* ed. Claude Coste (Paris: Seuil, 2002, 38). Benveniste does note the variance between $ρυθμος$ and $ρυσμος$, but says it is merely a question of "dialect" (fn 2. 312).

22. Barthes, *How to Live Together*, 7.

23. Martin Heidegger, *Being and Time*, trans. John Macquarrie and Edward Robinson (Oxford: Blackwell, 1962), 377.

24. Martin Heidegger, *Off the Beaten Track*, trans. Julian Young and Kenneth Haynes (Cambridge: Cambridge University Press, 2002), 277; translation modified. I have treated Heidegger's use of these cognates to think rhythm far more exhaustively in "The Art of Fugue: Heidegger on Rhythm." *Gatherings: The Heidegger Circle Annual* 2 (2012): 41–64.

25. Ironically, Heidegger notes Antiphon's debt to Democritus, and says of the *proton arruthmiston* that Antiphon, following Democritus, posits: "From the viewpoint of the history of being, 'materialism' as a metaphysical stance becomes apparent here" (*Pathmarks*, 205).

26. About Sophocles' *Antigone* he writes: "If we restrict ourselves to explicating what is directly said in the poetry, the interpretation is at an end. And yet with this the interpretation stands for the first time at the inception. The authentic interpretation must show what does not stand there in the words and which is nevertheless said." *Introduction to Metaphysics*, trans. Gregory Fried and Richard Polt (New Haven, Conn.: Yale Nota Bene, 2000), 173.

27. Benveniste, "The Levels of Linguistic Analysis," *Problems of General Linguistics*, vol 1, 110.

28. Martin Heidegger, "The Way to Language," in *On the Way to Language*, trans. Peter Hertz (New York: Harper and Row, 1971), 121. Heidegger adds an umlaut and hyphen to *Bewegen* (movement), saying this is a Schwabian archaism, distinct from the modern standard German word.

29. Mallarmé, *Divagations*, 208, 210.

30. Maurice Blanchot, "The Book to Come," in *The Book to Come* (Stanford, Calif.: Stanford University Press), 229.

31. Mallarmé, *Divagations*, 209.

32. Jacques Derrida, *Dissemination*, trans. Barbara Johnson (Chicago: University of Chicago Press, 1981), 178.

33. Jacques Derrida, *Voice and Phenomenon: Introduction to the Problem of the Sign in Husserl's Phenomenology*, trans. Leonard Lawlor (Evanston, Ill.: Northwestern University Press, 2011), 74–75.

34. Jacques Derrida, "Introduction: Desistances," in Lacoue-Labarthe, *Typography*, 32–33.

35. Kristeva, *Revolution in Poetic Language*, trans. Margaret Waller (New York: Columbia University Press, 1980), 26.

36. Ibid., 40.

37. Kristeva's strange dependence on the very "symbolic" realm that poetic language would unravel can be seen in her accounts of how this unravelling takes place: "These rhythmic, lexical, even syntactic changes [of poetry] disturb the transparency of the signifying chain and open it up to the material crucible of its production" (101); "the *unity of reason* which consciousness sketches out will always be shattered by the *rhythm* suggested by drives: repetitive rejection seeps in through 'prosody,' and so forth, preventing the stasis of One meaning, One myth, One logic." (148). What rhythm is set up against is "the signifying chain," is "reason" and oneness. And yet, what this does not lead to, for Kristeva, is an alternative form of meaning to signification, to an alternative form of reason to that of "one."

38. Blanchot, "The Book to Come," 226.

39. Deleuze and Guattari, *A Thousand Plateaus*, 320.

40. Deleuze and Guattari, *A Thousand Plateaus*, 315; See also Deleuze, *Difference and Repetition*, 21–22.

41. He writes: "rhythm is the language-organisation of the continuum of which we are made." Henri Meschonnic, "The Rhythm Party Manifesto," trans. David Nowell Smith, *Thinking Verse* 1 (2011): 165.

42. Heidegger, *On the Way to Language*, 160.

43. Mallarmé, *Divagations*, 235.

44. Blanchot, "The Book to Come," 241, translation modified.

45. Ibid., 225–26.

46. Ibid., 265–66, translation modified.

47. Heidegger, *On the Way to Language*, 149.

48. Heidegger, *Off the Beaten Track*, 27, translation modified.

49. Martin Heidegger, *Poetry Language Thought*, trans. Albert Hofstadter (New York: Harper and Row, 1971), 204.

50. This same link is what gives rise to Ezra Pound's celebrated aphorism: *DICHTEN = CONDENSARE*. Pound, *ABC of Reading* (New York: New Directions, 2010), 97.

51. *Off the Beaten Track*, 44.

52. Jonathan Culler, "The Language of Lyric," *Thinking Verse* 4, no. 1 (2014): 169.

53. Deleuze, *Difference and Repetition*, 22.

Sordello's Pristine Pulpiness

Simon Jarvis

Book Two of Browning's *Sordello* (1840) ends with a dazzling discard. The book has presented—and, at the same time, through verse-texture of a rich corrugation unmatched even in Browning's own other works, has thoroughly obscured—the most elaborate imaginable account of the poetics of the poet-hero, Sordello, of his own self-interrogations on this score, and of the way in which he takes his poetics to contrast with those of the rival poet Eglamor, whom Sordello has so efficaciously worsted in poetic agon as actually to kill him. At the end of this rich and strange meditation, Sordello apparently renounces poetry, or at least the public practice of it in which he has been so notably and so instantaneously successful. The renunciation of actually being a poet, of making and performing verses, is linked, in Sordello's mind, with the thought of a resumption of poetical, and perhaps even directly of political, power. In the very act of removing the poet's "crown," he remarks, apparently for his own benefit, "I shall be king again!" (ii.1001; L524).[1]

Although expected to officiate as poet at an important public event in Mantua next day, Sordello doffs the scarf set round him for a prize, and "into the font he threw / His crown." (ii. 1002-3; L524). The poet simply fails to turn up.

> Next day, no poet! Wherefore? asked
> Taurello, when the dance of Jongleurs masked
> As devils ended; don't a song come next?
> The master of the pageant looked perplext

> Till Naddo's whisper came to his relief;
> His Highness knew what poets were: in brief,
> Had not the tetchy race prescriptive right
> To peevishness, caprice? or, call it spite,
> One must receive their nature in its length
> And breadth, expect the weakness with the strength!
> So phrasing, till, his stock of phrases spent,
> The easy-natured soldier smiled assent,
> Settled his portly person, smoothed his chin,
> And nodded that the bull-chase might begin.

Sordello's jettisoning of his crown and scarf is matched and trumped here by a throwaway of Browning's own. The whole deeply worked poetics of verse which this Book has elaborated in verse is permitted, comically, to be effaced at once by Taurello's light enquiry, whose note is authentically that of a hunting English country squire, circa 1839: "Don't a song come next?" No poet? What a pity. Still, on with the bull-chase. The entire deep meditation set out in the rest of this Book on poetry's possible efficacy, on its relationship to power, spiritual and political—on what might now be called poetry's "criticality"—and on the relation of all these to verse composition itself, is deleted with a shrug.

The title of the book which you have in your hands—or, perhaps, some part of which, only, you have on your screen—seems to wish to make a distinction. The rhythm or rhythms in which it is to be interested are to be "critical." The adjective seems to say that rhythm might often, or even ordinarily, be received or experienced as uncritical, or even as the opposite of critique; that the specific difference which is to be made by this intervention is to conceive ways in which rhythm might have a critical force, instead, perhaps, of a lulling or assuaging or ideological one. No individual title, naturally, consisting of a mere phrase as it usually must, and lacking the specifying syntax which might turn that phrase into a claim or proposition of any kind, can bear too much scrutiny of this kind. Yet a title's freedom from syntax, its slogan-like or mythical excerptedness from such a context, can be at the same time just what makes it all the more necessary that it be interrogated. A title is just the blurred point at which various and even mutually antagonistic thoughts or practices of thinking and writing can be recruited together under a single banner, as mute and as insistent as a photograph of a young soldier.

"Critical rhythm": the phrase, at first hearing, is oxymoronic. The family of terms associated with criticism and critique imply customarily that something will be tested and judged. In a historiography which is fully "critical" rather than antiquarian, evidence will be subjected to an examination of its credentials, rather than taken on trust; in a "critical" edition the nature and authenticity of manuscripts, printed texts, and so on, will be assessed independently before they are allowed to provide readings for the edited text; or in a "critique" of pure reason, the instrument of knowing is to be subjected to an assessment of its nature and limits before it is allowed to be let loose and actually to know anything. How might "rhythm," this eminently non-propositional quantity, be in any of these senses "critical"? Its force has very often been taken to imply the reverse, an anaesthetic or lulling appeasement of awkward questioning. The phrase "critical rhythm" implies that rhythm can, in certain circumstances, take on a para-propositional or a cognitive force: a force by which it would be able to show something, to unconceal something, or even to think something. It brings us, indeed, close to an ugly term from recent discussions in art history and the aesthetics of visual art, a term which those disciplines have nevertheless often found it hard to do without: "criticality."[2] The criticality of a work of art (a category which, of course, itself remains under critical interrogation or even erasure) would be that mysterious constellation of its features or operations by which its relation to the existing social order might be more than a *purely* ideological one; by which that work would exercise an implicit, but perhaps explicable, critique of the social order which has produced it and with which it remains necessarily complicit. In Adorno's paradox, art is "society's social antithesis."[3] "Criticality"—Adorno himself tended to prefer the bolder and more embarrassing term "truth-content"—would cover those aspects of the work of art which allow it to be understood as exercising a work of negation or interrogation upon that very society which is its own condition of possibility.

For Adorno, of course, it would be impossible to attribute this elusive critical force or truth-content to any single technical feature or set of features characterizing works of art. No aspect of a work of art's technical handling bears truth-content in and of itself, but only as a moment in the entire complex constellation of forces and materials constituted by a singular work of art. There is no such thing as a "critical" harmonic repertoire, for example. Even free atonality is not critical in and of itself, nor is diatonic harmony automatically conservative. These technical arrays take on these forces only as they happen to be exploited and developed in particular musical compositions, either successfully or unsuccessfully.[4]

In order to interrogate and develop this phrase, "critical rhythm," a little further, I want to consider together two texts not often read in each other's company: the poem already introduced, Robert Browning's

Sordello—a poem which I take to be the among the most virtuosic displays in the field of extended verse-composition extant in English—and Immanuel Kant's *Critique of Judgment*. The connection between the two is not argued, here, to be one of Kant's possible "influence" on Browning, even though the possibility of an indirect influence of the philosopher on the poet cannot be perfectly excluded, but rather that, in the aporetic core of Kant's third critique, important structural features of the situation later faced by the poem *Sordello* are laid bare. The new verse planet discovered by *Sordello*, in the new repertoire of verse instrumentations, rhythms and sentences which it brings into being, is one on which there can be neither a science of the beautiful nor any "beautiful science," but in which a new poetics of the ugly begins to emerge, a poetics in which meter, rhythm and rhyme are permitted to "corrugate" the verse surface so as to produce a complexity of verse texture well in excess of any possible mimetic or illustrative role for which it could be recuperated. The connection will be developed specifically, rather than generally, by investigating a passing moment in the *Critique of Judgment* in which Kant considers the question of versification itself. The consideration is evidence for a larger hypothesis which I have been examining elsewhere, that moments at which philosophers consider *verse* are very often more revealing than those in which they meditate upon *poetry*, because, whereas the difficulty of defining "poetry" leaves it almost infinitely malleable to the philosopher's own preoccupations and predilections, the constraint imposed by the idea of "verse" is instead specific enough to exert pressure upon the philosophical apparatus brought up to interpret it.[5] The sense of "rhythm" which will be considered is necessarily restricted, time and space being so too: I shall concentrate on the sense which "rhythm" is usually given in metrics, as what results, in verse, precisely from the interaction between an arbitrary and abstract metrical pattern, a pattern which it is in principle impossible for any individual line of verse "perfectly" to realize, and the individual words, phrases, and sentences which are made to count as instances of that pattern in a verse composition. By insisting upon the absolute entanglement of "rhythm" in this sense in patterns of instrumentation, syntax, semantics, and verse-composition in general, I shall hope to mortify the assumption that there can in isolation be such a thing as a critical rhythm, that (for example) irregular rhythms might be more, or regular ones less, "critical." But by specifying in part the verse physiognomy of Browning's *Sordello* I shall offer some reasons for speculating that the poem's critical work on the verse repertoires it inherits is in practice the vehicle by which it is able to allow verse to open up sealed aspects of historical experience.

1

The earliest reception of *Sordello* was almost unanimous—the exception was R. H. Horne's scintillating piece in the *Church of England Quarterly*—in deploring its narrative obscurity and the harshness of its versification.[6] More than one of Browning's detractors pointed to a passage from near the beginning of Book Five as displaying convolutions egregious even from among *Sordello*'s flock of bizarreries:

> Yet before they quite disband—a whim—
> Study a shelter, now, for him, and him,
> Nay, even him, to house them! any cave
> Suffices—throw out earth. A loophole? Brave!
> They ask to feel the sun shine, see the grass
> Grow, hear the larks sing? Dead art thou, alas,
> And I am dead! But here's our son excels
> At hurdle-weaving any Scythian, fells
> Oak and devises rafters, dreams and shapes
> That dream into a door-post, just escapes
> The mystery of hinges. Lie we both
> Perdue another age. The goodly growth
> Of brick and stone! Our building-pelt was rough,
> But that descendant's garb suits well enough
> A portico-contriver. Speed the years—
> What's time to us? and lo, a city rears
> Itself! nay, enter—what's the grave to us?
> So our forlorn acquaintance carry thus
> A head! successively sewer, forum, cirque—
> Last age that aqueduct was counted work,
> And now they tire the artificer upon
> Blank alabaster, black obsidian,
> Careful Jove's face be duly fulgurant,
> And mother Venus' kiss-creased nipples pant
> Back into pristine pulpiness, ere fixed
> Above the baths.
>
> (v.21-46; L656)

What?

Woolford and Karlin's gloss for the longer passage of which this is part is, as usual, crisp and immensely helpful: "still using the architectural metaphor, Browning points out that Sordello's error was to assume that social justice could be accomplished in a moment, whereas it must inevitably be a gradual achievement, as the move from cave to city historically was." [L656] If the passage, seen through this optic, immediately makes sense, what also becomes clear is the immense surplus of verse corrugation over any possible extent to which this texture might illustrate, amplify or exemplify this underlying idea. What might most perspicuously have been told as an indicative narrative in the past tense is instead orchestrated, in a way wholly characteristic of Browning, as a series of rhetorical questions, imperatives, and exclamations—or, for one of his detractors, "pitching, hysterical and broken sobs of sentences."[7] A mildly deranged routine of self-interrogation is at work ("A loophole? Brave!"). Verbs of the indicative mood are distinctly in the minority: the passage is dominated by imperatives, interrogatives, and subjunctives. One way of interpreting this sort of feature of *Sordello*'s verse manner, of course, has been to take it as a still unrecognized instinct for the dramatic monologue trying to get out. But these features of the passage's verb-mood and rhetorical organization need to be understood in their relation to its phonotextual and prosodic instrumentation if their significance is to be heard accurately. Rhetoric almost always has significant rhythmic consequences, especially in verse. Here it sets up, briefly, a polymetrical passage in which two sets are running at the same time. "They ask to feel the sun shine, see the grass grow, hear the larks sing" is already, printed as prose, a striking instance of rhetorical parallelism, but, as relineation can make clear, it is also a miniature incantation in which an intonational contour is precisely reproduced three times:

> feel the sun shine
> see the grass grow
> hear the larks sing

This is what Roger Fowler called a "metrical rhyme" within phrases: the same part of speech in each case falls at the corresponding part of the phrase and has an equivalent stress value: modal-verb the noun verb, modal-verb the noun verb, modal-verb the noun verb.[8] But this very marked syntactic and rhythmic recurrence is also having at the same time to do duty within the ordinary five-beat couplets which form the metrical set for the poem as a whole:

> They ask to feel the sun shine, see the grass
> Grow, hear the larks sing? Dead art thou, alas,

The violence of the line-break—always marked when it falls between the subject of a verb and that verb—is even more evident here because it cuts into the three-phrase rhythmic recurrence with the metrical set which is deployed for the poem as a whole.

The passage comes to a climax with the astonishing line and a half on Venus, or rather on the sculptures of Venus which are the work of the refined artificers of the highest stage of city-construction; these are also the lines of the most intensely patterned phonemic linking and echoing in the passage:

> And mother Venus' kiss-creased nipples pant
> Back into pristine pulpiness, ere fixed
> Above the baths.

A good deal of what is singular in *Sordello*'s manner is compressed into these lines. The overloading of line 44 with stress (six, here) is a feature of many lines of the poem; equally typical is the way in which this is combined with a neologism formed by combination: "kiss-creased." "Kiss-creased nipples" shunts three stresses together at the same time as it sets up congested echoes: "kiss" has its initial consonant repeated in "creased," and its stressed vowel in "nipp-"; the medial plosive in "nipples" then spits all the way through the next line ("pant," "Back," "prist-," "pulp-"), and, in general, this poem loves spitting, clicking, and coughing consonants, taking no care whatever to produce a liquidity or smoothness of texture, but, rather delighting in the reverse, in a foregrounding of the physical apparatus of speech production and its bodily mess.[9] Then this needs to be taken together with the strange reversal in the sense. We well understand, especially after reading these comically luscious lines, with their curious mingling of "mother" Venus' maternal and erotic aspects, how anyone might pant for Venus' nipples, but what does it mean for the nipples themselves to "pant"? Or is it rather "the artificer" who "pants," whether from lust for his own too plausible creation or from fatigue at the labors necessary to produce it—an exhalation so powerful as to restore Venus' nipples to their former pristine pulpiness? "Pulpiness" suggests the frankest and crudest eroticism imaginable, wanting to get its hands on Venus' breasts right away. Then "ere fixed / Above the baths" is a miniature metamorphosis. It mortifies any reader who might have become too transported with the living palpability of these nipples, of all this polymorphous panting and kissing. This is just a statue after all.

A. C. Swinburne, who seems to have known much of *Sordello* by heart, gets, in a long digression on Browning towards the beginning of his book on George Chapman, to the heart of what is distinctive about *Sordello*.[10] Swinburne's excuse for his digression is that he wants to show why Chapman really is often obscure in a pejorative sense, by showing why Browning is not. On the contrary, Swinburne suggests, Browning "is something too much the reverse of obscure; he is too brilliant and subtle for the ready reader of a ready writer to follow with any certainty the track of an intelligence which moves with such incessant rapidity, or even to realize with what spider-like sagacity his building spirit leaps and lightens to and fro backward and forward as it lives along the animated line of its labour, springs from thread to thread and darts from centre to circumference of the glittering and quivering web of living thought woven from the inexhaustible stores of his perception and kindled from the inexhaustible fires of his imagination. He never thinks but at full speed; and the rate of his thought is to that of another man's as the speed of a railway to that of a waggon or the speed of a telegraph to that of a railway."[11] These sentences are about Browning in general; when Swinburne comes to discuss *Sordello* in particular, even he finds it necessary to qualify his admiration. The poem's "manner of construction" does "not seem defensible" to him, he confesses. It "is like a structure in which the background runs into the foreground, the figures and the landscape confound each other for want of space and proportion, and there is no middle distance discernible at all." Just such analogies from painting—the rebuke of a naïve failure of perspective—had earlier in the century been objected to Keats' *Endymion*, the poem which, with real differences, is *Sordello's* true verse ancestor, and whose links with Browning's poem had already been recognized by Horne. Swinburne, though, goes on to make a still more fundamental point. The poem's style, he writes, is "neither a dramatic nor a narrative style, neither personal nor impersonal, neither lyric nor historic, but at once too much of all these and not enough of any."[12]

Swinburne at last joins the long tradition of depreciating *Sordello* by comparison with Browning's later securely achieved mode of dramatic monologue. "The best parts of this poem also belong in substance always and sometimes in form to the class of monodramas or soliloquies of the spirit; a form to which the analytic genius of Mr. Browning leads him ever as by instinct to return."[13] But there may be a danger of an evolutionary fallacy, reading *Sordello* from the retrospect of Browning's later achievements in dramatic monologue, in insisting that effects of this power and complexity must merely have been immature specimens of a still misunderstood talent for dramatic monologue. The imperatives, apostrophes, subjunctives, and so on, which striate Browning's conjectural history of an imaginary city given near the beginning of Book Five, need not be germs of drama, but might also be considered as marks of the poem's continual collision of narrative and *lyric* modes. *Sordello* has proved hard to assimilate even for its academic apologists, I suggest, because it is so difficult to subordinate its verse texture to a properly hermeneutic function. In the model still dominant, the texture of verse-composition is presumed, in order to earn its place in an analysis, to be in need of being shown to be in the service of some larger interpretative point. This procedural hierarchy often produces in its turn a misleading idea of how the composition of long poems itself works; it is often allowed to imply that everything remarkable about the poet's verse technique is remarkable as offering a series of exemplifications and enactments of a prior set of hermeneutic designs upon the reader. This poem renders inoperable the privileging of hermeneutics over poetics. In *Sordello* we find waged as perhaps nowhere else in the long poem in English a continuous and unremitting war to the life between line and design. The plot is quite extraordinarily complex, but, as generations of Browning commentators have shown, and, especially, as the massive interpretative achievement of the Longman editors of this poem has demonstrated, it is not arbitrary or absent: it works, and it is worked out, for all its complexity, with remarkable care and consistency. It would be no mean thing to follow this plot, with its confusingly various nomenclature, sudden shifts of time and place, and so on, were it set out in prose; but the poem's verse texture appears almost at all times to be taunting the reader by offering a competing series of traps for his or her attention, traps whose point is by no means to be in the service of or to clarify the plot, but rather, for all we can see, to distract readers from it, to make it impossible to keep their mind primarily on the "story."

2

In the *Anthropology from a Pragmatic Point of View* Kant makes a distinction between two meanings of the term "poetry." *Poetica in sensu lato*, that is, in a broad sense, "may include the arts of painting, horticulture and architecture, as well as the arts of composing music and verse." The latter, verse-making, is what Kant calls *poetica in sensu stricto*.[14] The only explicit mention of versification in the *Critique of Judgment* comes in section 43, "On art in general." Kant is specifying the concept of art by running through a series of oppositions. Art is distinguished from nature as doing is from acting in general; it is distinguished from science as practical is distinguished from theoretical ability or technic from theory; it is distinguished from craft as free self-activity is distinguished from alienated labor. It is in the course of explaining this last opposition that Kant's remarks about prosody are made. Having explained that free art can only succeed if it is agreeable on its own account, Kant now makes an important qualification. Art must be free, but not so free that it becomes entirely disembodied:

> It is not inadvisable to recall that in all liberal arts there is nevertheless required something compulsory, or, as it is called, a *mechanism*, without which the *spirit*, which must be *free* in the art and which alone animates the work, would have no body at all and would entirely evaporate (e.g. in the art of poetry, correctness and richness of diction as well as prosody and meter), since many modern teachers believe that they can best promote a liberal art if they remove all compulsion from it and transform it from labor into mere play.[15]

This is both a difficult and a significant sentence, with numerous echoes in Kant's wider authorship. First of all, it specifies the earlier suggestion that free art must be play. Free art must be "play, i.e., an occupation that is agreeable in itself."[16] But it must not be "mere play," as it would were all constraint removed. The distinction is close to that which Kant makes in the preface to the second edition of the *Critique of Pure Reason*, where he remarks that

> Those who reject his [Wolff's] kind of teaching and simultaneously the procedure of the critique of pure reason can have nothing in mind except to throw off the fetters of *science* altogether, and to transform work into play, certainty into opinion, and philosophy into philodoxy.[17]

Any poet attempting free verse, this connection suggests, would be enacting a kind of poetical equivalent of skepticism, a versificatory philodoxy. Art, like science, must be work, even if—unlike science, which can never in any case be beautiful—it may not be undertaken for the sake of pay. Secondly, the sentence on prosody from section 43 of the *Critique of Judgment* raises the difficult question of the relation between art's spirit and its body. This is a rare moment at which Kant takes advantage of that lexical connection between the philosophical and chemical senses of the term spirit which was so often exploited by eighteenth-century ironists—for example in Swift's "Dissertation on the Mechanical Operation of the Spirit." If there were no constraint or mechanism in art, Kant says, the spirit would have no body and would *evaporate* [*verdunsten*]. Meter and prosody, therefore, are figured here as a kind of reliquary. They contain something which is infinitely precious—for what could be more precious than a free spirit which animates something which, presumably, would otherwise be dead?—and yet they must also constrain this precious, animating liquid, which would otherwise vanish into thin air.

Two different kinds of possibilities, then, seem to be envisaged for verse. It might be a mechanism, something itself inert and non-living, whose whole point is that it should in some way *arbitrarily* constrain the free spirit of art, and where what matters is not any property which the mechanism might have on its own account, but the mere fact that free spirit meets a constraint and is therefore obliged to turn play into work. Or it might be a body, something in which the free spirit of art finds an altogether appropriate embodiment or incarnation, an embodiment without which it could hardly in any case produce a work of poetry, rather than vague feelings of poetical inspired-ness, at all. The choice of the word "mechanism" seems deliberately to emphasize the inorganic, the arbitrary nature of the constraint; but the fear that, without this mechanism, spirit might lack a body, seems to do the very reverse.

We cannot but be aware of the contrast between the way in which Kant treats the question of arbitrary constraints in his critique of established religion, and the way in which he treats them in the case of art. In Part Four of *Religion within the Boundaries of Mere Reason*, which bears the subtitle "Of Religion and Priestcraft," Kant cuts through the complacency which thinks of verbally articulated prayer as somehow less superstitious than more visibly embodied religious practices:

> Whether the devout individual makes his statutory visit at *church* or undertakes a pilgrimage to the sanctuaries in Loreto or Palestine; whether he takes his formulas of prayer to the heavenly authorities with his *lips*, or by means of a *prayer-wheel*, like the Tibetan (who believes that his wishes, even if set out in writing, will reach their end just as well, only provided that they be *set in motion* by some thing or another, by the wind, for instance, if written on flags, or by the hand, if enclosed in a canister as though in a slinging device), or whatever the surrogate for the moral service of God might be, it is all the same and of equal worth.[18]

Nothing visible or physical can ever stand in for the invisible. For Kant the lips which move in prayer might just as well be a prayer-wheel turned only by the wind. The lips can add nothing which the spirit has not already performed. But perhaps there is to be a moment, like that which we have just seen in the *Critique of Judgment*, in which the illusion of a pure and wholly unconstrained spirit will itself be turned upon and subjected to constraint? This possibility is in fact raised immediately afterwards, only to be decisively removed:

> But is there not also perhaps a dizzying *delusion of virtue*, rising above the bounds of human capacity, and might it not well be reckoned together with groveling delusion of religion, in the general class of self-deceptions? No. The disposition of virtue has to do with something *actual*, which is in itself well-pleasing to God and conforms to what is best for the world. True, a delusionary sense of superiority may attach itself to it—the delusion of regarding oneself adequate to the idea of one's holy duty. But this is only accidental.[19]

So, although there certainly are delusions that can attach to the disposition of virtue, these are "accidental." The delusion which attaches to any attempt to provide an outer manifestation of an inner state, however, is essentially a surrogate for virtue, whose very character is made up of delusion. The contrast with the *Critique of Judgment* is striking. There is no danger that the moral service of God will "evaporate" without a tangible embodiment. On the contrary, such embodiments are precisely what imperils that service.

Now, from one point of view, this is not at all surprising. For Kant, this just is the difference between acting morally and making a poem. What are significant for us, however, are the consequences of Kant's insistence on the radical nature of this separation. It means that, in the end, it makes no difference at all whether the scrap of contingency which is used to provide a constraint is an inert mechanism or a living body. Sing expressively or twiddle your thumbs: either is equally useless so far as rational religion is concerned. There can be no appropriate external form of worship because it is the very notion of an external form which is inappropriate. Conversely, in the case of prosody, there is no sense at all in Kant's account that one or another exercise of free spirit might be better or worse domiciled in one or another meter. Indeed, a friction between the two seems to be the whole point. The constraint is there just for the purpose of making the poet do some work, and so to prevent poetic inspiration from going up in smoke.

Central to the development of twentieth-century metrics was the clarification and codification of the difference between meter and rhythm. This is understood in different ways in different traditions, of course, but, crudely put, meter is a wholly arbitrary pattern which can in fact never be perfectly realized by any individual line of verse. Rhythm, in such accounts, is created precisely by the inevitable *tension* between a metrical set and individual lines of verse in individual delivery instances. In this process of the separation of meter from rhythm Kant plays both an admitted role, and an even more important unadmitted one. Many of the chief metricians, especially amongst the Russians, were directly influenced by early twentieth-century neo-Kantianism and by its aesthetics in particular. Zhirmunsky's *Theory of Verse* explicitly acknowledges its debt to Kant. But even where there is no explicit acknowledgement of Kant, the essential conceptual structure is one that I would suggest is hardly thinkable without Kant. Meter is continually described by metricians as a norm, yet one that can never be realized. Individual lines may be closer to or further away from this norm; they can never perfectly embody it, just because it is in the very nature of meter to be a more perfectly abstract pattern than we ever find in natural language. It is a "norm," that is, of a highly factical kind: it contains no particular values or properties except that of being laid down and of resisting all attempts to approximate to it. It is highly questionable, in fact, whether the word "norm" is at all of any further use in describing meter, because by metricians it is treated in practice just as Kant here treats it: as a purely mechanical constraint, whose whole point lies in its being mechanical. The current standard theory of the relationship between rhythm and meter bears, in fact, a strong resemblance to the idea of the asymptotic progression of the moral agent towards the good—but one which lacks the idea of the good, lacks the idea of moral agency, and lacks the idea of progression. In this sense, the implication of Kant's sentence on verse-making, that meter is not itself a shape of spirit but instead a purely external and mechanical constraint upon it, has come to dominate the field.

Hence the temptation to think of verse "rhythm" as the "critical" element of verse. Against meter's inhuman abstraction and constraint, rhythm would figure as the concrete, the living, the embodied, the organic, the spontaneous. Such a temptation is succumbed to whenever, as quite often happens, irregular or metrically defective lines are regarded, quasi-allegorically, as connoting or even as producing "subversion" or disturbance of some larger code of values or assumptions, a code which can then be implicitly identified with metrical regularity.

Kant's extremely brief discussion of versification in the *Critique of Judgment* has, for all its strangeness, and for all that it shows no evidence of any real understanding of or interest in versification on Kant's part, this merit: that it does not attempt to place meter in an organic or mimetic relationship to meaning. It regards meter as of a substance quite inorganically alien to the "spirit" of poetry, and takes this alienness to be meter's virtue. One need not follow Kant in thinking of meter as a kind of container to take a hint, nonetheless, from his insistence on the *antagonistic* element in the relationship between meter and meaning.

3

For Kant, then, a persisting antagonism between spontaneity and constraint is what makes poetry poetry, rather than a mere vanishing effusion of high spirits. Much of the poetics of verse elaborated in book two of *Sordello* is concerned with precisely this clash. But Browning's version of it is never as simple as the relation of the lid of a jar to the volatile spirits inside it. Browning's sense of the mutual antagonism of spontaneity and constraint is dynamic, a continuous love-fight in which neither opponent can remain unscathed.

Sordello's first brush with actual *poetica in strictu senso*, as opposed to that *sensu lato* which he has been cultivating just by being poetical and thinking deeply in and around Goito in book one, reads at first like a dream of spontaneous genius triumphant. Sordello has "wandered forth" to Mantua and happens to find the lady with whom he is in love, Palma, hearing with others a poetical performance by the "best Troubadour of Boniface," Eglamor.

> Has he ceased?
> And lo, the people's frank applause half done,
> Sordello was beside him, had begun
> (Spite of indignant twitchings from his friend
> The Trouvere) the true lay with the true end,
> Taking the other's names and time and place
> For his. On flew the song, a giddy race,
> After the flying story; word made leap
> Out word; rhyme—rhyme; the lay could barely keep
> Pace with the action visibly rushing past:
> Both ended. Back fell Naddo more aghast
> Than your Egyptian from the harrassed bull
> That wheels abrupt and, bellowing, fronts full
> His plague, who spies a scarab 'neath his tongue,
> And finds 'twas Apis' flank his hasty prong
> Insulted. But the people—but the cries,
> And crowding round, and proffering the prize!
> (For he had gained some prize)—He seemed to shrink
> Into a sleepy cloud . . .
>
> (ii. 78-96; L468)

All the elements of a juvenile fantasy of poetical success are present. Sordello's act of performance is not premeditated, but appears to come over him ("Sordello was beside him"). Despite the fact that this is his first outing, and, so far as we can tell, his first practical encounter with song and with verse in particular, rather than with the poetical in general, Sordello knows just what to do and how to do it. Acclaim is total, universal, and instantaneous. The people crowd round. The poetry connoisseur currently in possession of the field, Naddo, meanwhile, knows with horrified immediacy that he is in the presence of sacred inviolability (the "scarab"). Last, Sordello wins a prize for which he did not even know that he was competing ("some prize"). And his response is to shrink into a sleepy cloud, fleeing from the possible imputation of ever having wished for prizes, acclaim, and so forth. Never in the poem does Sordello sound more like his dreamy ancestor, Keats' Endymion, than in this cloudy retreat. The elements of mock which hover around the hero throughout *Sordello*, and which often make him sound like a Crispin *avant la lettre C* (compare "He pondered this") are just held at bay.

Yet a counter-song is also at work here, one in which the little bits and pieces of verse-making are not the passive materials upon which spontaneous genius exerts itself, but are instead themselves motors of invention, what bears Sordello's song up: "[W]ord made leap / Out word—rhyme, rhyme." Sordello's song does not in fact come out of thin air but as an act of what we could call rhapsody, in Gregory Nagy's precise sense that the rhapsode is the one who is able to take up the song wherever another leaves it, and who strives to outdo as he takes up.[20] Sordello takes Eglamor's "names and time and place / For his." The description of the performance does not depend upon the subordination of execution to invention, nor on a myth of their ineffable unity, but rather shows, in a barely intelligible way, each competing with the other. It is hard to know what it can mean to say that the song was struggling to catch up with the story, or that "the lay could barely keep / Pace with the action visibly rushing past," since the action can only rush past insofar as the lay makes it do so, and the whole story is sung. What seems to be meant, rather, is the felt antagonism of two different kinds of attention or practice, their necessary discrepancy and mutual competition, figured here as a race.

The description of Sordello's first success can hardly avoid taking on a metaprosodic force. It is likely immediately to remind us of aspects of Browning's own verse manner in *Sordello*. An instance is the poet's apostrophe to Dante, in which he explains that although we almost always think of Sordello in relation to Dante, he, the poet, wishes to detach Sordello from Dante and to consider him as he is in himself:

(If I should falter now)—for he is Thine!
Sordello, thy forerunner, Florentine!
A herald-star I know thou didst absorb
Relentless into the consummate orb
That scared it from its right to roll along
A sempiternal path with dance and song
Fulfilling its allotted period
Serenest of the progeny of God
Who yet resigns it not; his darling stoops
With no quenched lights, desponds with no blank troops
Of disenfranchised brilliances, for, blent
Utterly with thee, its shy element
Like thine upburneth prosperous and clear:
Still, what if I approach the august sphere
Named now with only one name, disentwine
That under current soft and argentine
From its fierce mate in the majestic mass
Leavened as the sea whose fire was mixt with glass
In John's transcendent vision, launch once more
That lustre? Dante, pacer of the shore
Where glutted hell disgorgeth filthiest gloom,
Unbitten by its whirring sulphur-spume—
Or whence the grieved and obscure waters slope
Into a darkness quieted by hope—
Plucker of amaranths grown beneath God's eye
In gracious twilights where his Chosen lie,
I would do this! If I should falter now—

(i. 347-73; L417-18)

The most immediately striking feature of this passage is the distended sentence beginning in its third line and continuing without any other punctuation than that of line end itself all the way through to the semicolon in the middle of line nine. Its syntax is compressed because, still more than is habitual with Browning, it omits many connectives which would ordinarily be present. This feeling of intense compression is compounded by the difficulty of parsing the sentence: "Relentless," for example, seems to be an adjective qualifying "thou," but, because it appears immediately after the verb "absorb" made prominent by line-end, we wonder briefly whether it might be an archaic adverb qualifying that verb; or, again, if it be an adjective, whether it might even qualify the "herald-star" and not "thou" at all. Then there is the frequent impersonal pronoun "it," which we need to keep referring back to the "herald-star," even though it is closer to the "orb." The level of paraphrase, meanwhile, continues almost immeasurably distant: faced with the difficulty of getting these lines out so as to make syntax and meter work at once, readers are hardly in a position to work out what is perfectly clear once the passage has been paraphrased, that "thou" is Dante and the herald-star Sordello, and that the poet is saying that Sordello has tended to be overshadowed, or, rather, over-illuminated, by Dante.

What accounts for this passage's peculiar power, I think, is that a high degree of difficulty in construing the sentence, a degree of difficulty ubiquitous in *Sordello*, meshes or collides at this point with a melodic pattern at once rapid and incantatory. Consider lines 349–54:

Re	lent	less	in	to	the	con	sum	mate	orb
That	scared	it	from	its	right	to	roll	a	long
A	sem	pi	ter	nal	path	with	dance	and	song
Ful	fill	ing	its	all	ott	ed	pe	ri	od
Se	re	nest	of	the	pro	ge	ny	of	God

From the third to the fifth syllables of these lines there is only one clear primary stress: on the "ter" of "sempiternal." For most of this sequence, in other words, Browning omits to accent the fourth, a place which usually is accented in the English heroic line and, as can be seen from the rest of this long passage, is usually accented even in Browning's heroic line. "Relentless into the consummate orb" begins this series with a line of startling rapidity—phenomenologically rapid, that is, in the experience of speed which the appearance of five weak syllables in a row induces, since there is no real evidence that such lines take less time to speak than lines full of stresses—and it then begins what we could think of as a kind of rhythmic rhyme, to adapt a term of the poetician Roger Fowler, running through the next four lines. Yet there is no hint at all of syntactic rhyme, that feature which Fowler so clearly illustrates from Marlowe's *Tamburlaine*, in which rhythmic repetitions would be precisely matched by syntactic ones.[21] Instead the part of speech which in each case occupies the repeated rhythmic formula is continually varied. So, virtuosically, are polysyllables and monosyllables. "Relentless into the consummate orb" draws part of its springiness from the two polysyllables, which provide a completely unambiguous pattern of accents to carry us across this line with only three of them. But two lines later, the poet is able to achieve the same effect with an almost entirely monosyllabic line: "That scared it from its right to roll along."

If, so far, syntax has in a certain sense been subordinated to rhythm, made to fit itself as best it can into a tune, the verse now reverses that priority by offering us a place at which the role of syntax in specifying intonation is, precisely, foregrounded: at "for, blent/ Utterly with thee" the pointed comma after "for" demands an accentuation which we might otherwise forgo in order to avoid the extreme irregularity of having both nine and ten but not eight stressed, and runs, in turn, into a rhythmic problem in the next line, where we should like, in order to make the best sense, to emphasize "thee" (since it is hardly clear what point there would be in emphasizing the fact that Sordello is blent *with* Dante rather than through him or into him or around him), yet making the line work as a metrical instance pushes us towards just that accentuation.

Swinburne, we remember, thought that it was the poem's *style* which was "neither lyric nor historic." It is at the level of the poem's melodics, the intonational system of its verse syntax, that its generic collisions are most obtrusively present. The song-like melody of the earlier, barely punctuated, part of the passage accompanies the densest possible thicket of syntax and reference; the instructions issued by punctuation, later on, seem momentarily to make prose argument into the dominant factor. If it is the case that verse delivery is suspended between song and speech, then characteristic of Browning's melodics is to make that delivery perform hairpin turns between one and the other, to perform with extreme abruptness those transitions which had, even so recently as Wordsworth's comments on the versification of "Tintern Abbey," been considered as more characteristic of the greater lyric, than of the narrative long poem.

How critical these qualities are to *Sordello* can be appreciated when we consider Browning's revisions to the poem. They certainly fall far short of what he once envisaged, that process which in a letter of 1856 to the American publisher James T. Fields he referred to as "simply *writing in* the unwritten *every-other-line* which I stupidly left as an amusement for the reader to do—who, after all, is no writer, nor needs be" (L355). Browning abandoned this plan. Yet what he did do does have a powerful impact upon the poem's melodics, because Browning punctuates much more heavily in his later texts. Even very slight alterations can have an important effect upon verse texture. Here is the 1888 text of the same passage:

(If I should falter now)—for he is thine!
Sordello, thy forerunner, Florentine!
A herald-star I know thou didst absorb
Relentless into the consummate orb
That scared it from its right to roll along

> A sempiternal path with dance and song
> Fulfilling its allotted period,
> Serenest of the progeny of God—
> Who yet resigns it not! His darling stoops
> With no quenched lights, desponds with no blank troops
> Of disenfranchised brilliances, for, blent
> Utterly with thee, its shy element
> Like thine upburneth prosperous and clear.
> Still, what if I approach the august sphere
> Named now with only one name, disentwine
> That under-current soft and argentine
> From its fierce mate in the majestic mass
> Leavened as the sea whose fire was mixt with glass
> In John's transcendent vision,—launch once more
> That lustre? Dante, pacer of the shore
> Where glutted hell disgorgeth filthiest gloom,
> Unbitten by its whirring sulphur-spume—
> Or whence the grieved and obscure waters slope
> Into a darkness quieted by hope;
> Plucker of amaranths grown beneath God's eye
> In gracious twilights where his chosen lie,—
> I would do this! If I should falter now![22]

The changes are apparently of the most minor, yet they make a very important difference to the melodics of the passage. 1840's five sentences have now become seven. At the middle of the passage, the colon after "clear" has been replaced with a full stop, thus breaking the passage's huge central sentence into two and offering a more marked resting place. The most significant change, however, is that to the end of the long incantatory series at the beginning of that sentence, from "A herald-star I know thou dost absorb" to "Who yet resigns it not." A comma now appears after "period" and a dash after "God." These little alterations represent a tiny failure of nerve in the poem's melodics. The achievement of sustaining in the air thus many lines without punctuation, held together by syntactic relation alone, has given way, now, in the last few lines, to a looser or paratactic connection, in which, therefore, "Serenest of the progeny of God" is now merely an addition to the list of Sordello's properties instead of precisely that manner in which Sordello is to be understood *as* "Fulfilling his allotted period."

Although many of Browning's revisions concern what might once have been thought of as "accidentals," therefore, they in fact completely alter the substance of the poem by transforming its melodics. They do this along just the axis intuited by Swinburne—that of genre or mode, but mode sounding in the smallest details of intonation.

4

If we decline, then, to follow the consensus in understanding the undecidability of *Sordello*'s mode as a symptom of a poet with a genius for dramatic monologue struggling to get out, and instead regard it as the vital element from which a masterpiece of "corrugation" is precipitated, we may begin to think of the strange relationship between line and design in this poem as one of its central achievements. It is convenient to think of the relationship of individual lines to the poem of which they are made up as a relationship of parts to whole, bricks to a building. Yet this convenience also misleads, because metrical constraint (and, where it pertains, the constraint of rhyme too) are *compositional* factors. Under these constraints, word makes leap out word, rhyme rhyme. They inevitably induce phrases, ideas and even arguments or narratives which might not have been envisaged in just this shape in any work of plotting or designing undertaken by the poet before composition. Therefore the poem is a force field of antagonisms between modes of thinking constrained by very different requirements, modes which are not necessarily guaranteed to be in a harmonious or stable relationship with each other. The unity a poem has is as much like the unity of a war or a boxing match as it is like that of a building. Some practices of verse composition seem to allow the line (which, after all, is also at its level a whole with parts) to claim its own value as a composition in itself. In such poems, it feels untrue to say that each line has its value only subordinately, in relation to the whole. It seems to be just as much the case that elements of "the whole"—itself, of course, unable to avoid being a moment of synoptic abstraction—are in the service of these "parts," these thousands of works of art all squaring up to each other in the poem's arena.

Although Browning's interest in Shelley is much more fully attested than that in Keats, and although Browning's earlier poetry had been in various ways clearly derivative of Shelley's, it is quite clear that at the decisive level, the compositional level of verse syntax, *Endymion*'s is the crucial presence. Browning's further advance or further decline on Keats, however, is clear. Browning's syntax is at once much more complex and more propulsive than Keats', so that we are driven on through these couplets with a force which in English verse is paralleled only, perhaps, in Milton. Matthew Campbell described the poem as "the most exhaustive, and exhausting, early Victorian attempt to sound a rhythm of will," an idea which certainly captures our sense that this is verse which leaves no muscle unstrained.[23] The invitation to delicious diligent indolence which is held out by Keats' labyrinthine verse sentences is thus replaced in Browning by something much less inviting; as Herbert Tucker comments, "despite the poem's reputation for bewilderment, it is harder in this feel-good sense to get lost in *Sordello*" than in any other poem Tucker's book discusses.[24] *Sordello*, in fact, is the poem in which Keats' "undersong of disrespect to the public" becomes something like an oversong, a descant. Ugliness is allowed into the texture of the verse itself, and this, perhaps, explains the paradox that Browning's descriptions of perfectly obscure episodes in the wars of the Guelfs with the Ghibellines produce a verse mode more alert to the repulsive contingencies of war, and more able to keep them in view, than any other one can think of in English in the first half of the nineteenth century:

> So! but the midnight whisper turns a shout,
> Eyes wink, mouths open, pulses circulate
> In the stone walls: the past, the world you hate
> Is with you, ambush, open field—or see
> The surging flame—they fire Vicenza—glee!
> Follow, let Pilio and Bernardi chafe—
> Bring up the Mantuans—through San Biagio—safe!
> Ah, the mad people waken? Ah, they writhe
> And reach you? if they block the gate—no tithe
> Can pass—keep back you Bassanese! the edge,
> Use the edge—shear, thrust, hew, melt down the wedge,
> Let out the black of those black upturned eyes!
> Hell—are they sprinkling fire too? the blood fries
> And hisses on your brass gloves as they tear
> Those upturned faces choking with despair.[25]

Browning's ability to produce a detail as peculiar and yet as compelling as blood frying on hot brass gloves in the act of smashing up a face is made possible, curiously, not by any determined effort at reportage, but, rather, by the advanced involutions of his verse melodics and by the acute indirectness of the narrative approach which those involutions compel. This passage—Swinburne's favorite—is part of the interior reflection of the professional soldier Taurello Salinguerra. It is from a passage in which Taurello is mentally addressing the Ghibellin lord with whom he has long campaigned, Ecelin Romano. Ecelin has retired to a monastery, and Taurello is sceptically wondering whether it will really, in his pious retreat, in the event be possible for Ecelin quite to shut out every memory of what he has done and known in war. All the most unpleasant and disenchanting events in the poem—all the events in the poem as such, one is tempted to say—are introduced in this way in the course of someone's thinking about or remembering or alluding to something else, but just this seems to be the condition of their power. What is powerful here is not some attempt bracingly to break into the reader's cozy home with the real graphic horror, but, rather, the imagination of the point where fantasy runs out—Browning imagining Taurello imagining one little chink in Ecelin Romano's ability to imagine away what he has actually been. Leavis once complained of Browning's "corrugated surface," implying that the roughness was superficial; but, in *Sordello*, this is a surface which goes all the way down.

In a famous report of a conversation between Shelley and Byron, Shelley is supposed to have advanced the theory that each line of verse might be in itself an individual work of art. It is easy to paraphrase away this idea, by saying to ourselves that, for example, Shelley might have meant only that each line is crafted with a great deal of care and attention; if one takes the idea literally, however, it captures a necessary antagonism at the heart of every long poem, the antagonism between line and design. Here are a few instances that seize on memory and return to the mind in the street or the committee meeting: "Of infinite and absent Tyrolese," "Crowned with what sanguine-heart pomegranate blooms," "Though no affirmative disturbs the head," "By their selected evidence of song," "From the wet heap of rubbish where they burned," "Of the huge brain-mask welded ply o'er ply," "Bloom-flinders and fruit-sparkles and leaf-dust," "Tufting the Tyrrhene whelk's pearl-sheeted lip," "Amass the scintillations for one star," "When just the substituting osier lithe," "Eyepits to ear one gangrene since he plied," "Clove dizzily the solid of the war," "And hisses on your brass gloves as they tear" and, in the passage with which I began, "Relentless into the consummate orb." No responsible reader of the poem would read like this, of course: these lines not only cannot be interpreted without restoring their contexts to them, but their expressive force, too, depends upon that local web of patternings and interruptions in which they are caught. But the difficulty is that no reader of *Sordello* would want to or even can be a responsible reader unless she has first been an irresponsible reader, unless she has first given in to the most various series of seductions and repulsions which lines of these kinds seem to hold out like individual works of art. In *Sordello* it is sometimes as though the entire ensemble had been articulated so as to throw up lines so immensely striking, so ugly, even, that they captivate our attention, making it impossible to keep our mind on the larger design which our superego keeps insisting shall be the kernel beneath that shell. It is as though the lines were to refuse to be mere constituent parts of this edifice of lines, and the swell and surge of Browning's carry-on were instead to exist precisely for the sake of these peculiar configurations of foam, these fugitive works of art. This is why it is, I think, that so many of the lines concerned are lines in which there is no punctuation of any kind. Their effect is quite different from that of the unpunctuated lines of standard mid-twentieth-century free verse, say, because they are wrested from sentences which do indeed aspire to work as parsable syntactical concatenations; yet what is thus wrested is something which wants not only to do its syntactical day-job, but also to break out in song or screeching.

Kant's aporetic account of judging the beautiful in the third critique —an account in which there is no science of the beautiful, and yet in which it is not satisfactory, either, to say that one does not know anything about the beautiful but one knows what one likes—is matched, as is less often noted, by an aporetic account of making the beautiful. Just as there is no science of the beautiful, there is no fine science either. Yet art must not be allowed to be sheer play. Poetry requires a verse constraint if it is not to be the literary equivalent of skeptical philodoxy. *Sordello*, in throwing up its myriad verse-crustaceans, strange and pocked and beautiful or ugly, seizes this aporia for itself at the level of technical production. It understands that only one part of a poem's work on history can be done by research, even by research so elaborate as that which the poet undertook in preparation for this poem. A poem's most powerful relationship to history lies in those supposedly purely technical but in fact intimately historical materials, the verse sentences, manners, repertoires, and formulae it inherits and on which it works by changing them. The poet as critic of an outworn word or melody or rhyme is at one and the same time the poet as critic of the historical experience which those verse materials cannot but have sedimented within them. Browning's *Sordello* is five thousand, eight hundred and ninety-six works of art in which a new poetics of verse becomes audible. It is a poetics still far in advance of any of the machinery which has so far been brought up to contain it, and whose consequences for current verse thinking have, perhaps, still fully to be unfolded.

Notes

1. References to *Sordello* give the book and line numbers followed by the page reference to *The Poems of Robert Browning, 1826-1840*, ed. John Woolford and Daniel Karlin (London: Pearson, 1991).

2. The term is ubiquitous in, for example, the volume of James Elkins' "Art Seminar" devoted to *Art History Versus Aesthetics* (New York and London: Routledge, 2006).

3. See T. W. Adorno, *Ästhetische Theorie* (Frankfurt am Main: Suhrkamp, 1970), and Lambert Zuidervaart, *Adorno's Aesthetic Theory* (Cambridge, Mass.: MIT Press, 1991).

4. For further elaboration, see S. Jarvis, "Truth-content in Music and Literature," in *Adorno: A Critical Introduction* (Cambridge: Polity Press, 1998), 124–47.

5. "For a Poetics of Verse," round table eds. Cathy Caruth and Jonathan Culler, in *PMLA* 125, no. 4 (October 2010): 931-35; "Unfree Verse: John Wilkinson's The Speaking Twins," *Rhythm in Literature after the Crisis in Verse*, eds. Peter Dayan and David Evans, special issue of *Paragraph* 33, no. 2 (2010): 280–95.

6. Richard Hengist Horne, "Robert Browning's Poems," *Church of England Quarterly* (October 1842): 464–83. Repr. in *Robert Browning: The Critical Heritage*, ed. Boyd Litzinger and Donald Smalley (London and New York: Routledge, 1968), 73–75.

7. From an unsigned review, *The Atlas: A General Newspaper and Journal of Literature* (28 March 1840) 724, no. 15; repr. in *Robert Browning: The Critical Heritage*, 63.

8. Roger Fowler, "Three Blank Verse Textures," in *The Languages of Literature* (London: Routledge, 1971).

9. For more on Browning and impeded speech, see now Ewan Jones, "'Let the rank tongue blossom': Browning's Stuttering," *Victorian Poetry* 53, no. 2 (2015): 103–32.

10. Algernon Charles Swinburne, *George Chapman, A Critical Essay* (London: Chatto and Windus, 1875), 15–32.

11. Ibid., 16–17.

12. Ibid., 28.

13. Ibid.

14. Immanuel Kant, *Anthropology from a Pragmatic Point of View*, ed. and trans. Robert B. Louden (Cambridge: Cambridge University Press, 2006), 144.

15. Immanuel Kant, *Critique of the Power of Judgment*, ed. Paul Guyer, trans. Guyer and Eric Matthews (Cambridge: Cambridge University Press, 2000), 183.

16. Ibid.

17. Kant, *Critique of Pure Reason*, ed. and trans. Paul Guyer and Allen W. Wood (Cambridge: Cambridge University Press, 1999), B xxxvii.

18. Kant, *Religion within the Boundaries of Mere Reason*, ed. Allen Wood and George di Giovanni (Cambridge: Cambridge University Press, 1998), 168.

19. Ibid., 168–69.

20. See Gregory Nagy, *Plato's Rhapsody and Homer's Music: the Poetics of the Panathenaic Festival in Classical Athens* (Washington, D.C.: Center for Hellenic Studies, 2002).

21. See Fowler, "Three Blank Verse Textures," in *The Languages of Literature* (London: Routledge and Kegan Paul, 1971).

22. Robert Browning, *Poetical Works*, vol. 1 of 17 (London, 1888), 65–66.

23. Matthew Campbell, *Rhythm and Will in Victorian Poetry* (Cambridge: Cambridge University Press, 1999), 96.

24. Herbert F. Tucker, *Epic: Britain's Heroic Muse, 1790-1910* (Oxford: Oxford University Press, 2008), 292.

25. Robert Browning, *Sordello* (London: Edward Moxon, 1840), 159.

BODY, THRONG, RACE

The Cadence of Consent: Francis Barton Gummere, Lyric Rhythm, and White Poetics

Virginia Jackson

In American poetics, lyric and rhythm share a history—and since this is America, it is a racialized history. When Cleanth Brooks and Robert Penn Warren wrote in 1938 (in the first edition of *Understanding Poetry*) that "the systematic ordering of rhythm we call verse," their simplified abstract "we" stood in for many different thinkers about poetry over several previous decades—and, as history would have it, this consensus has remained more or less in place through the present decade.[1] In this enduring formulation, *rhythm=verse=poetry=lyric*. The readers who have abided by this equation have all tended to think that in view of the many disagreements over what poetry is or was or should become, the one thing on which everyone can agree is that rhythm is what poetry's got—and if there is another point of consensus, it is that most poetry has become essentially or de facto lyric poetry. On one hand, in the first decades of the twentieth century, this agreement was the symptom of the erosion of other forms of prosodic debate, since with the rise of the New Poetry and free verse, the abstraction of rhythm became an ordering principle more capacious than meter; it was also the symptom of the abstraction of particular verse genres (ballads, elegies, songs, psalms, epistles, odes, etc.) into a large idea of poetry as lyric. On the other hand, this agreement actually emerged from a theory of poetry, of rhythm, and of lyric with which most modern thinkers about poetry would be embarrassed to find that they continue to agree.

Before we get to some of the sources of that potential historical embarrassment, let's go back to our apparent equivalence (*rhythm=verse=poetry=lyric*) and examine it one part at a time. The word "systematic" is worth pausing over in Brooks and Warren's common sense statement. Someone or something needs to organize rhythm so that it can become verse, and so that verse can then become lyricized poetry. Yet as Niklas Luhmann would write, a "system operates on its own terms."[2] In modernity, a system is by definition self-organizing; thus if the twentieth-and-twenty-first-century idea of verse as a rhythm system does not attribute that organization to an actor, or even to a network—that is, to a poet or to a genre or to a mode—then what accounts for such systematic self-fashioning? For much of the nineteenth century, such questions might have been referred to an organic, or natural principle of creation and limitation, but in the twentieth century, that organic logic shifted to social relations, to human systems. As an organizing and defining principle of poetry as such, rhythm became a cultural rather than a natural system—and, not incidentally, this transition took place just as "the culture concept" (which is to say, the modern discipline of anthropology) took hold, in the first decades of the twentieth century.[3]

Consider the example of *Poetic Rhythm: An Introduction* (1995), a book that at the end of the twentieth century made prosody accessible in the way that *Understanding Poetry* had made the reading of individual poems a matter of general educational practice earlier in the century. In his introduction to this *Introduction*, Derek Attridge wrote that "to understand and enjoy poetry means responding to, and participating in, its rhythm—not as one of a number of features that make up the poetic experience, but as the heart of that experience."[4] Attridge's metaphor suggests that rhythm is organic in origin, but when he defines rhythm as "a patterning of energy simultaneously produced and perceived; a series of alternations of build-up and release, movement and counter-movement, tending toward regularity but complicated by constant variations and local inflections," his description moves from an evocation of natural heartbeats or hot sex to an invocation of cultural patterning, complication, inflection, variation, and locality.[5] Indeed, for two hundred and sixty-six pages, Attridge will go on to graph the elaborate phrasing, measuring, marking, stressing, x-ing, \-ing, and /-ing of poetic rhythm. Such elaboration makes it clear that once made "poetic," rhythm must be a cultural rather than a natural principle, must be learned and notated rather than felt and danced. The imaginary intimacy between natural rhythm and cultural regulation on which this influential view of poetic rhythm depends speaks volumes about the kinds of social relations or human systems we continue to conjure in the idea of "poetic rhythm." This much is clear, yet the history of that imaginary intimacy, of those imagined social relations, has remained invisible. There may be good reasons why we have not wanted to know too much about that backstory.

Although Attridge's book was published in the U.K., it is widely taught in the U.S. as the modern model of English prosody.[6] As Attridge and many others have pointed out, there is a history of precedents for a pedagogy so many have come to take for granted, but one precedent that is never invoked in such accounts is the work (between the 1880s and 1910s) of a once prominent though now relatively obscure American theorist of proto-modern poetics, Francis Barton Gummere. There is ample evidence of Gummere's influence in early twentieth-century poetics, especially in academic circles, but the reason that it is worth returning to Gummere's work is not merely its historical interest but its symptomatic and, as it turned out, field-defining emphasis on rhythm as the *socializing* principle of poetry. By "socializing," I mean the idea that poetic rhythm not only emerges from social origins but that poetic rhythm enables social "participation" (to use Attridge's word). At the intersection of German *Volksgeist* philology with the emerging disciplines of ethnography and psychology, an intersection that was instrumental in forming the new discipline of English literary study, Gummere's work occupied a transition zone between theories of poetic rhythm as natural and theories of poetic rhythm as a cultural system. "Poetry, like music, is social," according to Gummere; "like its main factor, rhythm, it is the outcome of communal consent, a *faculté d'ensemble*; and this should be writ large over every treatise on poetry."[7] As Max Cavitch has suggested, Gummere's turn-of-the-century declaration that rhythm is "the essential fact of poetry" capped off a long history of associations of rhythm with fantasies of racial identification, but Gummere marks a difference in that history when he makes the socializing influence of rhythm the explicit principle of modern poetics.[8] The French phrase serves to index the enlightened sociality of Gummere's theory, as does the key word "consent," to which we will return. Gummere is important because he emphasized the inherited idea that rhythm is at the heart of poetic experience, but also because his insistence on the ideally community-forming agency of poetic rhythm has become a secret hidden in plain sight in modern accounts of what poetic rhythm is or should be.[9]

Michael Golston has noted that "competing notions of rhythm have been the flash points for many of the controversies involving poetry in the twentieth century," and he has pointed to the background of those controversies in what he calls the racialized science of "Rhythmics" in the early twentieth century.[10] Gummere was the predecessor of the developments that Golston traces, of Harriet Monroe's declaration that rhythm is "an unalterable law" as well as of Pound's 1912 credo of "absolute rhythm."[11] But Gummere's account is instructive not so much because a direct genealogy descends from it, but because he modeled a conflict or confusion that has come to define modern poetics after it. To put simply the contradiction I will explore in the pages that follow: if rhythm is thought to be the defining principle of verse, and if (as we shall see in Gummere's theory) that defining principle is traced back to a social, ideally communal rather than natural origin of poetry we have lost in modernity, *and* if by recovering rhythm we might recover some of the socializing, communal force of those origins (as Gummere put it, "in order to draw the mind of the reader from the warped and baffling habit which looks upon all poetry as solitary performance"[12]), then does poetic rhythm become a racially reinforcing inheritance or an agent of social progress ? Since "culture" in the decades in which Gummere wrote was in the process of detaching itself from racial genealogies, what does the challenge of imagining poetic rhythm as racial in origin and post-racial in effect mean for thinking about modern American poetics? As Erin Kappeler has eloquently written about Gummere's influence on the first decades of the twentieth century and the rise of "the New Poetry" associated with Monroe and *Poetry Magazine*, "the idea of the New Poetry emerged at a time when the concept of multiculturalism as we understand it had not yet crystallized, meaning that a celebration of poetic diversity could as easily be used to champion racialist logic and American exceptionalism as to promote cross-cultural understanding."[13] Curiously, Gummere addressed this emerging uncertainty by suggesting that the eventuation of all poetry into the modern lyric individualizes and abstracts rhythm's communal racial origins, yet of course that individualization and abstraction does not solve the problem (indeed, as the language above indicates, Gummere often worried that it just makes the modern predicament that much worse, and as Kappeler suggests, it actually did). It is my argument here that some version of Gummere's double bind may continue to shape current definitions of the modern lyric and of poetic rhythm more than we would like to think. As recently as 2015, Jonathan Culler suggested that "rhythm gives lyric a somatic quality that novels and other extended forms lack—the experience of rhythm linking it to the body and, perhaps to the rhythms of various natural processes."[14] By returning to Gummere's now historically obscure logic, we might begin to trace the overdetermined origins of such versions of lyric rhythm as natural culture and to imagine an alternative history of American poetics, a history of the poetics of rhythm not modeled on naturalized (and thus racialized) concepts of culture or on English prosody or on common sense, an alternative that acknowledges the contradictions of any notion of a shared Anglo-American rhythm or shared Anglo-American poetry, a history in which the idea of rhythm remains central, but central as symptom rather than central as solution.

In 1905, Gummere became the fifteenth president of the MLA, an organization he helped to build. He spent his teaching career at Haverford College, though Harvard, Johns Hopkins and Chicago all tried to hire him several times; he wrote that he felt that teaching at a small college left more time for his research career (and he was committed to the values of Quaker education). This is to say that Gummere was a specialist's specialist, an academic's academic, and the special province of his work (like that of his mentor Francis Child in the first Department of English at Harvard, and of *his* mentor, Henry Wadsworth Longfellow, in the first department of Modern Languages at Harvard) was the poetry of the people, or poetry before it became the province of the academic specialization in poetics that Gummere (on the shoulders of Longfellow and Child) helped to create. According to Gummere's turn-into-the-twentieth-century poetics—particularly in his fourth book, *The Beginnings of Poetry,* published literally at the turn into the twentieth century, in 1901—what modern poetry has lost is a communal function. Whereas poetry once sprang from "the improvisation of verses in a singing and dancing throng," as Gummere wrote (and wrote often, as "throng" became his key word for the imaginary social experience organized by rhythm) in modernity "a solitary habit of thinking has made itself master of poetry, particularly of the lyric . . . Poetry [has passed] to a personal note of thought so acutely individual that it has to disguise itself, wear masks, and prate about being objective."[15] In Gummere's account, by the beginning of the twentieth century, not only had poetry become a decadently solitary enterprise, but it had become so "acutely individual" that in order to address a public it resorted to disguising its actual social situation. If in that idea you hear echoes of Adorno's "Lyric and Society" *avant la lettre,* that is no accident, since like Adorno's Marxism, Gummere's theory of intellectual and social history was Hegelian (though his poetics owed much to Herder). Like Longfellow and Child before him at Harvard, Gummere studied literary history in Germany (he received his Ph.D. in Philology at the University of Freiburg in 1881), where he adopted a dialectical understanding of the progress of history "as a steady advance . . . At each fresh occasion at which the individual isolates himself from society, he takes with him the accumulated force that society, by its main function, has stored up from traditions of the past."[16] This is to say that for Gummere—as for

Adorno—the radically isolated individual subject of the modern lyric carries within himself the traces of that "dancing throng," the traces of a language of men between whom the barriers had fallen (or between whom the barriers had not yet been built). For Gummere as for Adorno, the alienated modern subject of lyric may be redeemed from his isolation through the very medium of his isolation. But whereas for Adorno, that utopian horizon can be discerned in the alienated, objective language of the modern poem, according to Gummere, even in the modern isolated lyric, pre-lyricized, shared popular song may still be felt in the poem's rhythm. Modern poetry may have been reduced to lyric, but this lyric remnant carries traces of a lost communal past, and if we attend to that rhythmic trace we will be able to imagine a way out of decadent modern liberal individualism, may be able to glimpse in poetry, of all places, a world in which things could be different.

In 1987 Gerald Graff suggested that by the 1880s, the romantic theories of cultural origins associated with Herder and the Brothers Grimm had become "embarrassing" to the new Departments of English that had just been founded on them.[17] When discussing the history of "the Culture Wars" in 1991, Geoffrey Hartman referred to Gummere as the representative of "an older philological tradition that recognized the theories of folk or communal origin" behind Propp's analysis of the folktale, which Hartman described as "the crucial scholarly event between Grimm and Guattari."[18] This sort of double refusal and acknowledgement at the end of the twentieth century of the continuing influence of the ideas that formed the study of poetics at the end of the nineteenth century certainly owes much to the catastrophic consequences of some of those ideas in the first half of the twentieth century. How could those consequences not produce aversion and ambivalence? It is no wonder that such ideas seem more attractive to contemporary literary theorists in Adorno's Marxist version than in Gummere's *Volksgeist* version. Yet the utopian strains of Gummere's theory of not only the communal origins but the communal horizon of poetic rhythm may be more central to our inherited critical assumptions than we have wanted to acknowledge. As Steve Newman has argued, "individualist definitions of lyric and individualist antidemocratic politics go hand in hand" for Gummere, but it does not follow that in this view the modern lyric forfeits the socializing agency of rhythm, the potential to restore communal life. Rather, for Gummere, the lyric remains "flexible and progressive still, welcoming the new individual idea while it retains the old sympathy, the old cadence, form and phrases."[19] Can the old sympathy give rise to a new sympathy, can the old cadence become a modern beat? That is the question that hangs fire for Gummere, and for American poetics ever after him.

Gummere's description of how and why the spectral survival of popular song may be felt in the break, may be imagined where it can no longer be read or heard is worth reading in detail, since it makes visible some preconditions for later apparently commonsensical assumptions about the equivalence of rhythm and verse, and of modern verse and lyric:

> The modern artist in poetry triumphs mainly by the music of his verse and by the imaginative power which is realized in his language, often merely by the suggestion of his language; for poetry, as Saint-Beuve prettily remarked, lies not in telling the story but in making one dream it. For present purposes, then, it will be enough to look at the formal quality of rhythm and the more creative quality of imagination . . . one must see in rhythm, or regularity of recurrence due to the consenting cadence of a throng, the main representative of communal forces . . . Because the critics take rhythm and verbal repetition largely for granted in the work of any great poet, and look rather to his excellent differences in thought and variation of style, one must not ignore the immense significance of those communal forces in the poetry of art. It is not the mere rhythm, grateful, exquisite, and powerful as that may be, but it is what lies behind the rhythm, that gives it such a place in poetry; it appeals through the measures to the cadent feet, and so through the cadent feet to that consent of sympathy which is perhaps the noblest thing in all human life.[20]

In the break, "through the measures," rhythm emerges at the beginning of the twentieth century as what poetry's got, but also as what modern poetry is in danger of losing.[21] According to Gummere, the modern poet and modern critics value everything in poetry (music, imaginative power, differences in thought, variation of style) *except* rhythm and verbal repetition. These verse basics are taken "largely for granted in the work of any great poet," and in a way, that makes sense, since "it is not the mere rhythm" that defines poetry as such. No, "it is what lies behind the rhythm, that gives it such a place in poetry." In order to understand rhythm as the defining principle of poetry in Gummere's terms, it is necessary to enter into Gummere's philology of rhythm: Gummere does not, like Attridge, propose an overview of how poetic rhythm works on the page, but proposes something stranger, a genealogy of poetry before the page. Rhythm "appeals through the measures to the cadent feet," according to Gummere, in another odd turn of phrase that grants poetic rhythm the agency of address, the ability to interpellate us into a system of cultural origins. In that culture system, "the cadent feet" are both the metrical arrangements of modern poems and the dancing feet of the primitive "throng," residual in modern meters. Yet in these terms, poetry's appeal is not just primitive and somatic, but a "consent of sympathy" that civilizes, that has the agency to transform primitive, affective somatic response into "the noblest thing in all human life." That is quite a lot for poetic rhythm to do, since in it Gummere invests not only the redemption of the otherwise isolated modern lyric but the revision of modern social relations. "Conditions of production as well as of record" may have changed, Gummere writes, "the solitary poet has taken the place of the choral throng, and solitary readers represent the listening group; but the fact of poetry itself reaches below all these mutations, and is founded on human sympathy as on a rock. More than this. It is clear from the study of poetic beginnings that poetry in its larger sense is not a natural impulse of man simply as man. His rhythmic and kindred instincts, latent in the solitary state, found free play only under communal conditions, and as powerful factors in the making of society."[22] Poetic rhythm may lead to an origin story, yet for Gummere (as for Schiller, and a long line of romantic thinking about poetics) that story is not only an account of individual affective response but of "rhythmic and kindred instincts," a sympathy of kin and kind that made culture in the first place and could make it anew.

But what culture, what kind, and what kin? The word that Gummere uses to name the communal forces he wants to invoke as origin as well as utopian horizon of poetic rhythm yields some curious answers to that question. According to the OED, the word "throng" derives from

> Middle English *þrang, þrong*, probably shortened from Old English *geprang* throng, crowd, tumult, derivative from verbal ablaut series *pring-* , *prang-* , *prung-* : see THRING *v.*: compare Middle Dutch *dranc(g-)*, Dutch *drang*, Middle High German *dranc* (earlier *gedranc*), German *drang* throng, pressure, crowd; Old Norse *prǫng* (feminine), throng, crowd. *Throng* noun, verb, and adjective appear about the 13–14th cent., the adjective being the latest.

This etymology would have been important to Gummere, not only because the OED itself was the product of the mid-nineteenth-century comparative philology that formed his own training, but because Gummere was a scholar of Anglo-Saxon and Old English verse (his translation of *Beowulf* was a best-seller); Gummere's dissertation and first published book was *The Anglo-Saxon Metaphor* (1881), in which he wrote that "the passionate nature of the Germanic race is thoroughly opposed to the use and development of the simile. The lack of the latter in Anglo-Saxon is entirely natural, and explains itself."[23] In his third book, *Germanic Origins: A Study in Primitive Culture* (1892), Gummere claimed that "the Germanic race is the source of English life, and that the Germanic invaders of Britain may be fairly styled founders of England."[24] Thus "throng," the word that appears hundreds of times in *The Beginnings of Poetry*, condenses in its etymology the racial inheritance embedded in this view of the English language itself. The implicit violence of that view in the context of America in 1901 *almost* registers in Gummere's prose. "What lies behind the rhythm" are the echoes of the "cadent feet" of white people, but does this racial origin story mean that the "consent of sympathy which is perhaps the noblest thing in all human life" is restricted to white people, or that only those descended from the Germanic/English throng can groove to the primitive rhythms that survive in modern poetry? While in 1885 Gummere suggested to the new Modern Language Association that Anglo-Saxon meters be taught in elementary education in order to "train up a race or scholars" informed by their own racial heritage ("What Place," 171), by 1911, when he wrote *Democracy and Poetry*, Gummere wanted to shift his earlier focus on racial communal origins to the future consensual effects of poetic rhythm. In Gummere's theory of rhythm as the basis for all poetry, we can see the transition from race to culture in action. Like Adorno, Gummere wanted to believe in the progressive historical potential for the modern lyric, but unlike Adorno, Gummere did not claim that potential on the basis of a negative dialectic. If Gummere's fantasy of the dancing throng stood for an imaginary natural cultural rhythm, his hope that poetic rhythm could produce "a consent of sympathy" in modernity proved more difficult to articulate. Perhaps this difficulty arose because a community based on "consent," or elective affinity, could no longer be imagined in the U.S. in the early twentieth century. Or perhaps the issue for Gummere was that such a shared public rhythm could exist *only* in imagination—only as an idea. In this sense, the social agency of poetry in a pre-modern communal past becomes an idea of what poetry might be in a future that has not yet come to pass. It is this transformation of poetry from genre to idea, from a set of social practices to a utopian horizon of social promise that would prove central to modern American poetics. Not incidentally, Gummere locates the trace of this shift in the simultaneously pragmatic and imaginary phenomenon of poetic rhythm, and he locates that rhythm in a poetry that has devolved into the lyric.

This is to say that while on the one hand Gummere's attempt to make the lyric the repository of a virtual community set the stage for the twentieth-century versions of lyric reading that would come after him, the part of Gummere's view later poetics would not share may be even more instructive. By 1957 John Stuart Mill's 1833 definition of poetry— "feeling confessing itself to itself, in moments of solitude"[25] —had become so normative that Northrop Frye could define the lyric simply as "preeminently the utterance that is overheard" without allusion to Mill.[26] Gummere, however, vehemently rejected Mill's version of the modern lyric. "Something overheard?" Gummere asks,

> I mean, [Mill] explains, that "all poetry is in the nature of soliloquy," is the natural fruit of solitude and meditation. Now this is sheer nonsense, although more than one critic has hailed it as an oracle; of that which comes down to us as poetry, a good part is anything but soliloquy or the fruit of solitude. "Read Homer," cried out Herder, perhaps at the other extreme, but certainly with better reason than Mill, "as if he were singing in the streets!" . . . Poetry is a social fact.[27]

If the modern lyric is to address a public, is to be "a social fact" and not "in the nature of soliloquy," how might this be possible, short of returning to Greek choral epic or to Herder's "other extreme"? In 1911, in *Democracy and Poetry*, many decades before Benedict Anderson made the phrase famous, Gummere wrote that "only the individual poet, going back to *the imagined community* for his strength and his hope of a better issue, leaning on the communal sympathy and taking the communal rhythm, undertakes to justify the ways of God to man, eschewing, however, that poetical justice, as one calls it, which is born of the democratic hope that the community will at last attain the perfection of justice and social order."[28] The difficulty of theorizing a basis for "the communal sympathy" that may or may not survive in modern poetics is palpable in this prose. "The individual poet," or the lyric descendent of "the choral throng," can no longer rely on the "communal conditions" that once produced poetry, so the modern lyric poet must produce "the imagined community" as a placeholder for the community that is no longer there. Is that placeholder pure fiction? How such a fantasy allows the poet to lean "on the communal sympathy," much less to "take" "the communal rhythm" is at best unclear, since those lost worlds can presumably only be invoked in "hope of a better issue," a better and differently communal future.

If the community on which modern lyric rhythm depends is an optimistic imaginary, is Gummere's derivation then pure fantasy? If so, does the modern lyric poet draw upon this fantastic rhythm in order to conjure a social life of poetry, or does the lyric poet produce a vision of communal poetics in order to conjure an imaginary rhythm? As the fabrication of an ethnographic logic of poetic rhythm gives way to a history of the present, Gummere's account of poetic rhythm wavers. At the beginning of the second decade of the twentieth century, Gummere can forecast that shared rhythmic "poetic experience" only proleptically, as something lost that might yet again come to pass. The allusion to Milton seems bizarre in this context, as if only faith could bring about the revolutionary political conditions that would make poetry matter. Gummere is quick to distinguish that order of emphasis from a banal form of poetic justice, from a version of poetics in which "the perfection of justice and social order" would be available *only* in poetry. The conversion that proves hard for Gummere to think through is the transformation of his earlier version of a racially coherent experience of poetic rhythm into a community of "rhythmic and kindred instincts" no longer based on race. In this "imagined community," elective consent rather than racial genealogy will or would or could make rhythm the basis of an experience that will or would or could be "poetic" in the sense that it is *of* poetry but also in the sense that poetry would make it possible. Whereas for Benedict Anderson, a nation "is imagined because the members of even the smallest nation will never know most of their fellow-members, meet them, or even hear of them, yet in the minds of each lives the image of their communion"[29], in Gummere's precedent use of the concept (which Anderson, as an anthropologist drawing on many of the ethnographic concepts that influenced Gummere may well have known), readers of modern poetry share an imagined community only insofar as they are able to forget that this "image of their communion" is based on social relations they do not actually share.

Thus for Gummere as for a long tradition of American poetics after him, the virtual community lyric rhythm offers the modern reader is full of pathos and disappointment. According to Gummere, Whitman's lyric failure is a case in point: "No great poet ever put his naked Me into verse . . . The 'I' of every lyric poet is conventional, however sincere the utterance, however direct the confession."[30] By refusing all convention, Gummere writes, "Whitman deliberately refuses to keep step:

> and all the great poets do keep step, mainly in a very simple kind of march. They lead; but they lead in the consent of a consenting, coherent band. If Whitman's verse can be proved to be artistic, regular, governed by any definite law, then this objection breaks down. But proof of such artistic restraint, such definite law, in Whitman's verse I have not yet seen. He cannot be the poet of democracy in its highest ideal who rejects the democratic idea of submission to the highest social order, to the spirit of the laws, to that imagined community."[31]

One part of this view is the familiar complaint that, as a British reviewer had put it in 1856, "Walt Whitman is as unacquainted with art, as a hog with mathematics," but Gummere was writing in 1911, two decades after Whitman's death and long after his transformation into the Good Grey Poet.³² Although "free verse" would not be coined as such until 1915, Whitman's verse was no longer so startlingly unconventional as it had seemed half a century earlier. Indeed, one might think that Whitman, the laureate of social relations based on queer elective affinities, would represent the perfect alternative to Mill's version of poetry as "the fruit of solitude." Certainly if any American poet ever wrote "as if he were singing in the streets," it was Whitman. But Whitman's verse "refuses to keep step" with what Gummere calls "the consent of a consenting, coherent band," a refusal that turns out to be a refusal of a common rhythm. To recall the equation with which we began, if Gummere's work is one forgotten chapter in the story of how *rhythm* came to =*verse*, which came to=*poetry,* which came to=*lyric*, then the problem with Whitman's verse in this view was that it did not find the conventions that could make lyric rhythm a shared experience, and so could not effect this equation. And what would those conventions be, if they could be found? As we have seen, the logic of the imagined community relies on a rhythm that can only be virtual; thus Whitman's rejection of "the democratic idea of submission to the highest social order" is just that—an *idea*. Gummere is not complaining that Whitman did not write in, say, pentameter lines or ballad stanzas. Gummere instead uses Whitman as an example of a modern predicament in which the "social fact" of poetry is that we no longer feel that we are part of a rhythm system, whoever "we" may be; Whitman's failure to invoke the cadence of consent is a sign that what modern lyric readers consent to is not a shared rhythm but a shared sense that there is not a shared rhythm, that there is no "consenting, coherent band" except as "that imagined community" we have agreed to call poetry.

   Except as "that imagined community" we have agreed to call poetry. Meredith Martin has shown that during the first decades of the twentieth century, English prosody began to be simplified and "rhythmitized" into what she has called "the military metrical complex," or the creation of a distinctive "English beat" that could rally the troops marching into Europe's Great War.³³ Gummere's invocation of "a very simple kind of march" as the convention with which "Whitman deliberately refuses to keep step" betrays a desire for such an American beat, but unlike his contemporary British prosodists and poets, Gummere cannot name such a rhythm. Instead, his name for what an American rhythm would *not* be is "Whitman," who is not "governed by any definite law." Although Gummere's own theory of modern lyric's imagined community would make such a definite law impossible in practice, that theory also demands that the idea of a rhythmic law be the stuff of which the American rhythm will be made. Thus when in 1912, a year after *Democracy and Poetry*, Ezra Pound wrote, "I believe in an 'absolute rhythm,' a rhythm, that is, in poetry which corresponds exactly to the emotion or shade of emotion to be expressed. A man's rhythm must be . . . his own,"[34] he was certainly, as Martin argues, replying to the emerging idea of "a collective, national 'metrical' identity . . . with an even more individualized idea of rhythm" in the British context, but he was also offering a solution to an impasse in American poetics.[35] Gummere saw that solution coming and declared in advance that it wouldn't work, but Gummere's alternative to each man's "absolute rhythm" was a lyric rhythm that was a contradiction in terms, that could only work in our shared sense of its only virtual (or lyrical) possibility, as "that imagined community" we have agreed to call poetry.

As I have argued elsewhere, over the last part of the eighteenth, all of the nineteenth, and the first part of the twentieth centuries, the last three terms in our equation (verse, poetry, and lyric) converged through a gradual and uneven process I have called lyricization. Basically, the process of lyricization was a process of abstraction. While Gummere's account of the emergence of the modern lyric is a (somewhat fanciful) chronicle of the loss of communal life and the isolation of the individual, I would argue that modern ideas of poetry became lyricized because stipulative verse genres (ballads, odes, elegies, epistles, epitaphs, drinking songs, psalms, hymns, riddles, etc.) collapsed into an idealized version of poetry as lyric. Gummere was right that Mill was instrumental in this idealization, though not because Mill made poetry into "the fruit of solitude" so much as because he imagined lyric poetry as "more eminently and peculiarly poetry than any other," yet sought in vain for an adequate representative of a lyric poet among his British contemporaries.[36] I have been suggesting that Gummere shares something of Mill's (and Hegel's, and for that matter, Whitman's) idealized utopian horizon of lyric possibility, and I have been further suggesting that what Gummere adds to the nineteenth-century process of lyricization is a focus on rhythm as the agent of this generic abstraction. How and why did verse genres with particular objects of address and particular modes and economies of circulation begin to blend together to form one big idea of Poetry? And how and why did that big idea of Poetry become identified with the lyric? Because the process of lyricization took place over centuries and took many different forms in many different places, there is no one, totalizing answer to such questions. Instead, there are several different answers, and one of them might be the abstraction of rhythm and the equation of rhythm with lyric that I have been tracing in Gummere's poetics. For Gummere—and, as I have been suggesting, for a long line of thinkers about poetics who followed him without knowing his name—lyric became a repository of the socializing effects of rhythm at the same time that lyric indexed the loss of the communal, racial origins of that rhythm. Just as the development of the figure that came to be known as the impersonal lyric "speaker" in the early twentieth century solved the problem of particularly raced and gendered poetic identities, blending all bodies into a fictional dramatic persona, the early twentieth-century idea of a rhythm as the imaginary horizon of a virtual community deferred the problem of social "consent" between actual persons in actual political conflict. To return to the definition from *Understanding Poetry* with which we began, if we understand "the systematic ordering of rhythm" as what poetry *is*, we can stop worrying about what poetry, and what we, might have become, since the idea of rhythm, like the idea of lyric, always promises a future in which we will be different.

And who are "we"? If for Gummere in 1911 "the cadence of consent" could just barely be imagined as post-racial, the after-effect of that post-racial turn has been the abstraction of the idea of lyric rhythm into another form of whiteness, into the whiteness of the unmarked impersonal, of the disembodied, because unrealized, imagined community that we continue to associate with (of all things) lyric poetry. The problem of reclaiming that abstract, white, and impossible idea of rhythm for actual and non-white communities is at least as old as that idea itself. In 1903, W. E. B. Du Bois wrote a book that, like Gummere's work, grew out of the *Volksgeist* theories he had learned at Harvard.[37] In that book, Du Bois famously wrote of "the Negro folk-song—the rhythmic cry of the slave ... not simply as the sole American music, but as the most beautiful expression of human experience born this side the seas."[38] The beauty of these songs is in their pathos, as Du Bois' name for them, "the Sorrow Songs," makes clear, but in view of the turn-into-the-twentieth-century American poetics I have been discussing here, Du Bois' understanding of the virtual promise of the "cadences" of that pathos is especially striking:

> Through all the sorrow of the Sorrow Songs there breathes a hope—a faith in the ultimate justice of things. The minor cadence of despair change often to triumph and calm confidence. Sometimes it is faith in life, sometimes it is faith in death, sometimes assurance of boundless justice in some fair world beyond. But whichever it is, the meaning is always clear: that sometime, somewhere, men will judge men by their

souls and not by their skins. Is such a hope justified? Do the Sorrow Songs sing true?[39]

Du Bois leaves the question hanging fire at the end of that early book, and at least part of this suspension can be traced to the lyricized theory of rhythm Du Bois shared with Gummere. The much-discussed juxtaposition of lines and stanzas of lyric poetry from the Western canon with bars of music from the Sorrow Songs that stand as epigraphs to each of the fourteen chapters of *The Souls of Black Folk* could be read as the assimilation of folk rhythms to predominantly white lyric rhythms or it might be read as the reiterated difference between the two. Consider just the first instance of this practice (Figure 1).[40]

THE
SOULS OF BLACK FOLK

I

OF OUR SPIRITUAL STRIVINGS

O water, voice of my heart, crying in the sand,
　All night long crying with a mournful cry,
As I lie and listen, and cannot understand
　　The voice of my heart in my side or the voice of the sea,
O water, crying for rest, is it I, is it I?
　All night long the water is crying to me.

Unresting water, there shall never be rest
　Till the last moon droop and the last tide fail,
And the fire of the end begin to burn in the west;
　　And the heart shall be weary and wonder and cry like the sea,
All life long crying without avail,
　As the water all night long is crying to me.
　　　　　　　　　　　　　ARTHUR SYMONS.

FIGURE 1. Musical and poetic epigraph from *The Souls of Black Folk*, 1. First Edition, 1903. Poem is "The Crying of Water" by Arthur Symons. (Scan by Beinecke Library)

Not all of the verse choices in *Souls* are as lyric or as white or as odd as the opening selection from Arthur Symons, from a poem published in 1903, and only in the U.S.[41] Curiously, this first-person "lyric" has often been read as the "voice" of Du Bois or of the "black folk," as when Cornel West writes that "the hearts of a heartless slave trade cry out like the sea: 'All life long crying without avail / As the water all night long is crying to me.'"[42] Although the race and situation of the "I" are not identified or identifiable in the poem, precisely this lack of specificity allows West's lyric reading of Symons' decadently and artfully varied pentameters and daring triple cadences as the somatic beats of "the hearts of a heartless slave trade." This is not a lyric reading based on rhythmic traces but on pure rhythmic fantasy; similarly, West reads the musical bar from the spiritual "Nobody Knows the Trouble I've Seen" as "inexplicable lyrical reversal:

> *Nobody knows the trouble I've seen,*
>   *Nobody knows but Jesus*
> *Nobody knows the trouble I've seen*
>   *Glory hallelujah.*"[43]

Just as West (and a long history of lyric readers) make Symons' lines the vehicle of a tenor that is not actually there, so West (and a long history of lyric readers) imagine a community singing a spiritual that is not actually on the page. All that is on Du Bois' page are the first three bars of music, or the transcription of the tune to the first line of the song; there are no words, and we would need to read the music to sing the tune. The quarter notes, eighth notes, sixteenth notes, and half notes in the musical bars remain stubbornly untranslated from musical notation to poetic rhythm (probably a varied hymnal or ballad stanza of alternating tetrameter and trimeter lines) in Du Bois' text. The "lyrical reversal" that takes place in West's reading of the lines not apparent on the page is an imagined community in which the Sorrow Song indeed promises "the ultimate justice of things." But is that what the graphic rhythmic dissonance of Du Bois' epigraphs promises? The conversion of an idea of a raced folk into a consenting group, the transformation of communal song into the individual lyric that proved difficult for Gummere's distinctly white poetics became a stark contrast in Du Bois, and this dramatic disjunction has proven productive for modern black poetics.[44] As Brent Edwards has written, "the lyric is not a timeless, universal form; it is marked by history—and its history couches a threat."[45] For Edwards that threat is "to the enunciation of black subjectivity," but I have been arguing here that this threat might also be hidden in the place we would least expect to find it: in a modern theory of rhythm as what marks poetry as raced and at the same time frees poetry from racial constraints, a theory of lyric and of rhythm that draws on a lost communal past at the same time that it promises a communal future that can exist only in poetry. To understand rhythm as "the heart" of "the poetic experience" in America, to understand lyric as the heart of poetry, and to understand American culture as the system that organizes lyric rhythm, we would need to understand that not even in poetry—especially not in poetry—will we find rhythms we all can share.

Notes

1. Cleanth Brooks and Robert Penn Warren, *Understanding Poetry* (New York: Henry Holt, 1938), 213.

2. Niklas Luhmann, *Art as a Social* System (Palo Alto, Calif.: Stanford University Press, 2000). I do not cite Luhmann here to invoke all of systems theory, but to index a recent salient endpoint in a historical trajectory of thinking about systems as self-organizing social phenomena. It will be clear that this essay does not share Luhmann's structuralist approach to analyzing that self-organization, especially when it comes to poetics (about which Luhmann is consistently and rather eccentrically wrong).

3. See Mark Manganaro, *Culture, 1922: The Emergence of a Concept* (Princeton, N.J.: Princeton University Press, 2002) for an introduction to the history of the culture concept. The original definition of the culture concept is usually attributed to E. B. Tylor, who wrote in 1871 that culture is "that complex whole which includes knowledge, belief, art, morals, law, custom, and any other capabilities and habits acquired by man as a member of society." *Primitive Culture: Researches into the Development of Mythology, Philosophy, Religion, Art, and Custom* (New York: Gordon Press, 1871). Tylor was one of Gummere's most important sources, and his definition is still posted as the current Wikipedia definition of "culture": http://en.wikipedia.org/wiki/Culture.

4. Derek Attridge, *Poetic Rhythm: An Introduction* (Cambridge: Cambridge University Press, 1996), 1.

5. Ibid., 3.

6. Most (though not all) of Attridge's examples are British rather than American, and all but two are by white poets. Attridge tends to stress British history as the history of the language (which is especially interesting in view of Attridge's South African education and scholarship). Given those emphases, it is worth wondering how and why his examples have been taken to apply so easily to American examples.

7. Francis Barton Gummere, *The Beginnings of Poetry* (New York: Macmillan, 1901), 101.

8. Max Cavitch, "Slavery and its Metrics," in *The Cambridge Companion to Nineteenth-Century American Poetry*, ed. Kerry Larson (Cambridge: Cambridge University Press, 2011), 103. Cavitch's brilliant phenomenology of race and rhythm elaborates the history this essay only begins to trace.

9. This is to say that Gummere participated in an emerging discourse on rhythm as the simultaneous identification with and liberation from racial and cultural determination. He should be read in the company of Nietzsche, Kittredge, Lanier, Du Bois, and many others in this period. Jack Kerkering's *The Poetics of National and Racial Identity in Nineteenth-Century American Literature* (Cambridge: Cambridge University Press, 2003), begins to map this discourse, though he does not emphasize the importance of rhythm as its central term.

10. Michael Golston, *Rhythm and Race in Modernist Poetry and Science* (New York: Columbia University Press, 2008).

11. In 1912, Ezra Pound wrote, "I believe in 'absolute rhythm,' a rhythm, that is, in poetry which corresponds exactly to the emotion or shade of emotion to be expressed. A man's rhythm must be interpretive, it will be, therefore, in the end, his own, uncounterfeiting, uncounterfeitable" ("Prolegomena," in *Poetry and Drama*, ed. Harold Monro, 1912). Harriet Monroe's 1916 remarks are reprinted in *Poets and Their Art* (Freeport, N.Y.: Books for Libraries Press, 1967), 54.

12. Gummere, *Beginnings*, 101.

13. Erin Kappeler, "Editing America: Nationalism and the New Poetry," *Modernism/Modernity* 21, no. 4 (2014): 900. Kappeler's important essay traces some of the immediate consequences of Gummere's logic for modern American poetics.

14. Jonathan Culler, *Theory of the Lyric* (Cambridge, Mass.: Harvard University Press, 2015), 134.

15. Gummere, *Beginnings*, 139.

16. Ibid., 465.

17. Gerald Graff, *Professing Literature: An Institutional History* (Chicago: University of Chicago Press, 1987), 76.

18. Geoffrey Hartman, *Minor Prophecies: The Literary Essay in the Culture Wars* (Cambridge: Harvard University Press, 1991), 49.

19. Gummere, "Originality and Convention in Literature," in *Quarterly Review* 204 (1906): 44. See Steve Newman, *Ballad Collection, Lyric, and the Canon: The Call of the Popular from the Restoration to the New Criticism* (Philadelphia: University of Pennsylvania Press, 2007).

20. Gummere, *Beginnings*, 465–66.

21. I take the phrase "in the break" from Fred Moten, *In the Break: The Aesthetics of the Black Radical Tradition* (Minneapolis: University of Minnesota Press, 2003). My use of the phrase here may stand as shorthand for the black radical tradition that would emerge in dialectical response to the history of white poetics.

22. Gummere, *Beginnings*, 473.

23. Francis Barton Gummere, *The Anglo-Saxon Metaphor* (Halle: Karras, 1881), 10.

24. Francis Burton Gummere, *Germanic Origins: A Study in Primitive Culture* (New York: Scribner, 1892), 4.

25. John Stuart Mill, "Thoughts on Poetry and its Varieties," in *Autobiography and Literary Essays*, vol. 1 of *The Collected Works of John Stuart Mill* (Toronto: University of Toronto Press, 1981), 348.

26. Northrop Frye, *Anatomy of Criticism: Four Essays* (Princeton, N.J.: Princeton University Press, 1957), 249.

27. Gummere, *Beginnings*, 52.

28. Francis Burton Gummere, *Democracy and Poetry* (Boston and New York: Houghton Mifflin, 1911), 298. Italics mine.

29. Benedict Anderson, *Imagined Communities: Reflections on the Origin and Spread of Nationalism* (New York: Verso, 2006), 6–7. 2nd ed.

30. Gummere, *Democracy and Poetry*, 127.

31. Ibid., 125.

32. Anon., *The Critic* [London], April 1, 1856, 170.

33. Meredith Martin, *The Rise and Fall of Meter: Poetry and English National Culture, 1860-1930* (Princeton, N.J.: Princeton University Press, 2012). Martin's verb "rhyth-

mitize" marks the ways in which meter was abstracted and converted into rhythm, an argument too complex to summarize here, but one that applies to the American case as well, though in different forms, as this essay hopes to show.

34. Ezra Pound, "Prologomena," in Harold Monro's *Poetry and Drama* (1912), later collected as "credo" in "A Retrospect," *The Literary Essays of Ezra Pound* (New York: New Directions, 1918), 9.

35. Martin, *The Rise and Fall of Meter*, 181.

36. Mill, "Thoughts on Poetry and Its Varieties," 354.

37. For a good overview of Du Bois' Harvard debt to Gummere's teacher Francis Child's curriculum at Harvard, see David Levering Lewis, *W. E. B. Du Bois 1868–1919: Biography of a Race* (New York: Henry Holt, 1994). Du Bois' education in Berlin also brought him into contact with the *Volksgeist* theories that Gummere encountered in his German education.

38. W.E. Burghardt Du Bois, *The Souls of Black Folk: Essays and Sketches* (Chicago: A. C. McClurg & Co., 1903), 251.

39. Ibid., 262.

40. Du Bois, *The Souls of Black Folk*, 1.

41. Symons' poem appeared only in *Lyrics*, published by the Maine publisher T. B. Mosher in 1903.

42. Cornel West, *The Cornel West Reader* (New York: Basic Civitas Books, 1999), 102.

43. Ibid., 103.

44. It should also be said that Du Bois' *mise en page* has proven productive for literary criticism, which as Daniel Hack has recently pointed out, has tended "to see the pairing of the epigraphs as graphically modeling the overcoming" of "the gulf between black and white America." In the context of my reading of the genealogy of a discourse on American rhythm, the epigraphs don't work that way. Hack makes the excellent point that the critics who want them to work that way do not consider the tradition of what Hack calls *"African Americanizing* citation," a tradition Hack's book makes visible. See Daniel Hack, *Reaping Something New: African American Transformations of Victorian Literature* (Princeton, N.J.: Princeton University Press, 2017), 179–80.

45. Brent Edwards, "The Seemingly Eclipsed Window of Form," *The Jazz Cadence of American Culture*, ed. Robert G. O'Meally (New York: Columbia University Press, 1998), 596.

Contagious Rhythm: Verse as a Technique of the Body

Haun Saussy

Ringing Grooves

Nineteenth-century science loved to speculate about origins—the origins of language, of species, of law, of mythology, of private property, the family, and the state. To the extent that our academic institutions are nineteenth-century creations, we too live in spaces outlined by those phantasms of origin. The "singing and dancing throng" claimed by once-influential theorists to be the origin of English lyric displays in multiply overdetermined ways this zeal for origins.[1]

"What is Progress?" asked Herbert Spencer in 1857, and offered an example from embryology:

> The investigations of Wolff, Goethe, and von Baer, have established the truth that the series of changes gone through during the development of a seed into a tree, or an ovum into an animal, constitute an advance from homogeneity of structure to heterogeneity of structure. In its primary stage, every germ consists of a substance that is uniform throughout, both in texture and chemical composition. The first step is the appearance of a difference between two parts of this substance; or, as the phenomenon is called in physiological language, a differentiation. Each of these differentiated divisions presently begins itself to exhibit some contrast of parts: and by and by these secondary differentiations become as definite as the original one. This process is continuously repeated—is simultaneously going on in all parts of the growing embryo; and by endless such differentiations there is finally

produced that complex combination of tissues and organs constituting the adult animal or plant. This is the history of all organisms whatever. It is settled beyond dispute that organic progress consists in a change from the homogeneous to the heterogeneous.

Now, we propose in the first place to show, that this law of organic progress is the law of all progress. Whether it be in the development of the Earth, in the development of Life upon its surface, in the development of Society, of Government, of Manufactures, of Commerce, of Language, Literature, Science, Art, this same evolution of the simple into the complex, through successive differentiations, holds throughout. From the earliest traceable cosmical changes down to the latest results of civilization, we shall find that the transformation of the homogeneous into the heterogeneous, is that in which progress essentially consists.[2]

Cosmology, geology, paleontology, linguistics, economics, politics, ethnography, and the history of civilization furnish Spencer illustrations of his doctrine of evolution from the simple to the complex, published two years before Darwin's *Origin of Species*. Progress stretches out on a timeline a hierarchy still observable, for Spencer, in the present: "The infant European has sundry marked points of resemblance to the lower human races."[3] Music and poetry develop along the same lines.

In the co-ordinate origin and gradual differentiation of Poetry, Music, and Dancing, we have another series of illustrations. Rhythm in words, rhythm in sounds, and rhythm in motions, were in the beginning parts of the same thing, and have only in process of time become separate things.

Among existing barbarous tribes we find them still united. The dances of savages are accompanied by some kind of monotonous chant, the clapping of hands, the striking of rude instruments: there are measured movements, measured words, and measured tones. . . .

[T]he first musical instruments were, without doubt, percussive—sticks, calabashes, tom-toms—and were used simply to mark the time of the dance; and in this constant repetition of the same sound, we see music in its most homogeneous form.[4]

Music as a whole is a differentiation or specialization of the primitive cry, in keeping with the pattern of heterogeneity emerging from homogeneity.

We have seen that there is a physiological relation, common to man and all animals, between feeling and muscular action; that as vocal sounds are produced by muscular action, there is a consequent physiological relation between feeling and vocal sounds; that all the modifications of voice expressive of feeling are the direct results of this physiological relation; that music, adopting all these modifications, intensifies them more and more as it ascends to its higher and higher forms; that, from the ancient epic poet chanting his verses, down to the modern musical composer, men of unusually strong feelings prone to express them in extreme forms, have been naturally the agents of these successive intensifications. . . .

[W]hat we regard as the distinctive traits of song, are simply the traits of emotional speech intensified and systematized. In respect of its general characteristics, we think it has been made clear that vocal music, and by consequence all music, is an idealization of the natural language of passion. . . . [T]he dance-chants of savage tribes are very monotonous; and in virtue of their monotony are more nearly allied to ordinary speech than are the songs of civilized races.[5]

But what is rhythm? Seen physically (one of the advantages of Spencer over his more conventionally educated contemporaries is his lack of regard for distinctions between the physical and the cultural), rhythm is "a necessary characteristic of all motion,"[6] the self-limiting action of a force working through a medium.

A stick drawn laterally through the water with much force, proves by the throb which it communicates to the hand that it is in a state of vibration. Even where the moving body is massive, it only requires that great force should be applied to get a sensible effect of like kind: for instance the screw of a screw-steamer, which instead of a smooth rotation falls into a rapid rhythm that sends a tremor through the whole vessel. The sound which results when a bow is drawn over a violin-string, shows us vibrations produced by the movement of a solid over a solid. In lathes and planing machines, the attempt to take off a thick shaving causes a violent jar of the whole apparatus, and the production of a series of waves on the iron or wood that is cut. Every boy in scraping his slate-pencil finds it scarcely possible to help making a ridged surface.[7]

If music derives from emotional language, rhythm marks the rise and fall of emotional energy, for in a finite body, energy cannot go on increasing indefinitely.

Rhythm . . . is seen during the outflow of emotion into dancing, poetry, and music. The current of mental energy that shows itself in

> these modes of bodily action, is not continuous, but falls into a succession of pulses.... One possessed by intense grief does not utter continuous moans, or shed tears with an equable rapidity; but these signs of passion come in recurring bursts.[8]

So in Spencer's theory of expression, rhythm modulates and limits the force of the proposition that "music is an idealization of the natural language of passion."

But a heterogeneity that derives from a homogeneous beginning could always, presumably, be reduced back to its homogeneity. Western contrapuntal music might be considered the apex of complexity achieved thus far in that art, but when Spencer comes to explain its development, the appearance of internal heterogeneity turns out to be nothing more than a layering and overlap of components in themselves simple.

> It was not until Christian church-music had reached some development, that music in parts was evolved; and then it came into existence through a very unobtrusive differentiation. Difficult as it may be to conceive *a priori* how the advance from melody to harmony could take place without a sudden leap, it is none the less true that it did so. The circumstance which prepared the way for it was the employment of two choirs singing alternately the same air. Afterwards it became the practice—very possibly first suggested by a mistake—for the second choir to commence before the first had ceased; thus producing a fugue. With the simple airs then in use, a partially-harmonious fugue might not improbably thus result: and a very partially-harmonious fugue satisfied the ears of that age, as we know from still preserved examples. The idea having once been given, the composing of airs productive of fugal harmony would naturally grow up, as in some way it *did* grow up, out of this alternate choir-singing.[9]

The voices meeting in canon or counterpoint could always be brought back to the same beginning, be scored in unison. Nothing essentially new has emerged from the temporal deferral or rhythmical differentiation among the musical lines. But the imagined primitive throng has not yet arrived at the "mistake" that initiates a new musical complexity: their essential trait for the purposes of these demonstrations is to be simple.

Thus the history of poetry, as a subset of the history of all progress in the universe, returns us for our explanations to the singing and dancing throng. In it singing and dancing are as yet undifferentiated, rhythm is a natural impulse of the muscles, and words have hardly begun to distinguish themselves from music; different classes and professions are not yet to be discerned in it; and if it is an English throng, its words must be the Saxon roots, direct in their onomatopoeia.[10] The ballad-theorists Francis Barton Gummere and George Lyman Kittredge, who spread such conceptions, had their disciples. Some of them were influential. But the history of poetry that they extract from folkloric examples, making primitive poetry flow from a single ethnic, linguistic, and rhythmical origin, convinces only insofar as it excludes.

Forms That Err

In a lecture about "Techniques of the Body" delivered in 1934, the anthropologist Marcel Mauss told a few stories about how he discovered that *habitus* or learned behavior saturates the body, making what might seem to be a biological or natural object a social and cultural one.

> You know that the British infantry marches with a different gait from ours: with a different cadence, a different length of stride.... The Worcestershire Regiment, having distinguished itself in the battle of the Aisne alongside the French forces, was awarded a company of French drummers and buglers and requested royal permission to incorporate them. The outcome was discouraging. For nearly six months, long after the battle of the Aisne, I saw the following spectacle in the streets of Bailleul: the regiment had kept its English style of marching and tried to fit it to a French rhythm.... This unfortunate regiment of tall Englishmen could no longer parade. Everything in its march was discordant. When they attempted to fall into step, the music was out of step. In the end, the Worcestershire Regiment had to drop its French military band.[11]

Mauss' discovery of culturally distinct modes of walking started, as so often happens, from something going wrong: the British soldiers tangled up in their own feet, unable to match their strides to the beats of a French music squad. Presumably they would have had no trouble marching in time to an English military band, the beats and pace of which would have been designed to accompany their way of walking.

This might have remained just a curious story from the front, or the foundation-myth of the Ministry of Silly Walks, were it not for a bout of dysentery that Mauss suffered while on a visit to New York in 1926.[12]

> A sort of revelation came to me in the hospital.... I wondered where I had seen young ladies walking like the nurses on my ward. I had plenty of time to think about it. Finally I realized that it was at the

movies. Once I was back in France, I began to notice, especially in Paris, that this style of walking had become frequent. French young ladies were walking in that same way. As it happened, American ways of walking had begun to circulate among us thanks to the cinema. This was an idea that I could extrapolate. The position of the arms and hands during the act of walking are a social peculiarity—not simply the product of some purely individual, almost entirely mental arrangements or mechanisms. For example, I believe I can recognize a convent-educated young woman. She will typically walk with closed fists. And I can still hear one of my high school teachers shouting at me: 'You stupid animal, stop flapping your big hands as you walk!" So walking derives from a form of education.[13]

And thus, Mauss realized, the ways people have of moving around, of holding tools, their postures and stances in movement and rest are culturally acquired pieces of knowledge. We readily agree that there is such a thing as Greek, Basque or Ukrainian dancing, but no one ever heard of Greek, Basque or Ukrainian walking. Walking, being so basic, should belong to everybody, should just be walking. But Mauss found that this attitude is wrong. To get a sense of what "the American walk" might have looked like for French observers of the 1920s, the reader may wish to consider the Mary Pickford short from 1918, "100% American." In this film, Mary Pickford's character decides not to spend her money on clothes and bus fare, but to save it and buy Liberty Bonds. After looking in a shop window, she turns and walks away under a long portico, attracting the admiring gaze of an idle old man. The heroine doesn't let her clothes hobble her. You see her shoulders thrown back and her arms moving in proportion to her long, purposeful strides. This is a walk expressive of an *ethos*—but not just an individual ethos. Her gait, no less than the special feminine saunter known among the Maori as "onioi," must have been learned from someone.[14] It is not shown as specific to Pickford's character. Her friend who spends money on clothes and hats walks in a similar way, with big strides and elbow action; so the female American Walk is not for a single personality type, but general. Walking is of course a practical behavior, one of our basic bodily actions, but it also communicates: it tells the world something about who we are and what we do, and it communicates itself from body to body by processes of imitation.

So, Mauss hypothesizes, such techniques of the body as walking, standing, sitting, sleeping, eating, not to mention the postures adopted while climbing trees, swimming, chopping wood, having sex, and so forth, do not happen as a matter of course but have to be installed (*montés*) in a body through training.

More technically, Mauss calls any technique of the body an *engrenage* or gearing-together of subordinate routines, a "physio-psycho-sociological assembly of acts in series."[15] (This *engrenage* later becomes the core idea of André Leroi-Gourhan's *Le Geste et la parole*, under the name "chaîne opératoire."[16])

> The body is the first and the most natural tool of mankind. . . . Prior to the techniques using tools, there is the class of techniques of the body. . . . This constant adaptation to a physical, mechanical or chemical aim is carried out in a series of pre-installed acts (*actes montés*), installed in the individual not only by his own volition, but by his whole education, by the whole society to which he belongs . . .[17]

Mauss insists on the cultural particularity of these patterns, on the idea that there is no such thing as mere sitting or sleeping *per se*, but that every human group codes a certain set of behaviors as normal and desired, and considers departures from those norms unfortunate or even sinful. Techniques of the body vary, but every culture has them.

But what is a body? Doesn't everybody already know that? It might seem that the body, as a topic, is as close to home as anything can be, and therefore as far as possible from estrangement. Indeed the classic theories of alienation, from Hegel through Feuerbach to Marx and Lukács, always presuppose the body as the axis from which alienation departs.[18] Techniques of the body, in line with this understanding, are said to be historically and presumably conceptually "prior to the techniques using tools." But let us take a second look at the experiences by which Mauss learned to recognize the technical and cultural specificity of these ways of inhabiting a body. A body trained to march to a certain rhythm is already not a natural body. Troops march in an artificially precise way, which is scored and formatted by military music, among other things. Is it that some kind of national biological characteristic accounts, as a common factor, for both British marching and British drumming? Certainly not. Mauss is arguing that the body is not simply material and therefore predictable in its psychological realizations: rather, the social is the level at which you will find the explanations for behavior. Rules that we learn in society make our material bodies operative.

With a slight difference in emphasis, I reach for the vocabulary of phenomenology. A rhythm, for example a four-four march time, is an intentional object projected into the future, a rule that anticipates and regulates the behavior of those who accept it: *one*-two-three-four, *one*-

two-three-four, until a halt is called. And a different rhythm, for example a waltz, sets out a different rule and formats future behavior in different ways. A "recurrent figure of sound" (Gerard Manley Hopkins) orients and projects.[19] The soldiers of the Worcestershire Regiment found themselves with legs and feet trained to one projected rule, and ears receiving a different rule: they had a two-body problem or even a four-body one.

Techniques of the body come to consciousness because something goes wrong in a specific way, in the very way that scholars of comparative literature are apt to notice: the clash of codes. There is thus something to compare, a culturally specific remainder that arises when the two patterns don't mesh seamlessly, but leave margins of code unaccounted for on both sides. But it's too simple to describe the Worcester Regiment's problem as a clash between British and French rhythms. The maladjustment happens rather among four patterns of rhythm: the British step and the French music, of course, but, no less, the missing British music and the French way of stepping that the French music was meant to accompany. These are normative behaviors. They reveal themselves to consciousness as techniques, as artifices, when things do not go according to plan—and they would not do this if the bodies were simply carrying out successful goal-directed actions according to a technique. Estrangement, *ostranenie*, as Viktor Shklovsky called it, occurs.[20] We could not speak here of homogeneity developing into heterogeneity by progressive differentiation. Rather, heterogeneity comes crashing in on the homogeneous. Two throngs merge with no single rule to guide their movements. Their encounter is historically new and irreversible.

Techniques of the body always involve at least two bodies, an experienced one and a projected one. Exceptional circumstances allow Mauss to see the two bodies as two rather than as one. The nurses who cause the patient to re-experience his hours spent in the cinema, as if they were quoting the evanescent figures on the silver screen, exhibit their bodies in double, as praxis and as norm. This the stumbling soldiers also do, although in their case, the norm is unattained, and the signals proper to two conflicting norms haunt and confuse their practice. Along with these revelatory moments of failure, the discovery of the technical body is also enabled by media. It is notable that cinema, in Mauss' account, has transmitted bodily gestures and disciplines—the "American walk"—across oceans and continents without at the same time transmitting the people and bodies who originated them. Parisian women learn from the cinema how to walk the brisk American walk, just as, if other circumstances had favored it, they might have learned how to walk the Maori "onioi."

The cinema is just one of the great nineteenth-century mimetic technologies that permit the separation of acts, voices, gestures—in a word, *habitus*—from the bodies that issued them. Thanks to the cinema, or more precisely thanks to the originator of time-sequenced photography, Étienne-Jules Marey, we can give a positive answer to the famous question posed by Yeats and reiterated by Paul de Man, "How can we know the dancer from the dance?"[21] It would be a mistake to call cinematic representation the dance in itself, or to confuse it with the whole dance, but enough of the dance can be captured that it can be repeated and transmitted by mechanical means; it becomes textualized. As Walter Benjamin put it, cinema, like technical reproduction in general, "substitutes a mass existence for a unique existence. And in permitting the reproduction to reach the recipient in his or her own situation, it actualizes that which is reproduced."[22] By 1920, viewers of cinema could perform the walks of foreigners just as they could learn to perform a piece on the piano with the help of sheet music.

This contagious, re-citable property of media, implying a wider definition of textuality, opens up for us a definition of the body that will not require a common-sense, you-know-what-I'm-talking-about, essentialist or fundamentalist definition of the body at the center of our talk of corporeal techniques. As an alternative to that path, we have another path that says that what will count as a body is an effect of the representational or discursive means available to incarnate it. The body operative in our discourse is whatever we have the ability to speak, chart, compute, or perform—walk, dance, shimmy—into being.

And for this reason the characteristics of this body are apt to change every time a new imaginative or representational technique emerges. Marey is responsible for more than one such change. Well before his work with successive photographs of the movement of bodies in space brought him to the threshold of the cinema, he had first made his name as an inventor of devices for capturing physiological change and movement within living creatures. Marey's strategy was to make the biological phenomena write themselves. He hitched an oscillating penholder to an arrangement of springs, cords and tubes connected to the organs of interest, and made the organs move the indicator in proportion to their normal physiological action.[23] On the side of the output, Marey's strategy was to reduce what must be measured to one or more variables of space, and plot changes in that variable against an axis of time. The result was a two-dimensional table. Graphs representing quantitative change over time had been appearing here and there since William Playfair's charts showing the recent growth of the British national debt in 1801, and indeed a musical score is a kind of time-series chart.[24] Marey's original contribution was in permitting the flesh to speak—or rather, write—its actions rather than be spoken about by an observer.

And in time Marey's externalization of the body's processes onto paper came to be applied to language, incorporating what it had sought to displace—words. Philologists and linguists have always been dissatisfied with existing alphabets. No two languages use the letters in the same way; a single language will use them differently from one period to another, or from one region to another. Desirous of the precision that was making possible recent advances in physiology, a linguist, Pierre Jean Rousselot, and a laryngologist, Charles Rosapelly, attempted to use the devices Marey had developed in his laboratory to transcribe the subtle, coordinated movements of the vocal tract. Rousselot's adaptation of Marey's physiological recording devices made the tongue, the nose and the larynx write their own displacements onto paper, leaving a trace even more detailed and individualized than the sound recordings on wax cylinders that soon began to appear. (Edison first demonstrated his phonograph four years after Rousselot and Rosapelly published their study of the muscle movements in language.) Psycho-physiology framed the human body itself as an analogue and confirmation of such mimetic extra-corporeal technologies as the phonograph and cinema. Capturing and replaying motion was its signal ability. Man was once more "the most mimetic of animals."[25]

Just what kinds of distinctions the human perceptive apparatus is able to capture, and what it makes of them next, is the question that experimental psychology was set up to resolve. From the laboratories of Fechner, Wundt, Helmholtz, and Marey, devices for evaluating human response to sensory stimuli proliferated and found a home in all forward-looking universities. Reaction time, sensory discrimination, and other features of mental life could be measured in setups combining a human subject and a variety of inscribing and calibrating devices.[26]

Rhythm particularly lent itself to such investigations. A strictly quantitative stimulus could be established on the machine side of the setup—for example, a series of mechanically generated clicks—and the human responses evaluated for subjective qualities such as inferred groupings or supposed accentuation.[27] Imagine the laboratory set up for an investigation of the psychology of rhythm. At the center is a human body (then as now, a student volunteer). This body is coupled on one side with a device producing regular, uniformly paced clicks, and on the other side, with a device allowing the body to record an output reflecting what it hears, for example by tapping on a telegraph key. The output might (and usually did) reveal rhythmical groupings, accents, and other features of order that had been supplied by the subject, not given in the original stimulus.

People thrive on pattern. Robert MacDougall, writing in 1903 from William James's lab at Harvard, observed that

> the rhythm form is not objectively definable as a stable type of stimulation existing in and for itself; the discrimination of true and false relations among its elements depends on the immediate report of the consciousness in which it appears. . . . The artistic rhythm form cannot be defined as constituted of periods which are "chronometrically proportionate" . . . It is not such in virtue of any physical relations which may obtain among its constituents, though it may be dependent on such conditions.[28]

R. S. Woodworth in 1907 noted that "a uniformly spaced series of equal sounds . . . is often heard in rhythmic form, and the same series may be heard in different rhythms. For example, a series of seven sounds may be heard either in 3/4 rhythm or in 6/8 rhythm. These differences are not contained in the stimulus, which is equivocal. . . . The groupings are not describable in sensory or motor terms, but are non-sensory qualities."[29] Richard Wallaschek, the author of *Primitive Music* (1895), contended that

> the muscular sense is not directly and in itself the cause of enjoyment in music, but becomes the case not only of enjoyment but of high mental edification when forming the basis of a cortical process which consists in arranging a certain number of sensations in time-periods, and perceiving them as whole united groups. Through this mental process the otherwise mere sensuous enjoyment rises to the higher rank of artistic value, while without it the musical performance would have to be placed on the same level with gymnastics or, as in the savage world, with beating and fighting . . .[30]

The question hanging over these investigations is whether rhythm is necessarily a physical thing or an intellectual thing. Posed in these terms, the alternative is false, for a socialized body, as Mauss would have said, is a physical thing that performs cultural work on itself and its environment. The body attentive to rhythm is, we can say without too much metaphorical exaggeration, a transformer. It takes a flow of energy (sonic pulses) and packages it into a specific form of current that is best able to travel in its particular cultural milieu. Among infantrymen, it will be a four-four measure; among hearers of ancient Greek epic, it will be dactylic hexameter; among singers on the Scottish-English border, it will be the ballad stanza; and so forth. The body does not introduce new quantities of matter or energy that are not already in the environment, it merely alters the form of the material given it, but it does so in a way that secures consensual uptake by other receivers similarly prepared.[31]

The transformer that is the socialized body gives to heard sound an order that renders the sound memorable or that predisposes it to significance in relation to other sounds experienced in the hearer's milieu. In short, transforming sound into meter is the work of the perceiving body. This is cultural work. The choice whether to parse a series of sounds as falling into 3/4 or 6/8 meter is unthinkable without prior exposure to music in those time signatures, and the same must surely be said of McDougall's or Wallaschek's aesthetic syntheses. A rhythm is, to repeat, an intentional object, and a collective one at that.

The biomechanical hybrid—what Mauss calls an "assemblage of physio-socio-psychological acts in series"—thus delineated is in an epistemological feedback relation with a general model of "energetics" shared by physicists, biologists, social theorists, philosophers of art and cosmologists in the years around 1900.[32] In a universe heading inexorably toward disorder, why should anything be permanent? More specifically, why should anything in such a universe be remembered or repeated?

It takes some expenditure of energy to maintain cultural forms (failing which, they would simply dissolve or become indifferent). Repetition and the enforcement of norms go with the conservatism of most pre-industrial cultures. Even William Carlos Williams, in accounting for the modernist poetic movement in which he took a leading part, explains it chiefly as an effect of decay: traditional "measures . . . were synonymous with a society [that was] uniform, and made up of easily measurable integers, racial and philosophical,"[33] but "our lives . . . have lost all that in the past we had to measure them by, except outmoded standards that are meaningless to us."[34] Accordingly, "they should be horrible things, those [modernist] poems. To the classic muse their bodies should appear to be covered with sores. They should be hunchbacked, limping. And yet our poems must show how we have struggled with them to measure and control them."[35] The pathos of decline here assumes victory over premodern sensibility and conventions accomplished. And yet "to break the pentameter" took a "heave."[36] Once a cultural form—a rhythm for example—is launched and has been adopted by many people, it will take effort to dislodge it. Where does this countervailing energy come from?

Consider what is being offered to our listening and reciting bodies by the following:

> If I should die, think only this of me:
> That there's some corner of a foreign field

That is for ever England. There shall be
In that rich earth a richer dust concealed . . .[37]

You will have recognized Rupert Brooke's famous sonnet "The Soldier," reprinted during the Great War in newspaper leaders and recited from pulpits across Great Britain. Iambic pentameter, precise rhymes, elevating sentiment, patriotism, nostalgia: "the military-metrical complex," as Meredith Martin has called it, on parade.[38] Another example of war poetry from 1915, however, refuses to fall in step:

Here we are, picking the first fern-shoots
And saying: When shall we get back to our country?
Here we are because we have the Ken-nin for our foemen,
We have no comfort because of these Mongols.
We grub the soft fern-shoots,
When anyone says "Return," the others are full of sorrow.
Sorrowful minds, sorrow is strong, we are hungry and thirsty.
[. . .]
Horses, his horses even, are tired. They were strong.
We have no rest, three battles a month.
By heaven, his horses are tired. [. . .]
We come back in the snow,
We go slowly, we are hungry and thirsty,
Our mind is full of sorrow, who will know of our grief?[39]

The second example comes from *Cathay*, Ezra Pound's book of translations or quasi-translations from the Chinese. The reader has little sense of being led on by a familiar rhythmic pattern, as one does with the Brooke sonnet. Each line has to be scanned individually; the stresses clump or disperse as they will; despite a predominance of feminine endings, the lines are end-stopped in obedience to the blunt, paratactic statements being made rather than to demands of rhyme or meter. The "recurrent figures of sound" (Hopkins) that permit us to recognize rhythm are rare: when the phrase "hungry and thirsty" echoes the last two feet of a Homeric hexameter ($-\smile\smile \mid -\smile$), it is like a raft sighted on a wide sea. The lines stumble. We might as well be marching with the Worcestershire Regiment, except that the French military band has now been exchanged for a seemingly arrhythmic Chinese one. Its origins in national myth so distant as to be a mere outline, its meter for the most part unidentifiable and asymmetrical, and its sentiments far from sacrificial idealism, *Cathay* broke with the inherited patterns that we see so boastfully on display in Brooke's sonnet. *Cathay* has been described as anti-war poetry.[40]

It is so more than thematically: the repudiation of war goes so far as to rout marching cadences from the verse itself. A new technique of the body here clashes with poetic "rhythm" as understood by most English speakers of the time. As Virginia Woolf put it: "In the vast catastrophe of the European war our emotions had to be broken up for us, and put at an angle from us, before we could allow ourselves to feel them in poetry or fiction."[41]

Whatever Pound was translating, he wasn't transferring Asian meter into English. Pound could hardly have had any idea of the Chinese metric of his original. Not only did he lack Chinese, he had access only to a Japanese transcription that rendered the last few lines just cited in this form:

Jū-sha, ki-ga / shi bo gyō gyō.	戎車既駕，四牡業業。
Gai kan tei kyo / ichi getsu san sho.	豈敢定居？一月三捷。
Ga hi shi bo / shi bo ki ki.	駕彼四牡，四牡騤騤。
Kon ga lai shi / wu setsu hi hi.	今我來思，雨雪霏霏。
Kō dō chi chi / sai katsu sai ki.	行道遲遲，載渴載飢。
Ga shin shō hi / baku chi ga ai.	我心傷悲，莫知我哀。 [42]

Nothing here to imitate, apparently. But the strange syllables may have suggested a heavy, hesitant step that broke the confident marching iambics of Brooke. In any case, Pound definitely saw and put aside a draft translation of the same poem by Ernest Francisco Fenollosa that began:

Picking the ferns, picking the ferns,
    ferns that grow in the forest.
Speaking of home, speaking of home,
    the year grows old in the desert.
. . .
Picking the ferns, picking the ferns,
    Ferns that here are so tender,
Speaking of home, speaking of home,
    Hardens the soul with its sorrow.

Sorrow of mind, tears of the mind,
    and body in hunger and thirst—
But men return, don't ask to return
    we must clear the enemy first.[43]

Fenollosa (whose notebooks on Chinese poetry remained Pound's main source for his entire engagement with Asian models) had noted the verse form of the poem's Chinese original, a four-syllable *a b a b* stanza, and tried to render it as a ballad stanza in English. Though he hadn't worked out the rhyming words yet, Fenollosa had a definite rhythmic pattern in mind. Absurdly, it's 4/3/4/3 ballad stanza that reads as a waltz in 6/8 time:

<u>Pick</u>-ing the <u>ferns</u>, (da da) <u>pick</u>ing the <u>ferns,</u> (da da)
• • • • • • | • • • • • • | |
<u>Ferns</u> (da) that <u>here</u> are so <u>ten</u>- (da da) der (da da) . . .
• • • • • • | • • • • • • | |

Although Fenollosa knew that the forms, rhymes, meters, and stanzas of Chinese poetry had histories of their own, and had systematic associations with other parts of Chinese culture, he must have thought that in order to make the documents from China look and sound like poetry, those cultural specificities had to be replaced with features of the English-language tradition that also coded positively for the quality of "being poetic." This was exactly the wrong choice, a choice imposed by inertia, a mechanical tick-tock imposed by centuries of precedent. Pound's breaking of the rhythm made the marching bodies wake up ("Here we are . . .") and wonder what they were doing and when they could get back to their country. Stumbling was by far the more honorable thing to do, both as regards the war theme and the dignity of the Chinese classical poem. When Pound turned some forty years later to translate the three hundred and five Confucian Odes into ballad stanza and a simulacrum of Appalachian *Volksdichtung* peppered with blackface-minstrel japes, he may have done it out of sarcasm, or else sought to mark his own regression, as a guest of St. Elizabeths, to the state of Gummere's throng.[44]

Comes a Vapour from the Margin

Manifestos for Imagism presented its prosody as psychological and individual, an alternative to the mechanical, collective drumming of traditional meter. As Pound put it variously between 1912 and 1917:

> As regarding rhythm: to compose in the sequence of the musical phrase, not in sequence of a metronome. . . .
> I believe in an 'absolute rhythm,' a rhythm, that is, in poetry which corresponds exactly with the emotion or shade of emotion to be expressed. A man's rhythm must be interpretative, it will be, therefore, in the end, his own, uncounterfeiting, uncounterfeitable. . . .
> I think one should write vers libre . . . only when the 'thing' builds up a rhythm more beautiful than that of set metres, or more real,

more a part of the emotion of the 'thing,' more germane, intimate, interpretative than the measure of regular accentual verse . . .⁴⁵

Pound was simultaneously practitioner, theorist, and publicist. Some confusion of roles is to be expected. His calls for the breaking of traditional meter promise a rhythm that will be "germane, intimate, interpretative"—a musical reflection of personality. But his space of argument is polemically narrowed: in it, one must choose whether to write in obedience to "the musical phrase" or to "a metronome."

Cathay rejects the metronome, but its "absolute rhythm" is not purely psychological and interpretive either: its mimesis of emotional states is complicated by reminiscences of French free verse, American prose transcribing Japanese glosses on Chinese poems, and some faintly heard Sino-Japanese meters. Rhythm becomes palimpsestic. It becomes, to cite Pound again, "an 'Image,' [or] that which presents an intellectual and emotional complex in an instant of time."⁴⁶ Note that there is nothing necessarily visual in this definition of the "Image." It is rather a psychophysical apparatus through which the memory of past events can be fixed and transmitted, as Bergson proposed in *Matière et mémoire*:

> Here I am in the midst of images, in the vaguest sense that can be given to the word, images that are perceived when I open my senses, unperceived when I close them. . . . It is entirely as if, in this collection of images that I call the universe, nothing really new could ever be produced save through the intermediation of certain particular images, of which the pattern is given me by my body. . . .
> The body, interposed between those objects acting on it and those on which it exerts influence, is no more than a conductor, disposed to collect movements, and to send them on, when it does not halt them, to certain motor mechanisms. . . . It must therefore be as if an independent facility of memory gathered up images along the course of time as they are produced, and as if our body, with its environment, was only one of these images: the ultimate image. . . . So it is in the form of motor apparatus, and of motor apparatus alone, that [the body] can store up past actions.⁴⁷

Poetic rhythm, a "technique of the body" involving stored and repeated schemata, is an "image" in this sense. Visual imagery projects representation into space, which, in the Bergsonian language used by T. E. Hulme in articulating the Imagist poetic and emulated by Pound, is the realm of mechanistic causality and stereotyped language, as opposed to time, where creative freedom can occur. "It is important to see that the inability under which we suffer, of being unable to conceive the existence of a real change in which absolutely new and unpredictable things can happen, is entirely due to that fixed habit of the intellect which insists that we shall analyse things into elements, and insists on that because it will have a picture in spatial terms."[48] Thus the common etymology of the term "Imagism" is based on a *faux ami*, as is the usual explanation for the popularity of "imagistic" Chinese poetry as a model for modernist poetry in English.[49]

Verse, like dance, transmits a pattern of movement from body to body, or from a body at time T to the same body at time T+1. The transmission process does not simply go from inside to outside (the assumption imported into Imagist rhetoric from Bergsonian vitalism); since all bodies receive rhythms from outside, and there are many such rhythms (relayed, for example, by different languages and poetic traditions), verse can and must be perturbed even while seeking an "absolute rhythm." Our understanding of the history of poetry could do with less thematics and more attention to the contagious, repetitive logic of inscription.

Laudable attention has been paid in recent years to prosody, rhythm and meter in English.[50] Unfortunately the discussion has too often been provincial. By neglecting the foreign contributions to English verse we risk giving credence to the idea that a nation's poetry "progresses" straightforwardly from initial homogeneity to a later heterogeneity (with this heterogeneity being always decomposable into pure elements, as was the choral counterpoint of Spencer's example). Pound with his customary abruptness stated in 1913 that "The history of English poetic glory is a history of successful steals from the French."[51] This is a general truth—substitute what national labels you like. "The history of X's poetic glory is a history of successful steals from Y." French *vers libre* was a successful steal from various sources, including Whitman.[52] In the case of Whitman, as soon as the French had stolen him away, a group of American poets led by Pound and Eliot stole him back, in the guise of Laforgue, whose rhyme and meter, along with a great deal else, are unmistakable in "Prufrock" and *Hugh Selwyn Mauberley*. And *Cathay* is a storehouse of steals from France, China, and Japan. Pound's lines are bent and dented by the irreversible impact of the foreign.

If we recognize poetry as being "the most provincial of the arts,"[53] the verbal art with the least easily broken commitments to the language in which it is written, cross-linguistic influence is going to pose a problem. And nonetheless it happens. How? As with the hapless soldiers of the Worcestershire Regiment, any prosodic influence across languages is going to involve at least four overlapping systems. To understand, for example, how Whitman could affect French versification one needs to understand, at a minimum, how Whitman's prosody works; how French prosody at the time of contact or importation worked; then how Whitman's prosody seemed to work to French speakers (which may not be the same thing as how Whitman's prosody works for English speakers); then how the effects of one registered on the other. Contact between languages in verse form is a contact not between objects in themselves, but between the forms they take through comparison and reflexivity. The forms taken over from other languages will necessarily make the receiving language stumble, will break the inertia of its forward movement. This is not easy to understand without a commitment to the foreign languages, and it suggests, at least as far as poetry is concerned, that "English" is a mirage. At its historical turning points, verse is a technique of the stumbling body led on by alien bands.

Notes

I am grateful to the editors of this volume and to the reviewers for many suggestions. Conversations with Timothy Billings and Lucas Klein helped me work through the argument here, and invitations from Justyna Beinek and David Damrosch gave it shape.

1. On this "throng," see Francis Barton Gummere, *The Beginnings of Poetry* (New York: Macmillan, 1901), 139. By the late twentieth century, "the imaginary singing and dancing throng was a joke among folklore students in the United States" (Lee Haring, "The Oral Literature Researcher as a Foreign Expert," *Cahiers de littérature orale* 63–64 [2008]: 428. For the emergence of ideas of collective authorship in German romanticism (Herder, Grimm), and their role in debates of the early twentieth century, see Louise Pound, *Poetic Origins and the Ballad* (New York: Macmillan, 1921) and Haun Saussy, *The Ethnography of Rhythm: Orality and Its Technologies* (New York: Fordham University Press, 2016), 47–56.

2. Herbert Spencer, "Progress: Its Law and Cause" (1857), in *Essays Scientific, Political, and Speculative,* vol. 1 (New York: Appleton, 1904): 9–10. Punctuation unaltered.

3. Spencer, "Progress," 18.

4. Ibid., 30, 32.

5. Spencer, "The Origin of Music," in *Essays: Scientific, Political and Speculative,* vol. 2 (London: Williams and Norgate, 1891): 420, 414.

6. Spencer, "The Rhythm of Motion," *First Principles* (London: Williams and Norgate, 1867): 271.

7. Spencer, "The Rhythm of Motion," 251.

8. Ibid., 266.

9. Spencer, "Progress," 33.

10. On Saxon onomatopoeia, see Spencer, "The Philosophy of Style," in *Essays,* vol. 2: 333–369. Writers in English should choose "Saxon" over "Latin" terms in the interest of psychological efficiency: "Regarding language as an apparatus of symbols for the conveyance of thought, we may say that, as in a mechanical apparatus, the more

simple and the better arranged its parts, the greater will be the effect produced. . . . The greater forcibleness of Saxon English, or rather non-Latin English, first claims our attention" (338).

11. Marcel Mauss, "Les Techniques du corps," in Mauss, *Sociologie et anthropologie* (Paris: Presses universitaires de France, 1950), 367; original publication in *Journal de Psychologie normale et pathologique* 32 (1936). An English translation appears in *Incorporations*, ed. Jonathan Crary and Sanford Kwinter (New York: Zone Books, 1992), 455–77; here I venture my own. See also Jean-François Bert, ed., *"Les techniques du corps" de Marcel Mauss: Dossier critique* (Paris: Publications de la Sorbonne, 2012).

12. On this episode, see Marcel Fournier, *Marcel Mauss* (Paris: Fayard, 1994), 528–31.

13. Mauss, "Les Techniques du corps," 368.

14. On the "onioi" as presented in Mauss, see Carrie Noland, *Agency and Embodiment: Performing Gestures / Producing Culture* (Cambridge, Mass.: Harvard University Press, 2009), 26–29. For the film, see https://www.youtube.com/watch?v=u4_Xaswo BmM.

15. Mauss, "Les Techniques du corps," 384.

16. André Leroi-Gourhan, *Le Geste et la parole, I: Technique et langage. II: La Mémoire et les rythmes* (Paris: Albin Michel, 1964–65).

17. Ibid., 372.

18. Consider Marx's suggestion that "The criticism of religion disillusions man . . . so that he will move around himself as his own true sun. Religion is only the illusory sun which revolves around man as long as he does not revolve around himself." "Zur Kritik der Hegelschen Rechtsphilosophie. Einleitung" (1844), in Karl Marx and Friedrich Engels, *Werke*, vol. 1 (Berlin: Dietz Verlag, 1976): 378–91.

19. "Verse is . . . speech wholly or partially repeating the same figure of sound." "Poetry and Verse," in *The Journals and Papers of Gerard Manley Hopkins*, ed. Humphrey House and Graham Storey (London: Oxford University Press, 1959), 289. This phrase becomes a key refrain in Roman Jakobson's famous "Closing Statement: Linguistics and Poetics," in *Style in Language*, ed. Thomas Sebeok (New York: Wiley, 1960): 350–77.

20. Viktor Shklovsky, "Art as Device," in Alexandra Berlina, ed. and trans., *Viktor Shklovsky: A Reader* (New York: Bloomsbury, 2017), 80.

21. William Butler Yeats, "Among School Children," cited in Paul de Man, *Allegories of Reading* (New Haven, Conn.: Yale University Press, 1979), 12.

22. Walter Benjamin, "The Work of Art in the Age of its Technological Reproducibility," second version, trans. Edmund Jephcott and Harry Zohn, in Benjamin, *The Work of Art in the Age of Its Technological Reproducibility and Other Writings on Media*, ed. Michael W. Jennings, Brigid Doherty, and Thomas Y. Levin (Cambridge, Mass.: Harvard University Press, 2008): 22.

23. On Marey's wider circles of influence, see Robert Brain, *The Pulse of Modernism: Physiological Aesthetics in Fin-de-Siècle Europe* (Seattle: University of Washington Press, 2016).

24. See Edward Tufte, *The Visual Display of Quantitative Information* (Cheshire, Conn.: Graphics Press, 1983).

25. Aristotle, *Poetics* 1448 b 10.

26. See Laura Otis, "The Metaphoric Circuit: Organic and Technological Communication in the Nineteenth Century," *Journal of the History of Ideas* 63, no. 1 (2002): 105–28; Robert Brain and W. Norton Wise, "Muscles and Engines: Indicator Diagrams

and Helmholtz's Graphical Methods," 124-48 in *Universalgenie Helmholtz. Rückblick nach 100 Jahren*, ed. Lorenz Krüger (Berlin: Akademie Verlag, 1994).

27. For examples of early physiological rhythm research, see G. Stanley Hall and Joseph Jastrow, "Studies of Rhythm," *Mind* 11 (1886): 55-62; Thaddeus L. Bolton, "Rhythm," *American Journal of Psychology* 6, no. 2 (1894): 145-238; Robert MacDougall, "The Structure of Simple Rhythm Forms," *Harvard Psychological Studies* 1 (= *The Psychological Review*, Monograph Supplements, 4) (1903): 309-411; Raymond Herbert Stetson, "Rhythm and Rhyme," *Psychological Review Monograph Supplements* 4 (1903): 413-466, and "A Motor Theory of Rhythm and Discrete Succession," *Psychological Review* 12, no. 4 (1905): 250-70; P. F. Swindle, "On the Inheritance of Rhythm," *American Journal of Psychology* 24, no. 2 (1913): 180-203; Lionel Landry, "Le Rythme musical," *Revue philosophique* 102 (1926): 223-38; Pierre Fraisse, "Contribution à l'étude du rythme en tant que forme temporelle," *Journal de psychologie normale et pathologique* 39 (1946): 283-304. Nicolas Abraham, *Rythmes de l'œuvre, de la traduction et de la psychanalyse*, ed. Nicholas Rand and Maria Torok (Paris: Flammarion, 1985), begins with an evocation of such quantitative studies. For a general historical discussion, see Pascal Michon, "Notes éparses sur le rythme comme enjeu artistique, scientifique et philosophique depuis le milieu du XIXe siècle," *Rhuthmos*, 9 November 2012, available at http://rhuthmos.eu/spip.php?article540; consulted 3 August 2013. For a study of modern American poetry incorporating measurements of pitch, stress and duration, see G. Burns Cooper, *Mysterious Music: Rhythm and Free Verse* (Stanford, Calif.: Stanford University Press, 1998).

28. MacDougall, "The Structure of Simple Rhythm Forms," 310.

29. R. S. Woodworth, "Non-Sensory Components of Sense Perception," *The Journal of Philosophy, Psychology and Scientific Methods* 4:7 (1907), 171.

30. Richard Wallaschek, "On the Difference of Time and Rhythm in Music," *Mind* n.s. 4 (1895): 33.

31. On rhythm as synchronization and information-packaging, see Frederick Turner and Ernst Pöppel, "The Neural Lyre: Poetic Meter, the Brain, and Time," *Poetry* 142,5 (1983): 277-309. Karl Bücher, like Herbert Spencer, sought a social explanation of rhythmic art forms as originating from the movements of communal labor, e.g., flailing, pounding, winnowing, and washing, synchronized first for practical efficacy and then for aesthetic pleasure. See Bücher, *Arbeit und Rhythmus*, 3rd ed. (Leipzig: Teubner, 1902).

32. See Danièle Ghesquier-Pourcin, ed., *Énergie, science et philosophie au tournant des XIXe et XXe siècles*, 2 vols. (Paris: Hermann, 2010); Brain, *The Pulse of Modernism*, 37-63.

33. William Carlos Williams, "VS" (1948), cited in Michael Golston, *Rhythm and Race in Modernist Poetry and Science: Pound, Yeats, Williams, and Modern Sciences of Rhythm* (New York: Columbia University Press, 2007), 213. Williams repudiated Pound's indulgence in foreign languages and rhythms, presenting his own poetry as the record of a distinctly American rhythm (212-14).

34. Williams, *Selected Essays*, 337-8, cited in Golston, *Rhythm and Race*, 215.

35. Williams, cited in Golston, *Rhythm and Race*, 214-15.

36. Ezra Pound, "LXXXI," in *The Cantos of Ezra Pound* (New York: New Directions, 1972), 518.

37. "1914," part V, "The Soldier," in *The Collected Poems of Rupert Brooke* (New York: John Lane, 1918), 111.

38. Meredith Martin, *The Rise and Fall of Meter: Poetry and English National Culture, 1860-1930* (Princeton, N.J.: Princeton University Press, 2012), 139, 144. I find Martin's account of Modernism after the war less convincing.

39. "Song of the Bowmen of Shu," from Ezra Pound, *Cathay*, in Pound, *Poems and Translations*, ed. Richard Sieburth (New York: Library of America, 2003), 249.

40. See for example Hugh Kenner, *The Pound Era* (Berkeley: University of California Press, 1971), 201–3; Zhaoming Qian, *Orientalism and Modernism: The Legacy of China in Pound and Williams* (Durham, N.C.: Duke University Press, 1995), 60–61.

41. Virginia Woolf, "On Not Knowing Greek" (1925), in *The Common Reader, First Series*, ed. Andrew McNeillie (London: Hogarth Press, 1982), 34.

42. "Cai wei" 采薇 (*Shi jing* 167), from the notebooks of Ernest Fenollosa (Yale University Collection of American Literature, Beinecke Library), as reproduced in Timothy Billings, ed., *Cathay: A Critical Edition* (New York: Fordham University Press, 2018). The Japanese pronunciation is owed to Ariga Nagao 有賀長雄, Ernest Fenollosa's tutor in 1898–99.

43. Ernest Fenollosa, draft translation of "Cai wei" 采薇 (*Shi jing* 167), from the Ezra Pound Papers (Yale University Collection of American Literature, Beinecke Rare Book and Manuscript Library), box 100, folder 4228.

44. Ezra Pound, trans., *The Confucian Odes: The Classic Anthology Defined by Confucius* (Cambridge, Mass.: Harvard University Press, 1954).

45. Pound, "A Retrospect," 3–14 of *Literary Essays of Ezra Pound*, ed. T. S. Eliot (London: Faber & Faber, 1954), 3, 9, 12. These remarks date from 1912–1913. Pound continued to use the term "Imagism" even after his disaffection from the so-called movement, around 1915.

46. Ibid., 4.

47. Henri Bergson, *Matière et mémoire*, in *Oeuvres* (Paris: Presses universitaires de France, 1959), 169–70, 223–24, 180–81.

48. See T. E. Hulme, "The Philosophy of Intensive Manifolds," in *Speculations*, ed. Herbert Read (1924; rept., New York: Harcourt, Brace, n.d.), 197.

49. "The art of translating Chinese poetry is a by-product of the Imagist movement.... The element of poetry which travels best is of course concrete imagery.... Fortunately, most Chinese poetry is extremely concrete." A. C. Graham, *The Poetry of the Late T'ang* (Harmondsworth: Penguin, 1977), 13–15.

50. See for example Derek Attridge, *Poetic Rhythm: An Introduction* (Cambridge: Cambridge University Press, 1996); Meredith Martin, *The Rise and Fall of Meter*; Golston, *Rhythm and Race*; Simon Jarvis, "Prosody as Cognition," *Critical Quarterly* 40, no. 4 (1998): 3–15. The selections included in Virginia Jackson and Yopie Prins, eds., *The Lyric Theory Reader* (Baltimore: Johns Hopkins University Press, 2013), bear almost exclusively on theme and genre. My contention here is that theme and genre do not determine rhythm. Or perhaps theme and genre are supposed to do so in periods of "normal" (Spencer might have said "homogeneous") poetic development. But (and this is the noteworthy thing) formal features such as rhythm periodically upset the dominance of such top-down determinants. If I were writing literary history, the clashes would dominate and the periods of stability be reduced to parentheses.

51. Ezra Pound, "The Approach to Paris" (1913), reprinted in *Ezra Pound's Poetry and Prose Contributions to Periodicals*, ed. Lea Baechler and A. Walton Litz, vol. 1 (New York: Garland, 1991):154.

52. René Taupin, *L'influence du Symbolisme français sur la poésie américaine de 1910 à 1920* (Paris: Champion, 1929); Betsy Erkkila, *Walt Whitman among the French: Poet and Myth* (Princeton, N.J.: Princeton University Press, 1980).

53. According to W. H. Auden in *The Dyer's Hand and Other Essays* (New York: Random House, 1968), 23.

Constructing Walt Whitman: Literary History and Histories of Rhythm

Erin Kappeler

Whitman studies in the twentieth century have shown us the truth of Whitman's declaration, "I am large, I contain multitudes." There is a Whitman for every artistic and social need: the aesthetic Whitman liberates poetry from the shackles of its past; the queer Whitman challenges heteronormative structures; the historic Whitman registers the rapid technological and media shifts of modernity; the political Whitman shows us the promise of liberal selfhood. There are British, Spanish, German, Brazilian, Portuguese, Italian, Polish, Swedish, and Russian Whitmans, as Gay Wilson Allen and Ed Folsom show in *Whitman and the World*, each of which responds to distinct cultural trends and historical events. Whitman's varied legacies can make it seem as if "Whitman is mere *bathybius*; . . . literature in the condition of protoplasm—an intellectual organism so simple that it takes the instant impression of whatever mood approaches it," as the British critic Edmund Gosse half-seriously proposed in 1896.[1] Contemporary critics have been attentive to the constructed nature of these various Whitmans, particularly following the publication of the seminal essay collection *Breaking Bounds* in 1996, which was intended to direct critical focus to "the performative and staged dimensions of the figure 'Walt Whitman' and the constructedness of his reputation."[2] And yet, there is one Whitman who critics continue to accept as a natural fact: Whitman the father of free verse, who liberated American poetry from the confines of "traditional" poetry. This figure has been so fully naturalized that even the critics who are most attuned to Whitman's shifting place in history are still unable to recognize that the alignment of Whitman with free verse happened at a particular historical moment. David Reynolds, for instance, whose carefully historicized work is otherwise sensitive to Whitman's protean reputation, states as fact that, as the "father of free verse," Whitman "changed the course of poetry" by "liberat[ing] poetry from rhyme and meter, opening it up to the flexible rhythms of feeling and voice."[3] Even Betsy Erkkila, the editor of *Breaking Bounds*, literalizes this figure by explaining that Whitman "broke away from the form and content of traditional verse" to found a new tradition of poetic rhythm.[4] To be sure, Whitman's own writings seem to authorize this vision of Whitman as the father of a new poetic form; as he put it in the preface to the first edition of *Leaves of Grass*, the American poet's job was to "[see] the solid and beautiful forms of the future where there are now no solid forms."[5] But to claim that Whitman's new form was free verse is to take for granted that we know what free verse was and is, and, in the process, to simplify a complex history of debates about poetic rhythm. Whitman's poetry was not called "free verse" with any regularity until the 1920s, and even then, arguments about the nature of free verse abounded. American scholars in the 1910s and 20s hotly contested the formal identity of Whitman's writing, turning to scientific studies of linguistic rhythm to solve the problem of free verse once and for all. In what follows, I argue that Whitman's position in literary history as the father of free verse began to be constructed in this critical moment, and that this construction was a much more complicated and contentious process than has been realized. Focusing primarily on the critical work of Fred Newton Scott, Amy Lowell, and Mary Austin, I show that these arguments about Whitman's rhythm were motivated by concerns about constructing an American identity. As the second great wave of immigration increased the diversity of the American population and stimulated anxiety about the country's ability to absorb multiple immigrant bodies into a coherent national body, debates about Whitman's rhythms became debates about an imagined American race. In the process, these debates produced key ideas about the nature of free verse and modern poetry that continue to circulate in the academy today in deracinated, decontextualized forms. This significant moment in the country's "absorption" of Whitman as a generative figure thus provides a particularly rich site for rethinking the relationship between poetic rhythms, national ideologies, and literary history.

Scott, Lowell, and Austin may seem like minor figures in the development of free verse in America, but their work represents a dominant strain of poetic thought in the early modernist era—a strain of thought that tells a much different story about the emergence and reception of free verse than the familiar narrative of metrical constraint and liberation.

The study of poetry in the American academy during this time was largely concerned with a theory of generic evolution that grew out of nineteenth-century ballad scholarship. According to this theory, poetry had begun at the dawn of civilization as a heavily rhythmical, embodied, communal practice, and had evolved into an abstract, print-mediated, individualized experience. Nineteenth-century ballad discourse imagined pre-literate, pre-capitalist cultures to possess an authenticity and a unity that had been fragmented by the fall into mechanized print. In this schema, highly rhythmical oral poetry was the basis of genuine national literary traditions and a reflection of unified folk cultures; as Susan Stewart argues, ballad scholars believed that oral ballads provided "a legitimating point of origin for all consequent national literature" and culture.[6] This theory of the communal origins of poetry was reanimated and modified by early twentieth-century scholars, who saw free verse as an attempted return to the immediacy and organicism of the earliest poetry and as the true beginning of an American literary tradition. It is often acknowledged that the "balladic fantasy about a singular folk" was particularly powerful in the postbellum United States, as Michael Cohen has shown,[7] but it is less often noticed how integral this fantasy was to the construction of Walt Whitman as the fountainhead of American free verse. Indeed, Whitman's current place in literary history has been understood as a function of the institutionalization of the New Criticism rather than as an ongoing negotiation of the imagined relationship between rhythm, literary form, and national identity. Scott MacPhail, for instance, argues that the "lyric-nationalist readings of Whitman"[8] as the fountainhead of American poetry stem from the simultaneous emergence of the New Criticism and American studies in the mid-twentieth-century American academy.[9] MacPhail's analysis highlights how the New Critical ideal of the lyric as the genre that transcends history and ideology, when applied to Whitman's poetry, helped to "[serve] the ideological needs of [mid-century] state structures of power" by providing a seemingly rational, coherent articulation of American nationalism.[10] But an exclusive focus on this era's construction of Whitman misses the many other times that Whitman—and, more specifically, Whitman's rhythms—became a useful figure for the propagation of narratives of national progress.

By arguing that Whitman's poetry was not always understood as free verse, and that free verse is an unstable, changeable category rather than an empirical literary form, I hope to emphasize the imaginary, constructed nature of poetic rhythm itself. This is precisely the radical and unsettling understanding of meter that many scholars of Victorian poetry have been advancing in recent years; studies of American poetry from the same era, however, have been slow to integrate the insights of this work.[11] Many scholars of Victorian poetry take for granted that there is no unified system of "conventional" English meter, and that prosody names, not "an aesthetic category . . . distinct from the political or cultural sphere," but rather any number of contradictory "way[s] of thinking" about "gender, class, and national structures."[12] Scholars such as Isobel Armstrong, Jason David Hall, Matthew Reynolds, Meredith Martin, and Yopie Prins have investigated how definitions of meter, rhythm, prosody, and versification shifted throughout the nineteenth century, and how these fields were imagined as forces that could construct and support ideal forms of English national identity. This work shows that, although accentual-syllabic systems of scansion, based on the foot as the most fundamental metrical unit, have come to seem like both the natural way to approach the formal study of English-language poetry and the natural foil to more organic free verse forms, such systems only achieved hegemony in the twentieth century. The complicated, multivalent history of prosodic debate this scholarship illuminates shows that there was no singular metrical tradition from which free versifiers could break away until they helped to invent it; as Gertrude Stein quipped, "there is nothing to cut loose from . . . know this when there is no more to tell about what prose and poetry has been."[13] Building on this scholarship, I track changes in Whitman's reputation as a rhythmical innovator not to find the answer to the question of how to understand his rhythm, but rather to understand why certain approaches to the study of his rhythm became appealing at a particular historical moment. If, as Martin argues in *The Rise and Fall of Meter*, meter is never "merely the measure of the line," but always also "operates as a powerful discourse that interacts with and influences discourses about national culture,"[14] recovering early critical arguments about Whitman's metrical forms can help to illuminate just how imbricated rhythmic and nationalistic discourses have been in American poetics, suggesting the importance of attending to the politics as well as the aesthetics of prosody.

Fred Newton Scott's Whitman: Rhythm as National Symbol

Whitman simply proclaimed that he had created a new form of national poetry, but many scholars in the early twentieth-century American academy believed that their investigations into the origins of poetic rhythm had finally proved that this was so. Fred Newton Scott became one of the first academics to argue that Whitman had successfully created an entirely new, and entirely American, verse form when he published "A Note on Walt Whitman's Prosody" in *The Journal of English and*

Germanic Philology in 1908. Scott was a hugely influential figure in English studies in the early 1900s. He served as president of the Modern Language Association in 1907, founded the department of rhetoric at the University of Michigan, co-founded the National Council of Teachers of English and the Linguistic Society of America, and authored an impressive number of textbooks, critical studies, and scholarly articles, including the widely used *Introduction to the Methods and Materials of Literary Criticism*. Scott was particularly interested in the problem of differentiating the rhythms of poetry from the rhythms of prose, and his work in this area led him to believe that he had discovered the solution to the problem of Whitman's irregular form (though, importantly, he did not call that form free verse).

Scott's reconceptualization of Whitman grew out of his engagement with an unlikely pair of theorists: Francis Barton Gummere (whose career Virginia Jackson outlines elsewhere in this volume) and John Stuart Mill. As Jackson's essay shows, Scott's pairing of Gummere and Mill was truly strange, since Gummere fought a losing intellectual battle against Mill throughout his long career. Gummere strenuously objected to Mill's definition of poetry as "feeling confessing itself to itself in moments of solitude" because such a definition failed to account for the vital social functions of poetic rhythm. Mill's assertion that to "[confound] poetry with metrical composition" was "vulgar"[15] seemed to Gummere to be a catastrophic error; if cultural identity was an effect of poetic rhythm, as Gummere believed it to be, then uncoupling rhythm from poetry would fragment a once-coherent nation. Scott had no trouble combining aspects of these oppositional theories, however, because he believed that poetry was a unified, coherent genre, and that academic investigators could discover the "primal causes" and universal principles that governed its evolution.[16] He believed that Gummere was correct in arguing that poetry had begun as a social practice grounded in rhythm, but that it had evolved into an individualistic art form with little connection to early communal rhythms, meaning that Mill's definition was an accurate description of modern poetry. In eliding the distance between Gummere and Mill, Scott ignored the fissures and pressure points in prosodic discourse, thereby contributing to the growing sense that there was one "right" way to read poetry rather than multiple ways to approach different genres and metrical forms.

Scott's version of "right" reading is, curiously, both an artifact of turn-of-the-century evolutionary science as well as a source of many influential ideas about the organic rhythms of modern poetry. Scott accepted Gummere's theory of poetic evolution along with Mill's famous distinction between eloquence and poetry, and he posited that this distinction held the key to finding the fundamental difference between the rhythms of prose and the rhythms of poetry. Scott explained that speakers who wanted to communicate information were more attuned to the social function of poetry, since they had to factor in the response of their audience. He argued that the back-and-forth of communication led to "a swaying, fluctuating movement of a seemingly irregular kind."[17] Speakers who wanted to express emotion, on the other hand, had only to account for their own feelings, and so tended to produce "a fairly regular series [of sounds] subject to changes in tempo and pitch corresponding to the successive moods of the speaker."[18] If written prose and poetry had developed as modes of communication and expression, respectively, as Scott believed both Mill's and Gummere's theories proved, then it stood to reason that the rhythms of prose would be made up of long non-repeating units, based on the back-and-forth movement of communicative speech, while those of poetry would be made up of short recurring units based on the more regular movement of individualistic expressive speech. In premodern poetry, Scott explained, the short units of poetic rhythm corresponded to the stamping feet and clapping hands of the throng described by Gummere. In modern poetry, the units of rhythm were derived from the "physiolog[y] and psycholog[y]" of individual bodies.[19] To Scott, this theory seemed to prove that the most fundamental units of English-language poetry were not syllabic units (iambs, dactyls, anapests, etc.), as many prosodists believed, but rather temporal units derived from the rhythms of the human body. Syllabic units could be rightly understood as abstractions imposed upon those basic bodily rhythms—abstractions that could easily distract poets and their audiences from what he saw as the real rhythms of poetry, which were the rhythms of the body in motion.

Scott's attempt to substitute temporal units for syllabic units had many precedents in the nineteenth century—most famously, in E. S. Dallas' 1852 assertion that meter was simply "time heard" and in Coventry Patmore's 1857 elaboration that meter was made up of "'isochronous intervals,' or units of time."[20] These temporal units were so often tied to the rhythms of the body that, as Jason Rudy argues, "the history of Victorian poetry is in no small part a history of the human body."[21] If Scott was aware of this rich prosodic history, however, he did not let on. He presented his theory as an entirely new discovery that was only possible thanks to advances in modern science. He appealed to his own amateur experiments and to popular evolutionary theories to justify his approach to rhythm, which helped to give his prosodic theory the appearance of a disinterested, scientific discovery. He presented "data" drawn from his encounters with animals to prove that his rhythmical laws held for all vocalizing animals, explaining that, when he managed to overhear the songs of birds and the cries of cats without their noticing (meaning they had no audience and were only attempting to express themselves to themselves, to paraphrase Mill), their vocalizations came "in a rhythmical (one might almost say a metrical) series," but that, once his subjects noticed his presence and realized they had an audience, their cries became "harsh, strident," and "less regular," echoing the irregular rhythms of prose communication. He noted that his anecdotes about mewling cats and chirping birds opened him to "smiles and gibes," but he remained confident that "the researches of Darwin, Groos, and others concerning the genesis of expressive signs" proved the validity of such evidence.[22] To Scott, it was clear that his observations, combined with other studies in evolutionary science, plainly showed that the same set of rhythmical laws governed all languages, from the non-human to the primitive to the modern, and that his generation of theorists was the first to have discovered this fact. In Scott's account, poetic rhythm was an empirical, verifiable phenomenon, and classical prosodic terminology obscured this fact.

Scott argued that the discovery of these universal rhythmical rules meant that the answer to the question of how to interpret Whitman's idiosyncratic cadences was finally at hand. He posited that Whitman's unusual long lines were the result of a blending of the wave-like rhythms of prose (which he called "motation") and the steadier rhythms of poetry (which he called "nutation"). According to Scott, Whitman's natural "delight in large *free* movements and rushes of sound made him impatient of the *short* units, the quickly recurring beats, of the nutative rhythm. He wished to embody in his verse the largo of nature," and so he "sought to make [these natural sounds and movements] the very foundation of his prosody, the regulative principle of his rhythm."[23] Whitman had asserted that his poems were the best expression of democratic freedom, but Scott found scientific proof that Whitman's poetry was indeed more "large" and "free" than the "short," cramped, and stifling movements of "regular" meter. Scott thus helped to naturalize the opposition between "traditional" foot-based systems of prosody and more organic forms of meter.

At the same time, Scott's theory was able to locate the genesis of this new metrical freedom in the language of the American people. He explained that Whitman's hypersensitivity to the unique beauty of American speech helped him to see that he had to create an entirely new idiom in order to adequately express its "peculiar genius," and that it was his ear for "the pitch-glides and speech-tunes" of prose that allowed him to develop his new, hybrid poetic form.[24] In revaluing American speech as a tool of literary innovation, Scott's theory responded to a strain of British criticism that viewed Whitman's prosodic originality as an unfortunate effect of his insufficient metrical education. According to this view, Whitman was simply not educated enough to know that there were already metrical forms suitable for the expression of his ideas. Percy Smythe, 8th Viscount Strangford, put forth this argument most bitingly in 1866. In a satire couched as a defense, Smythe explained that Whitman had "somehow managed to acquire or imbue himself with not only the spirit but with the veriest mannerism, the most absolute trick and accent, of Persian poetry." Smythe argued that Whitman's uneducated state led him to translate this spirit into an undisciplined "yawp," but if he had had the good luck to attend an English preparatory school, and if "Persian verse-making had been part of the Haileybury course, after the manner of Latin alcaics and hexameters in an English public school," then Whitman might have been another Edward FitzGerald, translating mystical Eastern poetry into proper English forms.[25] Smythe's offhand references to specific Latin (and, elsewhere in the piece, Persian) meters are meant to give a sense of exactly how little metrical knowledge Whitman possessed. Not only did poets in the nineteenth century have access to countless English meters; the metrical traditions of all of the languages of the world were increasingly being translated and adapted for use by English-language poets. In ignoring these possibilities, Whitman proved his status as an uncultured American who could only "yawp" irregularly. It was clear to nineteenth-century critics like Smythe that Whitman was foregoing a world of metrical possibilities, and that his refusal of the metrical past required either condemnation or an explanation.

Whitman's defenders in the 1880s and 90s did little to justify his metrical project; they tended to assert that Whitman was an important innovator and defender of democracy without providing proof of their own, simply quoting Whitman's poetry in the belief that it spoke for itself.[26] It was not until Scott and other scholars of American literature set out to prove that their objects of study formed a coherent national literary tradition that critics began to attempt to explain and categorize Whitman's metrical innovations in a systematic way. Scott's account of Whitman's speech-based rhythms seemed to provide particularly compelling evidence that American poetry had finally become an organic expression of a unified national culture rather than an imitation of British poetry. As such, the poetic tradition that Whitman inaugurated could help to maintain the unity of the nation, creating a feedback loop between national identity and its literary expression. In Scott's opinion, as in Gummere's, social and artistic institutions were intimately linked. He argued that poetry and government were ruled by the same principles, explaining that,

> the relation between art and nature is like that between a people and its government ... The people can become free and remain free, only by submission to restraint. They can preserve their coherence, their communal individuality, their organic life and opportunity for unlimited expansion of that life, only as these things incessantly find expression in traditional, law-observing, law-embodying institutions.[27]

Prior to Whitman, no American poet had been able to devise a poetic law that could give expression to the American people's unique "organic life," and so American literature had failed to successfully cohere as a national tradition. The realization that Whitman had been creating within the bounds of rhythmic law rather than simply "yawping" without a sense of poetic rules meant that he could take his rightful place as the fountainhead of a modern American literary tradition, and that scholars of American poetry could finally prove that their discipline was a vital area of research.

Though Scott followed Gummere in arguing that a nation's literature and its identity were inseparable, his sense of the relationship between poetic rhythm and identity was slightly different. Gummere believed that national identity was an effect of rhythm, but Scott understood rhythm to be a figure for the functioning of a nation. If Scott's conflation of prosody and social relations was less absolute, it was no less powerful, for Whitman's prosody as a figure for the body politic provided a model for reconciling the potential chaos and heterogeneity of a truly democratic society with the supposed lack of freedom in any other social system. Scott put forth this model in parable form, explaining, "when I read Whitman's poetry in light of [the] conception" of Whitman's prosody as an interweaving of the long, irregularly recurring rhythms of prose and the short, repeating rhythms of poetry,

> a fantastic myth passes through my mind. I seem to see in Whitman some giant-limbed old heathen god who has descended to the earth fain to take part in the dance of mortals. He begins by practicing the waltz, but soon tires of the mincing steps and quick gyrations. He wants a larger, freer movement. He then tries marching and running and leaping, only to find that what his soul hungers for is the undulating movement of the waltz. So, devising a kind of colossal minuet, with woven paces and with waving arms, he moves through it with a grandiose, galumphing majesty peculiar to himself, fling-

ing his great limbs all abroad and shedding ambrosia from his flying locks, yet with all his abandon keeping time to the music, and in all the seeming waywardness of his saltations preserving the law and pattern of the dance.[28]

Scott advanced this parable of Whitman the dancer god as the foundational myth that America had been searching for since its colonial days. The motative movement of prose, with its potentially lawless irregularity, stands in for the heterogeneous individuals that make up the American people. These fractious individuals are brought under control by the regular, lawful nutative steps that allow bodies to move together in "the rhythm of consent" that Gummere had theorized, thereby becoming a unified people. For Scott, the "discovery" of Whitman's prosody was also the discovery of the first American throng. By finding their rhythm, he believed, the American people had found a way to overcome the social divisions and pressures that always threatened a democratic society. The "waywardness" and "abandon" of willful individual subjects would be harmonized in the pattern of the "colossal minuet" that was *Leaves of Grass*. For Scott, Whitman was useful not so much as the familiar figure of metrical revolution—the Whitman who liberated the line and "broke new wood" for Ezra Pound—as the figure of metrical reconciliation—the benevolent dancing giant who would bring his national community together.

Alternatives to Whitman: Rhythm as "Racial Fact"

Scott believed that the question of Whitman's rhythm and his consequent place in literary history was a settled affair. But for the majority of critics in the 1910s, the issue was far from resolved. According to prominent critics including Amy Lowell and William Morrison Patterson, a professor of English at Columbia University who researched how speech rhythms influenced poetic forms, the same scientific investigations into rhythm that proved to Scott that Whitman had invented a new and uniquely American verse form instead showed that he had failed to go far enough in his formal experimentation. Like Scott, Lowell and Patterson, who worked together to investigate poetic rhythm, believed that speech rhythms were the physical basis for the rhythmic patterns of both poetry and prose. But unlike Scott, they argued that Whitman had simply brought together the distinctive rhythmic curves of the communicative and expressive speech of the American people without adequately synthesizing them into a coherent poetic form. In her 1914 article "*Vers Libre* and Metrical Prose," published in *Poetry* magazine, Lowell explained that a misunderstanding of the nature of English meter was causing critics to overvalue Whitman's work and to overlook the truly groundbreaking prosodical experiments being carried out by contemporary poets. This was clearly a self-interested claim on Lowell's part, but her understanding of English prosody was shared by many of her contemporaries, as we will see. Lowell explained that Whitman had not invented a new poetic rhythm, but had rather stumbled into what she called "metrical prose."[29] She argued that *vers libre* had, confusingly, become a catch-all term for innovative poetry, which obscured the significant differences between French and English versification, as well as the notable divergences between different types of modern experimental poetry. In French poetry, Lowell argued, with its "firm and inelastic rules," it was "difficult . . . to escape monotony," and so French *vers librists* had rightly rebelled against the constraints of traditional meter.[30] English prosody, on the other hand, was "so much freer, and permits of so much more change," that translating the rhythms of *vers libre* into English was almost impossible.[31] According to Lowell, most poets who attempted this feat—including Whitman—ended up producing "metrical prose" rather than free verse. Sounding much like Scott, Lowell argued that the rhythms of speech, which were the basis of all poetic rhythms, formed a spectrum, from the long "wave lengths" of prose to the short, repeating "curves" of poetry, and that Whitman's rhythmical "wave lengths" showed that his most experimental passages were prose rather than poetry. The curves of Whitman's lines were "very long," but with a clear "return," which stood in marked contrast to the curves of *vers libre*, which were "much shorter" with an "excessively marked" return.[32] Lowell believed that the difference between the wave lengths of prose and the curves of poetry was absolute, and that mapping these rhythmical patterns could show beyond a shadow of a doubt whether a piece of writing was prose or poetry. Whitman's writing contained too many prose "wave lengths" to be classified as poetic, according to Lowell. If much of his poetry was not even poetry, but rather metrical prose, then he was clearly an unsuitable father figure for an American tradition, in spite of Scott's protestations to the contrary.[33]

Lowell believed that her hypothesis was verified in 1916, when she collaborated on a series of experiments with Patterson in his lab at Columbia University. Lowell read poems aloud into a state-of-the-art "sound-photographing machine" that "measure[d] the time-intervals" between her vocalizations.[34] Patterson and Lowell interpreted the results of these experiments somewhat differently (Patterson believed that the rhythms of *vers libre* could be translated into English; Lowell did not), but they agreed that they proved that Whitman was not the metrical innovator Scott believed him to be. Patterson explained that Whitman's poems were "mosaics," which he defined as a genre in which "the several kinds of verse and prose . . . alternate successively," creating an unsynthesized blend of multiple types of rhythmic curves. Not only did Whitman's writing rely too heavily on unmodified prose rhythms to be considered poetic; the poetic rhythms he did incorporate "drop[ped] into rather futile regularity" too often to truly break free from the constraints of "traditional" meter.[35] By placing the rhythms of prose and poetry side by side without fusing them, Whitman had pointed to the limits of, but had not transcended or transmuted, poetic form.[36] And if Whitman had been unable to synthesize the diverse American speech rhythms that Lowell and Patterson, like Scott, believed he had taken as his starting point, then his poetry would certainly not be able to accurately represent and reflect a coherent national character.

In his influential 1915 polemic *America's Coming-of-Age*, Van Wyck Brooks supported the idea that Whitman's rhythmic experiments had failed, though he posited a more complicated reason for Whitman's failure. It was not that his prosody was too free and unsystematic to constitute a national rhythm; rather, Whitman could not have represented the American character in the form of his poetry because that character did not yet exist. Brooks explained that America in the 1850s and 60s—like America in the 1910s—was a collection of "chaotic raw materials," and until the unassimilated immigrant groups that made up the population had been turned into a distinct American "race," no poet could create the representative form capable of founding a native tradition. Whitman had done all he could by diagnosing the problem with American poetry, which was that it was the product of a derivative, "genteel" culture that promoted the outmoded ideals of European romanticism.[37] Until "the American character" had been "determined . . . as a racial fact," no poet could do anything more.[38] For Brooks, the very condition of an American literary tradition was its perpetual deferral; if the American people needed a representative poet to show them their character, and if such a poet needed to have a coherent racial type to represent in his poetry, then American poetry was defined by its continual striving for an ideal that could only ever be imagined. Brooks' account turned American poetry into a utopian horizon rather than a discrete body of literature, helping to institutionalize the longstanding idea that American poetry could only cohere once an American identity had been located.[39]

For their part, Lowell and Patterson, like Scott and Gummere, saw the relationship between poetic form and national identity as a reciprocal one, in which poetic rhythms could help American readers to discover something like the American racial identity that Brooks saw as a moving target. Patterson argued that the free verse experiments of Imagist poets were a return to the "ancestral cadence" of the earliest English throngs who had chanted and danced their poetry, and as such they offered a powerful vision of rhythmic community that was illustrative for America as a nation of diverse immigrants.[40] Lowell concurred, arguing that it was the abstraction of meter as marks on a silent, printed page that had deafened modern readers to the "exceedingly subtle rhythmic effects" that early humans naturally felt in their bodies; consequently, rag-time, as an "instinct in the Negro race, a memory of the Congo," was more rhythmically complex than most popular newspaper poetry, and Franz Boaz had proven, in his study of the Kwakiutl tribe, that "the American Indian exhibits extreme facility in the execution of syncopating rhythms" that white Americans no longer possessed.[41] By tapping into the physical basis of poetic rhythm, Lowell and Patterson believed, modern poets would also necessarily touch the community-building functions of the earliest poetry.[42] Lowell was a particular champion of Vachel Lindsay, Carl Sandburg, and other so-called New Poets, who she believed had most successfully transmuted primitive rhythmic impulses into modern forms. Whitman may not have been able to harness the power of such rhythms, but these later poets, armed with studies like Lowell's and Patterson's, could return to the pre-literate physical origins of rhythm and the vital, primitive sociality of the Gummerian throng.[43]

In the 1910s, then, the question of what types of rhythms Whitman had included or created in his writings was inextricable from the question of American identity and its literary expression. Like Lowell and Patterson, the prolific critic and political activist Mary Austin responded to these questions with a crusade to show that a new tradition of American poetry had been created in the modern era, but that this tradition had not—indeed, could not have—begun with Whitman. Austin is best remembered as a regional, local color author and as a radical feminist and environmentalist. Her role in advancing an evolutionary view of poetic rhythms is less often noted, even though her theory of rhythm was a touchstone for F. O. Matthiessen in *The American Renaissance*. In *The American Rhythm*, first published in 1923, Austin argued that the endless search for a representative American poet by scholars from Emerson to Brooks to Lowell had missed the significant fact that, "[a]ll this time there was an American race singing in tune with the beloved environment, to the measures of life-sustaining gestures, taking the material of their songs out of the common human occasions, out of the democratic experience."[44] Native American poetry, Austin believed, had grown organically out of the American landscape, and the harmony between its rhythms and the environment meant that Native American poetry was almost a mimetic representation of America. Austin fantasized that the connection between the land and native poetry was so absolute that she could, simply by listening to the rhythms of "Amerindian languages," which she did not speak, "refer them by their dominant rhythms to the plains, the deserts and woodlands that had produced them" (18–19). While English-language poetry had become increasingly literary and book-bound, she argued, Native American poetry had developed organically, providing a template for the type of community-organizing poetry Gummere dreamed of.

Austin believed that Native American rhythms were the only basis on which a distinct American poetry could be founded because poetic rhythms were rightly derived from the rhythms of daily life. The rhythms of work and play in America were necessarily different from the rhythms of life in England; "the foot pace on the new earth, ax stroke and paddle stroke," gave rise to movements and patterns that were distinctly American (12–13). Because immigrants to the United States had experienced "an emotional kick *away* from the old [i.e., European] habits of work and society," Austin explained, "a new rhythmic basis of poetic expression [was] not only to be looked for, but [was] to be welcomed" as "evidence of the extent to which the American experience has 'taken,' among the widely varying racial strains that make up its people" (9). Derivative poetic rhythms were, for Austin, material evidence of a colonial mindset, while new rhythms were the sign of a new people beginning to feel their distinct identity. She argued that American poets had to be careful about the types of primitive rhythms they developed, however, as certain rhythms encouraged idiosyncrasy and fragmentation while others encouraged group cohesiveness. Austin was particularly wary of jazz rhythms because they were "a reversion to almost the earliest type of [rhythmic] response of which we are capable," and consequently "[implied] a certain amount of disintegration of later and higher responses, which would make an excessive, exclusive indulgence in jazz as dangerous as the moralists think it" (152).[45] An overdose of Whitman's rhythms was almost as bad as an overdose of jazz, according to Austin, because Whitman simply listed the diverse materials of American society without organizing and synthesizing them into a cultural type. Austin explained that "the genius of Whitman [was] not so much to be a poet as to be able to say out of what stuff the new poetry was to be made." He was "seldom far from the rutted pioneer track . . . Out of [its] dust, sweaty and raucous, we hear him chanting, principally of what he sees, so that his rhythms, more often than not, are mere unpatterned noise of the street" (17). No less than jazz rhythms, Whitman's poetry was "bond-loosening" and "soul-disintegrating" rather than community-building (32).

A genuine American poetry would draw on the rhythms that promoted communal identity rather than those that mimetically reflected the fragmentation and racial heterogeneity of twentieth-century America, and, according to Austin, Native American poetry was the only communally-oriented form available to American poets. She argued that Native Americans never used poetry "for the purpose of conveying information"; instead, "the combination of voice and drum in the oldest Amerind usage is *never for any other purpose than that of producing and sustaining collective states*" (23). Austin cited many of the same ethnologists as had Gummere to argue that democratic societies were the products of environmentally-influenced poetic rhythms; she explained that, "if we go back in the history of the dance we find the pattern by which men and women, friends and foes, welded themselves into societies and became reconciled to the All-ness. Here we find economy of stress giving rise to preferred accents, and social ritual establishing the tradition of sequence" (9). By dancing and chanting together, in other words, members of a group produced a sort of tacit social contract that resulted in the production of a coherent group identity. Austin argued that "rhythmic performances" were in fact the only way to convince individuals to subsume their interests under the interests of a group, and to orient themselves communally rather than self-interestedly. As Austin colorfully phrased it, "the poetic orgy . . . is the only means that has ever been discovered of insuring the group mind" (36). Free verse, or early attempts at the creation of free verse like Whitman's, did not have the same power to organize a group.

Like Lowell and other, more self-interested promoters of the new poetry, Austin believed that contemporary American poetry marked a return to the primitive roots of poetic rhythm, and as such it constituted a more truly American literature than anything Whitman had written. She argued that the "extraordinary, unpremeditated likeness between the works of such writers as Amy Lowell, Carl Sandburg, Vachel Lindsay and Edgar Lee Masters, exhibiting a disposition to derive their impulses from the gestures and experiences enforced by the American environment, to our own aboriginals" showed that a distinct American poetic tradition could finally be identified (46). The similarities of form between the new and the old American poetry showed that modern poets had finally realized that, "American poetry must inevitably take the mold of Amerind verse, which is the mold of the American experience shaped by the American environment" (42). If Whitman's prosody was useful at all, it was only as a negative example of the centrifugal rhythms that would keep the American community from cohering.

Changes in Whitman's reputation were not linear, of course, and at the same time that Austin, Brooks, Lowell, and likeminded critics condemned Whitman's attempt to create an organic American poetry as a failure, critics such as Ruth Mary Weeks championed Whitman's rhythms as the first truly modern innovation in poetry. Weeks had studied under Scott at the University of Michigan in the 1910s, and in her 1921 article "Phrasal Prosody," she took up the argument he had advanced in "A Note on Walt Whitman's Prosody." At first glance, Weeks' article seems to support the standard narrative of Whitman as a metrical innovator who broke with tradition; hers was one of the first academic studies to call Whitman's poetry free verse,[46] and she predicted that Whitman's rhythms would be a vital part of the future of American poetry. But early academic accounts of free verse such as Weeks' were more complicated than the polemical accounts advanced by poets such as Ezra Pound. For Weeks, free verse was not a break with the metrical past, but rather a step towards an ultimate poetic harmony that would reconcile "Procrustean classic" meters with the innovative rhythms of modern life. Weeks, like Austin, held to the Gummerian view that poetic rhythms evolved in tandem with the rhythms of everyday life, so that "primitive" poetry was strongly rhythmical and communally oriented, while modern poetry was irregularly rhythmic and individualistic. These idiosyncratic rhythms were an inescapable part of modern life, but they needed to be reconciled with the needs of the American community if poetry was to become a useful force in contemporary life. Drawing on Scott's preferred metaphor, Weeks argued that, "[t]he new day has new needs; the long free stride of democracy cannot accommodate itself to classic dancing measures," and that Whitman had created the new measure of modernity by taking the "vocal wave" as his "rhythmic unit."[47] Unlike Scott, however, Weeks believed that the vocabulary of "traditional" metrical poetry, based on syllabic feet, was compatible with Whitman's "new rhythmus." She argued that he had "attempted to use the various types of [vocal waves] as other poets use arbitrary groups of syllables to produce rhythmic effects," shifting the emphasis from the syllabic unit to what she called the "phrasal unit." Whitman had invented many types of "phrasal feet," she explained, including the "trochaic emphasis foot," and Amy Lowell's "delicate trochees," Sandburg's "resounding dactyls and amphibrachs," Edgar Lee Master's "hesitating minor iambs," and Ezra Pound's "mixed measures" were simply "perfecting this new and more flexible rhythmic unit."[48] To Weeks, preserving the vocabulary of "classic meters" as a means of describing free verse was important because it hinted at the ongoing evolution and the ultimate unity of poetic verse forms. She explained that free verse would not overtake "classic" meter, but would instead dialectically incorporate it, helping poets to develop "a richer, more pulsing measure than we have known, various yet sustained, combining syllabic and phrasal accent, pitch, time, pause, and rhyme—all the rhythmic values of spoken English" into a singular "rhythmus." Free verse was not a disruption or a break with the past, but "a new and beautiful note [in] the composite chord of the coming poetic harmony."[49]

Weeks extended Scott's utopian horizon beyond national boundaries; in her opinion, the rhythms Whitman invented had the potential not only to unify the heterogeneous national body of America, but, more broadly, to reconcile the past with the present, bringing the evolution of social life to a new pinnacle. If the gains of modern civilization had been offset by the loss of "the habit of social experience" that primitive civilizations had manifested in their tribal dances,[50] as Weeks, like Gummere, believed, then modern man needed the "golden strand of meter" to bind that ancient, communal mode of sociality to the present. Because rhythmic and social harmony were one and the same, Weeks argued, a completely harmonized poetry could overcome the fragmentation and alienation that had been ushered in by mechanized print and hastened by the industrial revolution.[51] Whitman's free verse pointed the way to this new incarnation of an Ur-rhythm, but only as part of a holistic vision of poetry that included both the embodied rhythms of free verse and the more abstract patterns of "classic" meter as integral parts of modern culture.

Bathybius whitmanii: Rhythm as Evolutionary Principle

The wildly different conclusions about Whitman's rhythms and his place in an American poetic tradition that Scott, Lowell, Patterson, Austin, and Weeks reached allow us to see the cultural work that prosodical fantasies did in the early twentieth century. For critics such as Weeks and Scott, poetic rhythms could point the way to an abstract social harmony, while for Austin, Lowell, and Brooks, among others, prosodical systems had very concrete effects on the evolution of the American "race." I have offered extended readings of these competing visions of American poetry because attending to these fantasies of rhythm not only allows us to better understand modernist poetic movements in context; it also allows us to see the ways in which these seemingly scientific approaches to rhythm have shaped the study of American poetry later in the twentieth century.

When Edmund Gosse joked in 1896 that Whitman was "mere *bathy-*

bius," he was unable to anticipate how apt his characterization would turn out to be. The *bathybius haeckelii* affair was one of the more notable scientific events in the nineteenth century, as it provided a rallying point for anti-Darwinians. In 1868, the British biologist Thomas Henry Huxley began to study sediment samples collected during the installation of the first transatlantic telegraph cable in 1858. Huxley believed the samples contained a sort of primordial ooze that was the missing link between inanimate and animate matter, and he quickly published his findings. It was not until 1875, when the Challenger Expedition undertook a sustained analysis of the ocean floor, that scientists realized that Huxley had mistaken a simple precipitate for the common ancestor of all living organisms. In many ways, this story is the perfect analogue to the story of Whitman's canonization. F. O. Matthiessen is the Huxley figure, promoting a vision of linear evolution from a single organism into the multiplicity of modern life. In his field-shaping work *The American Renaissance* (1941), Matthiessen relied heavily on the evolutionary theories of rhythm espoused by Gummere and Austin to argue that Whitman was the first modern poet to realize the physical basis of all poetic rhythm. Whitman understood that words had to be "grasped" with the senses before they could be effectively deployed, according to Matthiessen, and this understanding freed American poetry from the confining concept of "language as something to be learned from a dictionary." Indeed, Matthiessen went so far as to argue that Whitman had actually undergone a "crude re-living of the primitive evolution of poetry" from its "origin . . . in the dance, in the rise and fall 'of consenting feet' (in Gummere's phrase)" to the modern day. Whitman's primary "experience of natural rhythm" as the most basic source of poetry allowed him to move away from what Matthiessen, citing Austin, called the "conventional" poetry "of instructed imitation" to "the internal pulsations of the body, to its external movements in work and in making love, to such sounds as the wind and the sea," and so to forge an entirely new poetic tradition out of those primary sense experiences.[52] Whitman's poetry was consequently "more authentic than something Longfellow read in a book and tried to copy,"[53] and was thus far more suited to founding a truly native poetic tradition. As the product of an organic evolution of rhythm, Whitman's poetry was the foundational text that would create a new species of poetry that was better adapted to the rhythms and demands of modern life.

The endless critiques of Matthiessen's American canon have not lessened the power of his interpretive paradigm for later scholars of modernist poetry and poetics. The idea that primitive poetry could point the way to more socially effective modern rhythms remains particularly strong in the contemporary discourse of ethnopoetics, as can be seen in Jerome Rothenberg's 2002 introduction to the "Ethnopoetics" section of Ubuweb, a website devoted to archiving twentieth- and twenty-first-century avant-garde poetry and art. Rothenberg argues that modernist artists in the early twentieth century found analogues to their avant-garde practices in the traditional cultural practices of many of "the world's deep cultures—those surviving *in situ* as well as those that had vanished except for transcriptions in books or recordings from earlier decades." According to Rothenberg, such practices have historically helped Western artists to change the perception of formal innovations that "have been seen and heard as radical, even disturbing departures from conventional practice" by showing that such practices in other contexts have been viewed as "traditional" and "culturally acceptable."[54] Like the evolutionary view of Whitman, Rothenberg's pluralist vision encourages a naturalization of the unconventional as a way to prove the relevance of avant-garde art to contemporary life.

The idea that embodied rhythms, whether imagined as "primitive" inventions or modern rediscoveries, can revitalize metrical traditions that have become too constraining or too far removed from everyday life, has become a part of modern poetics, and there is no excising the effects of this idea from contemporary debates and discussions. But as Scott's coda to his article on Whitman indicates, imaginary constructions of rhythm can be registered as such even as they continue to shape the material practices of poets and critics. As he closed "A Note on Walt Whitman's Prosody," Scott noted that his vision of Whitman's prosody was only powerful if other readers believed in it—and he had his doubts that they would. He explained that even for him, Whitman's poetry did not hold up to multiple readings, making it unlikely that "his mode of versifying would pass into the consciousness of the race and seem as much a matter of course as iambic pentameter." Scott's moment of doubt, which he narrated as a moment that "[shook his] faith,"[55] indicates that, in some way, he understood his abstraction of social relations into poetic rhythm to be an ideologically motivated wish rather than a description of an empirical phenomenon. For many critics working later in the century, this belief hardened into dogma, crystallizing Scott's fantasy of a poetically mediated social order into truth. Returning to Scott's moment of doubt helps us to see how prosodies, as systems of belief, help to create and uphold the imagined continuities and lineages that make up our literary histories. By attending to the multiplicity of these systems of belief rather than pitting metrical tradition against rhythmical revolution, it will be possible to construct alternative lineages and histories that might tell different stories about the metrical past and the metrical present than those to which we have become accustomed.

Notes

1. Edmund Gosse, *Critical Kit-Kats* (New York, 1896), 97.
2. Betsy Erkkila, introduction to *Breaking Bounds: Whitman and American Cultural Studies*, ed. Erkkila and Jay Grossman (New York: Oxford University Press, 1996), 9.
3. David Reynolds, *Walt Whitman* (Oxford: Oxford University Press, 2005), ix.
4. Erkkila, *Breaking Bounds*, 7.
5. Walt Whitman, preface to the first edition of *Leaves of Grass*, in *The Portable Walt Whitman*, ed. Michael Warner (New York: Penguin, 2004), 334.
6. Susan Stewart, *Crimes of Writing: Problems in the Containment of Representation* (Oxford: Oxford University Press, 1991), 107.
7. Michael Cohen, "Popular Ballads: Rhythmic Remediations in the Nineteenth Century," in *Meter Matters: Verse Cultures of the Long Nineteenth Century*, ed. Jason David Hall (Athens: Ohio University Press, 2011), 206.
8. Scott MacPhail, "Lyric Nationalism: Whitman, American Studies, and the New Criticism," *Texas Studies in Literature and Language* 44, no. 2 (2002): 137.
9. Ibid., 133-34.
10. Ibid., 139-40.
11. Notable exceptions include Max Cavitch's "Stephen Crane's Refrain," *ESQ* 54, no. 1-4 (2008): 33-54, and Patrick Redding's "Whitman Unbound: Democracy and Poetic Form, 1912-1931," *New Literary History* 41, no. 3 (2010): 669-90. Cavitch notes that the narrative of "[p]oetry's liberation from the shackles of meter" remains popular even though the "long and complex history of versification in English is poorly suited to teleological narratives of liberation" (33), while Redding looks to "non-Whitmanian theories of democratic poetics" to explore the multiplicity of late nineteenth and early twentieth-century American poetics (670).
12. Meredith Martin and Yisrael Levin, "Victorian Prosody: Measuring the Field," *Victorian Poetry* 49, no. 2 (2011): 150, 153.
13. Gertrude Stein, *Narration: Four Lectures* (Chicago: University of Chicago Press, 2010), 17.
14. Meredith Martin, *The Rise and Fall of Meter: Poetry and English National Culture, 1860-1930* (Princeton, N.J.: Princeton University Press, 2012), 5.
15. John Stuart Mill, *Dissertations and Discussions* (New York: Henry Holt, 1874), 89.
16. Fred Newton Scott, "The Most Fundamental Differentia of Poetry and Prose," *PMLA* 19, no. 2 (1904): 254.
17. Ibid., 262-63.
18. Ibid.
19. Ibid.
20. Jason David Hall, "A Great Multiplication of Meters," in *Meter Matters: Verse Cultures of the Long Nineteenth Century*, ed. Hall (Athens: Ohio University Press, 2011), 7.
21. Jason Rudy, *Electric Meters: Victorian Physiological Poetics* (Athens: Ohio University Press, 2009), 2. Any number of prosodic tracts posit a link between the body and temporal units of meter; see, for instance, Oliver Wendell Holmes' "The Physiology of Versification," *The Boston Medical and Surgical Journal* 92, no. 1 (7 Jan 1875):

6–9. Holmes posited that "the respiration and the pulse . . . are the true time-keepers of the body," which directly influence "the structure of metrical compositions" (6). See also Alice Meynell's *The Rhythm of Life and Other Essays* (London: Elkin Mathews and John Lane, 1893), which argued that the "rhythmic pangs of maternity" influenced the meters used by female poets (6).

22. Scott, "The Most Fundamental Differentia of Poetry and Prose," 259–60.

23. Fred Newton Scott, "A Note on Walt Whitman's Prosody," *The Journal of English and Germanic Philology* 7, no. 2 (1908): 149. Emphasis added.

24. Ibid., 149.

25. Percy Ellen Frederick William Smythe Strangford, (8th Viscount), "Walt Whitman," in A Selection from the *Writings of Viscount Strangford on Political, Geographical, and Social Subjects*, ed. Viscountess Strangford (London, 1869), 298–300.

26. See, for instance, Edward P. Mitchell, "Walt Whitman and the Poetry of the Future," *New York Sun*, November 19, 1881, http://whitmanarchive.org/criticism/reviews/lg1881/anc.00082.html, and the anonymous "Review of *Leaves of Grass* (1891-92)]," *Poet Lore*, (1892): 286–87, http://whitmanarchive.org/criticism/index.html.

27. Scott, "A Note on Walt Whitman's Prosody," 137.

28. Ibid., 149–50.

29. Amy Lowell, "Vers Libre and Metrical Prose," *Poetry* 3, no .6 (1914): 214.

30. Ibid.

31. Ibid.

32. Ibid., 215–17.

33. Lowell intensified her criticism of Whitman in later years; see Lowell, *Poetry and Poets: Essays* (New York: Biblo and Tannen, 1971) for the text of "Walt Whitman and the New Poetry," a lecture delivered at the Contemporary Club of Philadelphia in 1920, in which she declared that "Walt Whitman fell into his own peculiar form through ignorance . . . Whitman never had the slightest idea of what cadence is . . . he had very little rhythmical sense," and that he "did not write in metre" (63, 70). She argued that the more intellectual new poets promoted true democracy, while Whitman's work was "as dangerous as a Bolshevik pronunciamento" (75). See also Melissa Bradshaw, *Amy Lowell: Diva Poet* (Burlington, Vt.: Ashgate, 2011). Bradshaw notes that Lowell's negative stance on Whitman was prompted in large part by her anxieties about socialism, which was causing unrest among workers in her family's mills (84).

34. Patterson praised Lowell's "vigorous sense of 'swing,'" an "undeniable [gift]" that made her the ideal vocalizer for their experiments (William Morrison Patterson, "New Verse and New Prose," *The North American Review* 207, no. 747 [1918]: 264); Lowell reported that Patterson called her "aggressively rhythmic" (Lowell, "Some Musical Analogies in Modern Poetry," *The Musical Quarterly* 6, no. 1 [1920]: 130).

35. William Morrison Patterson, "New Verse and New Prose," 264.

36. Such conclusions were not isolated to English departments. P. M. Jones, who taught modern French at University College of South Wales, Cardiff, and Cambridge in the 1910s and who established himself as an authority on Whitman's influence in France with two articles on the subject in *The Modern Language Review* in 1915 and 1916, argued that *vers libre* and Whitman's innovations were two distinct developments in two separate national traditions. He explained that the principles of *vers libre* had been "innate in French versification from the earliest times," and so *vers librists* were simply helping French versification to realize its entelechy. Whitman was, at most, "a foreign master who had accomplished a revolution in poetical art similar to that which

[French *vers librists*] . . . were attempting," but his experiments were necessarily distinct from those that were shaped by the rules of French prosody ("Influence of Walt Whitman," 192–94). Whatever Whitman had created, in Jones' opinion, was not *vers libre*. See Jones, "Whitman in France," *The Modern Language Review* 10, no. 1 (1915): 1–27, and Jones, "Influence of Walt Whitman on the Origin of the *'Vers Libre*,'" *The Modern Language Review* 11.2 (1916): 186–94.

37. Van Wyck Brooks, *America's Coming-of-Age* (New York: B. W. Huebsch, 1915). Brooks' polemic was a variation on a theme established by George Santayana in his 1911 address "The Genteel Tradition in American Philosophy." Santayana had similarly argued that Whitman's poetry was a formal failure, though he believed that this was due to Whitman's "unintellectual, lazy, and self-indulgent" personal character (53). See George Santayana, "The Genteel Tradition in American Philosophy," in *The Genteel Tradition: Nine Essays by George Santayana*, ed. Douglas L. Wilson (Cambridge: Harvard University Press, 1967), 37–64.

38. Brooks, *America's Coming-of-Age*, 10.

39. See Michael Cohen, "Poetry of the United States," in *The Princeton Encyclopedia of Poetry and Poetics*, ed. Stephen Cushman and Roland Greene, 4th ed. (Princeton, N.J.: Princeton University Press, 2012): 1480–85, for the long history of this idea, from Elihu Hubbard Smith's *American Poetry, Selected and Original* (1793) to twenty-first-century anthologies of American poetry.

40. Patterson, "New Verse and New Prose," 266.

41. Lowell, "Some Musical Analogies in Modern Poetry," 130.

42. Lowell and Patterson's nostalgia for an imagined state of primitive rhythmic experience is part of the strand of American poetic thought Virginia Jackson traces elsewhere in this volume, wherein, "lyric became a repository of the socializing effects of rhythm at the same time that lyric indexed the loss of the communal, racial origins of that rhythm." Though Lowell and Patterson are not explicitly concerned with the lyric, their work extended what Jackson names as Gummere's "field-defining emphasis on rhythm as the socializing principle of poetry," as well as the convoluted logic involved in "imagining poetic rhythm as racial in origin and post-racial in effect."

43. This was the thesis behind some of the most influential collections of the New Poetry, including Harriet Monroe and Alice Corbin Henderson's *The New Poetry: An Anthology*, (New York: Macmillan, 1917), which posited that modern poets were trying to "return to [poetry] at its great original sources, and to sweep away artificial laws . . . which have encumbered it" (xii). Louis Untermeyer's competing collection *Modern American Poetry: An Introduction* (New York: Harcourt, Brace, and Howe, 1919) similarly posited that modern poets were not creating something entirely new; they were "respond[ing] to indigenous forces deeper than their backgrounds" (xi). See Erin Kappeler, "Editing America: Nationalism and the New Poetry," *Modernism/modernity* 21, no. 4 (2014): 899–918.

44. Mary Austin, *The American Rhythm* (New York: Cooper Square Publishers, 1930), 18. Subsequent citations of this text are given parenthetically.

45. Austin's ambivalence toward "primitive" poetic rhythms was typical; many white scholars and critics during this era were careful to distance themselves from the racial otherness of "primitive" rhythms at the same time that they embraced the "primitive" as a source of cultural renewal.

46. Whitman's poetry had been casually named *vers libre* and free verse in critical articles published in non-academic magazines prior to Weeks', but academic studies

published in specialized journals during this era largely concurred that Whitman had not written free verse.

47. Ruth Mary Weeks, "Phrasal Prosody," *The English Journal* 10, no. 1 (1921): 14–15.
48. Ibid., 17–18.
49. Ibid., 19.
50. Ibid., 13.
51. Ibid., 19.
52. F. O. Matthiessen, *American Renaissance: Art and Expression in the Age of Emerson and Whitman* (Oxford: Oxford University Press, 1941), 564–65.
53. Ibid., 567.
54. Jerome Rothenberg, "Ethnopoetics," *Ubuweb*, October 2002, ubu.com/ethno/index.html.
55. Scott, "A Note on Walt Whitman's Prosody," 153.

Beat and Count

The Rhythms of the English Dolnik
Derek Attridge

1

The field of "historical prosody" can be understood in two ways: as an investigation of the changing norms according to which poets, consciously or unconsciously, handle the rhythmic properties of the (changing) language in their writing, or as an investigation of the governing prosodic theories of different periods, whether or not these reflect actual poetic practice. The focus on the specificity of both the deployment and the theorization of poetic rhythm in their historical contexts has been highly valuable: it has increased our understanding of many aspects of prosody, including the dependence of poets on prevailing aesthetic conventions and technological capabilities, the close connection between language change and shifts in metrical norms, and the embeddedness of prosodic theorization in the socio-political environment of the time.

However, an emphasis on historical change can obscure the remarkable longevity of some verse-forms in the English; in the case of such a verse-form, a contemporary reader can pick up a poem written several centuries ago and immediately recognize and participate in its rhythmic patterning. This persistence over time is in need of explanation just as much as the changes that metrical norms undergo through history. We may take the case of Thomas Wyatt as an example of a poet whose verse illustrates both metrical change and metrical continuity over time. Wyatt was writing in a period of prosodic uncertainty: alterations in the English language, especially the disappearance of the pronounced final *–e* that was an important metrical resource for Chaucer and his contemporaries, had produced a break in metrical traditions that necessitated a new start in the process of harnessing the rhythms of the language in poetic forms. The following sonnet by Wyatt, for instance, though it may have a particular appeal to ears accustomed to the freer forms of the past century, remains metrically puzzling:

> Avising the bright beams of these fair eyes,
>> Where he is that mine oft moisteth and washeth,
>> The wearied mind straight from the heart departeth
>> For to rest in his worldly paradise,
> And find the sweet bitter under this guise.
>> What webs he hath wrought well he perceiveth
>> Whereby with himself on love he plaineth
>> That spurreth with fire and bridleth with ice.
> Thus is it in such extremity brought:
>> In frozen thought now and now it standeth in flame;
>> Twixt misery and wealth, twixt earnest and game
> But few glad and many divers thought
>> With sore repentance of his hardiness:
>> Of such a root cometh fruit fruitless.

I quote this example from an article by George T. Wright,[1] though I have modernized the spelling. Wright argues that it can be scanned as metrical using classical prosodic feet if we accept that the decasyllabic line in Wyatt's time allowed for a variety of different patterns, alternative forms of the pentameter inherited from Lydgate that were soon afterwards ironed out by Henry Howard, Earl of Surrey to become the norm forever after. The problem with this claim is that *any* stretch of language can be pronounced metrical by assigning different foot types and invoking elision, shifted stress and other such licenses. Nonetheless, Wright may well be correct in supposing that Wyatt knew exactly what he was doing and that his first readers, when he circulated his poems in manuscript, did not register these lines as failed attempts at regular accentual-syllabic verse as we are likely to do. It is certainly true that, given the linguistic changes that had taken place by the early sixteenth century, there was no standard of "regular" long-lined verse to compare them with. The fact remains that to modern ears—indeed to mid-sixteenth-century ears, as evidenced by the regularizations of Wyatt's verse undertaken by Richard Tottel or his editor[2]—these lines don't sound like rhythmically regular verse.

When the contemporary ear encounters a poem of Wyatt's in shorter lines, however, there is no such sense of rhythmic jarring:

My lute awake! perform the last
   Labor that thou and I shall waste,
   And end that I have now begun;
   For when this song is sung and past
      My lute be still, for I have done.

As to be heard where ear is none,
   As lead to grave in marble stone,
   My song may pierce her heart as soon;
   Should we then sing or sigh or moan?
      No, no, my lute, for I have done.

These are the opening stanzas of one of Wyatt's most famous poems, which, for the contemporary reader and, we must assume, all readers since Wyatt's time, has an unmistakable rhythmic swing to it. The major metrical difference between the two poems is, of course, that the first is in some kind of five-beat verse and the second in four-beat verse, which, in view of the strictness of the arrangements of stressed and unstressed syllables, we can characterize more narrowly as iambic tetrameter. Wright points to this discrepancy as a puzzle needing to be solved: "[M]any shorter-line poems are not only regular but seem expert in their handling of rhythms. How then can we believe that so assured a master would, in effect, go to pieces metrically when confronted with the decasyllabic line, and then only in some poems?".[3]

Wright's rhetorical question overlooks the major differences between four-beat and five-beat rhythms: whether the lack of rhythmic regularity in many of the longer lines is due to conscious craftsmanship or an uncertain grasp of the form, it reflects the fact that five-beat lines present a distinct set of challenges and opportunities that have little to do with the world of four-beat verse. Let us rephrase the question as a real, not a rhetorical, one: how was Wyatt able to write short-lined verse—and "My Lute Awake" is typical of his poems of three or four realized beats per line—with a regularity that allows it to be unproblematically grasped today when his longer lines strain against any attempt to make them conform to a familiar norm? We might suppose that Wyatt was following a prior literary model in this shorter-lined verse, but if so it's one that is not easy to identify. Although Gower had written regular four-beat verse with a strict syllable-count a little over a century earlier, the disappearance of pronounced final *-e* would have rendered it irregular to Wyatt's ear. (The phonetic change in question was not understood until several centuries later.) His immediate predecessor, John Skelton, had developed his own distinctive short-lined verse-form, based on two or three, or occasionally four, beats, but he wrote nothing like Wyatt's syllabically strict tetrameters.

We can be sure, however, that the four-beat rhythm on which these poems are based was the staple of *popular* song and verse, as it had been since at least the beginning of the thirteenth century—the lyric "Nou goth sonne under wode" was first recorded in 1240, and a number of popular romances in four-beat meters can be dated from around the same time. These traditions did not observe a fixed number of syllables per metrical unit, so may seem an unlikely source for Wyatt's tetrameters; Wyatt was aware, however, of other verse traditions, notably the Italian, in which the exact syllable-count was a crucial requirement. Putting the two together would have produced the kind of octosyllabic verse we have from Wyatt's pen. Not surprisingly, he preferred a rising (or iambic) rhythm to a falling (or trochaic) rhythm, and a duple to a triple rhythm, both choices being closer to the natural rhythm of spoken English. The result was a verse-form that had the syllabic strictness of Italian poetry and the easily perceived rhythm of popular English verse. The longer line, by contrast, did not tap into this popular source and did not, to the early sixteenth-century hearer, have a strong rhythmic shape; Wyatt probably did not perceive a huge difference between lines that conformed to what was later to be called iambic pentameter and those that did not. Or, to be more precise, he would have perceived a difference but was happy to exploit it in his poetry, the "iambic pentameter" not having achieved canonic status. (This metrical form became more established in Surrey's poetry, though its status as the preeminent long line for English verse was challenged for many decades by poulter's measure, a version of four-beat verse that grouped two short lines together and no doubt sounded more rhythmical to many hearers than the unfamiliar pentameter.)

It is interesting to note that at this early point in the history of accentual-syllabic verse in modern English Wyatt, when writing four-beat verse, discovered some of the most common variations from the strict alternation of stressed and unstressed syllables that were to be the staple of poets from then on: in the lines quoted above, there is initial inversion ("Labor..."), promotion ("As to be"), and demotion ("No, no"). The same poem includes examples of line-internal inversion, both rising ("thorough love's shot") and falling ("lie withered and"; "know beauty but").[4] All these variations observe the conditions that would be followed by later poets writing accentual-syllabic verse, the form in which they have their natural home. As we shall see, four-beat verse that doesn't observe a syllable-count is less hospitable to them.

If Wyatt's longer line was written in a verse-form which is now, as a felt experience of rhythmicality, inaccessible to us (whether or not we are able to justify it intellectually in terms of variant forms of the pentameter), how is it that we can transcend the centuries between Wyatt's time and our own in the case of the shorter line? Part of the answer must lie in the four-beat rhythm itself as one of the most fundamental forms of rhythmic behavior in numerous cultures, whether it be in verse, music or dance.[5] And part of the reason for this near-universality must spring from the simplicity of the four-beat rhythmic unit, which is built up from two two-beat units, themselves merely the repetition of the basic beat. (Most three-beat lines as used by Wyatt imply a fourth, unsounded beat, as musical settings testify.) Wyatt's experiments with five-beat lines mark an attempt to escape from the dominance of the four-beat rhythm, to achieve something less like song and more like impassioned speech, a capability the dramatists later in the century were to capitalize on. Our ability to respond to Wyatt's poetry—and to much earlier verse in four-beat forms—also arises out of the historical continuity of the stress-rhythms of the English language itself, rhythms which underlie all major regular verse-forms and determine what hearers will find insistently rhythmical. That medieval verse in four-beat forms still sounds strongly rhythmical is one indication of the stability of this aspect of the language while other aspects, notably vowel-sounds, have changed enormously.

2

As I've noted, Wyatt's short-lined poems observe a strict syllable-count, and in this respect differ from the popular tradition that may have been one of the sources he drew on: lyrics such as the aforementioned "Nou goth sonne" and the popular romances were in a four-beat form that did not observe a fixed number of syllables. However, verse in this meter is just as easily identifiable and enjoyable as Wyatt's (and later) regular tetrameters. It is a form familiar to anyone who has grown up in an English-speaking household, since it is characteristic of the most popular nursery rhymes. The following example is typical of hundreds. (Beats, including the felt beats that are not spoken, are indicated by "B"):

```
Hark, hark, the dogs do bark—
  B    B        B       B
  The beggars are coming to town;
     B          B       B      [B]
```

```
Some in rags and some in jags,
  B         B        B       B

And one in a velvet gown.
     B       B    B      [B]
```

The four-beat meter—realized here as units of 4, 3, 4, 3 with a felt, or virtual beat, at the end of the second unit and echoed, mentally, at the end of the fourth—is immediately perceptible, and its strong rhythm has an effect on the pronunciation of the words.[6] The reader is likely to give more weight to the syllables taking a beat than would be the case in a prose rendition, and the interval between the beats is accorded roughly the same duration in pronunciation, whether it contains no syllables ("Hark, hark"), one ("dogs do bark"), or two ("coming to town"). The entire sequence of sixteen beats is experienced as a hierarchy: a major division after eight beats (signaled by the rhyme and strong syntactic break), lesser divisions after every four (reflected in the way the verse is set out on the page), and in lines 1 and 3 slight divisions after two (emphasized by internal rhyme). Each line ends emphatically on a break in sense, and rhyme plays an important part in accentuating the stanza's structure. These aural characteristics are particularly evident in the kind of recitation a parent might give a child, and emerge strongly if a group of readers is asked to read together without a leader.

As we've seen, one constraint that features in almost all literary verse does not apply here: the requirement that the meter observe fixed numbers of syllables. In this example, the varying number of syllables between the beats results in lines having 6, 8, 7, and 7 syllables, in spite of the fact that the first and third lines have four realized beats (or in traditional prosodic terms, four feet), while the second and fourth have three. Far from rendering the verse less emphatically regular, less catchy in its rhythm, these variations make it more so. If we rewrite the rhyme in regular alternating verse (iambic tetrameter and trimeter), the effect is still one of regularity but the distinctive rhythmic spring of the original has gone:

> Beware, beware, the dogs are there—
> The beggars near the town,
> A few in rags and more in jags,
> They seek a velvet gown.

The rhythm is relatively colorless now, the picture of the marauding troupe of beggars less vivid.

Various names have been applied to the type of verse exemplified by "Hark, hark, the dogs do bark," a type of verse characteristic of nursery rhymes and of many other popular forms, including ballads and advertising jingles. The most common label is probably "loose iambic"—though it could often be equally well termed "loose trochaic," "loose dactylic," or "loose anapestic."[7] Sometimes it is called "strong stress" or "accentual" verse, highlighting the importance of the stressed syllables carrying beats; but these terms miss the particularity of the verse-form we're considering here, as they apply equally to various types of alliterative verse that lack its distinctive rhythm. In order to signify that distinctiveness it is useful to have a term that doesn't imply the form is simply a variety (perhaps a crude variety) of an established meter. Marina Tarlinskaja adopts the Russian term for a similar type of verse, "*dol'nik*," which, slightly anglicized as *dolnik*, is a serviceable alternative.[8]

To insist on the distinctiveness of the dolnik rhythm is not to claim that it has clearly defined boundaries as a form: there are intermediate poems that are neither wholly in strict accentual-syllabic meter nor wholly in dolnik meter.[9] For instance, such poems may introduce into the alternations of syllabically regular verse an occasional variation in the number of syllables between beats (such as so-called "trisyllabic substitutions" in iambic verse), or begin otherwise strict lines with a variety of openings. Other poems have a typical dolnik distribution of stressed and unstressed syllables but use run-on lines to counter the strong shaping imparted by its hierarchical rhythm (Wyatt's "last / Labor" is an example). But dolnik verse proper has a number of definite properties: it is always in four-beat measures (including the possibility of the fourth beat's being virtual), is always rhymed, and always varies in the number of inter-beat unstressed syllables. And, importantly, the variations in those syllables always produces a strong rhythm. By contrast, five-beat verse with the same variations is perceived not as more strongly rhythmic than strict iambic pentameter but less.

At first blush, dolnik meter seems easy to define, then: four stressed syllables with any arrangement of one, two, or no unstressed syllables before, between, and after them. (As occasional variations, a stressed syllable may be allowed between beats, though in performance it will lose some of its normal emphasis; and the number of syllables between beats may be increased to three.) The following poem, Gerard Manley Hopkins' "Inversnaid," illustrates these rules; it also demonstrates the poetic power of which dolnik verse is capable. (I indicate beats and between them the number of—usually unstressed—syllables.)

```
This darksome burn, horseback brown,
  1   B    1    B   0 B    1    B
```

```
His rollrock highroad roaring down,
 1   B   1    B    1    B   1    B

In coop and in comb the fleece of his foam
 1   B    2    B    1    B     2    B

Flutes and low to the lake falls home.                    4
   B    1   B    2    B    1    B

A windpuff-bonnet of fáwn-fróth
1 B    1     B    2   B  O B

Turns and twindles over the broth
   B   1    B    1  B   2    B

Of a pool so pitchblack, féll-fröwning,
 2   B   1   B    1       B  O B  1

It rounds and rounds Despair to drowning.                 8
 1   B    1    B      1    B  1    B  1

Degged with dew, dappled with dew
   B    1    B O B    2     B

Are the groins of the braes that the brook treads through,
 2    B    2    B   2     B    2    B    1      B

Wiry heathpacks, flitches of fern,
 B 1 B     1       B    2   B

And the beadbonny ash that sits over the burn.           12
 2    B    2    B   2    B    2   B

What would the world be, once bereft
  B    2    B    1   B   1   B

Of wet and of wildness? Let them be left,
 1   B   2   B    1     B    2   B

O let them be left, wildness and wet;
1  B    2   B O B    2    B

Long live the weeds and the wilderness yet.              16
  B    2    B   2    B   2      B
```

The whole poem displays the classic four-beat structure: lines of 2 + 2 beats (often divided by a pause, sometimes by an offbeat realized by a pause); stanzas of 2 + 2 lines (signaled by rhyme); and the whole made up of 2 + 2 stanzas, signaled by a shift in rhythm. (Hopkins increases the number of double offbeats in the second pair of stanzas—from 3 and 3 to 9 and 8.) Yet the rhythmic variety achieved within this four-square structure is remarkable. Hopkins uses fourteen different rhythmic patterns: line 11 repeats the pattern of line 6 and line 14 repeats the pattern of line 3; otherwise each line is a unique arrangement. The dolnik variations make for both a firm, easily felt, rhythmic base and great expressive flexibility. To take one example: there are three lines that have no double offbeats and thus no triple lilt to lighten the movement—the opening pair, with their somber, fierce description, and the darkest line of the poem, "It rounds and rounds Despair to drowning." By contrast, the sprightliest rhythmic movement, achieved by means of four double offbeats, is given to the cheerful line "And the beadbonny ash that sits over the burn." Although literary dolnik verse (under any name) is often associated with light verse, and its conspicuous rhythms do unquestionably render it appropriate for humor, Hopkins shows that its potential is much wider than this association would suggest. Among the many poets who have deployed dolnik for serious purposes are Coleridge (most famously in "Christabel"), Scott, Shelley, the Brownings, Tennyson, Dickinson, Swinburne, Hardy, de la Mare, and Frost.[10]

3

Two lines of Hopkins' "Inversnaid" disrupt the easy swing of the dolnik: lines 5 and 7 end with compounds that produce successive stressed syllables, "fáwn-fróth" and "féll-frówning." Both, of course, are Hopkins' coinages, and it's noteworthy that both are accorded diacritics indicating two strong accents, the only occurrence in the poem of the symbols the poet liked to add to his lines. Hopkins was clearly aware that to sustain the dolnik rhythm he needed two beats at this point, and that in normal pronunciation one of the stresses in a compound would be weakened. We have to read these compounds as if they were separate words, then; this mode of pronunciation introduces a slight pause between the stresses and allows them both to be experienced as beats. It's not obvious why the image of airy lightness in line 5 should be expressed in rhythms that disturb the easy flow of the dolnik, but it's certainly appropriate that in the dour lead-up to that line about "Despair" the rhythm should falter.

This is not the end of the story, however. Even with Hopkins' diacritics urging us to override normal pronunciation in favor of verse rhythm, the placement at the end of the line of two beats without a syllable between them detracts from the smoothness of the dolnik rhythm. It seems that our initial definition of the form will not do: there are restrictions on the disposition of stressed and unstressed syllables, restrictions that are hard to identify because composers of dolnik verse—most of whom never put their names to their compositions—were not conscious of them as rules; they simply avoided arrangements that didn't work, choosing instead those that enhance the dolnik rhythm.

For example, Hopkins' other lines with a zero offbeat—1, 9, and 15—place it in the middle of the line at a syntactic break: the result is strongly rhythmic, balancing the line across the gap:

```
O let them be left, wildness and wet;
1 B      2    B   0 B      2     B
```

A rewritten version of the line with the gap filled is still rhythmic, but without the lift that the zero offbeat provides:

```
O let them be left, the wildness and wet;
1 B      2    B    1   B      2    B
```

However, if we keep the arrangement of stressed and unstressed syllables unchanged but do away with the medial pause, the result is distinctly uncomfortable:

```
O let them be kept wild and untamed;
1 B      2    B  0 B     2     B
```

Another example of a variation that gives the dolnik rhythm a distinctive flavor is the use of a stressed monosyllable between two stresses. There are two instances in Hopkins' poem:

> Flutes and low to the **lake falls home**
> Are the groins of the braes that the **brook treads through**

It's not by chance that this rhythmic figure occurs in both instances at the end of the line; this is the position dolnik poets have always favored, providing the line with a climactic triple emphasis. Although the monosyllable in the middle loses some of its weight in a strongly rhythmic performance, it still slows the line down at its end. Compare a rewritten line:

> Are the groins of the braes that the **stream**let **spans**

Here there is no emphatic close to the line. This figure can occur anywhere in the line, but it provides less reinforcement of the rhythm elsewhere:

> The **brook treads gently** the groins of the braes
> The brook in the **deep groins treads** its way

A full analysis of the handling of rhythm in dolnik verse has never been undertaken, and would require an extended treatise to do justice to the complexity of the form; in the remainder of this essay I can do no more than make some initial suggestions.[11] Nursery rhymes furnish some of the best examples of highly rhythmic verse that exploits to the full the variety possible in the dolnik form, and they present a useful starting point for any such analysis.

Since one of the main characteristics of dolnik verse is the variation between types of offbeat, and in particular between single and double offbeats, it may seem that it is a form that does not distinguish, as accentual-syllabic verse does, between a duple and a triple rhythm—or that it constantly shifts between the two. This is not the case, however; there are two fundamental types of dolnik, depending on whether the underlying rhythm is duple or triple, and the way a dolnik poem is voiced will depend on which of these the reader adopts. It is almost always an unconscious choice, since the distinction I am describing is not one that readers are generally aware of; it operates at a deep psycho-physical level. Many poems allow of being read in either way, but the choice is a perceptual one akin to that between duck and rabbit in the famous drawing: the reader has to opt for one of the two types of rhythm. Which is most suited to the words being read usually emerges very early in the poem, though occasionally in reading a new poem it becomes necessary to adjust one's performance. Poems rarely shift from one type of rhythm to the other, or, to be more accurate, readers, having settled into one mode of reading seldom change it during the course of the poem. Musical settings of dolnik verse have to make the same choice between a duple and a triple meter.

To give full weight to the rhythm in true dolnik verse, then, is to find oneself adopting either a **one**-two-**one**-two sequence or a **one**-two-three-**one**-two-three sequence. Take the following example:

> Diddle-diddle-dumpling, my son John
> Went to bed with his trousers on.

Like all dolnik verse, this is based on groups of four beats, but its specificity lies in what happens between (and before and after) those beats. If the lines are read rapidly and with a strong rhythm, everything between the beats is unstressed:

```
Diddle-diddle-dumpling, my son John[12]
  B        3       B    1   B   1  B

Went to bed with his trousers on.
  B   1  B    2     B    1   B
```

But if we slow down our reading and pay more attention to those inter-beat syllables, a subsidiary rhythm emerges:

```
Diddle-diddle-dumpling, my son John
B       b       B    b      B  b   B     [b]

Went to bed with his trousers on.
B    b  B    b       B   b   B    [b]
```

This is dipodic verse, so called because every pair of "feet" constitutes a rhythmic unit in itself. What the more detailed analysis shows is that the rhythm of these two lines is fundamentally duple, its sixteen beats arranged in alternations of stronger and weaker beats: everything occurs in twos. One large part of the body of dolnik verse follows this pattern, including such nursery rhymes as "Hark, hark, the dogs do bark," "Baa, baa, black sheep," "Mary, Mary, quite contrary," and "Pease porridge hot" and such poems as "Nou goth sonne under wode," Shelley's "The Cloud," and Hardy's "Neutral Tones." A. A. Milne made brilliant use of duple dolniks in poems like "Disobedience" and "Happiness."

Many other nursery rhymes observe a fundamentally triple rhythm. The following example asks to be read with a **one**-two-three-**one**-two-three movement:

```
Hey diddle diddle, the cat and the fiddle,
B    2      B    2     B   2    B  1

The cow jumped over the moon.
 1  B    1     B    2   B    [B]
```

Unlike duple dolnik verse, this verse can't be further analyzed into weaker beat-offbeat patterns. If one imagines these lines set to a simple melody, the triple rhythm emerges clearly. Another large part of the body of nursery rhyme verse falls into this rhythmic norm, including such favorites as "Three Blind Mice," "Little Bo-Peep," and "Humpty Dumpty." Triple dolnik in literary verse is rarer, just as triple accentual-syllabic meter is rarer. We'll turn to an example in due course.

Although it's obvious that triple dolnik tends to have a larger proportion of double offbeats than duple dolnik, it should be noted that *both* forms can use single, double, and occasionally triple or zero offbeats. When a double offbeat occurs in duple dolnik, one of the two syllables takes a subsidiary beat, as in the case of "with" in the earlier example:

```
Went to bed with his trousers on.
B    b  B    b       B   b   B    [b]
```

The two words "with his" occupy the same temporal space as the other beats in the line, both strong and weak. (Of course, in talking about these exact timings one is talking about a rigidly rhythmical performance, as one might chant to a child; in literary verse, the reader or reciter is likely to be more flexible—though in a good reading this underlying rhythm will always be felt.) We can show this temporal arrangement by means of symbols under the beats: each square represents the same amount of time, the black squares indicating beats. When double offbeats occur in duple dolnik, the white square indicates the beginning of the inter-beat temporal unit, as is the case with "with his" in the following line:

```
Went to bed with his trousers on.
 B   b   B   b        B  b  B     [b]
 ■   □   ■   □        ■  □  ■      □
```

We can think of this as *rhythmic* scansion, complementing the *metrical* scansion of beats and offbeats. To bring out the rhythm in performance, it helps to tap regularly on the temporal units, giving the black squares more emphasis than the white.

A slightly rewritten line shifts the placing of the second weaker beat, which now occurs on the *second* syllable of the double offbeat, but doesn't alter the rhythm:

```
Went to market with trousers on.
 B   b   B      b     B  b  B     [b]
 ■   □   ■      □     ■  □  ■      □
```

Now it is "market" that fills the temporal space of a beat, as does "with" on its own.

Triple dolnik, conversely, can cope happily with a single offbeat; again, the rhythmic scansion shows how this happens:

```
The cow jumped over the moon.
 1   B   1      B   2    B       [B]
 □   ■□  □      ■□   □  ■       □ □ ■
```

Here "cow" takes as long to pronounce as the disyllable "over"; the extra length—two temporal units—is indicated by ■□, allowing "jumped" to be destressed and given the same time as "-er" or "the." (It's a feature of spoken English that the stress-rhythm can override syllabic distinctions: we have no difficulty in reducing "jumped" to the length and weight of those apparently much shorter syllables.)[13]

As an example of a rhyme that doesn't reveal immediately which of these two rhythmic types it belongs to we may take the following:

Doctor Foster went to Gloucester
In a shower of rain.
He stepped in a puddle right up to his middle
And never went there again.

The first line invites a firm duple reading, and the second line can be made to fit, especially if "shower" is treated as a monosyllable:

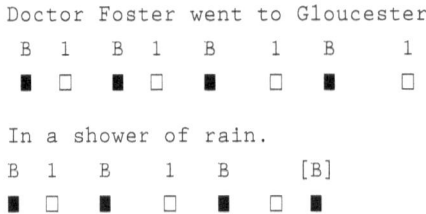

But the following lines are unmistakably triple (it becomes clear that the rhyme is, in fact, shaped as a limerick, a verse-form that is regularly triple):

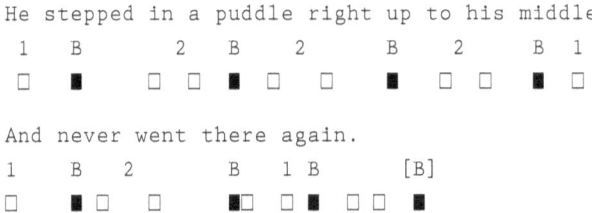

And if we go back to the first two lines and read them with the same triple rhythm, they acquire a spring lacking in the rather mechanical **one**-two-**one**-two of the duple reading:

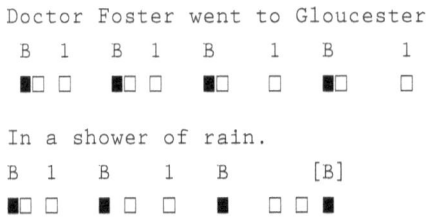

Note that this manner of reading extends many of the stressed syllables to double their length; "Doctor Foster" changes from a four-square pronunciation with unstressed syllables taking as long as stressed syllables to one that gives stresses appropriately extra emphasis. Note, too, that scansion without any indication of temporal relations has no way of representing these different rhythms. (Foot-scansion, of course, would merely record a succession of trochees for two lines followed by an indeterminable series of feet that could be dactyls, amphibrachs or anapests; it would not capture the rhythm of the lines at all.) Interestingly, YouTube offers musical settings of this rhyme in both two-four time and three-quarter time; to my ear, the latter is more engaging.[14]

One major difference between accentual-syllabic verse and dolnik verse is the handling of metrical variations. We noted in Wyatt's "Awake, my lute" instances of promotion and demotion; these departures from the strict alternation of stressed and unstressed syllables do not require vocal adjustment. As long as the three syllables of "As to be" are given the same weight in pronunciation they will function rhythmically as offbeat-beat-offbeat. Equally, "No, no" can be read as two syllables with the same emphasis and still feel metrical (though a perfectly plausible reading would be to give the second more weight). In dolnik verse, promotion and demotion are rare: the strong rhythm encourages the voice to reduce the emphasis on stressed syllables occurring in offbeat positions and to increase the emphasis on unstressed syllables occurring in beat positions. The former is a more common occurrence than the latter, especially in triple dolnik verse; in the verse we have looked at the word "son" in "my son John" loses some of its weight when we read with a pronounced rhythm. Similarly, as we have seen, the word "jumped" in "cow jumped over" is likely to be destressed. These are not, therefore, instances of demotion, strictly speaking. An example of a normally unstressed syllable that takes a beat and is therefore likely to be given additional weight is the first syllable in "In a shower of rain"; again, this is different from promotion as it occurs in accentual-syllabic verse. In "my son John," there is no question of treating "my" as anything but a strongly stressed syllable, though the meaning doesn't require it. Inversion, as in Wyatt's "thorough loves shot" (rising inversion) and "lie withered and" (falling inversion) is even rarer in dolnik verse, occurring only if the meter temporarily shifts into something more like accentual-syllabic verse.

4

Let us return now to Hopkins' "Inversnaid." The rhythm of the opening settles quickly into a duple rhythm:

```
This darksome burn, horseback brown,
 1   B    1    B   O B    1      B
 □   ■    □    ■   □■     □      ■
```

```
His rollrock highroad roaring down,
 1  B   1   B    1   B   1   B
 □  ■   □   ■    □   ■   □   ■

In coop and in comb the fleece of his foam
 1  B   2   B    1   B    2    B
 □  ■   □        ■   □    ■    ■

Flutes and low to the lake falls home.
  B   1   B   2   B   1   B
  ■   □   ■   □   ■   □   ■
```

What this means is that the few double offbeats—"and in," "of his," and "to the"—can be read quickly and lightly, as befits their relative lack of importance. As we've noted, however, the third and fourth stanzas have an increased number of double offbeats. This raises a question: should we adjust our reading of these two stanzas to introduce a triple rhythm into the poem? Such a reading would be scanned as follows:

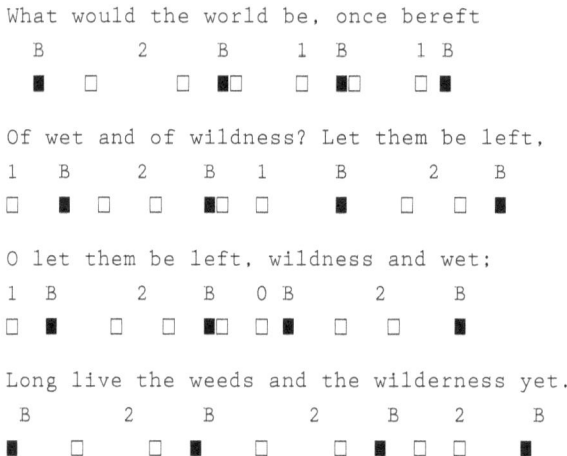

This reading is certainly possible, but to my mind such a shift would introduce a lilting quality out of keeping with more serious tone of these lines. A duple reading gives the stressed syllables greater weight:

```
What would the world be, once bereft
  B      2    B    1 B    1 B
  ■      □         ■  □   ■  □ ■

Of wet and of wildness? Let them be left,
 1  B   2   B   1    B    2   B
 □  ■   □       ■    □    ■   □    ■
```

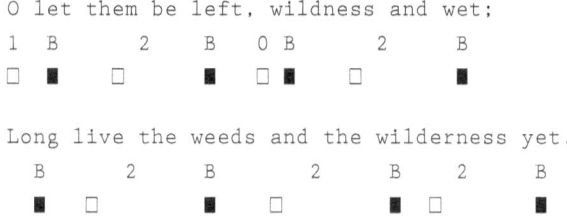

Hopkins's plangent prayer for the unkempt portions of the natural world is all the stronger for its musicality: only two of the sixteen syllables taking beats do not begin with /w/ or /l/ ("once," of course, begins with the former phoneme), the middle two lines form a pleasing chiasmus, and the expansion of "wildness" to "wilderness" functions wonderfully to bring the poem to a satisfying close. The duple dolnik rhythm is part of this music: it combines strong rhythmicality with a lightness of movement that turns the poem, at its end, into something like an incantation.

Does an understanding of dolnik rhythm help us to approach the meter of that most discussed of all dolnik poems, Tennyson's "Break, break, break"? It's another example of a poem that can be read either as duple or as triple dolnik, with different results. I show both possibilities under the opening lines:

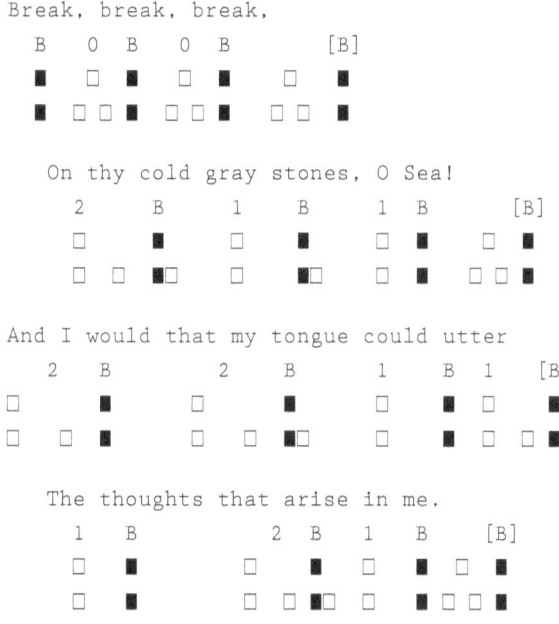

```
    O, well for the fisherman's boy,
    1    B    2    B    2    B        [B]
    □    ■    □         ■    □    ■   □   ■
    □    ■    □    □    ■    □    □   ■   □ □ ■

         That he shouts with his sister at play!
              2         B         2    B    2    B         [B]
              □         ■         □    ■    □    ■    □    ■
              □    □    ■         □    □    ■    □    □    ■    □ □ ■

    O, well for the sailor lad,
    1    B    2    B    1    B    [B]
    □    ■    □         ■    □    ■    □    ■
    □    ■    □    □    ■□   □    ■    □ □ ■

         That he sings in his boat on the bay!
              2         B    2    B    2    B         [B]
              □         ■    □    ■    □    ■    □    ■
              □    □    ■    □    □    ■    □    □    ■    ⊔ □ ■
```

The opening three words give nothing away, and a reciter doesn't have to decide between duple and triple. But the second line immediately presents alternatives: are we going to give "On" and "thy" the same length as "cold," and prolong "cold" and "stones" to double the length of "gray" in order to sustain a triple rhythm? Or does the line go better in a duple rhythm, moving more quickly of "On thy" and giving "cold," "gray," and "stones" equal durations? My preference is for the latter, and even when the poem becomes more fully triple as far as metrical analysis is concerned—that is, in terms of beats and offbeats—a duple dolnik rhythm sustains the emphasis on the three stressed syllables of each line while moving rapidly over the unstressed syllables. This is how Sir John Gielgud reads it, in a highly moving performance;[15] and the choral setting by Stuart Vezey also treats it as duple to good effect.[16]

We may end with a dolnik poem that, in contrast, encourages a triple reading. Here are the first two stanzas of Blake's "Nurse's Song" from *Songs of Experience*, with metrical and rhythmic scansion:

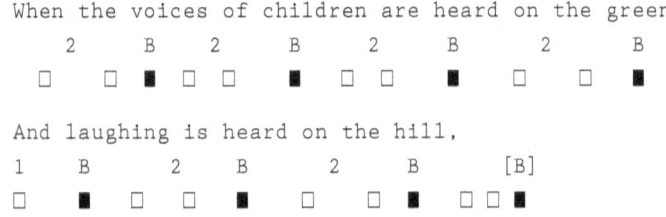

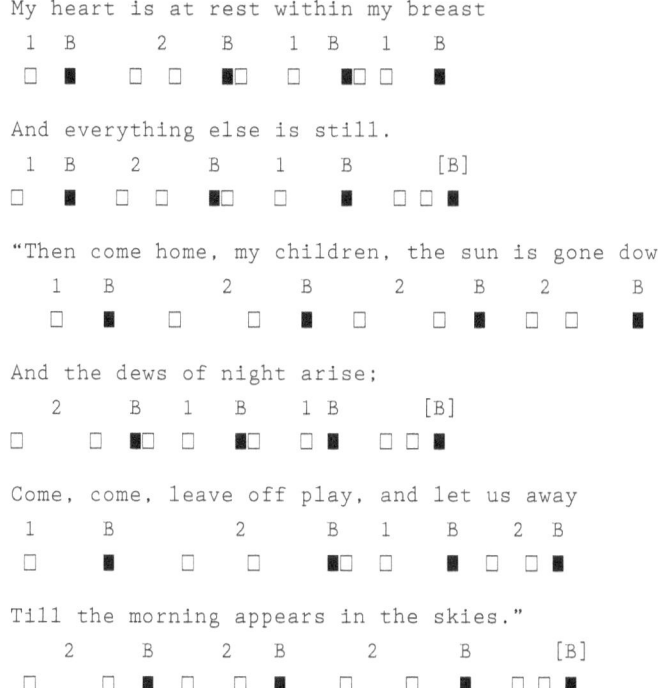

Though it would be possible to read these lines with a duple rhythm, the result would do Blake's poetry much less justice. Take this line, for example, shown here in a duple reading:

```
Come, come, leave off play, and let us away
1       B       2       B  1   B   2   B
□       ■       □       ■   □   ■   □   ■
```

In a triple reading each of the words in "leave off" have the same length as the syllables taking beats, so that "come, leave off play" is felt as **one**-two-three-**one**; but in a duple reading the whole phrase "leave off" is only a single temporal unit and feels rushed. Moreover, in a triple reading "play" is extended, and thus highlighted, but not in a duple one. The same lengthening occurs, very appropriately, in a triple rhythm reading of "rest," "dews," and "night." Blake no doubt held in his head a large stock of popular verse in dolnik meters in both types of rhythm, and drew on this stock without having to reflect consciously on which type was more appropriate to the poem he was writing.

To ascertain exactly what properties of poems propel readers toward duple or toward triple underlying rhythms would require an extensive survey of both popular and literary verse. Nor is it obvious that readers would always agree on which of the two was preferable in particular cases. But if the study of prosody is to advance, the distinctive characteristics of dolnik verse need to be taken fully into account, as a rhythmic form that has endured for eight or more centuries and shows no sign of falling into disuse.

Notes

1. George T. Wright, "Wyatt's Decasyllabic Line," *Studies in Philology* 82 (1985): 129–56.

2. The collection of poems known as *Tottel's Miscellany*, first printed and perhaps edited by Richard Tottel in 1557, included several works by Wyatt that had been altered to make them conform to standard iambic pentameter.

3. Wright, "Wyatt's Decasyllabic Line," 131. As one indicator of Wyatt's willingness to diverge from the decasyllabic model, Martin Duffell, analysing Wyatt's 22 sonnets, finds that 40 percent have more or fewer syllables than ten. *A New History of Metre* (London: Legenda, 2008), 120.

4. Here and throughout I use the terminology developed in Derek Attridge, *The Rhythms of English Poetry* (London: Longman, 1982), and *Poetic Rhythm: An Introduction* (Cambridge: Cambridge University Press, 1995).

5. See Andy Arleo, "Counting-out and the Search for Universals," *The Journal of American Folklore* 110 (1997): 391–407; Robbins Burling, "The Metrics of Children's Verse: A Cross-linguistic Study," *American Anthropologist* 68 (1966): 1418–41; Andreas Dufter and Patrizia Nel Aziz Hanna, "Natural Versification in French and German Counting-out Rhymes," in *Towards a Typology of Poetic Forms: From Language to Metrics and Beyond*, ed. Jean-Louis Aroui and Andy Arleo (Amsterdam: John Benjamins, 2009), 101–21; Attridge, *Rhythms*, 81–84 and *Poetic Rhythm*, 53–57.

6. Though I find it unavoidable in referring to particular poems, I would prefer not to speak of "lines" in discussing popular four-beat verse since this verse-form is more a matter of sequences of beats occurring in a rhythmic hierarchy than separable entities that might be shown visually as such on a page. Poulter's measure and its near relation, the fourteener, are conventionally lineated so as to combine two short "lines" into one long one.

7. An example of the kind of multi-syllabled nonsense that arises when rhythmically straightforward verse of this type is treated as if it were a complex construction created out of classical feet is Timothy Steele's assertion that a short, playful poem of Keats' in this form is made up of "two catalectic trochaic tetrameters, two acatalectic trochaic tetrameters, and two iambic tetrameters" (http://learn.lexiconic.net/meter.html).

8. Marina Tarlinskaja, *Strict Stress-Meter in English Poetry Compared with German and Russian* (Calgary: University of Calgary Press, 1993), and "Beyond 'Loose Iamb': The Form and Themes of the English 'Dolnik,'" *Poetics Today* 16 (1995): 493–522. I acknowledge that the term sounds foreign to ears accustomed to the traditional terminology of English prosody, but I believe it's important to be able to designate this verse-form by means of a label with no implication that it is merely a variant of accentual-syllabic or strong-stress meter.

9. The distinction between "rhythm" and "meter" is notoriously uncertain, and the subject of much dispute. My use of "meter" is meant to indicate an arrangement of language according to set rules, while "rhythm" refers to an experience registered by the

performer both mentally and physically. The standard meters of English establish, for the reader or speaker, regular rhythms; some more recherché meters, such as syllabics, do not. All utterances have a rhythm, however, and there are tendencies towards regularity even in ordinary speech. To speak of "dolnik meter" or "iambic meter," therefore, is to emphasize the operation of rules; to speak of "dolnik rhythm" or "iambic rhythm" is to emphasize the experiential dimension of the verse. "Dolnik verse" or "iambic verse" is poetry written according to the rules of a meter and experienced as having the rhythm produced by those rules.

10. For a discussion of the dolnik as a major presence throughout the history of medieval and modern English verse, see Derek Attridge, *Moving Words: Forms of English Poetry* (Oxford: Oxford University Press, 2013), chapter 7.

11. There are, broadly speaking, two ways of approaching this question: one is to accumulate a large amount of data in order to identify the most common patterns in dolnik verse, the other is to test existing texts against rewritten versions to determine the effect on the rhythm of various possibilities. Both approaches have their weaknesses: the former fails to engage with the non-occurring patterns and thus is unable to determine which are most detrimental to the rhythmic integrity of the verse; the latter depends on a single pair of ears. I hope it goes without saying that in following the latter course, I am offering my own judgments for testing by readers.

12. We may note here the characteristic triple stress at the end of the line.

13. There is nothing to prevent a rhythmic analysis of this type being undertaken for accentual-syllabic verse, but it doesn't reveal anything that is not shown by metrical analysis: iambic and trochaic verse is in duple rhythm, dactylic and anapestic verse is in triple rhythm.

14. https://www.youtube.com/watch?v=k1EKfP7x_JE; https://www.youtube.com/watch?v=fOthsY6Aguo

15. https://www.youtube.com/watch?v=CEMZYEvqLUM

16. https://www.youtube.com/watch?v=pyCKAIaF-3w

How to Find Rhythm on a Piece of Paper

Thomas Cable

A Rift in English Prosody

In 1959 W. K. Wimsatt, Jr., and Monroe C. Beardsley published "The Concept of Meter: An Exercise in Abstraction," an essay that summarized and crystallized an influential approach to poetic form.[1] As the authors insisted, their essay offered little new but presented common wisdom that had become obscured or forgotten and needed restatement. Yet their clarity, succinctness, and wit made it arguably the high-water mark of New Critical approaches to meter and one of the most important metrical statements of the twentieth century. It continues to be a point of reference and departure.

The collaboration of a literary critic (Wimsatt) and a philosopher (Beardsley) resulted naturally enough in two main strands of argument reflecting their disciplines, although it is clear that the authors shared literary and philosophical ideas. As for the literary, their taxonomy of the history of English poetic form is a wonderfully clear description of the two main traditions of English prosody. The first comprises the old "strong-stress" medieval meters (*Beowulf* and *Piers Plowman*), aspects of which have been sporadically revived, especially in the nineteenth and twentieth centuries. The second comprises the "syllable-stress" meters (especially iambic pentameters and tetrameters from Chaucer to the present). Pedagogically, the taxonomy works neatly in surveys of British and American poetry even as its historical and theoretical ideas have been rejected and superseded.[2]

For most of what follows, our concern will be broadly ontological. On this matter, Wimsatt and Beardsley had two points of departure. They took issue with structural linguistics for not being abstract enough when discussing poetic meter, and with "temporal" (including "musical") approaches for imposing a score extraneous to the text. What all these methods had in common, according to Wimsatt and Beardsley, was attention to an individual performance that might be plausible but was something different from the enduring text from which other performances might derive; hence their title, "an exercise in abstraction."

They saw linguistic approaches as hugging the phonetic ground too closely, not stepping back to take advantage of categories in meter analogous to the concept of the phoneme in the flourishing phonology of the time. (The phoneme as used by linguists cited in the essay—Harold Whitehall, Seymour Chatman, George L. Trager, Henry Lee Smith—is an abstraction that ignores the differences in the pronunciation of, for example, a consonant like /p/ to capture the features that distinguish /p/ from /t/, etc. So should a metrical description, said Wimsatt and Beardsley, have a level of abstraction that systematically ignores certain differences in, for example, the degree of stress on stressed syllables.) As it turned out, one of their two main targets, Seymour Chatman, showed to everyone's satisfaction that he was as abstract as Wimsatt and Beardsley, and seven years later with the founding of generative metrics by Morris Halle and Samuel Jay Keyser, no one complained about a lack of abstraction in linguistic prosody. Halle and Keyser did not begin with the familiar syllable but with the "position," ten positions to the line in iambic pentameter, to be filled by one syllable, two syllables, or no syllable according to a set of rules that mapped syllables of various degrees of stress onto the positions. In the years since, revisions and modifications have been offered by Paul Kiparsky, Gilbert Youmans, Bruce Hayes, Kristin Hanson, and many others.

Despite different assumptions between linguistic theory and Wimsatt and Beardsley's theory, the approaches have a crucial element in common: the priority given to linguistic stress over linguistic timing—often to the complete exclusion of linguistic timing. Collectively, these prosodists are called "stressers." By contrast, prosodists who emphasize either temporal or musical elements, or both, are known as "timers." Wimsatt and Beardsley's essay illustrated what was once again a central rift in English prosody of the past two centuries, between timers and stressers.

T. V. F. Brogan has a clarifying chart that traces the different branches of these schools of metrics in his monumental *English Versification, 1570-1980*.[3] Wimsatt and Beardsley are on the branch of "traditional stress metrics" while Chatman, Halle, Keyser and other structural and generative metrists are on the nearby branch of "linguistic stress metrics." For all of these, relative stress is the key—greater stress on one syllable than on an adjacent syllable. In iambic verse, by the traditional view, it is greater stress of whatever degree on the second syllable of the foot. The various branches of temporal metrics are on the far side of the page, the split in the family tree having occurred centuries earlier.

One problem was that not everyone heard relative stress the way Wimsatt and Beardsley did, and so it seemed that stressers were imposing an individual performance, in contradiction of the principles they espoused. A key to the difference in perception is the idea of the "beat," which timers invoke by analogy with the beat in measured music but which stressers generally disregard, dismiss, or conflate with linguistic stress. If we say, as timers do, that a beat can be perceived without a corresponding stress, we are putting the poem into a perceiving consciousness, something different from the enduring, unincarnated text imagined by Wimsatt and Beardsley, by New Critics generally, and by generative metrists.

Here we come to the question of what is added by consciousness in the act of reading a poem—or, more precisely, the various additions of various consciousnesses. A dictionary marks word stress. If that were all that is needed, the dictionary could be mechanically superimposed on the written text of the poem, along with a full theory of phonology aimed at describing the phrasal stress, emphatic stress, and so on, of ordinary talk. However, a long tradition of commentary going back to Wordsworth and Coleridge holds that the performance of a poem in metrical form will often have features that diverge from the features of simple conversation—a "metrical pause" within the line, for example.

Modern developments of this idea in the temporal tradition argue that without a realization and instantiation of those features, a line of poetry is incomplete. Among those who have taken this view over the past century and longer, it is impressive how much agreement there is on the specific metrical patterns that count. This reasoning can be carried to its logical conclusion in the spirit of Jorge Luis Borges on Pierre Menard:[4] identical sequences of words, written or oral, may become different lines of poetry among different readers, because a line is more than the sequence of syllables. Certain kinds of pauses are a structural part of the line, as much as any syllable. One reader may produce a version of the sequence of words that is complete (by the lights of temporal metrists); another reader of the same sequence of words may produce a line that is a fragment (because it lacks a non-syllabic structural element). These different versions, then, should not be called different "performances" of the same line but different "lines."

From these epistemological problems of perception and knowledge, difficult ontological questions arise, and they vex our understanding of both the production and reception of the poem. In New Criticism generally, and certainly in the metrics of that school, the words on the page counted for more than presumptions about either the author or the performer. The receiver was even further removed from flesh-and-blood humans—a vague, generalized construct without an anatomy to frame the doors of perception.

Even today, little experimental work has been done on the perception of poetry. However, increasingly sophisticated studies have been carried out during the past ten years on the perception of music, making use of new technology and revisiting old problems in phenomenology. The link between music and poetry in prosodical scholarship has long been a part of the temporal tradition. From an armchair perspective it might seem that technological advances in the neurosciences should not change the basic questions in poetics even if there are analogies with music: we've only got better instruments, one might say. However, the better instruments in the lab have necessitated a progressive refinement of assumptions, research strategies, and indeed basic questions about the perception of music. There are direct implications for the language of poetry.

It may clarify the exposition to anticipate two main points this essay will make: (1) it will downgrade the importance of the *line* for all periods of English poetry in favor of what is proposed as a metrically prior principle—a beat that continues whether line structure is present or not; and (2) it will invoke a rhythmical analogy from Baroque music to illustrate that principle and then link both the analogy and the principle to recent work in cognitive science. To illustrate the question of the line and the syllables it comprises, we will begin with the notebooks of Percy Bysshe Shelley.

Shelley's Stand-ins for Syllables and Beats

Shelley's brief lyric "A Lament" was worked out in three stages of a first draft, which appear to be separated by a period of months in a notebook now in the Huntington Library. This much of the process of composition was described in a 1932 essay by Bennett Weaver.[5] Shelley then resumed work and finished it—or nearly finished it—in a notebook now in the Bodleian Library, Oxford. The completed lyric was published by Mary Shelley in 1824:

A Lament
  O world! O life! O time!
   On whose last steps I climb,
Trembling at that where I had stood before;
   When will return the glory of your prime?
    No more—oh, never more!

Out of the day and night
 A joy has taken flight;
   Fresh spring, and summer, and winter hoar,
Move my faint heart with grief, but with delight
    No more—oh, never more!

  In the Huntington notebook, the first two stages of the first draft contain a mix of English words (*life, death, time,* etc.) and nonce syllables (*ni, nal, na,* etc.). Weaver makes three comments that are especially interesting for our purposes. Of the first stage of the first draft he writes: "Whether the words came in response to the rhythm or whether the rhythm was determined by the words who can say? It is a fact, of course, that the words precede the symbols of the rhythm; and consequently we might assume that some idea associated with the words began to throb in Shelley's mind and to take on measured motion."[6] To be sure, the words barely precede the "symbols," by which Bennett means the nonce syllables, *na, ni,* and so on with their diacritics. The very first line is "Ah time, oh night, oh day," and then the symbols are up and running for the next two lines: "Ni nal ni na, na ni / Ni na ni na, ni na." It is as though some rhythmic impulse in the poet alighted on a handful of English words, then lost its argument, and resorted to nonce syllables as placeholders.

  The third stage is interesting for recording only the iterated syllable *na* (and once *a*) through eleven lines varying from two to nine syllables with sporadic diacritics of accent, breve, macron, and circumflex; for example, the first stanza:

Na na, na na ná na
Nă nă na na na—nă nă
  Nă nă nă nă nā nā
Na na nă nă nâ ă na

These rhythmical notations are followed by a draft of ten lines with actual words, which are closer to the nonce syllables than the final poem is; they are still a poem in progress.

  Weaver says: "I would now assume that these symbols suggest a certain insistent rhythm and that the words on the opposite page are the result of an attempt to give this beating pulse a body in which to live."[7] A brief response is that the beating pulse already had a body in which to live—Shelley's. Shelley was looking for a way to externalize it in English words, convey it to others, and replicate it in their bodies.

Finally, Weaver notes that between the two versions of the third stage, four of the ten lines of English words have different numbers of syllables than the corresponding nonce lines, five lines follow the count, and one line is uncertain because of three syllables crossed out; in addition, "The most perplexing difference between the symbols and the words lies in the fact that there are eleven lines of the one and only ten of the other...."[8]

The explanation that suggests itself is that the final number and length of lines—whether measured in syllables or beats—come late in the process of a lyric such as this. After the fact, we speak of "iambic pentameter," "iambic tetrameter," and so on. These are the primary categories of the classifying metrist, and by common sense the place to start. However, there is something more basic, something, as we will see in the next section, akin to a "walking bass" in music.

Mary Shelley and subsequent editors ignored Shelley's indication of a missing foot in line 8—a space between "summer" and "&." She closed up the space and printed line 8 with nine syllables instead of ten.[9] There is a way of reading the line as an iambic pentameter—with a silent beat, a "virtual beat"—between "summer" and "and." However, this would be an extremely complex reading, especially because not all the lines of the stanza are iambic pentameter. The fascinating question that presents itself is whether it would be closer to Shelley's intention (1) to posit a silent beat in the text as printed; or (2) to insert one of the words that he wrote in an earlier draft but did not keep in the fair draft; or (3) to retain the space itself.[10] Because silent beats in such contexts do not occur elsewhere in Shelley's poetry, the second or third solution would arguably be closer to Shelley's intention, which would be a line of five beats, as in the corresponding third line of the previous stanza.

The point is that silent beats are as salient as any syllable. Empirically, we can determine that there are contexts where silent beats, though possible, would be unlikely, as in the line by Shelley. In other contexts they are as expected and as real as footsteps in walking. We will turn now to walking as a metaphor for much that has been said, especially about beats in poetry. However, as the essay proceeds, a more literal connection between beats and walking will emerge.

The Walking Bass

Bach's Feet: The Organ Pedals in European Culture is the title of a recent book by David Yearsley on rhythm in Baroque music and the instantiation of rhythm in bodily activity such as the movement of feet, whether on the pedals of the organ or on the road in walking. The book contains photographs of large-buckled shoes from the seventeenth and eighteenth centuries, which serve as a kind of metonymy for the "feet" of the title. "Feet," of course, show up in discussions of meter (*foot:* "*Prosody*... The term is commonly taken to refer to the movement of the foot in beating time"—*OED*). In addition to being an incomparable composer, Bach was a great organist and a great walker. From his youth he walked to other towns to hear famous organists. Once while employed as an organist at Arnstadt, he obtained a leave of a few weeks to go to Lübeck and hear Dieterich Buxtehude, the organist of St. Mary's Church. The journey on foot of 250 miles to Lübeck and the same distance back exceeded by three months the leave that his employers had granted—to their consternation—although Bach managed to keep his position.[11] Yearsley says this about the "walking bass" as manifested on the organ and on the land:

> In the idiom of pedal-playing, the feet progress as if they are walking. They alternate left and right, moving through their music in much the same way that they move through life. Nearly ubiquitous in the seventeenth and eighteenth centuries, this peripatetic musical figure remains the standard to this day. At the organ, the "walking bass" operates at both the literal and metaphorical level: organists' feet walk or run over the pedalboard, one foot and then the other, mimicking ambulatory motion in the act of conveying a musical sense of distance covered.[12]

An example of the walking bass is a familiar staple at weddings, Bach's "Air from Orchestral Suite No. 3 in D. Major."[13] Whether played on the organ or as arranged for violin and piano (often referred to as "Air on the G String"), the steps of the bass are as salient and as stately as the beats of iambic pentameter in a Shakespeare sonnet.[14]

The walking bass, in its metronomic regularity, establishes the meter. Between the steps of the bass, rhythmic figures give variety. Something similar happens in the walking bass of jazz.[15] As succinctly stated by Justin London: "Meter functions as a ground for rhythmic figures."[16] This idea will be developed as we proceed. First, however, let us consider the segmentation of linear units, as in the lines that Shelley heard.

Permeable Boundaries: Continua vs. Discrete Categories

Most of the examples of lines of poetry in this essay are offered to call into question the priority that has been given to a consistent *count per line* in English poetry—whether a count of syllables, beats, or feet. This is not to deny that the consistent counts are there. The iambic pentameter can be said, conventionally, to have ten syllables, five beats, and five feet (or whichever of these concepts a particular theory allows). What is called into question is whether the count per line is the ground for an understanding of *meter* and *rhythm*. What is basic and what is derived? Does the very term "iambic pentameter" close off an understanding of patterns that are prior to a division into lines?

Consider these lines from two poems by Swinburne, the first in hexameter, the second in trimeter:[17]

> Thou art more than the day or the morrow, the seasons that laugh or that weep;
> For these give joy and sorrow; but thou, Proserpina, sleep.
>
> (*Hymn to Proserpine* 3-4)

> And froth and drift of the sea;
> And dust of the labouring earth;
> And bodies of things to be
> In the houses of death and of birth.
>
> (*Atalanta in Calydon* 330-33)

In the 48 lines of this Chorus from *Atalanta in Calydon* most of the odd-numbered lines could be combined with the following line into one long line and popped into *Hymn to Proserpine* with no disruption—at least no disruption in the *meter,* which in its variable combinations of duple and triple rhythms has been called *mixed meter, iambic-anapestic meter, loose iambic, dolnik, strict stress-meter,* and *logaoedic.* Derek Attridge's notation shows this mix. The *B* represents a "beat," the *o* an "offbeat," and the *-o-* a "double offbeat." By Attridge's view, and by the view assumed here, the *B* aligns with a syllable on which tapping naturally occurs—whether the tapping of a finger, a pencil, a foot, a piece of chalk, or any other external time marker.[18] As will be argued, this tapping is more than an incidental accompaniment to a silent or oral reading of a poem.

> For these give joy and sorrow; but thou, Proserpina, sleep . . .
> o   B   o   B   o   B -o-   B   o   B -o- B
> And froth and drift of the sea; and dust of the labouring earth;
> o   B   o   B -o-   B   o   B   -o-   B   -o- B

The conflation of lines from the two poems may disrupt the sense, though there are those, including W. B. Yeats, who say that Swinburne in his most impressive flights of sound has already taken leave of sense.

If the line division of some nineteenth-century poetry is ambiguous when taken in by the ear, there are metrically similar medieval poems that show the ambiguity in written form. Here are two lines from the *Poema Morale*, c. 1200, in a meter known as "septenary," for the seven beats in each line that occur on syllables. Following Attridge's notation, a "virtual beat" is indicated at the end of each line:

Ich am nu elder þan Ich wes a wintre and a lore
o B o B o b o B o B o b o B o [B]

Ich welde mare þan I dude mi wit oh to be more
o B o B o b o B o o B o b o B o [B]

(Trinity MS. 1-2)

And here are four lines by Samuel Taylor Coleridge:

It is an ancient Mariner
o b o B o   B o b

And he stoppeth one of three.
  -o- B o   B o   B   [B]

"By thy long grey beard and glittering eye,
   -o- B   O B   o   B   -o- B

Now wherefore stopp'st thou me?"
 O   B o   B   o   B   [B]

(*The Rime of the Ancient Mariner* 1-4)

Finally here are four lines by Emily Dickinson:

The Brain—is wider than the Sky—
o B   o B o b o B

For—put them side by side—
o B   o   B o B   [B]

The one the other will contain
o B o   B o b o B

With ease—and You—beside—
  o B   o B   o B   [B]

(632)

Both the Coleridge and the Dickinson lines are in a form of ballad meter known as Common Measure: 4 3 4 3. However, if we follow Attridge's description of a "4 x 4" structure, that is, four lines of four beats, a "virtual beat" occurs at the ends of lines 2 and 4.[19] Furthermore, if the two lines from *Poema Morale* were each broken into two lines, as they are sometimes printed, they would appear to be in Common Measure too:

Ich am nu elder þan Ich wes
  o B   o B o   b   o B

a wintre and a lore
  o   B o   b o B o [B]

Ich welde mare þan I dude
  o B o   B o   b o B o

mi wit oh to be more
  o B   o b o   B o   [B]

It is obvious why the septenary has long been proposed as a source for ballad meter.

But although Attridge's supplement of [B] to represent a virtual beat is a step, literally, in the right direction, the division into four lines is still an abstraction from the continuous progression of beats in the brain: one can think of Bach's walk to Lübeck, and even in our imaginary landscape, a walk along a road lined with posts spaced a stride apart.

In the eighth line of Shelley's poem, a stride—a post, a virtual or silent beat—could conceivably occur between "summer" and "and":

Fresh spring, and summer, and winter hoar,
   O   B   o B   o [B] o B   o B

It would be analogous to the silent beat that has been posited in this line from Shakespeare's *Richard III*:

But, tell me, is young George Stanley living?
  o   B o [B] o   B   O   B o B o   (5.5.9)

Or in many of the dipodic lines in George Meredith's "Love in the Valley," as in line 3:

> Knees and tresses folded to slip and ripple idly
> B   o   b   o   B o [b] o B o   b o B o

Although a silent beat could theoretically occur between the two offbeats in Shelley's line, the practice of the poets argues otherwise. The silent beat, in which a stressed syllable bearing ictus is missing, is rare in English poetry beyond the ballad stanza and dipodic verse. It occurs occasionally in poetry of the drama but seldom in lyric poetry, including that of Shelley, who worked more variations on the iambic pentameter than most of his contemporaries.

The argument of this essay has been moving toward a consideration of some kind of clock in the human mind, as illustrated first by Shelley's nonce syllables as markers of rhythm existing before the actual words; and second by an analogy from Baroque music and jazz where the meter is counted out by a "walking bass." The last part of the essay will look at studies in cognitive science that have confirmed this clock, and we will ask about its relevance to the structure of a poem in meter.

Double Offbeats and the Ripples of Rhythm

First though with the poems before us, it is worth noting that in Coleridge's lines, but not in those of the other two poets, there are occurrences of the symbol *-o-*, as in the lines by Swinburne, indicating a "double offbeat": *And he, By thy, -ering-*. These patterns of two unstressed syllables have been designated by other names—for example, "anapestic substitutions" when scanned with the following beat. George Saintsbury, Edward Weismiller, Marina Tarlinskaja, Kristin Hanson, and Derek Attridge are among the prosodists who have urged attention to this pattern as one of the most important ways of achieving rhythmical variety in English poetry from Coleridge to the present.

Tarlinskaja's work is especially extensive and persuasive. An understanding of the variations in English metrical poetry during the past two centuries—and in much Middle English lyric poetry—must begin with the two metrically unstressed, homely syllables designated in the present study by *-o-*. They cause a distinct ripple in the tapping of the beats.

By this way of looking at it, the steady progression of posts along the roadside gives us the *meter*; the uneven surface between the posts is what we can call *rhythm*. If the ground between the posts were smooth, we would say that the meter and the rhythm of the language are in an isomorphic relationship. But the rhythm of English, like that of all natural languages, is filled with stony patches and potholes, gullies and small stumps.

Because of the disjunction between the melodies and rhythms that the poet hears and the sound patterns that the language offers, there is an inevitable *tension* along the ground separating the posts. In addition, the poet makes use of double offbeats and other "substitutions." The inverted first foot, the so-called pyrrhics and spondees, the caesura, the unstressed syllable at the end of the line, and so on, these occur before, between, and after the tapped beats, the posts.

Cognitive Approaches to Language, Music, and Poetry

But this tapping, whether of the fingers or the foot, the walking—aren't these manifestations of human behavior to the side of the poem itself, something the poem may or may not cause? Wimsatt and Beardsley had a very clear notion of the distinction between the poem and its accidentals:

> When we ask what the meter of a poem is, we are not asking how Robert Frost or Professor X reads the poem, with all the features peculiar to that performance. We are asking about the poem as a public linguistic object, something that can be examined by various persons, studied, disputed—univocally.[20]

By Wimsatt and Beardsley's view, the poem may evoke certain responses in some sophisticated readers but not in others. In replying to criticisms of their essay, they claimed not to hear "the element of 'ideal' temporally equal recurrence" that Elias Schwartz heard and which they said is "neither a part of objective linguistics nor of observable phonetic phenomena. This seems to place it safely beyond verifiable public discussion, where we have no wish to follow."[21]

In the decades since their essay, and especially during the past twenty years, the intersection of traditional phenomenology and cognitive science has done much to illuminate the private areas of consciousness, including the perception of rhythm, which Wimsatt and Beardsley showed little interest in. It has also called into question whether there is even such a thing as a "poem as a public linguistic object" in the way they meant.

Yet the specific, potential contributions of cognitive science have been more fully understood and applied to analogous problems in music than in poetics. Much current work in perception and music shows not only what is happening in the head but also how that neuronal activity connects to the movements of hands and feet that have been observed since the ancient Greeks and before.[22]

Little of this has made it into discussions of poetic meter. For example, for the link between music and poetry via cognitive poetics, Derek Attridge's otherwise exemplary entry for "Rhythm" in the fourth edition of *The Princeton Encyclopedia of Poetry and Poetics* cites only a handful of older studies, including groundbreaking work going back to the 1970s by Reuven Tsur, but nothing recent by psychologists and neuroscientists; nor does the entry on "Cognitive Poetics" by Tsur himself and T. Sovran.[23] (There is only so much one can do in an encyclopedia entry.) By far the fullest and most searching application of current work in music and the neurosciences to the rhythms of poetry is the 2012 dissertation by Nicholas Myklebust.[24]

One way of restating the problem—and suggesting a solution—is to ask exactly what it is that temporal metrists of a long tradition have perceived—this "beat" that is always referred to—and how it is perceived. To have some idea of what is processed by those who say they feel such a mental event will possibly help explain what is processed by those who say they do not.

First of all, it is important to ask whether the beat itself has any temporal duration. Music theorists have made the point that a specific kind of note is perceived only *after* it has been performed; a staccato note, for example, is known as such only after the fact.[25] During the moment of perception, when the note is present, there is no way of knowing how long it will extend (unless, of course, one knows the piece of music, and even then, performers offer various interpretations). The length of a legato note, similarly, will be known only when the note ends. Thus, there is a problem in understanding the perception of a "present" event, because it is fully perceived only when it is no longer present.

William James pondered this paradox and invoked a term from the psychologist E. R. Clay's work of 1882, "the specious present." James' elaboration of the idea influenced subsequent thinking, including that of Edmund Husserl. By James' view, present moments cannot be discrete entities like beads on a string, or there would be no sense of continuity. The "present" had to include both a reflection of the past and a projection into the future:

> In short, the practically cognized present is no knife-edge, but a saddle-back, with a certain breadth of its own on which we sit perched, and from which we look in two directions into time. The unit of composition of our perception of time is a *duration*, with a

bow and a stern, as it were—a rearward- and a forward-looking end.
... It is only as parts of this *duration-block* that the relation of *succession* of one end to the other is perceived.[26]

Interestingly for our purposes, James invokes the perception of various meters in poetry and melodies in music. He posits two stanzas of poetry in which a line in one stanza is of different length than the corresponding line in the other. James' hypothetical example captures the problem that we considered above for Shelley's two stanzas.[27] Because of stanza and rhyme structure, the line in the second stanza that was shortened by closing up the space is *heard* as shorter.

The perception of a melody was, in fact, Husserl's favorite example. According to Husserl a melody is not heard a note at a time, because then there were would be no continuity.[28] Yet, the perceptual moment is also not a block of temporal duration as James had proposed. Instead, it is perceived with a memory of the notes that have preceded and a projection of the notes to come. Husserl's three phases *of perception, retention* (short-term memory) and *protention* (anticipation) moved the object of study from the outside world to the interior of the mind, the locus of phenomenology.

If these ideas are transposed to literary meter, it should be clear that Husserl's assumptions and conclusions opposed a view such as that advocated by Wimsatt and Beardsley and a long line of "objective" metrists. The beats of the line of verse are not in the acoustic stream, much less on the page, but in embodied consciousness, and that is a matter of an individual's cognition. Yet aspects of Husserl's theory left nagging questions that were picked up by Maurice Merleau-Ponty and a tradition of phenomenologists to the present.[29] These investigations have direct relevance for metrics.

For example, Hubert L. Dreyfus points out that Husserl's system, though located within the mind, is oriented more toward the *analysis* of perception than toward perception itself; similarly, Shaun Gallagher points to Husserl's reification of the categories involving the temporal "phase." As Gallagher puts it, Husserl "tends to reify or hypostasize the phase and to treat it as something that is actually 'for itself' in consciousness."[30] A process often referred to in current work is "proprioception," the reception of stimuli produced within the body so as to register in the central nervous system the body's own limb position in space. This is different from the mind's conceptualization of such stimuli. It is sometimes argued that Husserl's phenomena are mediated by conception, contrary to the basic assumptions of phenomenology.

In addressing this problem, Merleau-Ponty's emphasis on perception within the body has been a frequent source of reference for philosophers of "embodied cognition."[31] Here is a promising nexus where the speculations of philosophers intersect with the empirical findings of current neuroscience. One recent team of researchers, McAuley, Henry, and Tkach, summarize their results in a publication of 2012:

> Increasing evidence shows that neural circuits involved in beat perception overlap with motor circuitry even in the absence of overt movement. The study investigated effects of tempo on beat-based processing by combining functional magnetic resonance imaging with a perceptual timing paradigm where participants made simple temporal judgments about short rhythmic sequences.[32]

They found that accuracy in the perception of beats varied with the tempo of the beats, less so at a slower tempo of 1,500 milliseconds than at a faster tempo of 600 ms. To recite "Gather ye rosebuds while ye may" at the rate of a beat every thirty seconds would not only destroy the beats, it would destroy the poem. This is not an aesthetic statement but an ontological statement: the sequence of words would be something other than a poem. Such dissolution would continue to happen, of course, at tempi incrementally faster than the absurd rate of a syllable per half minute. The beats of music and poetry occur within a narrow range in the ecology of human perception. The poem exists, then, in a certain band of time.

Some psychologists would say that what happens in the brain is "self-entrainment."[33] A mental clock becomes attuned to the meter of a piece of music or a poem. Merleau-Ponty had referred to it as "temps du corps, temps-taximètre du schéma corporel" (time of the body, taxi meter time of the corporeal schema).[34] Here is attestation of the interior clock that we feel when reading Emily Dickinson—or any other accomplished poet writing in meter. The main thesis that this essay offers is that the range within which the meters of poetry and music are perceived is quite narrow relative to the whole range of human rhythmic perception. It is analogous to the range of a wind-up metronome of wood and metal. The same kind of clock works for Dickinson's Common Measure, Milton's and Shakespeare's iambic pentameter, Byron's and Keats' ottava rima, Longfellow's trochaic tetrameter, Tennyson's and Swinburne's mixed meter hexameter, and so on.

But if the clock is always ticking at more or less the same tempo, and if the theory collapses the beats of all meters into a single progression of beats, what useful distinction can it possibly make? The answer is that it distinguishes the tempo of the entrainment of poetry from that of a slowly dripping faucet, or a jackhammer on the street. McAuley, Henry, and Tkach found perception of beats to be strongest, "around 100-120 beats per minute, which corresponds to a beat period between 500 ms and 600 milliseconds."[35] This is more or less the range within which beats in poetry have always been found to occur whenever empirical studies have been made, going back to William James' citation of evidence from nineteenth-century German psychologists, Ana Snell's often cited study of 1918, on up to Frederick Turner and Ernst Pöppel in 1983, and Nicholas Myklebust's own timing.[36]

Measurements by the clock, however, are more apt to be irrelevant, or even misleading, than helpful. Except for gross distinctions—comparisons of linguistic or musical periodicities with the periodicities of dripping faucets or jackhammers—the external clock really doesn't matter. Human cognition must deal with widely varying tempi as we bump about in the world, but the tempo of poetry and music, in relative terms, is more or less constant. For both forms it is within a fairly narrow band, and that is mainly what needs to be said.

More interesting than the measurements of the simple timing of beats is the response by neurons to the patterns of rhythmic variation between the beats. For example, in a collection of essays that takes Husserl's writings on time as a point of departure, Andy McGuiness and Katie Overy summarize the correlation of areas of the cerebral cortex and meters familiar in poetry:

> Another emerging theme is the accumulating evidence to suggest that motor regions of the brain are engaged during perceptual rhythm tasks. For example, Grahn and Brett (2007) have shown that the basal ganglia (involved in initiating movement) are activated while listening to stimuli with a strong sense of pulse, compared with stimuli without a steady pulse. Trainor *et al.* (2009) have shown that activation of the vestibular system (involved in balance) contributes to discrimination between duple and triple metres, while Thaut *et al.* (2009) have shown that particular regions of the cerebellum (involved in balance and fine motor control) are involved in different types of rhythmic task, such as isochronous versus non-isochronous tapping.[37]

The separate operations of the basal ganglia, the vestibular system, and so on reveal the complexity of hearing meter and rhythm. Furthermore, different hearers embody different neuronal activity: MRI results show what one might expect, that trained musicians make more connections for a melody than non-musicians.[38] As one proceeds along the spectrum away from trained musicians, there are different connections for listeners whose "mirror neuron systems" function less empathetically.

This raises a difficult question for both music and poetry. If meter exists by being embodied, there will be different embodiments among different perceivers. Some will be closer than others to the embodiment by the author—whatever value one might put on the author's embodiment.[39] Multiple "lines" of poetry can be derived from a single written *representation* of a line. It is always more difficult to make qualitative judgments about these variants in poetry than in music. A trained musician is more readily identifiable than a trained reader. The fact that immensely learned and sensitive authorities in poetry have split historically in ways that have been mentioned indicates the problem.

These considerations return us to a question touched on above with reference to Husserl and to the title of this paper: the relationships between *written representations, concepts*, and *the feel of meter and rhythm*. If a written line is a representation on paper, does it evoke analogous representations in the mind? Specifically, for our purposes, are meter and rhythm derived internally from some kind of mental representation? Or is there a more direct link within the body between the perception of the written line and the feel of the meter and rhythm? Hubert Dreyfus draws the analogy with playing tennis or chess, in which the neophyte is conscious of explicit "rules" in devising a tactic for performing an action (aside from the obvious rules of the game): in tennis, for example, posture, arm movement, and so on. The experienced player performs more intuitively, and a theory of rules and representations, is not only irrelevant but misleading. Proprioception, the body's direct knowledge without the mediating level of representation, is the operative concept (a concept in opposition to "concept," a word that appeared along with "abstraction" in the title of Wimsatt and Beardsley's essay, our continuing point of departure).

By this view, there are aspects of the structure of consciousness that happen before we know it and do not normally enter into the phenomenal content of experience in an explicit way. Gallagher uses the term "prenoetic" to describe this hidden aspect of consciousness (from Greek *noētikos* 'intellectual').[40] The cognitive (noetic or mental) processes of perceiving meter and rhythm are shaped prenoetically by the fact that they are embodied.

In summary, tapping is not a vague, indirect effect of meter on the human body caused by reflective consciousness. It is the direct external manifestation of neuronal activity in the basal ganglia and the cerebellum. All this can be said more succinctly.

Meter is the tapping.

Rhythm is everything in the language of the poem that distracts the tapping.

Between the two there is *tension*—to return to a favorite term of the New Critics. If the distraction is great enough, the tapping is lost: by some theories of meter, the language is said to be *unmetrical*. However, by the view assumed here, the meter is not in the language but in the body. Except for the initial priming of the pump, the winding of the clock or the metronome, the setting of the taxi meter, language does not cause tapping. Language reinforces or obscures what the body knows to do. Furthermore, by this view, we would not even say that meter causes tapping. Meter *is* the tapping. But suppose the poem is read with no bodily movement. Is there no meter? Of course there is, stillness being the normal way of reading. The tapping is in the brain. The limbs are held in check. The car is in gear, but the clutch is depressed. This is what recent studies of rhythm in the neurosciences have shown us.[41]

This idea returns us to the analogy with walking. It is too easy to reach for spatial metaphors, as I did with the posts along the road. Recent research suggests that we should forget the posts and the fences and focus on the internal feel of the movement of the limbs.

Maxine Sheets-Johnstone in *The Roots of Thinking* hypothesizes the evolution of consciousness in bipeds as an aspect of the "binary periodicity of the legs in walking or running."[42] In the latter part of this book and more fully in *The Primacy of Movement,* she applies these ideas of bodily movement and rhythm to extended criticisms of both Husserl and Merleau-Ponty for being insufficiently attentive to movement. In the account that she gives of the roots of consciousness, the prosodist and the musicologist will find evocative suggestions specifically of the bodily foundations of the meters of poetry and music—and ultimately the rhythms of Percy Bysshe Shelley and Johann Sebastian Bach:

> In corporeal terms . . . upright posture meant that a quadrupedal rhythmic complexity was reduced to *a simple binary periodicity.* Though consistently regarded as more complex because of the challenge to balance, the stress on supporting anatomical segments, and the like, upright posture was in another, concept-enhancing sense a radical simplification. Instead of four footfalls there were two, and instead of a variety of possible patternings of footfalls—trotting, galloping, and pacing, for example—there was basically one pattern variable only in terms of speed: walking and running. . . . Moreover it is

the binary periodicity of stride and arm swing as well as footfalls that is remarkable in bipedal as opposed to quadrupedal locomotion.[43]

To return to Bach's "Air on the G String": when performed by piano and violin, the walking bass line of the piano suggests the meter while the slow sweeping melody of the violin provides the rhythmical figures. Between the two there is tension, analogous in poetry to the tapping that is meter and the rhythm of language that distracts. The unruly rhythms of language and the harnessed variations of the poet's craft distract the consciousness from its focus on regular metrical progression—a progression from the present moment to the next moment—and in the distraction produce pleasure, which we then experience as beauty, elaboration, development, diminishment, complexity, and so on.

Conclusions

Much recent discussion of consciousness revives, continues, and gives empirical support to intuitions of the past two centuries. As Coventry Patmore put it in 1857, using, it might be noted, the familiar spatial image of a fence:

> These are two indispensable conditions of metre,—first, that the sequence of vocal utterance, represented by written verse, shall be divided into equal or proportionate spaces; second, *that the fact of that division shall be made manifest* by an 'ictus' or 'beat,' actual or mental, which, like a post in a chain railing, shall mark the end of one space, and the commencement of another. . . . Yet, all-important as this time-beater is, I think it demonstrable that, for the most part, *it has no material and external existence at all,* but has its place in the mind, which craves measure in everything, and, wherever the idea of measure is uncontradicted, delights in marking it with an imaginary 'beat.'[44]

We can venture this tentative conclusion: the forms of English poetry lie along various continua. The most important of these, from which all others can be derived, is the steady progression of beats, like a single row of posts extending across the landscape. However, this is a spatial metaphor, and it has the hazard of all spatial metaphors when talking about temporal events. Therefore, we should add to this image the image with which we began. The physical action of walking along the post-lined road can take place only in time.

To return to the metaphor once more, even Wimsatt and Beardsley invoke both a fence and the act of walking. However, the fact that the event takes place in time is mentioned only to dismiss it as irrelevant to meter and rhythm:

> But all measurement is not necessarily temporal measurement—even when the things measured occur in a temporal succession. If a person walks along the street hitting every third paling in a fence, he sets up a pattern, but he may or he may not do this in equal lengths of time. Better still, let every third paling be painted red, and we have a pattern which our person does not have to set up for himself but can observe objectively. He will observe or experience this pattern in time, but not necessarily in equal lengths of time.[45]

It is hard to know what to make of this, the idea of *seeing* painted palings in equal (or unequal) "lengths of time." In any event, it fits with metaphors that run through their writing, including the title of a collection of important essays, *The Verbal Icon*. Their "Note on the Title of this Book" roots the metaphor in visual experience and expands it from there in the direction of semiotics but not of temporal experience: an icon is "a verbal sign," "a visual image," "not merely a bright picture."[46]

Where does this leave the piece of paper in the title of this essay? The ink marks, too, exist in space. There is no rhythm in them. Only when they are perceived by an observer who is literate in the language of which the marks are a representation is there the possibility of rhythm. Even then, many irrelevant verbal events in time can be adduced from the writing (a performance of the poem as a list of words, a performance with the intonations of casual talk, and so on). Only a restricted set of events—a few styles of reading, whether silently or aloud—qualify as manifesting "the meter and rhythm of the poem" in correspondence with the meter and rhythm inside the body.

Notes

I am grateful to Natalie Gerber for her immensely helpful comments on this essay.

1. W. K. Wimsatt, Jr., and Monroe C. Beardsley, "The Concept of Meter: An Exercise in Abstraction," *PMLA* 74, no. 5 (1959): 585-98.

2. Discoveries in medieval English metrics of the past four decades—in Old English meter since 1970 and in Middle English meter since 1985—make the story unsustainable, although it is still the usual account in handbooks and anthologies. The problem is that extremely technical methods are needed to reconstruct a very simple *sound* of the poetry—at least for Middle English. For Old English poetry, the problem is worse: extremely technical methods are needed to arrive at a very complex sound.

3. T. V. F. Brogan, *English Versification, 1570-1980: A Reference Guide with a Global Appendix* (Baltimore: Johns Hopkins University Press, 1981), 142.

4. Jorge Luis Borges, "Pierre Menard, Author of the *Quixote*," trans. James E. Irby, in *Labyrinths: Selected Stories and Other Writings*, ed. Donald A. Yates and James E. Irby (New York: New Directions, 1964), 36–44.

5. Bennett Weaver, "Shelley Works Out the Rhythm of *A Lament*," *PMLA* 47, no. 2 (1932): 570–76. A convenient summary with additional information is in *The Norton Anthology of English Literature*, ed. Stephen Greenblatt and M. H. Abrams, 8th ed. (New York: Norton, 2006), A7–A9.

6. Ibid., 572.

7. Ibid., 574.

8. Ibid.

9. This final draft is in a notebook that Weaver apparently did not have access to. A facsimile has since been edited by Carlene A. Adamson, *Shelley's Pisan Winter Notebook (1820–1821): A Facsimile of Bodleian MS Shelley adds. e. 8,* The Bodleian Shelley Manuscripts, vol. 6 (New York: Garland, 1992), 341.

10. See Greenblatt and Abrams, A8–A9, notes 3–4.

11. David Yearsley, *Bach's Feet: The Organ Pedals in European Culture* (Cambridge: Cambridge University Press, 2012), 110.

12. Ibid., 107.

13. A very clear explanation of the walking bass with reference to this piece is the CD with accompanying "Course Guidebook" by Robert Greenberg, *Bach and the High Baroque*, Part 1, Disc 6, under the rubric "Rhythm and Meter" (Springfield, Va.: The Teaching Company, 1998). I am grateful to Natalie Gerber for pointing out that analogies between the musical bass and poetic meter have been made before, as by Stéphane Mallarmé, quoted by Timothy Steele in *Missing Measures: Modern Poetry and the Revolt against Meter* (Fayetteville: University of Arkansas Press, 1990), 3.

14. For reasons why the lines of Shakespeare's sonnets would likely have been slow and stately in the author's mind, see Thomas Cable, "Issues for a New History of English Prosody," in *Studies in the History of the English Language: A Millennial Perspective*, ed. Donka Minkova and Robert Stockwell (Berlin: Mouton de Gruyter, 2002), 134–46.

15. Matthew Butterfield describes what jazz musicians "gain from the near-isochronous pulse maintained by bass and drums and the near-simultaneity of their beat onsets. . . . This presents an opportunity for improvising soloists to generate PDs [participatory discrepancies] against the beat of the rhythm section for expressive purposes," in "Participatory Discrepancies and the Perception of Beats in Jazz," *Music Perception* 27, no. 3 (2010): 157–76.

16. Justin London, *Hearing in Time: Psychological Aspects of Musical Meter* (Oxford: Oxford University Press, 2004), 48.

17. Lines are cited from Algernon Charles Swinburne, *Major Poems and Selected Prose*, ed. Jerome McGann and Charles L. Sligh (New Haven, Conn.: Yale University Press, 2004).

18. Derek Attridge, *The Rhythms of English Poetry* (London: Longman, 1982). This essay will use the slight revisions of Attridge's system in Thomas Carper and Derek Attridge, *Meter and Meaning: An Introduction to Rhythm in Poetry* (New York: Routledge, 2003), 148–49. In its full elaboration, *B* represents an emphasized beat, *b* an unemphasized beat, *[B]* a virtual beat, *o* an unemphasized offbeat, *O* an emphasized offbeat, *-o-* a double offbeat, and *[o]* a virtual offbeat (also called a "metrical pause," distinct from the syntactic break or "caesura").

19. Attridge, *Rhythms*, 88.

20. Wimsatt and Beardsley, "The Concept of Meter," 587–88.

21. Wimsatt and Beardsley's reply to Elias Schwartz in the exchange of comments between the three authors in *PMLA* 77, no. 5 (1962): 674.

22. See, for example, Aniruddh D. Patel, *Music, Language, and the Brain* (Oxford: Oxford University Press, 2007) and the references in the rest of this essay.

23. R. Tsur and T. Sovran, "Cognitive Poetics," in *The Princeton Encyclopedia of Poetry and Poetics*, ed. Roland Greene, Stephen Cushman, et al., 4th ed. (Princeton, N.J.: Princeton University Press, 2012), 272-73; D. Attridge, "Rhythm," ibid., 1195–98.

24. Nicholas Myklebust, "Misreading English Meter: 1400–1514" (Ph.D. diss., University of Texas at Austin, 2012).

25. David Clarke, "Music, Phenomenology, Time Consciousness: Meditations after Husserl," in *Music and Consciousness: Philosophical, Psychological, and Cultural Perspectives*, ed. David Clarke and Eric Clarke (Oxford: Oxford University Press, 2011), 9.

26. William James, *The Principles of Psychology*, 2 vols. (1890, Cambridge, Mass.: Harvard University Press, 1981), 1: 574–75.

27. Following earlier usage, James refers to "lines" as "verses": "Divers verses may again be bound together in the form of a stanza, and we may then say of another stanza, 'Its second verse differs by so much from that of the first stanza,' when but for the felt stanza-form the two differing verses would have come to us too separately to be compared at all" (1: 576).

28. Edmund Husserl, *On the Phenomenology of the Consciousness of Internal Time (1893-1917)*, trans. J. B. Brough (Dordrecht: Kluwer, 1991), 376. See, for example, Eugene Montague, "Phenomenology and the 'Hard Problem' of Consciousness and Music," in *Music and Consciousness: Philosophical, Psychological, and Cultural Perspectives*, ed. David Clarke and Eric Clarke (Oxford: Oxford University Press, 2011), 34.

29. The problem of "absence" that had worried James remained even after Husserl had incorporated the ideas of retention and protention. It was the opening wedge in Jacques Derrida's deconstructive reading of Husserl's time manifold, as it also was in his reading of Saussure's concept of the phoneme: Jacques Derrida, *Speech and Phenomena, and Other Essays on Husserl's Theory of Signs*, trans. D. B. Allison (Evanston, Ill.: Northwestern University Press, 1973), 64-69.

30. Shaun Gallagher, *The Inordinance of Time* (Evanston, Ill.: Northwestern University Press, 1998), 65. See also Hubert L. Dreyfus, "Intelligence without Representation—Merleau-Ponty's Critique of Mental Representation: The Relevance of Phenomenology to Scientific Explanation," *Phenomenology and the Cognitive Sciences* 1, no. 4 (2002): 372.

31. Maurice Merleau-Ponty, *Phenomenology of Perception*, trans. Colin Smith (London: Routledge & Kegan Paul, 1962). See, for example, the six chapters in Part One, "The Body," and Chapter 2, "Temporality," in Part Three.

32. J. Devin McAuley, Molly J. Henry, and Jean Tkach, "Tempo Mediates the Involvement of Motor Areas in Beat Perception," in *The Neurosciences and Music IV: Learning and Memory*, special issue of *Annals of the New York Academy of Sciences* 1252 (April 2012): 77.

33. For example, Robert F. Port, "Meter and Speech," *Journal of Phonetics* 31, no. 3–4 (2003): 599–611.

34. Maurice Merleau-Ponty, *Le visible et l'invisible, suivi de notes de travail*, ed. Claude Lefort (Paris: Gallimard, 1964), 227.

35. McAuley, Henry, and Tkach, "Motor Areas in Beat Perception," 77.

36. See James, *The Principles of Psychology*, vol. I, 577–83; Ada L. F. Snell, "An Objective Study of Syllabic Quantity in English Verse: Blank Verse," *PMLA* 33, no. 3 (1918): 396-408; Frederick Turner and Ernst Pöppel, "The Neural Lyre: Poetic Meter, the Brain, and Time," *Poetry* 142 (August, 1983): 277–309; and Myklebust, "Misreading English Meter," 199.

37. Andy McGuiness and Katie Overy, "Music, Consciousness, and the Brain: Music as Shared Experience of an Embodied Present," in *Music and Consciousness: Philosophical, Psychological, and Cultural Perspectives*, ed. David Clarke and Eric Clarke (Oxford: Oxford University Press, 2011), 247.

38. See McGuiness and Overy, "Music, Consciousness, and the Brain," 247–49; Montague, "Phenomenology and the 'Hard Problem' of Consciousness and Music," 36; Gallagher, *The Inordinance of Time*, 96–97; London, *Hearing in Time*, 15.

39. On the transference of an author's patterns to the reader with specific reference to Robert Frost, see Gerber's essay "Beyond Meaning: Differing Fates of Some Modernist Poets' Investments of Belief in Sounds," in this volume.

40. Shaun Gallagher, *How the Body Shapes the Mind* (Oxford: Clarendon, 2005), 2.

41. See McGuiness and Overy, "Music, Consciousness, and the Brain," 248; McAuley, Henry, and Tkach, "Motor Areas in Beat Perception," 77.

42. Maxine Sheets-Johnstone, *The Roots of Thinking* (Philadelphia: Temple University Press, 1990), 78.

43. Sheets-Johnstone, *Roots*, 77. See also Sheets-Johnstone, *The Primacy of Movement*, 2nd ed., Advances in Consciousness Research, vol. 14 (Philadelphia: Benjamins, 2011).

44. Mary Augustine Roth, *Coventry Patmore's "Essay on English Metrical Law": A Critical Edition with a Commentary* (Washington D.C.: Catholic University of America Press, 1961), 15.

45. Wimsatt and Beardsley, "The Concept of Meter," 590.

46. W. K. Wimsatt, Jr., *The Verbal Icon: Studies in the Meaning of Poetry*, with two essays coauthored by Monroe C. Beardsley (Lexington, University of Kentucky Press, 1967), x.

Picturing Rhythm

Meredith Martin

If a man or a woman wants to write a poem it has to be as plain as two and two are four is how he is to do it.
—WILLIAM CARLOS WILLIAMS

1

In histories of English versification, the study of what we now call "syllabic" meter has received relatively little attention. By "syllabic" verse I mean verse that, in theory, has no discernable accentual pattern and is measured solely by syllable count; this verse would resemble prose except for the fact that the length of the line is determined by the number of syllables it contains. Robert Beum, a friend and interlocutor to William Carlos Williams, provides a succinct explanation of syllabic meter in his 1957 article "Syllabic Verse in English:"

> Syllabic verse is verse which disregards the foot system . . . and instead of being measurable metrically into small regularly recurring units within the line, takes the whole line as its metrical unit, each line (or in the case of a pattern of varying line-lengths, each mating line) containing the same number of syllables, while stress number and stress position are not fixed, and while the lines are end paused.[1]

Though Beum discusses syllabic verses of varying line lengths (different numbers of syllables in each line in a repeated pattern) and the most familiar practitioner of the varying line-length syllabic, Marianne Moore, he focuses his inquiry on poets like Dylan Thomas who use the same number of syllables in each line.[2] In an early edition of Lewis Turco's ubiquitous *The Book of Forms,* Turco only spends one sentence on his subsection "Syllabic Prosody" but spends several paragraphs on "isoverbal prosody."

In "isoverbal" prosody, the poem's lines are determined by the number of words in each line: "If one were to write stanzas that contained differing numbers of words in each corresponding line in succeeding stanzas, then one would be writing in quantitative isoverbal prosody."[3] Turco names William Carlos Williams' "The Red Wheelbarrow" as "the most famous quantitative isoverbal poem in English."[4] Turco ends his section on "isoverbal prosody" with Williams' poem, but gives no hint that "The Red Wheelbarrow" might also be syllabic.

> So much depends
> upon
>
> the red wheel
> barrow
>
> glazed with rain
> water
>
> beside the white
> chickens

Each of the four short stanzas contain three words followed by one word—isoverbal—with the syllabic equation of 4:2, 3:2, 3:2, 4:2; the first and fourth stanzas are "mated," in Beum's terms, as are the second and third. The one-word, two-syllable lines are set off visually before a stanza break. The visual image of the words themselves—"upon," "barrow," "water," "chickens"—alone above that space might stretch out—a bit—the amount of time it takes us to say them, or at least make us take a short pause. Williams wrote this poem before he elaborated his theory of "triadic verse." The "upon" rests above the remaining six lines, enacting its prepositional status and the precipice—the hovering between—that we might enact in the space between the short stanzas. Thinking about the poem itself as an image in addition to its status as an imagist poem, I began to think about how syllables were a function of imagism and how images were also a function of syllables. How might syllables produce concentration—like Pound's "complex"—and how might that complicate our understanding of modernist rhythm?

When we narrate the history of early twentieth-century poetic rhythm, we most often tell the story of the opposing forces of regularized accentual-syllabic verse and free verse. Ezra Pound's statement "As regarding rhythm . . . compose in the sequence of the musical phrase, not in sequence of a metronome" and "Don't chop your stuff into separate *iambs*" are, as Timothy Steele reports, "part of the narrative of how "20th-century poetic practice favors rhythm over meter."[5] Williams famously rejected Pound's ideas of bodily rhythm and Anglo-Saxon accents in favor of an abstract idea of "measure" that he wrote about everywhere but defined precisely nowhere. Syllabic verse is seldom part of this story, and though there are many historical moments when counting in poems becomes either controversial or traditional, syllabic verse at the beginning of the twentieth century has been particularly neglected by the historical record. Williams does not do much to help us with this. In his unpublished 1913 essay "English Speech Rhythms" (which Harriet Monroe refused for *Poetry* because she thought it was incomprehensible) Williams confusingly insists "Imagination creates an image, point by point, piece by piece, segment by segment—into a whole, living. But each part . . . exists naturally in rhythm . . . no work in words that is not regularly rhthmic [sic] and periodic can be of highest imagination and that workman who does not weld the rythm [sic] of his image into his material cannot be highest of his craft." Like Gerard Manley Hopkins, in this essay Williams believes that rhythm is a thing apart from language but upon which language rides: "Upon the wordy passions string sounds as they strain toward the perfect image." And "the rhythm must be maintained perfect, must continue even when the words scarcely can follow it across a roughness, as in a lullaby when the song halts from sheer weariness the cradle keeps swaying."[6] And counting syllables are "the bare makeshift for the appreciation of elapsing time . . . This makeshift counting of syllables— only possible because we were not capable of music and because none has yet been able to count time without it—is now expanded to meet the true necessity which is that time, not the syllables, must be counted."[7] It seems that Williams is aiming toward a theory of quantitative prosody: "the same rhythm, swift, may be of three syllables or if two are elided, of one: whereas, slow, it may consist of four or seven or any number that the sense agrees to. This is the flexibility that the modern requires."[8] But what is the real difference, for Williams and other poets, between quantitative and syllabic prosody? Does syllabic verse have a rhythm? Can we hear it? Detect it without seeing it on the page?

Beum, Yvor Winters, and other scholars (including the authors of the "syllabic verse" entry in the most recent edition of the *Encyclopedia of Poetry and Poetics*[9]) trace the beginning of syllabic verse not to the experiments of "modernism" but to the poet Ezra Pound associated most closely with the Victorian idiom—Robert Bridges.[10] Bridges is best known today as the editor of Hopkins' poetry. Poet Laureate of England between 1913 and his death in 1930, he was well respected by his peers as well as by the younger poets associated with literary modernism, who considered him the foremost metrist of his day. Bridges' best-selling 1929 book-length poem *The Testament of Beauty,* critics argue, is the first truly successful experiment in syllabic verse form.[11] Syllabics developed concurrently in the United States at the turn of the twentieth century and were part of a larger reconsideration in the United Kingdom, Germany, France, and the States of the efficacy of the classical foot-based system for measuring English verse. This essay explores a few forays into syllabics, most notably Bridges' earlier experiments with Neo-Miltonic syllabic verse, and connects these forays into abstract ideas about speech rhythm. I then move briefly to the perhaps unfamiliar American poet and prosodist Adelaide Crapsey, whose invention and popularization of the "cinquain" around the same time that Bridges was experimenting with syllabics also coincides with her fascinating quantification of syllable length as a potential key to poetic meaning. I conclude with a consideration of how William Carlos Williams, influenced by this discourse, revised and revamped theories of syllables as units of time in his verse line. By looking at alternative histories of early twentieth-century verse culture, I hope to show the importance of prosodic discourse in early twentieth-century literary history—a history that often assumes the importance of image at the expense of rigorous considerations of metrical or sonic experiments. Though scholars have recognized Pound's devotion to Anglo-Saxon strong-stress lines, or T. S. Eliot's ghosts of meter, it is only Marianne Moore's lines that have garnered widespread attention for their syllabic prosody. But what if we saw syllabics in the early twentieth century as a prosodic possibility, for poets like Bridges, Crapsey, and Williams, that might mediate not only between the visual and the aural dimensions of poetry but also between the science and aesthetics of verse form?

2

Syllabic verse is not the same as quantitative verse. Put simply, the first counts syllables and the second counts the amount of time it takes to say those syllables. They are related, and both rely on the complicated matter of pronunciation. In 1903, T. S. Omond published *A Study of Metre*, which posited replacing foot-based scansion with measure by "time spaces." Omond traced prosodists' obsession with time through the musical notation theories of Joshua Steele (1755) to American prosodist Sidney Lanier, who theorized in his 1880 *Science of English Verse* that metrical and musical time were the same.[12] Steele, Lanier, and a number of other prosodists attempted to solve the problem of (temporal) metrical notation by adopting musical notation. And yet Coventry Patmore, by far the most influential prosodist of the late nineteenth century, believed that the (English) mind could imagine these abstract spaces—what he called "isochronous intervals" between accents without any sort of visual mark.[13] How much time did it take to pronounce each syllable in English, a language with no common pronunciation? Patmore, Hopkins, and Bridges argued about these issues and, spurred by their conversations, Bridges devoted himself to correcting English pronunciation in order to eliminate ambiguity in pronunciation and therefore eliminate the need for metrical notation (a problem that had always dogged Hopkins). For Bridges, the problem of quantity in English was primarily a problem of how we see syllables on the page and how what we see tells us how to pronounce.

Nearly all of the prosodic discourse at the turn of the twentieth century was concerned with the problem of the visual versus aural perception of verse form. Prosodists and linguists did not agree—and still do not agree—about how to measure and mark equivalent spaces of perceived time in a verse line. Because English spelling is not phonetic, problems of measuring the length of time it takes to say a line (much less a word)—whether or not to elide syllables, and how or when to stress certain syllables became issues of notation. As Jason Hall argues, the scientific study of verse attempted to solve the problems of defining accent, pitch, and tone by using mechanical measurements that relied on the supposed objectivity of machine recording.[14] These measurements, however, conducted in laboratories and scrutinized by linguists in Russia, Germany, the United States, and France, simply confirmed the bias of the examiner and did not definitively solve the issue of how to measure accent in English in all its variety.[15] Despite the lack of agreement, linguists held out hope that science and even mathematics could rescue study of prosody from the abstraction of the literary disciplines. The increased attention to syllables by Bridges, Crapsey, and Williams overlaps with the discussion of the phonemic unit in linguistics first discussed in France in 1876 and explored more fully by Saussure in the decades after. Though controversial, phonemes were essentially a thing by the 1920s.[16] A phoneme is the smallest unit of sound that may cause a change in meaning within language but doesn't have meaning in itself—the "t" phoneme containing all of the sounds a "t" can make phonetically for instance. It is an indivisible unit of sound or, how we might decide to measure the borders of a string of letters that makes up a syllable. The desire for scientific precision in measuring prosody and the resurgent interest in syllabic counting as a model for versification correspond with new and controversial ways of thinking about sound in language in the nascent field of linguistics.

The modernist salvo, found in William Carlos William's poem "A Sort of Song": "no ideas but in things"[17] might be understood differently if we remember that phonemes become *things* at the beginning of the twentieth century. I simply want to mark this concurrence to think about how sound-units were being measured in ever more minute ways. For Bridges, reforming spelling to make it phonetic—and corresponding with *OED* editor Henry Bradley to beg that he adopt phonetic spelling in the dictionary—was crucially related to his interest in inventing a syllabic verse form that could accommodate a variety of different kinds of speech.

French verse-lines, with their strict rules for the number of syllables per line, caesura, and excluded words, were largely understood to be syllabic—so much so that the types of French verse were understood by number of syllables allowed in each line (twelve, or the alexandrine, ten, eight, seven, and six).[18] This ideal, of a purely syllabic non-accentual French versification, offered a structure for thinking about English prosody freed from accent and pronunciation that could then accommodate a variety of speech rhythms along the same lines as "free verse."[19] So, too did the rise of French "vers libre" and the idea of "symbolism" influence sonic and visual experiments in English verse form. The twin movements of literary decadence and literary jingoism in England were interwoven into competing ideas about literary form in the early decades of the twentieth century. On the one hand, French literary decadence manifested itself in France as a break away from regular alexandrines and toward freer sonic play. On the other hand, literary jingoism (patriotic and flamboyant in a different way) promoted the idea of an all-natural accent, a beat that was integral to the properly functioning national body. This turn of the century concept of "rhythm," derived earlier in the nineteenth century but brought to prominence by Frances Barton Gummere, promoted new ethnographically supported narratives of primitive throngs and primitive songs as natural history in order to justify and naturalize the marching rhythm of military drills in service of the nation.[20] We might, then, recontextualize the varieties of experiment that we blur into "free verse" and, among those varieties of experiment, see syllabic verse form as an escape—a new direction away from both decadence and jingoism and toward a more controlled verse that might bring something like an idealized objectivity of poetic form to modern poems, for both poets and for ever more discerning readers of poems.

The idea seemed to be, at the outset of the twentieth century, that if "modern" verse could be truly syllabic—counted by syllables only—then any language could fall into a syllabic rhythm, irrespective of pronunciation, emphasis, tone, pitch, or stress. And the precision of a strict syllable count mapped expressively onto the precision of imagism—the idea in a thing and the precise description of that thing distilled into an exactly counted verse line. Not only did syllabic verse avoid the patriotism and easy ideology of a national past, it also provided a kind of freedom to define its formal terms—not dissimilar to the fascination, for Pound, with Chinese and Japanese forms (often rendered syllabically in English).[21] Since true syllabics seemed nearly impossible, they allowed for a fantasy of poetic form that might avoid the dissolution into the boring regularity of the accentual-syllabic drum beat. Because syllabic verse demanded only speech stress as modulation it fit perfectly into the democratic ideologies of the "free verse" project as opposed to the necessity of understanding quantity or relying on an understanding of the correct placement of an accent to scan a line properly.[22] It seemed to be at once natural and perfectly strange—a constructed poetic form that would always draw attention to its constructedness. It could at once bear the mark of each individual poet and allow that poet to freely import quotations as long as these quotations could fit the syllable count. It wasn't that accentual meter needed to be actively suppressed, but because particular accentual-syllabic meters had become so ideologically weighted, syllabic verse could provide an alternative.

For Bridges, syllabic verse meant he could codify what he felt to be the "freest of free verse," and invent a verse line that could accommodate a variety of speech rhythms. Though he had failed in his attempts to convince the *New English Dictionary* editor Henry Bradley to help him reform English spelling, he continued to push for a clearer way to direct readers toward the correct pronunciation of his verses in his poetic experiments. Between 1912 and 1913, he began publishing in a new verse form he first called syllabic alexandrines (in an obvious reference to French verse but also referring to hexameters); he settled on the name "Neo-Miltonic syllabics." Bridges' first published foray into syllabic verse form occurred in the same year that he became Poet Laureate, 1913 (a year before *Des Imagistes* was published).[23] Bridges felt keenly that he had discovered a spontaneous new way to write his thoughts as freely as possible in a new verse form:

> Seeing then that to free the last foot it was only needed to forbid the terminal extrametrical syllable, and that Milton had, with so great effect, excluded it from every other place in his syllabic verse; it seemed to me that the next step that he would have taken (had he continued his work) would have been to forbid it also in the last place.
>
> I naturally wondered what the effect would be, and determined to experiment on it. One cannot originate a poem in an unknown

metre, for it is familiarity with the frame-work which invites the
words into their places, and this dilemma I happily remembered that
I had had for many years a poem in my head which had absolutely
refused to take any metrical form. Whenever I had tried to put it into
words the meter had ruined it. The whole poem was, so far as feeling
and picturing went, complete in my imagination, and I set to work
very readily on it, and with intense interest to see what would come.
I was delighted to find the old difficulty of metering it had vanished,
and it ran off quite spontaneously to its old title The Flowering Tree.[24]

What is important here is that Bridges feels that there was a poem he could feel and picture but that meter ruined it; the form he found counted only syllables. He signals the six syllable syllabic by indenting each alternate line, in case we miss the end rhyme that further emphasizes the six syllable lineation.[25] Do we have to see this poem to understand where and how to pause, how to count the syllables in each line? Here are the first few stanzas of "The Flowering Tree":

> What Fairy fann'd my dreams
>   while I slept in the sun?
> As if a flowering tree
>   were standing over me:
> Its young stem strong and lithe
>   went branching overhead
>
> And willowy sprays around
>   fell tasseling to the ground
> All with wild blossom gay
>   As is the cherry in May
> When her fresh flaunt of leaf
>   gives crowns of golden green.
>
> The sunlight was enmesh'd
>   in the shifting splendor
> And I saw through on high
>   to soft lakes of blue sky:

Though the syntax seems to be entirely archaic ("fann'd," "enmesh'd"), for Bridges, these apostrophed words were subtle directions intended to teach a reader how to both see and hear his new "unknown metre." How would a reader know how to read this? Bridges uses mostly monosyllabic words that could be ambiguously accented so as to avoid any regular pattern. "Its young stem strong and lithe," is audibly the same count (six) as "went branching overhead," and the visible line break between these help us *see* the parallel metrical structure so that the visual form of the syllabic line becomes a rhythmic guide (count to six) for the rest of the poem. And here we have the question of what counts *as* rhythm. Counting syllables hardly seems spontaneous, but if I heard enough syllabic lines, just as if I heard enough iambic pentameter lines, I might be able to "count" them seemingly spontaneously. That is the issue for Bridges—he works deeply inside of a form until it is not artificial to him (like he did with classical quantity) and then, even the fact that this line seems iambic becomes invisible to him. Could we read these lines without hearing them as iambic alexandrines? Almost every line is enjambed, so seeing *and then* perhaps hearing that these lines are written in six syllables as the rule might spur a reader to move—as one might in French verse—from "cher-ry in" to "cherryin" in order to keep the count of six syllables. And freed from a heavy stress (as on "**cher**ry") since stress is not the rule, the verse might elide quite a few sounds: "Flowering" could become "flowring," "tasseling" could become "tassling," and "willowy" could become "willwy." Again, we might not know how to elide these sounds—we still might not know—yet we are directed by our eyes to see that each line can only accommodate six syllables, and so we perhaps accommodate only six syllables on our pronunciation as well. This is, I think, what Bridges wanted to achieve.

The third syllabic experiment, "The West Front," is less rhythmically legible at first:

> No country know I so well
>   as this landscape of hell.
> Why bring you to my pain
>   these shadow'd effigys
> Of barb'd wire, riven trees,
>   the corpse-strewn blasted plain?

The elision of "know I" to make six syllables is hardly evident at the outset and it feels awkward to blur them. That odd grammar and the staccato of syllables of "corpse-strewn blasted plain" might alert a careful reader to the fact that Bridges is working hard to suppress what seems like an insistent accentual regularity. There is the obvious expressive meaning of the lost ability and will to count—the countless dead, the landscape that is only marked by "blast" and no order or, at least, not the old order. The first four lines seem faintly iambic according to the classical system (and indeed, he experimented quite a bit with the iambic hexameter in his translations of classical verse before moving on to the syllabic alexandrine) but by line five those monosyllables signal that we ought to perhaps be counting rather than stressing. What some careful readers might see as simply the influence of his collaboration with Gerard Manley Hopkins (a shadow of sprung rhythm, accents not separated by unstressed syllables), I see an evening out of accent across the lines. So that "barb'd wire, riven trees" and "corpse-strewn blasted plain" have a parallel rhythmic structure of five syllables, each one stressed but the penultimate. For this belabored reason, as well as the rhyme at the end of each line, the poem avoids simply devolving into broken alexandrines. Bridges calls these poems "sixes," and sets them off typographically in his books so we know that he's experimenting.

By the time he writes *The Testament of Beauty* in the late 1920s, he has worked out an explanation of the form and writes it in a phonetic spelling that normalizes his elision along the lines of what he argues Milton would have used. By 1929, that is, Bridges has enough clout to use his poem (which became a best-seller) to promote his system of phonetic spelling, thereby solving the problem of where and how to elide certain syllables so that the syllables in each line add up.[26] Bridges' publisher explains the new approach to spelling in an introduction he appended to the first edition, making sure that it was understood to be intentional—a guide to reading as well as an active attempt to normalize the author's hopes for reformed spelling. Bridges had been working on spelling reform since the turn of the century and he approached in a variety of official ways, most notably as a member and convener of the Society for Pure English before and during the First World War, and, also in 1929, as the author of the B.B.C.'s *Recommendations for Pronouncing Doubtful Words*. The publisher's note on the text states:

> The slight approach to a simplified spelling in this book is copied from the author's MS, which the printer was instructed to follow. The simplification, as will be seen, is mainly confined to two particulars, namely the final e and the doubled consonant. Since this e is invariable mute he would reserve it to distinguish heavy from light syllables: thus hav, not have, and liv, distinguished from live; and all the -ate, -ile, -ive, and -ite words can have their speech-values shown, as steril and pueril; and thus ther is no confusion there.

Indeed, ther is no confusion there. Bridges has built his syllabic meter and its proper pronunciation into the very spelling of his poem. He uses a "doubled consonant, which following the short vowel denotes its accentuation,"[27] stops rhyming (more or less) and uses far more multi-syllabic words, eliminating, also, most of the obvious caesurae. This final syllabic experiment is, I have been arguing, a combination of his few syllabic poems and his longer classical experiments like "Wintry Delights." That is, more than fifteen years after his more simple "sixes" were published, Bridges has advanced his understanding of syllabics into an entirely new domain. In order to read them clearly as "syllabics" at all, you must train yourself to master his rules of elision and pronunciation not unlike a poet translating from classical quantities must try to train him or herself to "hear" an imaginary equivalent quantity between Latin and English. The ability to "hear" the amount of time it would take to pronounce a syllable, by 1929, has become so complicated for Bridges that even looking at the first few lines of the poem it is not evident that the lines are "syllabic"—as in, have the same number of syllables in each line—at all.

> 'Twas late in my long journey, when I had clomb to where
> the path was narrowing and the company few,
> a glow of childlike wonder enthral'd me, as if my sense
> had come to a new birth purified, my mind enrapt
> re-awakening to a fresh initiation of life;
> with like surprise of joy as any man may know
> who rambling wide hath turn'd, resting on some hill-top
> to view the plain he has left, and see'th it now out-spredd
> mapp'd at his feet, a landscape so by beauty estranged
> he scarce wil ken familiar haunts, nor his own home,
> maybe, where far it lieth, small as a faded thought.

Though Bridges' "Poor Poll" appeared in 1923 (the same year as Eliot's *The Waste Land*) and was a more successful and less archaically constructed experiment in Neo-Miltonic syllabics, it is *The Testament of Beauty*'s 5,000 lines of sustained, subtle, controlled irregularity that have captured the attention of twentieth-century metrical historians. Yvor Winters, in *Primitivism and Decadence* calls *The Testament of Beauty* an attempt at a "carryall form" that could accommodate a variety of speech patterns. Winters, usually an admirer of Bridges, declares these lines as syllabic verses and good poetry a failure:

> The form is unrhymed duodecasyllables, dependent for their existence as such upon a definite and reasonably workable system of elision ... whether one attempts to scan the line accentually, or whether one follows Bridges and scans it syllabically (by all odds the preferable procedure, it successfully avoids the accentual-syllabic, avoids, that is, any pattern or norm underlying every syllable, so that, though one has constant change of movement from moment to moment, one has no variation, no precision of intention.[28]

Winters is, frankly, bored by the poem and believes it to be a failed attempt to combat the accentual fervor of Ezra Pound. What is lacking here in the long, four-book poem is "precision of intention." Though *The Testament of Beauty* has long been recognized as both the establishing and culminating poem in syllabic meter, it is, I think, the fact that we cannot all pronounce the poem in the same way that has prevented other poets from taking up the "Neo-Miltonic Syllabic" as a viable verse form. Mastering Bridges' rules for elision ends up complicating what is supposed to be a simplified scheme for pronunciation. Bridges merely adds to the long history of discourse about syllabic elision that begins as far back as the very first poet's handbooks.

3

The same years that Bridges was first experimenting with syllabics (1912–1913), the reputation of a now little known poet named Adelaide Crapsey (1878–1914) was on the rise. Crapsey was teaching at Smith College and perfecting the syllabic verse form called "the cinquain" that she had been working on since 1901. Crapsey's two books, *A Study in English Metrics* (Knopf, 1918) and a collection of poetry titled *Verse* (Manas, 1915; Knopf, 1922), were published posthumously. *Verse* was in its fourth edition by 1929, and Crapsey was the subject of a scholarly book by Llewellyn Jones in 1923. One of very few women to write a metrical treatise, Crapsey's interest in English metrics, like Bridges' interest, focused on the problem of pronunciation in print—the problem, in other words, of how to understand the history and future of English metrics without a stable system of pronunciation for the English language. She begins *A Study in English Metrics* with a series of questions reminiscent of Bridges' concerns:

> In the first place, even admitting it to be theoretically desirable, do we possess to-day a pronunciation sufficiently standardized to make possible the analysis of vocabularies on anything like the scale suggested? Variations in pronunciation are notorious. How can we be assured that a classification of the words in any given poem will represent the pronunciation of the poet who wrote? Is it not, rather, certain, that the analysis will depend upon the pronunciation of the critic who dissects, and that the results of the analysis will, consequently, vary with each new critic? And further, will not the difficulties be hopelessly increased when different historic periods are to be considered? No

attempt is made to minimize these difficulties, nor, for the present, to meet them in detail.[29]

If everyone understood the English language to be pronounced the same way, then there would be no controversy as to how to pronounce a poem. Whereas Bridges wanted to provide a verse form flexible enough to accommodate a variety of speech rhythms while still adhering to a general rule,[30] Crapsey wanted to think about syllables in the context of early linguistic science. Influenced by Paul Verrier, a French linguist and theorist of rhythm and meter, and E. W. Scripture, an American psychologist with a side interest in poetry and rhythm, Crapsey's obsession with syllables forms part of the new school of linguistic prosody emerging in the wake of Alexander Ellis, Daniel Jones, Henry Sweet, and their work on the study of phonetics. Crapsey's scientific investigations, then, are a crucial part of her development of the cinquain; a syllabic form that I see as a specimen and example of how the idea of counting syllables (however imprecise) hearkened toward a more direct and scientific treatment of the thing at the same time as it attempted to avoid the potential pathos (and variety) of accentual verse.

Though Crapsey's treatise was unfinished, her initial examination consisted of quantifying the number of mono-syllabic, disyllabic, and multi-syllabic words in nursery rhymes and poems. By examining words and counting the number of syllables based on her own estimate of their pronunciation, Crapsey argues that there are three types of verse ranging in structural complexity from mono-syllabic to poly-syllabic.[31] Her main thesis was that "an important application of phonetics to metrical problems lies in the study of phonetic word-structure." Crapsey presents her data in the form of 125 nursery rhymes (she calls this "experimental testing"), and analysis of poetry by Milton, Pope, Tennyson, Swinburne, Francis Thompson, and Maurice Hewlett. Though she is careful to avoid claims her data cannot support, Crapsey nonetheless presents her results in a series of tables that seem to argue for themselves. That is, we can clearly see from the table shown in Figure 1 that Milton uses a higher preponderance of polysyllables than does Pope. Bridges' failure to establish a new verse form via phonetic spelling as guidance becomes, to Crapsey's next generation, the attempt to fulfill the fantasy of objective reading, or a dream of pure analytics. And yet this pure analytics might be just as ideologically bound as the fantasy of a pure instinctually felt rhythm that pervades turn-of-the-century prosodic theories like those of George Saintsbury and Gummere. It is Crapsey who is doing the counting, after all.

But she knows that her own subjectivity is the problem with her

A STUDY IN ENGLISH METRICS 21

TABLE I.

MILTON	Total No. of words	Per cent Mono-dissyllabic	Per cent Polysyllabic
Paradise Lost I......	5,960	91.67	8.33
II......	7,917	92.24	7.75
III......	5,566	92.07	7.92
IV......	7,700	92.74	7.24
V......	6,804	92.01	7.99
VI......	6,773	90.95	9.03
VII......	4,774	91.40	8.58
VIII......	4,921	91.45	8.53
IX......	9,010	93.01	6.98
X......	8,370	91.74	8.24
XI......	6,859	92.48	7.50
XII......	4,930	91.78	8.21
Total..............	79,584	92.03	7.95
Samson Agonistes Dialogue..............	9,465	92.04	7.94
Choruses..............	3,427	90.92	9.08
Total..............	12,892	91.75	8.23

TABLE II.

POPE	Total No. of words	Per cent Mono-dissyllabic	Per cent Polysyllabic
Essay on Criticism......	5,744	94.91	5.08
The Rape of the Lock...	6,149	94.71	5.28
Elegy—Unfortunate Lady	652	95.86	4.14
Essay on Man I......	2,288	94.32	5.68
II......	2,251	94.32	5.68
III......	2,481	94.43	5.56
IV......	3,141	95.54	4.46
Total..............	10,161	94.72	5.27
Epistle to Dr. Arbuthnot	3,353	95.91	4.09

FIGURE 1. Table from Adelaide Crapsey's *A Study in English Metrics*, 1918.

method. As in almost all other prosodic manuals, Crapsey spends time going through her main prosodic predecessors (George Saintsbury, T. S. Omond) before asserting "what has now become apparent is that we soon reach . . . the limits of possible analysis based on simple observation 'by ear' or by our 'sense' of rhythm. The delicate and accurate study of the rhythmic groups of verse must, it is seen, be carried on by means of laboratory experiment."[32] Would Crapsey have seen her own syllabic "cinquains" as a rhythmic group or were they resistant to being read "by ear" or by a "sense" of rhythm?

Crapsey presents an undeniably scientific study of prosody by eschewing entirely the instinctual rhythmic discourse that pervades, say, Alice Meynell's 1893 *The Rhythm of Life*, in which Meynell elaborates a theory of rhythm relating to the periodicity of the planets, the tides, "a sun's revolutions and the rhythmic pangs of maternity."[33] If, for Meynell, rhythm is natural and embodied and for Bridges, syllabic verse—and any verse form—can be studied long enough so as to become easily evident to the practitioner and reader, for Crapsey rhythm must be considered as part of a more rigorous science. The posthumous introductions to her poems are careful to walk the line between the discourse of mere over-feeling poetess and an accomplished metrist conversant and participating in the broader (largely male) prosodic discourse of the age. Jean Webster describes Crapsey's poems in the preface to *Verse* as "of gossamer delicacy and finish, [and] are the stronger for the technical knowledge behind them. Likewise, her technical work possessed the more vigor because it was not the result of mere theoretical analysis, but also of the first-hand knowledge gained through her own creative achievement."[34] Webster describes Crapsey's study in metrics as "astoundingly objective and coldly unreflective of any emotional mood, so her own poems were at the other extreme, astoundingly subjective and descriptive of a mental state that found expression in no other form." Despite the incomprehensibility of her metrical theories, "the verse form which she calls "Cinquain" [that] she originated herself" Webster concludes, was incredibly comprehensible to the lay reader. Carl Sandburg, for one, championed the form of the cinquain—a five line syllabic form defined as having two, four, six, eight, and two syllables as a rule. Though overshadowed in literary history by Pound's experiments with Chinese ideograms or the poetry emerging out of imagism and its various schools (from Pound to Amy Lowell to William Carlos Williams), Crapsey's syllabic form was nonetheless a prescient example for many of the main tenets of imagism.[35] Beginning in the 1920s, a number of scholars began to trace her cinquains directly to Japanese sources.[36] Webster writes, "she reduces an idea to its very lowest terms—and presents it in a single sharp impression." Though Crapsey passed away the same year that *Des Imagistes* was published, it is clear that her interest in linguistic prosody in which words can and should be analyzed by constituent parts, and the idea that syllables themselves could convey an idea with a kind of simplicity all led to her development of her singular syllabic verse form.

Louis Untermeyer recognized Crapsey's debt to Japanese poetics; he published three of her poems in his 1919 *Modern American Poetry*.[37] Two of them were cinquains and one, "On Seeing Weather Beaten Trees," was a two-line poem in ten-syllable meter:

> Is it as plainly in our living shown,
> By slant and twist, which way the wind hath blown?

In all three poems she shows both her interest in and her mastery of syllabic meters; Untermeyer mythologizes that Crapsey began to write after a breakdown (contrary to the dating that Jean Webster provides for her cinquains in the *Miscellany*). "[T]hough she became instructor in Poetics at Smith College in 1911, the burden was too great for her. Prior to this time she had written little verse, her chief work being an analysis of English metrics . . . . In 1913, after her breakdown, she began to write those brief lines which, like some of Emily Dickinson's, are so precise and poignant. She was particularly happy in her 'Cinquains,' a form that she originated. These five-line stanzas in the strictest possible structure . . . doubtless owe something to the Japanese *hokku*, but Adelaide Crapsey saturated them with her own fragile loveliness."[38]

Here is one of her most well known cinquains, published in 1915 and 1922 but supposedly written in 1901.

> Niagara
> *Seen on a night in November*
>
> How frail
> Above the bulk
> Of crashing water hangs,
> Autumnal, evanescent, wan,
> The moon.

As we can see, the verse form as Crapsey first used it was not simply syllabic but also iambic. We have to see it (just as we are reading the record of "seeing" Niagara at a particular time) to apprehend the form. Two and four and six and eight and two syllable lines provide a variation on the quintain stanza (another quintain stanza of variable line length is the limerick, for example). The poems (without the title) are twenty-two precise syllables long. Like most imagist poetry the cinquain is clear and concise, but, like Williams's control in "The Red Wheelbarrow," the mastery of this poem is in its line breaks. "Frail," "bulk," "hangs," "wan," "moon": these are words that make an image of a waterfall in a nearly concrete example, cascading down the increasing syllable count with the moon impossibly still below—a reflection in a pool. (The "above" in line two is another prepositional pun.) The poem captures both movement and stillness, action and pause. And the poem displays the conflict between stillness and action; the crashing water "hangs" expressively in the middlemost line as if the waterfall were frozen by a trick of inverted syntax. It would be easy to rattle these off like so much bad haiku and, indeed, schoolchildren today do just that. But Crapsey, like Marianne Moore and William Carlos Williams, was paying attention to the control of a poem's movement across a line of variable syllable length: a new way of counting and a new way of figuring stillness and action at once in a poem.

4

Paul Ramsay, in 1971, characterized William Carlos William's metrical practice as dividing his language into "bright small bundles, or fragments, as a way of saying 'Look! At what is here to be seen (felt, heard).'"[39] The cinquain is certainly a bright small bundle of concision. Robert Beum, the theorist of syllabic verse I quoted at the beginning of this essay, corresponded with Williams for years; Mariani writes that "what Williams stressed in [his] letters to Beum was the need for American poetry to move decisively away from a prosody of stress and toward a 'prosody of the measurement of time,' (i.e., toward the qualitative sonorities of a Robert Bridges as demonstrated in *The Testament of Beauty* and away from what he called the vulgarities of Hopkins' "constipated" sprung rhythms)."[40] Natalie Gerber's recent work shows the veracity with which he rejected the "rigidity of the poetic foot"[41] and Mariani's important essay on metrical innovation before and around *Paterson*[42] shows how Williams presented his poetics in his poems more effectively than in his discourse about his poetry. Nonetheless Williams mentions syllables in a few key places. In 1954, he published "On Measure: An Essay of Cid Corman" in *Origin* magazine and states: "Verse—we'd better not speak of poetry lest we become confused—verse has always been associated in men's minds with 'measure,' i.e. with mathematics. In scanning any piece of verse, you 'count' the syllables. Let's not speak either of rhythm, an aimless sort of thing without precise meaning of any sort. But measure implies something that can be measured."[43] Later in the essay, he closes by saying "Without measure we are lost. But we have lost even the ability to count."[44] His discussion of the "variable foot" in this essay and elsewhere has long puzzled scholars; I will not attempt to tease it out here. What I will argue, however, is that the math of Williams' poetry, in 1922, should be considered as part of the trajectory of syllabic prosody I have outlined in England and America, despite Williams' own equivocation about counting by syllables between 1913 and 1935.

In 1922, Williams published *Spring and All* and in it, that ubiquitous poem about the red wheelbarrow. I wondered what would happen if this poem were an experiment in syllabics rather than the quintessential imagist poem. Recall that the syllables are 4/2, 3/2, 3/2, and 4/2. That, in itself, seems enough to show that Williams is counting and showing us how to count, participating in and continuous with the discourse about syllables as particular units of poetic rhythm as opposed to syllables as bearers of accent. Williams is known for setting up a formal expectation and then riffing on it; here, he sets up his syllabic stanza, retreats from it, repeats the retreat, and then repeats the initial syllabic stanza again in the end. We could read this as two "sixes" divided by two "fives," in any number of mathematical combinations:

So much depends
upon

a red wheel
barrow

glazed with rain
water

beside the white
chickens

Williams uses line breaks and spacing to direct the reader to pause just as Bridges used line breaks and elision to do the same. But what if the poem could be restructured even more severely? The total number of syllables was twenty-two. I found the original version of the poem in the facsimile edition "Spring and All," before editors—and Williams, retitled the poem to simply "The Red Wheelbarrow." There was no denying the math there—the poem appears in the twenty-second section, as if XXII were its title. Just as Crapsey's system for syllables reaches for pure analytics, so, too, does Williams's title "XXII" reach toward the fantasy of prosody as mathematics; the mathematical function becomes the title, the figure of meter at once a move back to the Roman numeral while simultaneously letting go of certain ambitions and toward other, more precise metrical ambitions. Williams may indeed have had occasion to come across Crapsey's 1915 volume *Verse,* or had seen them in Untermeyer's 1919 anthology, in *The Century Magazine* (which printed a cinquain in 1916), or any of a wide number of anthologies that reprinted her poems and thought about the form, or, even more likely, tracked her down after seeing her name again and again in a wide array of reviews.[45] Crapsey's literary celebrity between 1914 and 1922 by far exceeded Williams', and the "cinquain," was a popular form for imitations. Indeed, "XXII," convinces me to think more capaciously about how Williams' hope for prosody "as a measurement of time" was part of the same concern that Bridges and Crapsey brought to their experiments. The only way I could believe in an alternate syllabic form for "XXII," then, was to see it:

So much
depends upon
a red wheel barrow glazed
with rain water beside the white
chickens

I'd like to close with that poem, equally, in my mind, sacrilegious and curious, but I'd also quickly like to gesture to what we lose in this visual transformation; we lose what Hugh Kenner calls the words "disassociated to their molecules" in the original poem,[46] or what John Hollander describes as the cutting of "wheel barrow" and "rain water" into constituents. That is, *"with the implication that they are phenomenological constituents as well. The wheel plus the barrow equals the wheelbarrow, and in the freshness of light after the rain (it is this kind of light which the poem is about, although never mentioned directly), things seem to lose their compounded properties."*[47] Williams "'etymologizes' his compounds into their prior phenomena." But Williams does more than etymologize the compounded images; he makes the words into visible, countable syllables. Williams created a rhythmic picture for the ear and the eye made of these phenomenological constituents that, due to our focus on other stories about modernist form, we have, as Williams himself laments, lost our ability to count.

Notes

1. Robert Beum, "Syllabic Verse in English," *Prairie Schooner* 31 (Fall 1957): 262.
2. See the following for other relevant work on Williams' meter.: Stephen Cushman, *William Carlos Williams and the Meaning of Measure*; New Haven, Conn.: Yale Univer-

sity Press, 1985; Paul Ramsay, "William Carlos Williams as Metrist: Theory and Practice," *Journal of Modern Literature* 1, no. 4 (May 1971): 578–92; Mary Ellen Solt, "William Carlos Williams: Idiom and Structure," *The Massachusetts Review* 3, no. 2 (Winter 1962): 304–18; Kingsley A. Weatherhead, "William Carlos Williams: Prose, Form, and Measure," *ELH* 33, no. 1 (March 1966): 118–31; Philip Wheelwright, *Metaphor and Reality* (Bloomington: Indiana University Press, 1962), 159–61. Williams mentions syllables in several essays and letters, including but not limited to "Marianne Moore," repr. in *Imaginations* (New York: New Directions, 1970), 308–18; Letter to Marianne Moore, March 23, 1921, in *The Selected Letters of William Carlos Williams*, ed. John C. Thirlwall (New York: McDowell, Obolensky, 1957): 52–53; Letter to Kenneth Burke, March 23, 1921 and Letter to Kenneth Burke, July 19, 1955 in *The Humane Particulars: The Collected Letters of William Carlos Williams and Kenneth Burke*, ed. James H. East (Columbia: University of South Carolina Press, 2003): 10.v; "Federico Garcia Lorca," *The Kenyon Review* 1, no. 2 (Spring 1939): 148–58; *The Autobiography of William Carlos Williams* (New York: New Directions, 1967), 146; *Paterson,* ed. Christopher MacGowan(New York: New Directions, 1992); "On Measure—Statement for Cid Corman," repr. in *Selected Essays of William Carlos Williams* (New York: Random House, 1954), 337–40; Letter to Richard Eberhart, May 23, 1954, in *The Selected Letters*, 325-6; "Green Eyes" (1958) and "The Gossips" (1962), *The Collected Poems of William Carlos Williams*, vol. 2, *1939–1962* (New York: New Directions, 1988), 349, 415; "Measure—a loosely assembled essay on poetic measure," *Spectrum,* 3, no. 3 (Fall 1959); "Free Verse," *Encyclopedia of Poetry and Poetics,* ed. Alex Preminger (Princeton, N.J.: Princeton University Press, 1965), 288–90.

3. Lewis Turco, *The Book of Forms: A Handbook of Poetics: Including Odd and Invented Forms* (Hanover, N.H.: University Press of New England, 1986), 17.

4. Ibid.

5. Timothy Steele, from "Prosody for 21st Century Poets" on poets.org. See also Steele, *Missing Measures: Modern Poetry and the Revolt Against Meter* (Fayetteville: University of Arkansas Press, 1990).

6. From William Carlos Williams, "Speech Rhythms," quoted in Mike Weaver, *William Carlos Williams: The American Background* (Cambridge: Cambridge University Press, 1971), 82–83.

7. Ibid.

8. Ibid.

9. M. J. Duffel, T. V. F. Brogan, and R. B. Shaw, "Syllabic Verse," *Encyclopedia of Poetry and Poetics*, 1388–90.

10. Aside from some debatable Renaissance examples, the practice is a modern one, pioneered by Robert Bridges in the late nineteenth and early twentieth centuries. Bridges wrote nearly 5,000 lines of syllabic alexandrines, especially for New Verse (1925) and The Testament of Beauty (1929), the longest syllabic-verse poem in the language. In the 1910s, Adelaide Crapsey invented the cinquain. Beginning in the same decade Marianne Moore, the American poet best known for the practice, wrote poems in elaborate syllabic stanzas featuring wide variations in line length, complex patterns of rhyme or half rhyme, and conspicuous use of prose rhythms.

11. Robert Bridges, *The Testament of Beauty* (Oxford: Clarendon Press, 1929).

12. Joshua Steele, *Prosodia Rationalis; or, an Essay towards establishing the Melody and Measure of Speech, to be expressed and perpetuated by Peculiar Symbols* (London: J. Nichols, 1775); Sidney Lanier, *The Science of English Verse* (New York: Charles Scribner, 1880, 1908, 1920). T. S. Omond, *A Study of Metre* (London: Grant Richards, 1903).

13. Coventry Patmore. *Amelia, Tamerton church-tower, etc., with Prefatory study on English metrical law* (London: G. Bell and Sons, 1878).

14. For a detailed account of the impact of scientific machinery on the study of prosody, see Jason David Hall, "Materializing Meter: Physiology, Psychology, Prosody," *Victorian Poetics* 49, no. 2 (Summer 2011), 179–97.

15. William Carlos Williams himself recognized the historical nature of the issue, citing Campion and Chapman in his 1958 essay "Measure—a loosely assembled essay on poetic measure."

16. Saussure was lecturing in Geneva between 1906 and 1911 though the *cours de linguistic générale* was not published until 1916. *OED*: The first use of the term *phonème* is normally attributed to the French linguist Dufriche-Desgenettes (1873); it was subsequently used by F. de Saussure (*Mémoire* [1878/1879]), and hence (as German *Phonem*) by M. Kruszewski (*Über die Lautabwechslung* [1881]) (14–15). Daniel Jones acknowledges that between 1914 and 1922 "much attention has been given recently to the grouping of sounds into phonemes" (preface, *An Outline of English Phonetics* [Leipzig: B.G. Teubner, 1922]). My larger project examines the cross-currents between linguistic theories of phonemic sound groups, anthropological theories of rhythm, and historical prosody in Anglo-American verse.

17. "There's nothing sentimental about a machine, and: A poem is a small (or large) machine made of words. When I say there's nothing sentimental about a poem I mean that there can be no part, as in any other machine, that is redundant. Prose may carry a load of ill-defined matter like a ship. But poetry is the machine which drives it, pruned to a perfect economy." This is on the same page as "A Sort of Song" in his introduction to the 1944 *The Wedge*, and reprinted in *Paterson. The Collected Poems of William Carlos Williams*, vol. 2, *1939–1962* (New York: New Directions, 1988).

18. Rules about elision in appear in the earliest English prosodic handbooks, like Sir Edward Bysshe's *The Art of English Poetry*, 1702, who copied his handbook from the 1663 *Quatre Traites de Poësies, Latine, Françoise, Italienne, et Espagnole* by Claude Lancelot. Cf. Dwight Culler's "Edward Bysshe and the Poet's Handbook" *PMLA* 63, no. 3 (September 1948), 858–85. Bysshe was widely reprinted in Tom Hood's *Practical Guide to English Versification* and *The Rhymester* throughout the nineteenth century.

19. In his 1922 essay "Harum-Scarum: An Essay on Free Verse" printed concurrently in *North American Review* and *London Mercury*, Bridges writes "I wish to confine myself to English Free Verse, one cannot treat the subject at all without reference to French vers libre; because in France the revolt against the traditional form is in its threats and promises very similar to our own, and the theory of it has been more intelligently handled and analyzed there than by English critics, the best of whom borrow their reasonings, so far as I can find, from the French." Bridges, "Humdrum and Harum-Scarum." *North American Review* and *London Mercury* (1922). repr. in *Collected Essays*, no. 2; See also, Donald Stanford, *Robert Bridges and the Free Verse Rebellion* in *Journal of Modern Literature* 2, no. 1: 19–32; T.M. Kelshall, *Robert Bridges, Poet Laureate* (London: Robert Scott, 1938); John Sparrow, *Robert Bridges* (London: Longmans, Green & Co. 1962); William Johnson Stone, *On the use of Classical Metres in English* (London: Henry Frowde, 1899). Edward Thompson, *Robert Bridges 1844–1930* (Oxford: Oxford University Press, 1944); R. C. Trevelyan, "Prosody and the Poet Laureate," *The New Statesman* 24, London, December 13, 1924. 296–98.

20. Frances Barton Gummere, *The Beginnings of Poetry* (New York: Macmillan, 1901).

21. There are many accounts of Pound's fascination with Japanese hokku, most notably Hugh Kenner's observation that *The Pisan Cantos* "are full of hokku." *The Poetry of Ezra Pound* (New York: New Directions, 1951; repr., Lincoln: University of Nebraska Press, 1985), 63. See also references to Pound in Earl Miner, *The Japanese Tradition in British and American Literature*, 2nd ed. (Princeton, N.J.: Princeton University Press, 1958; rev., 1966; repr., Westport, Conn.: Greenwood, 1976); and Miner "Pound, Haiku, and the Image," *Hudson Review* 9 (1956–57): 570–84. For these and many other references I am grateful to http://themargins.net/bibliography.html.

22. See Erin Kappeler, "Shaping Free Verse: American Prosody and Poetics 1880-1920," (Ph.D. diss, Tufts University, 2014); Paul Ramsay, "Free Verse: Some Steps toward Definition," *Studies in Philology*, 65, no. 1 (January 1968): 98-108; "Free Verse," *Encyclopedia of Poetry and Poetics*, ed. Alex Preminger (Princeton, N.J.: Princeton University Press, 1965), 288–90.

23. Donald Stanford notes "'The West Front' was first published in *October and Other Poems*, 1920. The other eleven poems in neo-Miltonic syllabics, all of which appeared in *The Tapestry*, privately printed in London in 1925, with dates of composition are: 'The Flowering Tree' (1913), 'Noel: Christmas Eve' (1913), 'In der Fremde' (1913), 'Epitaph: Hubert Hastings Parry' (1920), 'The Tapestry' (1921), 'Kate's Mother' (1921), 'The College Garden' (1921), 'The Psalm' (1921) and 'Como se Quando' (1921)." Stanford *In the Classic Mode: The Achievement of Robert Bridges* (Newark: University of Delaware Press, 1978), 319.

24. "New Verse," in *The Collected Essays, Papers, of Robert Bridges, 1927-1936* (Oxford: Oxford University Press).

25. Bridges often used indentation, smaller typesetting, or various fonts to indicate metrical experiments in his published work.

26. Letter to Bridges, 1, February 1930: ". . . been reading and thinking about *The Testament of Beauty* a good deal in the last month. . . The metre eases me, flies me along, I find no trouble here, nor with the spelling, and I get such varied lovelinesses. . . " (*Selected Letters of E. M. Forster*, vol. 2, *1921–1970* (Cambridge, Mass.: Belknap Press), 89.

27. The Publisher's Note continues: "Inconsistencies (except for possible oversights such as shear for sheer in IV. 241 and ethic for ethick in IV. 353) are intentional, any rule being stayed at the point where it would needlessly distract the reader: thus nature appears in two spellings, of which the explanation is that the final syllable (whether the word be pronounced as may be indicated by the spelling nat-ur, or by nacher as recognized by our Southern-English authorities) is always light and unaccented; but since the syllable tur has an uncertain value and is very offensive to the eye, the common full spelling, ture, is always maintaind, except in those places where it suffers liquid synaloepha in the prosody, where the omission of the e guides the eye to the easy reading of the rhythm: and the author would explain that the use of –eth for the 3rd per. sing. of verbs is not an archaic fancy, but a practical advantage, indispensable to him, not only for its syllabic lightness, but because by distinguishing verbs from the identical substantives, it sharpens the rhetoric and often liberates the syntax."

28. Winters continues: "It has certain advantages, possibly, for the purpose to which it is put in the *Testament of Beauty* over the heavily accented meter of Pound: its very monotony gives it a certain coherence, the coherence, however, merely of undefined intention, yet its freedom from the constant recurrence of the heavy measuring ac-

cent does not commit it so closely to a particular range of feeling; but if Pound's best *Cantos*, the first six or seven, are considered, the meter of Bridges is far less interesting in itself. This is curious, for Bridges, in general, is incomparably the better metrist." He goes on to praise Bridges' daughter, Elizabeth Daryush, for a far subtler and more successful execution of syllabics in her poem "Still-Life." Yvor Winters, *Primitivism and Decadence: A Study of American Experimental Poetry* (New York: Arrow Editions, 1937), 139–40.

29. Adelaide Crapsey, *A Study in English Metrics* (New York: Knopf, 1918), 16.

30. And he does this *explicitly* in "Poor Poll," in which his macaronic verse in Neo-Miltonic syllabics shows that he can use Greek, Latin, Italian, German, French, *and* English. Cf. Meredith Martin, *The Rise and Fall of Meter* (Princeton, N.J.: Princeton University Press, 2012).

31. Though her writing style in this treatise is not part of my argument, her prose avoids any discussion of aesthetics, nor does it repeat any of the broad naturalizing or patriotic claims about rhythm that were conventional in many prosody handbooks. Crapsey expands in as detached and objective a tone as she can, marshaling pure statistics: "purely, or mainly, mono-dyssyllabic, *i.e.,* showing a characteristic occurrence of polysyllables running from 0 to 2%"; "a type of medium structural complexity *i.e.* showing a characteristic occurrence of polysyllables running from about 3% to about 5.5%, with a tendency to drop towards 2% and to rise towards 6&"; and "a type of extreme structural complexity, *i.e.,* showing a characteristic occurrence of polysyllables running from about 7% to about 8.5%, with a tendency to drop towards 6% and to rise toward 9.5% (or 10%)." *Note:* The term "polysyllable is used to include all words over two syllables in length" (7–8).

32. Crapsey, *A Study in English Metrics*, 34.

33. Meynell elaborates: "Nevertheless, before it is too late, let me assert that though nature is not always clearly and obviously made to man's measure, he is yet the unit by which she is measurable. The proportion may be far to seek at times, but the proportion is there." Alice Meynell, *The Rhythm of Life and Other Essays* (Copeland and Day: Boston, 1896), 6.

34. Jean Webster, preface to Adelaide Crapsey's *Verse* (Rochester, N.Y., Manas, 1915).

35. Webster dates her cinquains, including "Niagara," to 1901. "The Witch" appeared in *Century Magazine*.

36. Torao Taketomo, "American Imitations of Japanese Poetry," *The Nation* 110: 70–72; Royall Snow, "Marriage with the East," *New Republic* 27 (1921): 138–40; Josef Washington Hall, "The Pacific-Asian Influence on the Poets of the United States," *Anthology of Magazine Verse* (1926): 150–71; H. L. Seaver, "The Asian Lyric and English Literature," in *Essays in Memory of Barrett Wendell* (1926; repr., New York: Russell, 1967). I am grateful to David Ewick's invaluable website *Japonisme, Orientalism, Modernism: A Bibliography of Japan in English Language Verse of the Early 20th Century*; for this invaluable reference, see http://themargins.net/bibliography.html.

37. Triad

> These be
> Three silent things:
> The falling snow . . . the hour
> Before the dawn . . . the mouth of one
> Just dead.

The Warning

Just now,
Out of the strange
Still dusk ... as strange, as still ...
A white moth flew. Why am I grown
So cold?

38. Louis Untermeyer, ed., *Modern American Poetry* (New York: Harcourt, Brace and Howe, 1919), 206.

39. Paul Ramsay, "William Carlos Williams as Metrist," 582.

40. Paul Mariani, *William Carlos Williams: A New World Naked* (McGraw-Hill: New York, 1981), 598. Williams: "In the work of the poem, the joining of phrases, the trimming away of connectives, the joining of stone to stone, as a Greek column was joined, as the Incans joined their great wall—there is virtue. [Pound] calls it virtue, excellence—and continues to say that virtue is timely. It pays off in life in behavior, in poems—as it would pay off in many another thing, if we could learn from our poets." Mariani notes that Williams named a poem inspired by Robert Bridges's *Testament of Beauty* the "Testament to Perpetual Action" (597).

41. *Selected Essays of William Carlos Williams* (New York: New Directions, 1969), 289. See, for example, *Selected Letters*, 334–35; and Williams' unpublished 1913 essay "Speech Rhythms," reproduced in its entirety in Weaver, *The American Background*, 82–83. From Natalie Gerber, "Moving Against the Measure: Prosody in a Post-Metrical Age" (Ph.D.diss., University of California, Berkeley, 2001).

42. Paul Mariani, "The Poem as a Field of Action: Guerilla Tactics in *Paterson*," *The Iowa Review* 7, no. 4 (Fall 1976).

43. William Carlos Williams, "On Measure—Statement for Cid Corman," in *Selected Essays of William Carlos Williams* (Random House: New York, 1954), 337.

44. Ibid., 340.

45. Crapsey's poems appeared posthumously in William Stanley Braithwaite's *Anthology of Magazine Verse* (1916), and *Poetic Year for 1916: A Critical Anthology*; Alfred Kreymborg's *Others, An Anthology of New Verse* (1916); and *Selections from American Literature*, part 2, ed. Leonidas Warren Payne. The 1915 *Verse* was reviewed in *The Century* 91: 511; *Publisher's Weekly* 95, part 1, 300, *The Others* 1, no. 6, and 3, no. 6: 166; *The Independent* 86–87:144; *Harper's Weekly* 62: 62; the second edition (1922) was reviewed in *The New Republic* 33: 258; and Crapsey appeared in Jay Broadus Hubbell's *An Introduction to Poetry* (New York: Macmillan, 1922), 194.

46. Hugh Kenner, *A Homemade World: The American Modernist Writers* (Baltimore: Johns Hopkins University Press, 1989), 59.

47. John Hollander, *Vision and Resonance: Two Senses of Poetic Form* (New Haven, Conn.: Yale University Press, 1975).

Fictions of Rhythm

Beyond Meaning: Differing Fates of Some Modernist Poets' Investments of Belief in Sounds

Natalie Gerber

In an essay entitled "The 'Final Finding of the Ear': Wallace Stevens' Modernist Soundscapes," Peter Middleton argues that "[s]ound is secondary" and noncognitive and finds Stevens' and other modernist American poets' investment of belief in sound to be "utopian."[1] Of course, such investment was not limited to the American modernists. The romantic poet William Wordsworth speaks of the "power in sound / To breathe an elevated mood,"[2] and fellow romantic Samuel Taylor Coleridge qualifies a legitimate poem as one that, "like the path of sound through the air,"[3] carries the reader forward. Likewise, the nineteenth-century French Symbolist poet Stéphane Mallarmé aspired toward a musicalized language for poetry that would make the poet capable "not just of expressing oneself but of modulating oneself as one chooses."[4] Paul Valéry, Stevens' contemporary, believed, as Lisa Goldfarb writes, that "the poet must perceive the primacy of sound over meaning."[5] Hence American modernist poets like Robert Frost, Wallace Stevens, and William Carlos Williams could not claim uniqueness but rather obstreperous insistence upon both the primacy of sound and its value beyond the semantic.

These poets' willingness to believe that linguistic sound offers transparent access to our innermost thoughts, feelings, and emotions ought to be startling;[6] it certainly has been challenged and problematized by scholars pointing to both the constructed and the socially, historically, and politically situated contexts that produce both the poem and the poet's subjectivity.[7] Yet cognitive research proves that rich phonological representations are activated early in our processing of silent reading;[8] this so counters Peter Middleton's assertions about the nature of sound that we should reconsider these poets' appeal to prosody as a primary ground as perhaps not merely utopian or impressionistic, even if we recognize their statements to exaggerate the importance of sound over meaning.[9] While a full correlation of psycholinguistic findings in relation to some modernist poets' investments of belief in sound will have to wait for another essay, this one will prepare that ground by disentangling competing claims regarding sound among three particular American modernists (Stevens, Williams, and, especially, Robert Frost) and by offering a novel solution why Frost's claims have fared worse than these contemporaries', all of which are equally predicated upon the sound structure of a poem.

Stevens and Frost

As two preeminent American modernists writing metrical verse, Stevens and Frost might well share a limited legacy of formal innovation; and yet Stevens has been granted greater stature as a prosodic innovator and theorist. It is tempting to attribute this difference in reception to Frost's adamant rejection of newer modes of poetic rhythm, while Stevens practices free verse alongside metrical composition. Nonetheless, the difference is more likely attributable to the specific nature of their prosodic innovations, which differ significantly in the level of phonological representation involved, a difference that matters to the reception of their legacy.

As in his well-known remark in "The Noble Rider and the Sound of Words," Stevens' comments about sound focus on the sounds of individual words: "Above everything else, poetry is words; and . . . words, above everything else, are, in poetry, sounds."[10] Rarely, if at all, does he speak of larger linguistic units, such as the phrase, sentence, or line. Throughout Stevens' letters and his prose, we find statements such as "I like words to sound wrong,"[11] or "A variation between the sound of words in one age and the sound of words in another age is an instance of the pressure of reality."[12]

Likewise, as I have shown elsewhere,[13] much of Stevens' early and mid-career metrical innovations turn upon an inventive yet strictly rule-governed play with lexical stress, that is, with how words sound depending upon their linguistic, syntactic, and, of course, metrical environments. Stevens' placement of words into the meter in such a way that they "sound wrong"—i.e., altered from normative realizations—displays quite a sophisticated awareness of factors influencing lexical phonology; these run the gamut from historical pronunciations and cross-linguistic difference (particularly between French and English) to quite supple realizations of

English stress rules (for lexical, compound, and phrasal stress). For example, when Stevens writes,

```
              /   x   \
Of ocean, perfected in indolence                      (CPP, 85)
w  s w       s  w  s  w   s  w s
```

```
            /    x   \
More exquisite than any tumbling verse                (CPP, 29)
w    s  w  s      w   s  w  s    w   w
```

he is echoing usages of an earlier age, as in the second line of Robert Herrick's couplet from 1647, and John Clare's line from 1819:

```
Gods Grace deserves here to be daily fed,
                            /   x   \
That, thus increast, it might be perfected.   (Robert Herrick)
w     s     w    s    w   s    w  s
```

```
                      /    x   \
I dropt me down with exquisite delight        (John Clare)
w   s    w    s   w     s  w  s   w s
```

And when Stevens writes lines like those below, he is drawing on the use of French stress patterns, to motivate an alternate pronunciation:

```
                         \   x   /
Attach. It seemed haphazard *denouement*¹⁴            (CPP, 33)
w  s    w  s       w  s  w      s  w   s
```

```
           /    x   \
A vital, linear ambiance. The flare¹⁵                 (CPP, 327)
w  s w   s   w    s  w  s      w   s
```

In stark contrast, the next examples display Stevens self-consciously forcing a bungled Anglicization of a foreign word, a rhythmic tactic that contributes to the comic portraiture of the young poet:

```
When amorists grow bald, then *amours* shrink          (CPP, 12)
w    s w s     w    s     w    s  w       s
```

```
                          /
One eats one paté, even of salt, quotha                (CPP, 22)
w    s    w   s w   s  w   s      w   s
```

```
Sepulchral señors, bibbling pale mescal,          (CPP, 31)
  w s    w    s  w      s    w     s  w  s
```

Supple auditor of French that he is, Stevens' use of the rhythm rule to retract stress from the second syllable of *amour* to the first to avoid a stress clash with *shrink* displays a virtuosic multilingual wit, one echoed in the prior examples.

Were these examples not enough, one could examine Stevens' existential play with the stresslessness of nonlexical words to unmoor any certain meaning, and thus destabilize what otherwise ought to be a triumphant declaration: for example, in response to the question "What am I to believe?" in "Notes Toward a Supreme Fiction," the twelve-syllable, entirely nonlexical iambic-pentameter line "I have not but I am and as I am, I am"[16] winkingly refuses our desire to impose certain *iambs* and shapes on belief. Or we could look to evidence in "Sea Surface Full of Clouds" of Stevens' masterly orchestration of the full variety of circumstances that produce disyllabic words with initial stress. As the poem renders its serial, modulating impressions of the sea "In that November off Tehuantepec," the image brought to mind shifts from "rosy" to "chop-house," "porcelain," "musky," and, finally, "Chinese chocolate," as in "And made one think of chop-house chocolate."[17] Thus, within the metrical baseline "And máde one thínk of [/ x] chócoláte," we find activated supple rules for "'fitting . . . a selection of the real language of man in a state of vivid sensation'" to the meter:[18] these range from phonological rules governing segments (i.e., consideration of vowel length and its influence on stress [e.g., the underlying vowel length and lexical rhythm of *rosy* and *musky* are comparable to the vowel length and lexical rhythm of *Mary*, not *Marie*] and the reduction of sonorant sequences [*porcelain*]), to stress rules involving larger entities (e.g., compound stress [*chop-house*] and the rhythm rule, whose domain is the phrase [*Chinese* chocolate]).

In summary, we can isolate the word as a significant locus of Stevens' innovative metrical effects, discerning how his virtuosic meter intensifies our awareness of the variable rhythms that come from words' shifting relationships in linguistic context, grammar, syntax, and metrical placement.

In contrast with this exacting play with words by Stevens, Robert Frost treats words as plastic elements within larger compositional units, rather than individual lexical entities. Frost once remarked, "The strain of rhyming is less since I came to see words as phrase-ends to countless phrases just as the syllables *ly, ing,* and *ation* are word-ends to countless words."[19] Clearly, Frost came to regard words, for poetic purposes, as functionally equivalent to morphological adjuncts in language—they may be essential, but they are not the base.

That base, for Frost, lies in larger prosodic units like phrases and, especially, sentences, which Frost presents as the domain generative of meaning: "I shall show the sentence sound saying all that the sentence conveys with little or no help from the meaning of the words."[20] Indeed, when Frost speaks of words, he speaks of them as "other sounds" that may be strung upon the sentence sound, suggesting that, for him, sentence sound is primary: "A sentence is a sound in itself on which other sounds called words may be strung."[21]

As we might expect then, unlike Stevens, Frost rarely invites us to attend to individual words, to modulations in their stress accents or even finer adjustments in linguistic rhythm occasioned by their changing syntactic functions or metrical placement. Instead, Frost invites us to hear the possible shifts in either the nature or location of melodic accent—a higher-level accent that falls across sequences of words and reflects a speaker's or reader's sense of what holds the greatest informational, contextual, or emotional value.

Frost's acclaimed "Home Burial" exemplifies how his scaffolding of speech rhythms within the metrical template focuses attention on the intonational contours (that is, both on the possible locations of the tonic syllable and the potential for shifts in pitch height and direction on the tonic) and thus on the range of interpretive stances associated with the characters' statements. Its opening lines, with multiple possibilities for melodic accent,[22] mirror the poem's subject matter—a mobile and latently violent power struggle between the husband and wife. Whether we place melodic accent on either or both members of the contrastive gender pair (*he* and *her*, *she* and *him*) or upon the preposition *before* makes a tremendous difference to our interpretation of the poem's unfolding drama: "He saw *her* from the bottom of the stairs / Before she saw *him*."[23] That all of these decisions are enabled by the poem's metrical rhythm, a muted blank verse, means that readers must struggle with decisions regarding melodic emphasis as essentially matters of interpretation. The multivalent possibilities for pitch height and direction on the phrase "before she saw him" are essentially inferential: any single prosodic change also involves meaning. In contrast, the flat and falling tone of the neutral declaration, "She turned and sank upon her skirts at that," acts as a baseline for the expressive departures of the characters' speech.[24]

Another way to convey Frost's distinctive prosodic innovations is to say that whereas Stevens influences how we produce the stress contours of a word, which is the lowest level of our language's accentual structure,

Frost attempts to govern the reader's assignment of melodic accent to words that already possess stress, using the higher of the language's two levels of accentual structure, intonation.

This distinction is important because whereas word-stress (*stress accent*) is so familiar and apparently fixed that it can be represented in dictionary entries, melodic accent is inherently variable and is commonly held to be idiosyncratic and unpredictable. Thus, readers are far more likely to recognize and enjoy the shifts in lexical rhythm (stress accent) that Stevens' verse involves. But these same readers are likely to resist, resent, or, worse yet, entirely miss the shifts in melodic accent that Frost claims are essential to his verse.

Indeed, while no less overstated than Stevens', Frost's beliefs in the importance of certain properties of sound, are, by their nature, less easily defended. This is in large part because the sound combinations Stevens primarily engages lie at lower and more fixed levels of the prosodic hierarchy, the rhythmic organization of language:

> The Prosodic Hierarchy: Prosodic Domains in Language[25]
> Utterance
> Intonational Phrase
> Phonological phrase
> Phonological word
> Foot (Moraic Trochee)
> Syllable

Stevens' metrical experiments draw upon the prosodic organization of language at or below the level of the phonological word. They either vary the location of stress accent, as we saw with *denouement* or *ambiance*, or they call upon well-attested phonological processes (e.g., elision and the reduction of sonorant sequences) and the internal structure of syllables in English to compress additional phonological material into a single metrical foot.[26] We are far more likely to agree to the possibility of a poet's manipulating the placement of stress accent within a word, not only because of past precedent, but also because the accentual stresses of words themselves are predictable.

By contrast, Frost's sound of sense—his belief in the expressive force of "the intonation entangled somehow in the syntax idiom and meaning of a sentence"[27]—involves higher levels of the prosodic hierarchy that are, by definition, variable and responsive to an array of paralinguistic and other factors (For example, a reader's or listener's mapping of prosody onto intentions involves pragmatic issues beyond a speaker's [or author's] control,[28] as well as matters of "individual difference"[29]). These factors, along with our unfamiliarity with technical descriptions of intonational phonology, make us intuitively less likely to agree that a poet can fix melodic accent. Instead, we are likely to resist the idea that the arrangement of words on a page can so specify how the reader's voice should posture that a single articulation of the poetic line is not only possible but inevitable;[30] instead, we might agree with Dwight Bolinger, who so titled a seminal article on intonation, "Accent Is Predictable (If You're a Mind-Reader)."[31]

Frost and Williams

To suggest that Frost's and Williams' sound configurations are deeply similar would certainly have been rejected by both poets. Nonetheless, the parallels between Frost's theories and Williams' are even closer than those between Frost and Stevens. Williams, like Frost, intuits that the structure of speech sound can yield a new means of prosodic organization for the modern poem. Frost: "[M]y conscious interest in people was at first no more than an almost technical interest in their speech—in what I used to call their sentence sounds—the sound of sense. Whatever these sounds are or aren't . . . I say, I began to hang on them very young. . . ."[32] And Williams: "From the beginning I knew that the American language must shape the pattern; later I rejected the word language and spoke of the American idiom—this was a better word than language, less academic, more identified with speech."[33] The fact that Williams claims to harness the cadences of speech rhythm as a new measure displacing meter, whereas Frost claims to "get cadences by skillfully breaking the sounds of sense with all their irregularity of accent across the regular beat of the metre"[34] should not dissuade us from seeing these parallels, as is brought out in the following comments:

> When you listen to a speaker, you hear words, to be sure,—but you also hear tones. The problem is to note them, to imagine them again, and to get them down in writing. But few of you probably ever thought of the possibility or of the necessity of doing this.[35]

> You see, basically he [Williams] was listening to himself talk and listening to other people around him talk, and trying to find a way of putting it down on the page so that he'd be able to take advantage of all the beautiful little rhythms of medical office-kitchen-bathroom-street-grocery speech."[36]

These statements objectively reveal what the poems—with their differences of register and diction, syntactic structures, and tone—do not: the poets' shared interest in bringing to the page the sonic play of seemingly spontaneous speech. In poem after poem, particularly in early Williams, we find sudden changes in the direction or height of melodic accent. These are often prompted by a specific class of syntactic units, ranging from sentence adverbials ("Gold against blue"[37]), parenthetical elements ("this could be / applied fresh at small expense"[38]), and vocatives ("my townspeople"[39]), to social formulae ("Forgive me"[40]), moved constituents ("first the right / forefoot // carefully"[41]), and interjections ("phew!"[42]; "For Christ's sake"[43]), which are separated from adjacent or surrounding syntactic units by pauses and other factors. As a result, these irruptive sequences multiply the frequency and type of intonational phrases and tunes characterizing the statement. (By contrast, one might say a neutral declarative statement in American English possesses a single intonational contour with a fairly regular falling tune, but see discussion of "Never Again" in the next section of this essay.) Whether these effects successfully simulate actual speech or not, they encourage the reader to imagine that the poem is occurring in an actual discourse situation—one that possesses immediacy ("This Is Just to Say"), dramatic context ("Portrait of a Lady"), and, perhaps most elusively for modernist poets, audience ("Tract").

Frost's effects are both less obvious and less energetic. Typically, the diction is less idiomatic, the register more elevated, and the syntax more hypotactic. Nonetheless, Frost's extensive right-branching sentences employ conventions similar to those of Williams' briefer and more excitable sentences. Compare Williams' "Pastoral" to the start of Frost's "Directive." Both poems begin with one or more sentence adverbials that—by virtue of their distinctive intonational contours—create characteristic tunes (of course, they also serve to establish temporal and/or spatial context):

When I was younger
it was plain to me
I must make something of myself.

                (WILLIAMS, *CP*, VOL. 1, 64; ADVERBIAL ITALICIZED)

and

Back out of all this now too much for us,
Back in a time made simple by the loss
Of detail, burned, dissolved, and broken off
Like graveyard marble sculpture in the weather,
There is a house that is no more a house . . .

                (FROST, *CPPP*, 341; ADVERBIALS ITALICIZED)

Both poems also interrupt ongoing syntactic units with parenthetical asides

>   . . . all,
> *if I am fortunate,*
> smeared a bluish green
> (WILLIAMS, *CP*, VOL. 1, 64; MOVED CONSTITUENT ITALICIZED)

and again

> The road there, *if you'll let a guide direct you*
> *Who only has at heart your getting lost,*
> May seem as if it should have been a quarry—
> (FROST, *CPPP,* 341; MOVED CONSTITUENTS ITALICIZED)

While syntactically inessential, the asides convey affective values intrinsic to each poem's trajectory and semantic force. Frost's poems also achieve a range of tones by drawing upon a similar set of constructions, as do Williams' poems in general. Frost's subset of asides, however, is comprised less of the brief interjections and vocatives characteristic of Williams (although both are found in *North of Boston*) than of lengthy nonrestrictive appositives, parentheticals, and, especially, imperatives, whose "voicing" (i.e., pitch direction, height, and pacing) differs appreciably from the primarily declarative sentences with which they are interwoven.

Of course, none of this is to say that the *sound* of the two poets' work is similar. What is intriguing and perhaps has kept many scholars and readers from noting the strong parallels is just how different the effects of each poet's intonational contours are. Williams' lines tend to align with intonational phrases, turning intonational tunes into a prosodic measure: what we hear is the rise and fall of the voice, organized by line. In contrast, Frost's versification counterpoints a line's metrical stress and its ongoing syntax *against* the intonational contour or melodic accent of constituents within the line: what we hear is the play of tension between the more-or-less regular rhythms that the metrical organization of the verse occasions and the possibilities for distinctive melodic tunes that the text's speech rhythms suggest may be superimposed upon the metrical rhythms. In assessing Frost's theories, we should remember that while today we "hear" his verse as canonically metrical, his contemporary critics were misled by quite a few of his poems (arguably, many of the most interesting ones) to think he wrote "'vers libre, . . . an excellent instrument for rendering the actual rhythms of speech.'"[44]

In short, in order to assess Frost's claims vis-a-vis Williams', we must see past both well-worn narratives about Frost being a conventionally metrical poet as well as Frost's own posture vehemently rejecting free verse. Critics like John Sears and Tyler Hoffman have contended that this posture was at least partially motivated by Frost's need to proselytize and/or to distinguish himself from the Imagist poets.[45] I would remind us that Frost also recognized that free verse had some limited utility and first found "a voice of his own" in what I will, somewhat perversely, argue was for him the closest thing to a successful free-verse poem: "My Butterfly," a rhymed verse comprised of iambic lines of variable length.

Frost himself considered "My Butterfly" to be a breakthrough, especially its second stanza.[46] That stanza is where, after two lines of iambic pentameter, the poem torques away from its imitations of Keats, archaic diction, and a precious register through an abrupt change in tone and mood that propels the poem briefly in ways reminiscent of Williams' verse:

> The gray grass is scarce dappled with the snow;
> Its two banks have not shut upon the river;
> *But it is long ago—*
> *It seems forever—*
> Since first I saw thee glance,
> With all thy dazzling other ones,
> In airy dalliance,
> Precipitate in love,
> Tossed, tangled, whirled and whirled above,
> Like a limp rose wreath in a fairy dance.[47]

Like "After Apple-Picking," Frost's other early poem comprised of iambic lines of variable length, this poem uses a parsing line—a line of variable length that parses syntactic units into individual lines—to indicate factors typically linked with intonation: pacing, affect, tone. The effect is limited, as Frost said the effects of free verse are: "[Free verse is] good as something created momentarily for its sudden startling effect."[48] Nonetheless, Frost positions the poem penultimately in *A Boy's Will*, giving it a significance that lies as much in its prosody as its biographical relevance. For it was Reverend Wolcott's comment to Frost upon reading this poem among others that "the tone of [his] verses was too much like that of talk" that Robert Newdick reports to have galvanized Frost's poetic:

> That observation was to Frost like the drop of acid that magically brings down the precipitate from a chemical solution, for the tone of talk was precisely what he had been striving for without being quite conscious of it.... Now he realized, too, what he had found most

offensive in Lanier: the underlying concept of the aptness of musical notation for verse.[49]

Frost opposes a musical tune (or, for that matter, setting verse to music) because it lacks the expressive signification carried by intonational tunes. Yet, as he and Williams recognized, intonational tunes are ephemeral. By *North of Boston*, whose period of composition coincides with Frost's theorizing the sound of sense in letters, Frost will typically use "the very regular preestablished accent and measure of blank verse" to contain the comparably evanescent effects of the "very irregular accent and measure of speaking intonation."[50] Thus, Frost's election of seemingly so slight a poem as "The Pasture" as epigraph to his *Collected Poems* also becomes more plausible in light of his focus on intonational tunes. We may not agree with his assessment, but his belief in the poem's production of five tones in a single stanza—a "light, informing tone"; an "'only' tone—reservation"; a "supplementary, possibility"; and a "free tone, assuring" followed by an "after thought, inviting"[51]—makes it a fit introduction to an oeuvre to be judged primarily by its counterpoint of stress and melodic accent.

Frost's Legacy

Since Williams and Stevens, as well as Frost, all invest belief in theories about sound, we might well wonder why Frost's theories have fared the worst in critical estimations. Yes, Frost "fiddl[es] with his terminology," shifting terms much as Williams does. But none of these poets could, as Timothy Steele says of Frost, "focus his meaning to his own satisfaction."[52] Imprecise though it be, Frost's theory is, actually, better developed than at least these two contemporaries', neither of whom writes anything more than loosely assembled notes on meter, measure, and the like. Frost's discussion of intonation, tone, irregular accent, and how speakers underline their words even anticipates the language and markings of intonational phonology, albeit with one important caveat, that accent is or can be made reliably predictable, or that such an outcome would even be desirable.

This penultimate section will explore Frost's alleged desire for intonation to achieve a kind of transparent perlocutionary force through an investigation of "Never Again Would Birds' Song Be the Same," a poem that seemingly thematizes Frost's theory of sentence sounds and that is, in both critics' and Frost's own estimation, an accomplished text, even a "tour de force,"[53] yet one that fails to fulfill Frost's theory of sentence sounds, a point Frost himself seems to concede when he prefaces his reading of the poem for the *Yale Series of Recorded Poets* by saying, "[T]his does something that I don't usually approve of, like a statistical thing, sentence after sentence the same."[54]

The poem is comprised of six sentences, each of which except the last is qualified in some way by what Frost might call a "reservation" or "supplementary" tone.[55] While all the sentences are in the indicative, only two make direct positive statements of fact: the second half of "Be that as may be, she was in their song" and "And to do that to birds was why she came."[56] These two sentences are also among the only ones to coincide with a single line, a point to which we'll return later. The other sentences suggest a more imaginative mood or conditional statement (which in modern English is often conveyed by means of modal auxiliaries)—a willing suspension of belief which permits Adam to hear in the birds' song an oversound. Between the two kinds of propositions, we hear the pull of tones that critics have celebrated as giving the poem its virtuosic feel.

But this poem's pull of tones is less effortless or colloquial, per se, than in "Home Burial" or even "Mowing," for reasons that may lie in Frost's renovation of his source line.[57] From Hamlet's "So have I heard and do in part believe it," Frost introduces at least two important changes: the change of the verb *hear* to *declare,* and the change of the primary verbs *have* and *do* to the modals *would* and *could* ("He *would* declare and *could* himself believe"). Despite Frost's disapproval of the simple declarative statement,[58] his practice here shows that syntactically complex declarative statements do, in fact, possess multiple sounds, in part due to the range of verb choices possible within them. *Believe* belongs to *representatives*, a type of verb by which "the speaker is committed, in varying degrees, to the truth of a proposition," but *declare* belongs to *declarations,* by which "the speaker alters the external status or condition of an object or situation solely by making the utterance."[59] The implicit gap between the two—the failure of the speaker to alter the external status or condition solely by making an utterance (the kind of power implicit in chant and spells that Frost toys with in "Mending Wall") or by believing it (being committed to the proposition's truth)—opens into an exploration of varying degrees of commitment and affect that have important phonological as much as philosophical effects. Similarly, Frost's change to the modals *would* and *could* not only favors words that convey a speaker's stance or orientation toward his statement, it also participates in foregrounding a space between one's personal volition, habit, or intention, and one's degree of commitment in believing this same thing. In a love poem, the kind of poem that Frost surprisingly almost never wrote and that conventionally makes a simple declaration, such grammatical complexities are unexpected as well as sonically interesting.

When Frost reads the poem aloud, it is notable that he interrupts himself twice to mark shifts in tone. After the first line, he says "See the tone of it" and then repeats the line but with different words ("He could himself believe, he would aver"); next, he indicates a shift in tone that coincides with the sentence adverbial "admittedly."[60] A significant question is whether Frost is celebrating this poem for its evident shifts in tones, as he does "The Pasture," or whether he feels compelled to note the tone because the poem might not infallibly convey its intonational effects without additional notation (something Frost frequently chastised Vachel Lindsay for;[61] and something Williams tended to do both in readings and in letters). My subjective opinion is that this poem does, in fact, successfully indicate shifts in tone on the page but that it does so by means of the very foregrounded elements Frost singles out, rather than by a development of dramatic context.

In the two instances that Frost's remarks isolate, as well as in other cases in the text, which I've italicized below for emphasis, Frost uses fronted and moved adverbials, limiting adverbs, negative particles, and modals—stance words, i.e., familiar rhetorical markers, to create shifts in tone and therefore cadence (e.g., "he *would* declare and *could himself* believe"; "*probably* it never would be lost"; "*Admittedly* an eloquence so soft/ *Could only* have had an influence ... / *When* call or laughter"; "*Be that as may be*"; and, of course, "*Never again* would birds' song be the same"[62]). In this poem, he does not—as so frequently elsewhere—rely on the implied feelings of a posited lyric speaker to comb tonally ambiguous words such as *oh* or *no* or *yes* "into the ... single one of its meanings intended."[63] While the adverbials and modals found in "Never Again" can certainly be made to carry an oppositional meaning, as in irony, they are not as tonally multivalent. For Frost, "Never Again" uses rhetorical conventions to orchestrate tone: tone arises not from context (i.e., from dramatically developed setting and character, as in "Home Burial") but from underlying argument. The initial line with its use of contrastive emphasis (*would* and *could*; *declare* and *believe*) to more narrowly delimit the location of the focus (if not the direction of melodic accent on the focus syllable) is a good example; it presents a near-perfect balance of two somewhat opposed propositions—the commitment to declaring in the grammatical aspect of "habitual" or "durative" action ("He *would* declare") against the implicitly conditional state of belief in his own declaration ("and *could* himself believe"). The poem sustains both the doubt about its proposition and its avowed determination to believe in that proposition. The movement and the turn of the sonnet are a perfect balance of these impulses as well: "Be that as may be, she was in their song."

Here, the adverbial concessive clause, which begins with a relic of the subjunctive, is answered by the first unqualified declaration in the poem: "... she was in their song."

Leaving the issue of intonation for a moment, this effect—which makes the problem of sustaining belief, much akin to the problem of sustaining tone, central to the poem—is mirrored, as other scholars have noted, by the ways in which Frost's sentences here run over not only line breaks but also stanzaic boundaries, inviting us to hear both lineages of the sonnet in play. For while the rhyme scheme follows Shakespeare's exemplar, the poem's arc might better be described as Petrarchan: the problem of belief elaborated in the first eight lines is answered by an affirmation of love's effects, however qualified, in the last six, and, one might say, justified—sonically, albeit not logically, by the soaring contour of the final declaration in the second half of the final line. Against the definitive "Never again would birds' song be the same" with its falling contours and emphatic stress, is counterpointed, "And to do that to birds was why she came," in which the final nominal triumphantly soars and stays aloft; it imaginatively escapes postlapsarian time and the audible fall of declarative statements by triply erasing closure. At least in my hearing, its rising intonation soars above syntactic ending, line ending, and poem ending to keep the voice afloat. Here Frost accomplishes, by means of sonic equivalences what might not be accomplished by statements of fact, an achievement that accords with Frost's statements in other contexts: "The greatest satisfaction comes from weaving intonations together to make a work of art"[64] and "Statement yes but it is only as the poem and the sentence within the poem transcend{exceed} statement (not fall short of it) that poetry arises."[65]

If this sonnet succeeds in telling the voice how to intone, or at least in more narrowly identifying a range of postures than is true of other Frost poems, why should its success be troubling? Again, Frost says of this sonnet that it does "'a statistical thing.'"[66] Was he, perhaps, less committed to confining the reader to a single tune than he professed or than critics have interpreted his theory of sentence sounds to be? Like Tyler Hoffman and Timothy Steele before me, I'd like to suggest that the very possibility of mistaking vocal intonation in Frost is important and was important for Frost. Indeed, Frost is aware of the importance of context to specifying vocal intonation, as the following entries from his *Notebooks* attest:

> Tune (Sound and Soundness. Tone from context. Tune from tone and meter.[67]

> The question of how any intonations are made fast to the paper. By the context partly: partly by idiomatic signs.[68]

Whatever we believe about Frost's legacy and about the legacy of some other modernists, we may well resist the idea that the arrangement of words on a page can or should so specify how our voice should posture that a single articulation of the poetic line is not only possible but inevitable. Instead of a poetry that aims to dramatize affective states or to "confer . . . [the poet's] identity on the reader,"[69] more important may be the invention of new rhythms and new resources equally capable of representing affect or of constructing knowledge. In other words, recognizing a poem such as "Never Again . . .," which possesses a pull of tones but no real tonal ambiguity, to be a tour de force does not preclude the question of whether it is more than a set piece. If not, to what extent does its success in specifying a particular set of intonational contours constitute a limitation?

The answer may depend on how we interpret Frost's theory of the sound of sense. Do we take his statement "Never if you can help it write down a sentence in which the voice will not know how to posture *specially*"[70] as a directive to the writer that leaves space for individual difference and divergence by the reader? Or do we take this and other statements as transferring an "auditory image"[71] that shapes or even determines readers' prosodic experiences and thus their interpretations of the text?[72] And what are the ethical, as much as aesthetic, ramifications of success or failure? Here, we can point to well-known accounts of the failure of readers to interpret Frost's poems right until they heard him read it, as well as to Frost's apparent displeasure at these reports[73]; we can also point to contemporary accounts from psycholinguistics and popular media that provide both empirical data and anecdotal endorsements for the efficacy of explicit prosody, i.e., an author's own reading of his or her text (or even attributed qualities), on a reader's implicit prosody, that is, on how the reader then reads the same text or a subsequent one attributed to the same author.[74] The point is cognitive studies prove Frost and some other modernists right in their underlying assumptions about the functions of high-level prosodic information, but questions remain both about whether or not melodic accent is or can be made reliably transferable and whether doing so would be to the ultimate benefit of a poem or not.

Human and Non-Human Language Illuminated by Cognitive Studies

To explore these questions, I will draw upon cognitive studies of human and non-human language that hold profound implications both for Frost and for the "speech-based poetics" of modernism that similarly values the poem's ability to transcribe a poet's speech rhythms to the page.[75] Together, these studies suggest the epistemological as well as prosodic limitations inherent in such enterprise.

Ellen Bryant Voigt's study of rhythm and syntax, *The Art of Syntax*, cites brain studies of infants that demonstrate that the recitation of the alphabet or numbers is stored in one part of the brain, but knowledge in another. Thus, an 18-month-old who bursts into a riff of numbers "fourfivesixseveneight" "doesn't actually *count* that high: the string of sounds belongs not yet to meaningful speech but to song."[76] These same studies also show that different areas of the brain light up on an MRI when the same child sings these numbers versus when she uses them semantically.

Such discoveries pose significant issues for our understanding of Frost's theory of the sound of sense, as for our understanding of other modernists' investments of belief in sound, since these studies suggest that the intonation of linguistic strings reproduced in their entirety may belong to the realm of song, whereas the intonation of new language use belongs to the realm of knowledge. To the extent that we inhabit any poet's tunes, replicating their exact melodic contours, then much like the 18-month-old reciting the alphabet, we as readers may be limited to reproducing a song or tune (a simulation of the speaker's expressive values), rather than being engaged in the construction of new knowledge. Frost's (and Stevens') purported "indifference to language as a signifying system" is directly relevant here: as Frost scholar Tyler Hoffman says, "he [Frost] prefers to dwell on the felt structure of the sentence apart from the words that comprise it"[77]; that is, its pre-existing tune and tonal message.

A new study of the evolution of human language syntax, conducted by two linguists and a psychobiologist, confirms the cognitive separations implied above and suggests further issues for the limits of speech-based poetics as described by many of the modernists. According to this study, our infinite human language syntax emerges from

> the adventitious combination of two pre-existing, simpler systems that had been evolved for other functional tasks. The first system, Type E(xpression), is found in birdsong, where the same song marks territory, mating availability, and similar "expressive" functions. The second system, Type L(exical), has been suggestively found in non-human primate calls and in honeybee waggle dances, where it demarcates predicates with one or more "arguments." . . . Each layer, E and L, when considered *separately*, is characterizable as a finite state system. . . . When the two systems are put together they interact,

yielding the unbounded, non-finite state, hierarchical structure that serves as the hallmark of full-fledged human language syntax.[78]

The implications for Frost, and, to a lesser extent, for Stevens and Williams, are staggering. For Frost figures the poet's range of sentence sounds as analogous to a species of bird's characteristic tunes: "Just so many sentence sounds belong to man as just so many vocal runs belong to one kind of bird. We come into the world with them and create none of them. What we feel as creation is only selection and grouping."[79] To the extent that birdsong comprises only an expression layer, which imparts a single meaning to an entire song, rather than a lexical layer—that is, a range of sounds that can communicate essential information and, through the elaboration of an infinite syntax, construct variable arguments, Frost delimits verse and its readers to a partial range of actual human language functions, those focused upon a "limited, holistic range of intentions . . . [those that] convey messages, not meanings."[80]

In his exemplary poem "Never Again . . .," while the birds' song is described as never again being the same, the poem does not ask us to imagine it as now possessing a lexical layer. That might be the case, were Eve's influence described as rhetorical or argumentative. However, her distinctive "eloquence" is regarded as influential only (and even then, this influence is hedged as being conditional) "when call or laughter carried it aloft."[81] That is, it is influential only in the specific cases of non-phonemic sounds, such as laughter, or of the stylized sequences of tones characteristic of calling. It is particularly interesting to note that the latter sequences—which are termed "call contours" in the literature of intonational phonology[82]—are recognized as well-established conventional patterns that we might say, like birds' song, convey "messages, not meanings."[83] Indeed, the call contour with its stylized "sequence of two levels [of pitch] with the second lower than the first by approximately the musical interval of a minor third"[84] correlates with neuroscientific studies in the field of music showing that pitch changes according to a minor third have fairly universal, expressive values for the prosodic patterns produced by speakers of American English.[85] That is, it is thereby probably safe to say that far from adding a lexical layer to an expressive one, Eve's "voice" is abstracted away from the lexical and thereby syntactic combinations that give rise to novel meanings are instead constrained to a fairly fixed expressive value akin to music or nonlinguistic sound. To the extent that Eve's vocal influence stands in for Frost's notion of sentence sounds, her example suggests a poetics that prioritizes expression over argument, the acoustic dimension of sound over the phonemic.[86]

What we might take away from both studies is not only germane to Frost but also broadly implicative of the central problem of modernist poets' theorization of sound. For Frost's potentially desiring his readers to inhabit his individual intonational tunes and hence his construction of meaning, rather than claim their own, wherever the voice is too firmly scripted is a result that should remind us of Williams' own intonational-based measure—the late triadic-line verse or variable foot. Williams called this measure the crowning achievement of all his work; nonetheless, he eventually disavowed it, calling it "overdone, artificial, archaic—smacking of Spencer [sic] and his final Alexandrine."[87] Frost, who plies the intertwined resources of grammar, rhetoric, and intonation to create similar effects, stops short of disavowing what he has achieved, but, in recognizing that he can write something "statistical" that he still approves of, suggests the equal limitations of his prosodic theory.

Returning to the modernist dilemma of speech representation in general, we might see how all these modernist poets emphasize the plastic, i.e., expressive, qualities of linguistic sound, seeking in the prosodic organization of sound aesthetic satisfactions that exceed the semantic and aspire to confer values beyond meaning. The very proof from cognitive studies that we tend to reproduce an auditory image of a text once we are exposed to it suggests anew not the failure of these poets' astute accomplishments but rather a ground why subsequent generations of poets came to be suspicious of the modernists' beliefs in the purported transparency of "absolute rhythm," choosing instead to tilt their verse productions toward the materiality of language.

Notes

I owe tremendous thanks to Minda Rae Amiran and Tom Cable for acute remarks on drafts of this essay.

1. Peter Middleton, "The 'Final Finding of the Ear': Wallace Stevens' Modernist Soundscapes," in "Wallace Stevens and 'The Less Legible Meanings of Sound,'" ed. Natalie Gerber, special issue, *The Wallace Stevens Journal* 33, no. 1 (2009): 70.

2. William Wordsworth, quoted in Susan J. Wolfson, "Sounding Romantic: The Sound of Sound," in the volume "'Soundings of Things Done': The Poetry and Poetics of Sound in the Romantic Ear and Era," *Romantic Circles* (2008): par. 22, https://www.rc.umd.edu/praxis/soundings/wolfson/wolfson.html.

3. Samuel Taylor Coleridge, quoted in Wolfson, "Sounding Romantic," par. 2.

4. Stéphane Mallarmé, quoted in Lisa Goldfarb, *The Figure Concealed: Wallace Stevens, Music, and Valéryan Echoes* (Brighton, U.K.: Sussex Academic Press, 2011), 4.

5. Goldfarb, *Figure Concealed*, 15.

6. Consider, for example, Frost's vigorous appeal to the sonic contours of words in verse as an extra-semantic dimension essential to the poem's delivery: "I try to make each word serve two purposes; in addition to its own meaning it serves as a guide to

the voice in reading preceding and succeeding words. If this is not always true of each word, it is true of each phrase or each line." We might wonder at the purpose of such a guide, if Frost did not elsewhere elaborate that "By the arrangement and choice of words on the part of the poet, the effects of humor, pathos, hysteria, anger, and, in fact, all effects, can be indicated and obtained." Quoted in Robert Newdick, "Robert Frost and the Sound of Sense," *American Literature* 9 (1937): 297–98.

Now compare these statements to Stevens' similar ascription of power to a poet's selection and organization of what we might loosely term word sounds:

> And what about the sound of words? . . . The deepening need for words to express our thoughts and feelings, which, we are sure, are all the truth that we shall ever experience, having no illusions, makes us listen to words when we hear them, loving them and feeling them, makes us search the sound of them, for a finality, a perfection, an unalterable vibration, which it is only within the power of the acutest poet to give them.

7. See Marjorie Perloff, "The Return of the (Numerical) Repressed: From Free Verse to Procedural Play," *Radical Artifice: Writing Poetry in the Age of Media* (Chicago: University of Chicago Press, 1991), 134–70; and Dorothy Wang, *Thinking Its Presence: Form, Race, and Subjectivity in Contemporary Asian American Poetry* (Stanford, Calif.: Stanford University Press, 2014).

8. Studies in psycholinguistics demonstrate the many cognitive functions that implicit prosody plays even in silent reading, from the parafoveal previewing of a homophone speeding the access of an individual lexical item (Charles Clifton Jr., "The Roles of Phonology in Silent Reading: A Selective Review," in *Explicit and Implicit Prosody*, ed. Lyn Frazier and Edward Gibson [Berlin: Springer, 2015], 163), to the role of "both global and local rhythmic context guid[ing] segmentation and lexical access" (Mara Breen, "Empirical Investigations of Implicit Prosody," in Frazier and Gibson, *Explicit and Implicit Prosody*, 185). Importantly, at multiple levels of phonological representation, implicit prosody seems to play an early role in our processing of language, ranging from our ability to access lexical items (Clifton Jr., "Roles," 163) to our use of prosody to interpret syntactic relationships among constituents even before the content of these constituents is available (Eva Fernández and Irina Sekerina, "The Interplay of Visual and Prosodic Information in the Attachment Preferences of Semantically Shallow Relative Clauses," in Frazier and Gibson, *Explicit and Implicit Prosody*, 258).

Indeed, Frost's musing in his *Notebooks*—"The sentences must spring from each other and talk to each other even when there is only one character speaking Self repartee" (Robert Frost, *The Notebooks of Robert Frost*, ed. Robert Faggen [Cambridge, Mass.: Belknap Press, 2006], 45; spacing as in original)—bears significant parallels with empirical findings that while silent readers can recognize the contents of individual propositions without the benefit of prosodic information, implicit prosody facilitates our global comprehension of passages and helps silent readers make inferential judgments about relationships between propositions (Katy Carlson, "Clefting, Parallelism, and Focus in Ellipsis Sentences," in Frazier and Gibson, *Explicit and Implicit Prosody*, 77).

9. Whereas poets speak simply of prosody, that is, of the versification of a text, psycholinguists distinguish between explicit and implicit prosody. *Explicit prosody* refers to the production and analysis of prosodic contours in actual speech, whether "read speech," "spontaneous speech," or "'laboratory speech.'" Shari Speer and Anouschka

Foltz, "The Implicit Prosody of Corrective Contrast Primes Appropriately Intonated Probes (for Some Readers)," in Frazier and Gibson, *Explicit and Implicit Prosody*, 265. "Implicit prosody" refers to "a prosodic structure [a reader projects] onto what is read silently." Caroline Féry, "Extraposition and Prosodic Monsters in German," in Frazier and Gibson, *Explicit and Implicit Prosody*, 12. Importantly, studies of implicit prosody demonstrate some grounds for claims modernist poets have made about prosody on the page.

10. Stevens, *Collected Poetry and Prose*, ed. Frank Kermode and Joan Richardson (New York: Library of America, 1997), 663. Subsequent references are given as *CPP*.

11. Wallace Stevens, *Letters of Wallace Stevens*, ed. Holly Stevens (New York: Knopf, 1966), 340.

12. Stevens, *CPP*, 650.

13. For further discussion of these points, see Natalie Gerber, "Stevens' Prosody: Meaningful Rhythms," *Wallace Stevens Journal* 29, no. 1 (2005): 178–87; and Natalie Gerber, "'A Funny Foreigner of Meek Address': Stevens and English as a Foreign Language," *The Wallace Stevens Journal* 25, no. 2 (2001): 211-19.

14. *Dénouement,* first recorded by the *OED* in 1752, was anglicized in pronunciation by 1922, the date of the poem. Both the 1933 edition of the *OED* and the 1934 2nd edition of *Webster's New International Dictionary* give only the pronunciation with accent on the second syllable. Later Merriam-Webster's and other American dictionaries show a return to a first variant closer to French, with primary stress on the final syllable and secondary stress on one or both of the first two syllables. In his eccentric pronunciation, Stevens was ahead of his time.

15. Here and elsewhere, an underline indicates syllables that, through standard allowances (e.g., elision or the reduction of sonorant sequences), count as a single metrical position. Also, one might note that current Merriam-Webster's dictionaries show word accent only on the first syllable of *ambiance,* with no stress on the final two syllables—and for one variant, elision of the last two syllables (as in the preceding word *linear*). Yet in this line the final syllable, *-ance,* fills a strong position. This, of course, is not an unusual metrical variation in English poetry; and the variation between French and English doublets such as *honóur* and *hónour* dates back at least to Chaucer. Stevens' play here with the stress patterns of English words supports his well-known statement that "French and English constitute a single language." Stevens, *CPP*, 914.

16. Stevens, *CPP*, 349, 350.

17. Ibid., 82–85, 82.

18. Quoted in Stevens, *CPP*, 650.

19. Robert Frost, *Collected Poems, Prose, & Plays*, ed. Richard Poirier and Mark Richardson (New York: Library of America, 1995), 791. Hereinafter abbreviated *CPPP*; see also Frost, *Notebooks*, 42.

20. Ibid., 681.

21. Ibid., 675.

22. I follow linguist Anthony Fox in distinguishing *stress* and *accent*. *Accent* "refer[s] to the linguistic phenomenon in which a particular element of the chain of speech is singled out in relation to surrounding elements, irrespective of the means by which this is achieved" (*Prosodic Features and Prosodic Structure* [Oxford: Oxford University Press, 2000], 115). *Stress accent* or *accented syllable* refers to the presence of accent on a syllable, i.e., what is commonly "referred to as 'word-stress'" (145). *Pitch-accent* refers to the superordinate presence of melodic accent, or pitch, upon a syllable that has already

received prominence, i.e., stress accent, at a lower level (115). I use the term *melodic accent* because *pitch-accent* is better known to linguists than to critics, who might use *pitch* and *accent* distinctively.

23. Frost, *CPPP*, 55; emphasis added.

24. Ibid. For a parallel example in this poem, compare Mary's famous outcry, "'Don't, don't, don't, don't,' she cried" (56) to Frost's comment to Sidney Cox apropos of the vital sentence: "You recognize the sentence sound in this: *You,* you—! It is so strong that if you hear it as I do you have to pronounce the two you's differently" (681). By his own desiderata, Frost's meter succeeds when it forces distinctive variations in melodic accent, not lexical stress.

25. Marina Nespor and Irene Vogel, *Prosodic Phonology* (Dordecht: Foris, 1986), 16; Alan Cruttenden, *Intonation*, 2nd ed. (Cambridge: Cambridge University Press, 1997), 23–25.

26. Consider these conventional underlined examples from Stevens' verse, none of which diverges significantly from canonical metrical practice from Shakespeare forward:

```
The ephemeral blues must merge for them in one,      (Stevens, CPP, 12)
 w   s  w      s    w    s     w    s   w   s

The impossible possible philosophers' man,           (Stevens, CPP, 226)
 w   s  w      s   w   s    w   s    w    s

The inanimate, difficult visage. Who is it?          (Stevens, CPP, 336)
 w   s  w      s  w    s     w   s   w  s
```

27. Frost, *CPPP*, 670.

28. See Tanenhaus, Kurumada, and Brown for discussion of the "multiple challenges" listeners face in "mapping prosody onto intentions" and for the adaptive nature of interpretation based on pragmatic issues (Michael K. Tanenhaus, Chigusa Kurumada, and Meredith Brown, "Prosody and Intention Recognition," in Frazier and Gibson, *Explicit and Implicit Prosody*, 99).

29. For example, we find the statement that "Any study investigating sentence-level implicit prosody will likely have to deal with such individual differences" and the conclusion that "it may not be possible to study sentence-level implicit prosody without recourse to participants' overt prosody." Speer and Foltz, "Implicit Prosody," in Frazier and Gibson, *Explicit and Implicit Prosody*, 283. For a succinct, careful restatement of why "Such individual differences may be the reason why studies involving word-stress manipulations have so far yielded more consistent results than studies involving sentence-level prosodic phrasing regarding both the existence of an implicit prosodic contour generated during silent reading and information about what this implicit prosody may sound like," see 283.

30. At issue here is how we are to understand Frost's well-known statement "Never if you can help it write down a sentence in which the voice will not know how to posture *specially*" (Frost, *CPPP*, 666): Does Frost seek to delimit for the reader's voice or only for the writer's not only which word is the most salient in a linguistic string but also which pitch pattern is the most pertinent? In short, should each line of his verse tell us how to comb each word "into the . . . single one of its meanings intended" (Frost, *Notebooks*, 60)?

31. See Dwight Bolinger, "Accent Is Predictable (If You're a Mind-Reader)," *Language* 48, no. 3 (1972): 633–44.
32. Frost, *CPPP*, 684-85.
33. William Carlos Williams, *I Wanted to Write a Poem: The Autobiography of the Works of a Poet*, ed. Edith Heal (New York: New Directions, 1958), 65.
34. Frost, *CPPP*, 665.
35. Ibid., 687.
36. Allen Ginsberg, "Poetic Breath, and Pound's Usura," in *Allen Verbatim: Lectures on Poetry, Politics, Consciousness* (New York: McGraw-Hill, 1975), 165.
37. William Carlos Williams, *The Collected Poems of William Carlos Williams, Volume I: 1909-1939*, ed. A. Walton Litz and Christopher MacGowan (New York: New Directions, 1986), 3. Hereinafter abbreviated *CP*.
38. Williams, *CP*, vol. 1, 73.
39. Ibid., 73, 80.
40. Ibid., 372.
41. Ibid., 352.
42. Ibid., 73.
43. Ibid.
44. Ford Madox Ford, "Mr. Robert Frost and 'North of Boston,'" *Outlook* (London), June 27, 1914, 879–80.
45. See John F. Sears, "Robert Frost and the Imagists: The Background of Frost's 'Sentence Sounds,'" *New England Quarterly Review* 54 (1981): 467–80; also, Tyler Hoffman, *Robert Frost and the Politics of Poetry* (Hanover, N.H.: University Press of New England, 2001).
46. See Jay Parini, *Robert Frost: A Life* (New York: Henry Holt, 2000), 43.
47. Frost, *CPPP*, 36; emphasis added.
48. Quoted in Newdick, "Sound of Sense," 294.
49. Ibid., 290.
50. Frost, *CPPP*, 680.
51. Ibid., 688.
52. Timothy Steele, "'Across Spaces of the Footed Line': The Meter and Versification of Robert Frost," *Cambridge Companion to Robert Frost*, ed. Robert Faggen (Cambridge: Cambridge University Press, 2001), 146.
53. Quoted in Parini, *Robert Frost*, 323.
54. Quoted in Tom Vander Ven, "Robert Frost's Dramatic Principle of 'Oversound,'" *American Literature* 45 (1973): 239; Robert Frost, *Robert Frost Reads from His Own Work, Yale Series of Recorded Poets*, produced by the Yale University Department of English and Audio Visual Center, ed. RWB Lewis, recorded May 19, 1961 in the Pierson College Lounge, Yale University (Carillon Records, 1961), Audio, Side 2, Band x.
55. Frost, *CPPP*, 688.
56. Ibid., 308.
57. See Parini, *Robert Frost*, 323.
58. See Frost, *CPPP*, 665.
59. David Crystal, *How Language Works* (New York: Avery Trade, 2007), 277–78.
60. Frost, *Yale Series of Recorded Poets*.
61. See Frost, *CPPP*, 854, for example.
62. Frost, *Notebooks*, 308; emphasis added.
63. Ibid., 60. See also Frost on "the Os and Oh's of a play of Shakespeare" (165).

64. Quoted in Eric W. Carlson, "Robert Frost on 'Vocal Imagination, the Merger of Form and Content,'" *American Literature* 33, no. 4 (1962): 522.
65. Frost, *Notebooks*, 48.
66. Quoted in Vander Ven, "Frost's Dramatic Principle," 239.
67. Frost, *Notebooks*, 405.
68. Ibid., 124.
69. Stevens, *CPP*, 901.
70. Frost, *CPPP*, 666.
71. Speer and Foltz, "Implicit Prosody," in Frazier and Gibson, *Explicit and Implicit Prosody*, 282.
72. Chuck Clifton, Jr. recounts several psycholinguistic experiments presenting empirical evidence that (human) subjects who were primed by listening "to the supposed author of a written text, speaking aloud, before they read the text" then "mirrored the presumed actual voice of the source of the written material" when they read this material. Clifton Jr., "Roles," in Frazier and Gibson, *Explicit and Implicit Prosody*, 169.
73. Chatman's well-known study comparing the recordings of seven speakers to Frost's own recorded reading finds that many of the readers make important errors in reciting Frost. In particular, several readers crucially misread the penultimate line "The fact is the sweetest dream that labor knows" (Frost, *CPPP*, 26), choosing to emphasize the verb *is*, as in the idiom *The fact is . . .*, rather than emphasizing the noun *fact*, as Frost does. Chatman comments, "One can obviously misinterpret a poem—and I don't mean 'richly'—by using an inappropriate intonation pattern. This is not merely a question of emphasis; intonation patterns alone can distinguish a meaningful and sensitive performance from a trivial one." Seymour Chatman, "Robert Frost's 'Mowing': An Inquiry into Prosodic Structure," *Kenyon Review* 18, no. 3 (1956): 431.

Robert Newdick reports Frost's alleged displeasure "when some one told him, once after hearing him read his poems, that now they knew how to read them right, because they had heard his voice." Newdick continues, "Yet even Carl Van Doren has confessed that when Frost once read a poem to him: 'the sound of his voice for the first time explained his poetry to me.'" Newdick, "Sound of Sense," 298.

74. For cognitive studies, see Frazier and Gibson, *Explicit and Implicit Prosody*. For popular media, see Wyatt Mason, "Letter of Recommendation: Audiobooks Read by the Author," *New York Times Magazine*, July 13, 2016, https://www.nytimes.com/2016/07/17/magazine/letter-of-recommendation-audiobooks-read-by-the-author.html.
75. Perloff, "Return," 137.
76. Ellen Bryant Voigt, *The Art of Syntax: Rhythm of Thought, Rhythm of Song* (St. Paul, Minn.: Graywolf Press, 2009), 4.
77. Hoffman, *Frost and Politics*, 37.
78. Shigeru Miyagawa, Robert C. Berwick, and Kazuo Okanoya. "The Emergence of Hierarchical Structure in Human Language," *Frontiers in Psychology* 4, no.71 (2013): 1, https://www.ncbi.nlm.nih.gov/pmc/articles/PMC3577014.
79. Frost, *CPPP*, 681.
80. Miyagawa et al., "Hierarchical Structure," 2.
81. Frost, *CPPP*, 308.
82. Cruttenden, *Intonation*, 119–20.
83. Miyagawa et. al, "Hierarchical Structure," 2.

84. Cruttenden, *Intonation*, 120.

85. Meagan E. Curtis and Jamshed J. Bharucha. "The Minor Third Communicates Sadness in Speech, Mirroring Its Use in Music," *Emotion* 10, no. 3 (2010): 346, https://www.ncbi.nlm.nih.gov/pubmed/20515223.

86. Of course, neither Frost nor Stevens nor almost any other poet really thinks that the lexical content of a poem functions only as sound. But the research described above suggests both the primacy and insufficiency of sound in poetry.

87. Quoted in Stephen Cushman, *William Carlos Williams and the Meanings of Measure* (New Haven, Conn.: Yale University Press, 1985), 92.

Sapphic Stanzas: How Can We Read the Rhythm?

Yopie Prins

Sappho, Still

In 2014 news broke that several new fragments of Sappho had been identified and deciphered by papyrologist Dirk Obbink, Professor at Oxford: "SAPPHO: Two previously unknown poems indubitably hers, says scholar."[1] Word spread fast in headlines and blogs around the world: "Incredibly rare Sappho love poems discovered on tattered 1,700-year old papyrus" . . . "New poems of Greek poetess Sappho recovered" . . . "New Sappho poems set classical world reeling" . . . "Sappho sings again" . . . "A new Sappho poem is more exciting than a new David Bowie album."[2]

As classical scholars dove into the details of transcribing, editing, translating, and interpreting the fragments, the reading public followed the story with great excitement. In *The New Yorker*, Daniel Mendelsohn described the dramatic discovery of the papyrus "about seven inches long and four inches wide: a little larger than a woman's hand" and "densely covered with lines of black Greek characters." Of course the Greek characters on this papyrus were not actually written *in* a woman's hand, much less the hand of Sappho, but they could be clearly identified as one of her poems, as Mendelsohn went on to narrate:

> Judging from the style of the handwriting, Obbink estimated that it dated to around 200 A.D. But, as he looked at the curious pattern of the lines—repeated sequences of three long lines followed by a short fourth—he saw that the text, a poem whose beginning had disappeared but of which five stanzas were still intact, had to be older.

Much older: about a thousand years more ancient than the papyrus itself. The dialect, diction, and metre of these Greek verses were all typical of the work of Sappho, the seventh-century lyric genius whose sometimes playful, sometimes anguished songs about her susceptibility to the graces of younger women bequeathed us the adjectives "sapphic" and "lesbian" (from the island of Lesbos, where she lived). The four-line stanzas were in fact part of a schema she is said to have invented, called "the sapphic stanza."[3]

According to this narrative, although there were other pieces of internal evidence to associate the poems with Sappho, the identification depended first and foremost on recognizing a poetic form associated with the archaic Greek poet Sappho living on Lesbos sometime around 630 B.C. We might even say that the Sapphic stanza is a poetic invention of Sappho that makes possible our poetic reinvention of Sappho as "the seventh-century lyric genius," singing at the origins of a Western lyric tradition.

The recent discovery of "the new Sappho" repeats the drama of previous discoveries. Exactly one hundred years earlier, the headlines of 1914 also announced big news, first in the London newspapers and then in *The New York Times*: "Poem by Sappho, Written 600 B.C., Dug Up in Egypt" (Figure 1). Written by Joyce Kilmer (American poet and Man of Letters) this article begins enthusiastically:

> Out of the dust of Egypt comes the voice of Sappho, as clear and sweet as when she sang in Lesbos by the sea, 600 years before the birth of Christ. The picks and spades of Arab workmen, directed by Bernard P. Grenfell and Arthur S. Hunt of the Egypt Exploration Fund, have given the world a hitherto unknown poem by the greatest woman poet of all times.

And Kilmer ends even more hyperbolically:

> They have recovered, they have almost recreated, one of the greatest poems of the greatest poet of the greatest age of lyric poetry. It is already a classic, this little song, whose liquid Greek syllables echo the music of undying passion.

To illustrate how a scrap of papyrus is recovered from the past and "almost recreated" as a song echoing in the present, the article includes a picture of men digging in the sand ("Scene of the Discovery of the New Papyri of Sappho at Oxyrhynchus"), a photograph of papyrus fragments ("Three of the fifty-six pieces surviving from the roll which contained Book I of the Unknown Odes of Sappho"), a reconstruction of the Greek

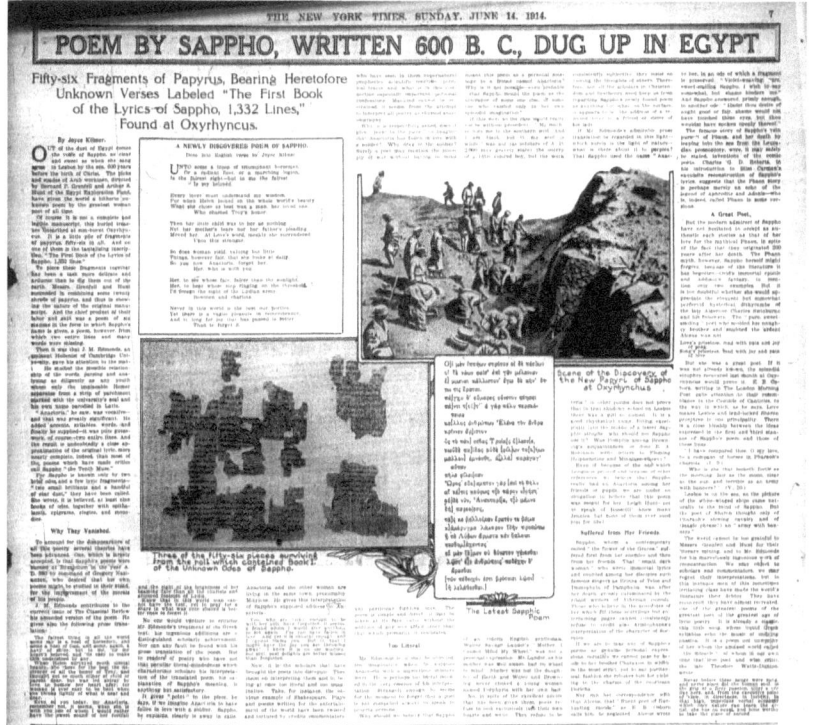

FIGURE 1. Joyce Kilmer, "Poem by Sappho, Written 600 BC, Dug Up in Egypt," *New York Times* (June 14, 1914), 7.

text from one of these fragments ("The Latest Sapphic Poem"), and a metrical translation of that text in Sapphic stanzas by Kilmer himself ("A Newly Discovered Poem of Sappho, Done into English verse"). From the composite image of this new poem (now known as Sapphic Fragment 16, to which we will later return) we are invited to imagine the voice of Sappho herself, "as clear and sweet as when she sang," transcending time through the perfectly measured time of her lyric meters.

The rhetoric around the recovery of new Sapphic fragments, at the beginning of the twentieth century and again at the beginning of our own, repeats a long history of invoking Sappho as a musical figure for lyric, proclaimed the Tenth Muse in antiquity because of the beautiful songs that were composed and performed by Sappho (or in the name of Sappho) for accompaniment by the lyre. But by the time they were collected and organized according to meter in nine volumes for the Alexandrian Library, Sappho's lyrics were no longer songs to be heard but rather poems to be read, producing an idea of Sapphic song as always already lost. And this silence is amplified by the historical fragmentation of the Sapphic corpus: out of scattered fragments, Sappho has been incorporated into many languages over many centuries, emerging as an exemplary lyric figure in nineteenth-century poetry as an exemplification of twentieth-century lyric reading.[4] Within this critical tradition, every discovery of a new Sappho is still the same old Sappho, still silent: we imagine her *as if* she could be heard, because we know how to read the Sapphic stanza.

Or do we? Even if we know how to recognize the schema of the Sapphic stanza, how can we read the rhythm? That is the question posed by this essay's title, which might be imagined as if it were a line in Sapphic meter. If we approach it as a rhetorical question, we have already given up on the possibility of scanning it: "Sapphic Stanzas: How **can** we read the rhythm?" But if we approach it as a practical question, we could try out different possibilities for scansion: "**Sapph**ic **Stanz**as: **How** can we **read** the **rhythm**?" Measuring the length of syllables, as in classical quantitative verse, we would scan: **long short long short long short short long short long [short]**. And if we decide to call this a choriambic line, we would look for a four-syllable foot in the middle, scanning "**how** can we **read**" as a choriamb: **long short short long**. To make the scansion work, we would have to assume that the final word "rhythm" has two syllables, and then treat the second syllable as either short or long (since we may not be sure about the rhythm of "rhythm"). Of course this would not be the only way to scan the line. If we were dividing it into feet, according to foot scansion, we would read: *trochee, trochee, dactyl and trochee trochee*. Or, if we were stressing accents, according to beat prosody, we would read: *five strong beats and also some well-placed offbeats*. Or, if we were counting syllables rather than stresses, as in syllabic verse, we would read: *this is just eleven syllabic units*.

But however we choose to scan the line, if we repeat its pattern three times we can construct a Sapphic stanza by adding on a shorter fourth line, like a refrain, to make a quatrain that can be schematized (with – marking long or stressed syllables, and ˘ marking short or unstressed syllables, and x marking the "anceps" syllable that is either stressed or unstressed) like this:

– ˘ – x – ˘ ˘ – ˘ – x

– ˘ – x – ˘ ˘ – ˘ – x

– ˘ – x – ˘ ˘ – ˘ – x

– ˘ ˘ – x

The shorter line at the end of the Sapphic stanza is called "Adonic" and it has five syllables: ***long short short long short*** (or ***long short short long long***). And zipahdeedoodah, with this final ***dactyl and trochee*** (or ***dactyl and spondee***), we have completed the stanza identified with Sappho, now the proper name for a metrical form that has been variously imagined and reimagined by generations of scholars and poets.[5] In reading and writing "Sapphics," they perform different ways to think about the relation between meter and rhythm, stanza and line, form and content.

Scanning the history of such conjectures would be another approach to the question posed by my title. We could run to the library to search for versification manuals and histories of prosody gathering dust on the shelves, or run a search through the Princeton Prosody Archive (PPA), inspired by T. V. F. Brogan's bibliography of English versification and brought into the digital age by Meredith Martin.[6] This full-text searchable database yields numerous references to "Sapphic stanzas," in metrical treatises and a wide range of metrical experiments to recreate the Sapphic stanza in English: for example, in Elizabethan quantitative verse, and in neo-classical Sapphics mediated by Catullus and Horace for imitation by eighteenth-century poets like William Cowper, and with increasing variability and frequency in Victorian poetry, as nineteenth-century poets and prosodists became obsessed with reading classical Greek meters in relation to English ideas about rhythm and meter.

Beyond the collection and quantification of these historical materials, the Princeton Prosody Archive invites us to consider: "What if literary concepts such as meter and rhythm are historically contingent and fundamentally unstable?"[7] This is the theoretical point of doing research in historical prosody. In addition to demonstrating the historical contingency of ideas about the Sapphic stanza, my purpose is to explore how these metrical imaginaries have served to produce allegories of rhythm, and vice versa, thus undoing a distinction between rhythm and meter that has become one of the central orthodoxies of English prosody. According to this orthodoxy, meter in poetry is an abstract paradigm that is realized in the rhythms of speech or embodied in a rhythmic performance or rhythmically perceived in the mind. Yet the phenomenology of poetic rhythm experienced in the present moment depends on how meter is theorized at different moments in history. Such metrical discourses attempt to materialize meter while also idealizing rhythm. Furthermore, this idealization of rhythm is central to ideas about lyric emerging toward the end of the nineteenth century, when Sappho was increasingly read as the very personification of lyric and the Sapphic stanza as its rhythmic perfection. To reflect critically on Sapphic rhythm, I propose a "meta-metrical" reading of several examples from the past two centuries and in contemporary poetics.

Allegories of Rhythm

At the turn of the twenty-first century, googling the phrase "Sapphic Stanza" leads us into a labyrinth of dictionary definitions and classroom instructions, Wikipedia entries and Facebook posts, Youtube videos and audio recordings, blogs for poets and poetry websites, including an essay posted online by the Poetry Society of America. Entitled "Marvellous Sapphics" and written by the poet Rachel Wetzsteon, the essay starts with a poetic performance of the Sapphic stanza that presents Sappho as the very embodiment of this metrical form:

> I would like to tell you about a lovely
> stanza form I've long been an ardent fan of:
> it was conjured up in a simpler time by
>   Classical Sappho.[8]

Wetzsteon presents the Sapphic stanza as a "show and tell," in both senses of "telling": she recounts the myth of its origin by carefully counting out syllables in three hendecasyllabic lines that lead up to the final Adonic: "Classical Sappho." Here we are asked to scan the name of Sappho in Sapphic meter, "conjured up in a simpler time," suggesting not only the archaic time of ancient Greece but also a time when verse was measured by temporal duration of syllables, in contrast to the modern measures of English accentual-syllabic verse. At the same time, by recreating the "Marvellous Sapphics" of the Sapphic stanza in English, the versification of Wetzsteon's poem transforms Classical Sappho into modern English meter, conjured up in the present and projected into the past. It's a lovely performance of a lovely form, to love and "be an ardent fan of."

Wetzsteon's essay goes on to describe how the process of reading and writing imitations of Sappho's meter leads to the internalization of a Sapphic rhythm:

> If you try your hand at this stanza, you should be warned that it's addictive. When you're in the middle of writing one, its rhythm—so close, after all, to a heartbeat—has a way of entering your bloodstream when you aren't looking. Get up from your desk and take a walk and clear your head, and you'll find that the stanza—the last line especially—is following you. Shave and a haircut; oboe concerto;

Emily Bronte; over and over; where am I going? It's insidious; it's unstoppable!

In her clever reiteration of final Adonics, over and over, there is a repetition compulsion that seems to embed Sapphic meter in the rhythms of the body, and the rhythms of life. Transforming the metrical form of the Sapphic stanza into a rhythmic figure, Wetzsteon imagines it "so close, after all, to a heart beat" that it seems to be "entering your bloodstream" and you can feel it running throughout your body: the pulse of your heart, the breath of your lungs, the pace of your feet (like a pop song stuck in your head, every breath you take, every move you make).

This idea of Sapphic rhythm is an incorporation of the metrical lessons that Wetzsteon learned from her teacher, the poet and critic John Hollander. In *Rhyme's Reason*, he offers a somewhat more pedantic poetic performance of the Sapphic stanza:

> *Sapphics:* four-line stanzas whose first three lines are
> Heard—in our hard English at least—as heartbeats,
> Then, in one more touch of a final short line,
>   Tenderly ending.[9]

Slipping from "heard," to "hard," to "heart," Hollander invites us to read the "hard beating" of English accentual verse as if we could hear a heart beating, but more softly, especially in the "touch" of the final short line, the Adonic that is "tenderly ending." The internal rhyme of this tender end enacts the etymological sense of the Latin verb *tendere*—to stretch out—by extending the length or duration of this syllable. Thus Hollander tries to achieve an effect reminiscent of the alternation of long and short syllables in classical quantitative verse.

In both examples, the imitation of the Sapphic stanza is thematized, explicitly turning meter into a figure for rhythm embodied in the heartbeat of the poem. And often this figurative logic is taken one step further, for example in *The Poem's Heartbeat*, a manual of prosody by the poet Alfred Corn. He suggests that a primal sense of rhythm ("before an infant is born it develops a sense of hearing, and the first thing it hears is the heartbeat of the mother") can be developed into a feeling for poetry, "as hearing with the inner ear, a kind of hearing that you will gradually acquire as you examine (and perform aloud) actual examples cited for study."[10] One of the examples cited in his manual is the Sapphic stanza, illustrating how we might learn to hear quantitative meter in English: "When directed to listen for this auditory feature we can, however, hear it . . . . **Oooom pa ooooom pa ooooom pa pa ooooom pa ooooom pa.**"[11] Listening to the Sapphic stanza as a variation on the poem's heartbeat, Corn seems to turn Sappho into the mother of poets, giving birth to his own poetic imitations of the Sapphic stanza, and perhaps even giving birth to poetry itself.

This kind of allegorical reading is further elaborated by Amittai Aviram in *Telling Rhythm: Body and Meaning in Poetry*, arguing that every poem presents "an interpretation or representation—an *allegory*—of the bodily rhythmic energy of poetic form," and that all poetry can be read allegorically as a manifestation of the sublime power of rhythm in the physical world.[12] In keeping with Aviram's argument, poets like Wetzsteon and Hollander are both "telling rhythm" as the essential meaning produced by the meter of their Sapphic imitations. But in doing so, they hearken back less to Sappho (whoever that was) than to a tradition of imitating Sappho (as the personification of a classical form), and especially English imitations of that form (circulating in the name of Sappho) in the nineteenth century. In other words, the "Classical Sappho" invoked by Rachel Wetzsteon turns out to be "Victorian Sappho," a figure produced by Victorian discourses about Sapphic meter, marking the emergence of a powerful metrical imaginary that persists in the imagination of "Sapphic rhythm" among poets in the twentieth century and beyond.

Imagining Meter

In the course of the nineteenth century, debates about classical models for English versification raged fast and furious among poets, prosodists, philologists, and pedagogues, all contributing to new ways to think about meter. In 1860, for example, an amateur classicist named Thomas Foster Barham published a treatise "On Metrical Time, or The Rhythm of Verse, Ancient and Modern." Although he admits his theories are but "the reflexions of an isolated country student, living remote from Academic halls and libraries" he insists on the practical utility of reciting meter as a way of learning how to recognize rhythm.[13] According to Barham, the "untutored ear" must be taught to hear the rhythms of poetry by learning first how to read and then how to recite meter: reading comes before speaking, thus predicting and indeed prescribing how English should be pronounced. He offers a quintessentially Victorian idea of metrical education for the perfection of speech, and claims to discover new rhythms for the modern world by recovering an idea of metrical time from the ancients. Barham goes on to exemplify his argument with reference to classical meters including "that beautiful and well-known

> The first shall be that beautiful and wellknown system named the Sapphic. This is commonly represented as consisting of three lines, technically termed *epichoriambic*, with a short portion superadded. They are formed however essentially of dactyls and trochays; and as originally written by the poetess, would seem to have been intended for three lines only, the two former trimeters, and the last a tetrameter.
>
> Φαίνεταί μοι κῆνος ἴσος Θεοῖσιν
> Ἔμμεν ὠνήρ ὅστις ἐναντίος τοι
> Ἰσδάνει, καὶ πλασίον ἀδὺ φωνεύσας ὑπακούει.
>
> With this rhythm, the effect of the metre is certainly considerably different from that of our ordinary mode of reading, but, as it seems to me, it is preferable.

FIGURE 2. Thomas Foster Barham, "On Metrical Time, or The Rhythm of Verse, Ancient and Modern" (1860).

system named the Sapphic." He proposes that we think of the Sapphic stanza "originally written by the poetess" as three lines instead of four, and quotes the first stanza of fragment 31, the famous *phainetai moi* ode (Figure 2). By visualizing these lines as two trimeters and a tetrameter, he imagines another way to read Sapphic rhythm: "With this rhythm, the effect of the metre is considerably different from that of our ordinary mode of reading, but, as it seems to me, it is preferable." But can we really hear this rhythm, even with a well-tutored ear, or is it a metrical effect that appeals to the eye?

This is but one of many ways to visualize the Sapphic stanza in Victorian England; we see another example in the popular 1885 edition of Sappho, introduced and translated by Henry Thornton Wharton, another amateur scholar.[14] He prints the Sapphic stanza as a metrical grid, a strophe with 4 lines of alternating short and long syllables (Figure 3). This image of the meter leads Wharton to imagine Sapphic rhythm not as the perfection of speech, but as a perfect song that he discovers in the poetry of Algernon Charles Swinburne: "Nothing repeats its rhythm to my ear so well as Swinburne's Sapphics," he writes at the end of this passage. The untutored ear can be attuned to Sapphic song by reading Swinburne's imitation of Sappho, according to Wharton:

> With such lines as these ringing in the reader's ears, he can almost hear Sappho herself singing:

the various divisions. The metre commonly called after her name was probably not invented by her; it was only called Sapphic because of her frequent use of it. Its strophe is made up thus:

$$-\cup-\bar{\cup}-\cup\cup-\cup-\bar{\cup}$$
$$-\cup-\bar{\cup}-\cup\cup-\cup-\bar{\cup}$$
$$-\cup-\bar{\cup}-\cup\cup-\cup-\bar{\cup}$$
$$-\cup\cup-\bar{\cup}$$

FIGURE 3. Henry Thornton Wharton, *Sappho: Memoir, Text, Selected Renderings and a Literal Translation* (1885).

> *Songs that move the heart of the shaken heaven,*
> *Songs that break the heart of the earth with pity,*
>   *Hearing, to hear them.*

In Swinburne's final Adonic, "Hearing, to hear them," Wharton imagines that Sappho herself can be heard again, or "almost," precisely because she is no longer heard. Swinburne's vision of Sapphic poets singing an elegiac strain in the wake of Sappho, forever echoing her song, is referred back by Wharton to an effect of meter that we must also strain to hear.

Moving from classical to musical models for imagining Sapphic rhythm, a Victorian treatise on the history of music by John Frederick Rowbotham dedicates an entire chapter to "the high state of perfection which Greek singing had reached under the influence of the Lesbian School of Musicians."[15] Rowbotham praises the "thrilling style" of Sappho in particular: "She was full of fire and passion, and is the acknowledged mistress of the Systaltic or 'Thrilling' Style of Music, of which very likely she was the inventress, and it is out of compliment to her introducing a new style into Music that Plato has called her the Tenth Muse."[16] According to Rowbotham, the musical thrill of Sapphic song is its melodic elaboration of epic meter. He suggests that the Sapphic stanza is "a woman's Hexameter," and compares a line in Sapphic meter to dactylic hexameter in order to illustrate how Sappho falls one foot short of Homer (Figure 4).

In contrasting epic and lyric meters, Rowbotham concludes that the Sapphic stanza is an example of "the feminine heroic." Rather than striking up the lyre as prelude to recitation of Homeric battles that went on and on, Sappho used the lyre as harmonious accompaniment to love songs that had greater melodic variation; because the lines were lacking

But when she chose to write in regular falls, and make symmetry of emphasis, no one could do it better than she could. And that which we know as the Sapphic Metre is an instance of this. And it is a woman's Hexameter. And there is a charming timidity about it which makes the difference; or perhaps she is not tall enough and cannot reach so high; for look, when we come to compare it with the real Hexameter, lo! it is one foot too short.

Hexameter. _ ∪ ∪ _ ∪ ∪ _ ∪ ∪ _ ∪ ∪ _ ∪ ∪ _ _
Sapphic.   _ ∪   _ ∪ _ ∪ ∪ _ ∪   _ ∪

FIGURE 4. John Frederick Rowbotham, *A History of Music* (1885–86).

one foot, they could be grouped into a longer stanza that Rowbotham describes as "the extension of the Musical Period and the protraction of the Cadence on the voice."[17]

The interplay of different metrical notations is even more visible in a slim pamphlet published in 1896 by Joseph Salathiel Tunison, entitled *The Sapphic Stanza: A Tentative Study in Greek Metrical, Tonal, and Dancing Art* (Figure 5). Tunison juxtaposes three different ways to visualize the Sapphic stanza, ranging from Diomedes (a Latin grammarian from the fourth century) to Buchanan ("the eminent Scotch Latinist" from the nineteenth century), and in each example the bar keeps shifting to divide the line into different kinds of feet.[18] The materialization of meter in graphic form produces a vision of the Sapphic stanza as a "tonal and dancing art" that can be incorporated into the rhythms of the voice and the body. By (choreo)graphing the meter, metrical feet can be mobilized as dancing feet and naturalized as embodied rhythmic movement. In his Preface, Tunison declares an interest in "primitive Greek music" connected to dance, and he goes on to argue that "the real advance marked by Sappho was in the art of rhythm."[19] Sapphic meter is best understood as the embodiment of rhythm, according to Tunison, who speculates that "her stanza suggests rapid movement thrice repeated, and a sudden complete change at the last. . . . like this: Forward, back, forward, then a mere flinging or swaying of the body while the dancer remained in one spot."[20] At this historical moment the metrical imaginary of Victorian poetics, marking the meter as a musical form, was moving toward the rhythmic

accurate description of the metrical formula. For example Diomedes took the following to be the correct prosodic notation:

$$\overline{}\,\smile\,|\,\overline{}\,\overline{}\,|\,\overline{}\,\smile\,|\,\smile\,\overline{}\,|\,\smile\,\overline{}\,\overline{}$$

though he admitted that others preferred to scan the stanza in this manner:

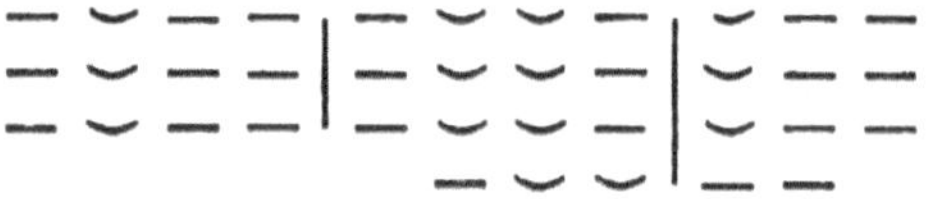

$$\overline{}\,\smile\,\overline{}\,\overline{}\,|\,\overline{}\,\smile\,\smile\,\overline{}\,|\,\smile\,\overline{}\,\overline{}$$

George Buchanan, the eminent Scotch Latinist, preferred the following ambiguous formula:

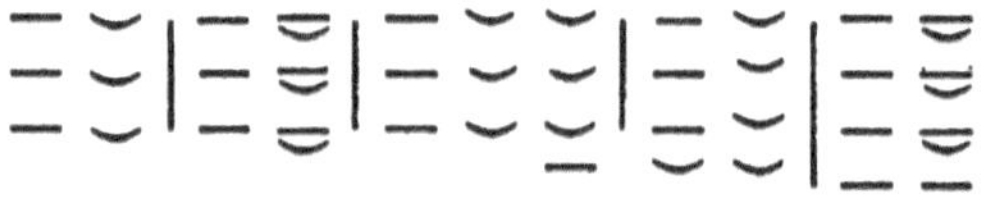

$$\overline{}\,\smile\,|\,\overline{}\,\overline{\smile}\,|\,\overline{}\,\smile\,\smile\,|\,\overline{}\,\overline{\smile}\,|\,\overline{}\,\overline{\smile}$$

Neue agreed with Buchanan but added accent marks to indicate the particular syllable on which the emphasis fell in recitation, thus: $\acute{\overline{}}\,\smile\,\overline{}\,\overline{}\,\overline{\smile}\,\|\,\acute{\overline{}}\,\smile\,\smile\,\overline{}\,\smile\,\overline{}\,\overline{\smile}$. On the other hand Dr. Ambros in his History of Music adopted the notation of Diomedes, while agreeing with Neue as to the proper places for the accents. Now, it is plain that whatever notion these various critics had of the relation between the long and the short syllable, they were agreed as to the cæsura. They would all have divided the verses into semicolons, to use the ancient grammatical phrase, with one important accent to each subdivision. These semicolons, each with its single strong syllable, answer respectively to the feet of the hexameter.

FIGURE 5. Joseph Salathiel Tunison, *The Sapphic Stanza: A Tentative Study in Greek Metrical, Tonal and Dancing Art* (1896).

imagination of twentieth-century prosody, producing a notion of primal rhythm for which Sappho serves as origin.

Thus, by the early twentieth century, some classical scholars were looking back to the Indo-European roots of Sapphic meter. In 1909 John Williams White published "The Origin and Form of Aeolic Verse," building on "a commonplace of Comparative Metre that the primitive poetic form in Aryan speech was a dimeter of eight syllables" and that "the language was quantitative, but the order of longs and shorts was not yet regulated (o o o o o o o o)."[21] Using each bubble to represent a syllable that could be either short or long, White suggests these syllables were regulated into patterns by a "rhythmicizing instinct that gave melodic form to the second half of the primitive dimeter first in India," and then "among the ancestors of the Ionian poets," and then "their brothers, who in course of time made their way and settled Aeolis" and "metrized differently."[22] According to White, Sappho's poetry represents the artistic perfection of an instinctively rhythmic and distinctively Aeolic impulse, as "their early bards sang to the people in forms that we first meet, at the end of a great period, in the highly developed verse of Alcaeus and Sappho." This interest in Aeolic syllable-counting marked the emergence of a "new metric" that sought to "catch glimpses of the growth of rhythms in the most primitive stages"; by imagining that "centuries before Sappho the Lesbian maidens sang their songs in the measure" of older Aeolic melodies, it became possible for scholars "to refer developed metrical forms back to more primitive previous stages of rhythm."[23]

Responding to such theories, a 1920 treatise entitled *Res Metrica* by W. R. Hardie notes that the discovery of new Sapphic fragments at the turn of the century was "metrically instructive" for generating new ideas about the Sapphic stanza.[24] But in a detailed excursus on Aeolic Verse, Hardie also expresses skepticism about "the 'Indo-European,' 'Aeolic,' or 'quadrisyllabic' theory which has had much vogue in recent years."[25] Although he accepts the claim that Indo-European verse was at first "syllabic"—i.e., although "syllables were merely counted, they were in no way regulated and might be long or short"—he disagrees that this "polyschematist dimeter" persists in the Sapphic stanza. He reprints a Sapphic line, in order to call into question a representation of meter in which the first four syllables appear as bubbles, open to interpretation (Figure 6).

In Hardie's view, this schematic representation is an historical impossibility because of the literary production of the Sapphic stanza; Sappho's verses were not only "things which could easily be sung to the lute" but "they must have been also *read*," and for this reason "the notion that a Sapphic line was in part unregulated or amorphous is the opposite of

> But recent metricians would not admit even as much as this. They regard 'quadrisyllabic' scansion or structure as much more lasting than that, and they find verses in the sixth and fifth centuries which they define as partly 'syllabic' or amorphous. One of them¹ even gives the scheme of a *Sapphic* line as
>
> $$\circ\,\circ\,\circ\,\circ - \cup\,\cup - \cup - -,$$
>
> and the 'polyschematist' dimeter is discovered frequently in the lyrics of the drama.

FIGURE 6. William Ross Hardie, *Res Metrica* (1920).

the truth."²⁶ This concern about the quantitative ambiguity of syllables reflects broader critical debates about quantitative versification in English, and about the relationship between rhythm and meter in modernist experiments with syllabic verse: the question of whether English syllables could be quantified or counted implied new ideas about rhythm. Looking back into the prehistory of the Sapphic stanza was a way of looking forward into the future of English poetry as well.

Meta-Metrics

With nineteenth-century ideas about Sapphic meter morphing into twentieth-century ideas about the Sapphic line, the discovery of a new Sapphic fragment (so enthusiastically announced by Kilmer in *The New York Times* of 1914) proved a critical turning point for English imitations of the Sapphic stanza, and the transformation of Victorian into modern poetics. A photograph of the papyrus is featured in *The Oxyrhynchus Papyri Part X,* and edited with transcription, translation, and notes by Grenfell and Hunt (Figure 7). Now known as Fragment 16, the papyrus is riddled with gaps and seems to be part of a longer poem. Grenfell and Hunt were able to construct a somewhat coherent translation in English prose, based on five and a half consecutive stanzas in Greek:

> Some say that the fairest thing on the black earth is a host of horsemen, others of foot, others of ships; but I say that is fairest which is the object of one's desire. And it is quite easy to make this plain to all; for Helen observing well the beauty of men judged the best to be that one who destroyed the whole glory of Troy, nor bethought herself at all of child or parents dear, but through love Cypris led her astray. [Verily the wills of mortals are easily bent when they are moved by

Fr. 1

No. 1231

FIGURE 7. Bernard P. Grenfell and Arthur S. Hunt, *The Oxyrhynchus Papyri Part X* (1914).

vain thoughts.] And I now have called to mind Anactoria, far away, whose gracious step and radiant glance I would rather see than the chariots of the Lydians and the charge of accoutered knights. We know well that this cannot come to pass among men . . .[27]

The fragment sets up a contrast between Homeric epic and Sapphic lyric, beginning with the rhetorical device of a priamel, differentiating between what "some say" in the world of Homer and what "I say," in the first person singular, in the world of Sappho: what moves the heart is not men on horse, not men on foot, not men on ships but rather whatever one loves (translated here as "the object of one's desire"). Turning away from men at war in the first stanza, the fragment turns toward women in love in the following stanzas, where Helen and Anactoria appear not only as objects of desire but as desiring subjects. The movement of desire is emphasized through verbs of motion, as stanzas 2 and 3 remember Helen's departure for Troy, and stanzas 4 and 5 remember Anactoria "far away." The memory of Anactoria with her "gracious step and radiant glance" is described as more desirable than the advance of Lydian charioteers and footsoldiers ("accoutered knights" is an awkward translation for the Greek word *pesdomachentas*, which contains the word "foot"). As an epic theme is thus transformed into erotic poetry, the fragment demonstrates the transformation of Homer's marching hexameters into the graceful feet of Sappho's meter, translating the measures of heroic epic into the melodic cadences of the Sapphic stanza.

Albeit in rather pedestrian prose, this flat-footed account of Fragment 16 opens up a meta-metrical reading that invites critical reflection on an allegory of meter, simultaneously projected into and out of Sappho's poem. For this reason Kilmer's article on the new fragment expresses special interest in Anactoria, not as an actual "girl so named" who was familiar to Sappho on Lesbos, but because "it is a good rhythmical name, fitting excellently into the middle of a lesser Sapphic strophe." For Kilmer, the very act of naming of Anactoria here presents the possibility of reading the Sapphic stanza meta-metrically, as a performance of meter. While giving due credit to Professors Grenfell and Hunt from Oxford for deciphering the poem (and dutifully citing Professor Edmonds from Cambridge as well, for producing another prose translation of the fragment), Kilmer sets aside "that peculiar literal-mindedness which characterizes scholars." Instead he calls to mind a more figurative translation into the form of the Sapphic stanza:

> Unto some a troop of triumphant horsemen,
> Or a radiant fleet, or a marching legion,
> Is the fairest sight—but to me the fairest
>   Is my belovéd.

What matters most (or seems fairest) to Kilmer is the meter, which he has "done into English verse" by finding an equivalent for Greek quantitative meter in accentual-syllabic lines. This metrical performance is especially pronounced in the Adonics at the end of each stanza (for example, in marking the accent on "Is my belovéd" in stanza 1) and in the manipulation of caesuras in stanza five:

> Her, to see whose face, fairer than the sunlight,
> Her, to hear whose step ringing on the threshold,
> I'd forego the sight of the Lydian army,
>   Bowmen and chariots.

In the reiteration of "Her, to see" and "Her, to hear," Kilmer visualizes the Sapphic stanza as an appeal to both the eye and the ear, hoping to make its metrical feet visible and audible again, like footsteps ringing on the threshold between past and present.

Fragment 16 prompted many more imitations of, and meditations on, Sapphic meter in the early twentieth century. No doubt this fragment had special appeal for readers in 1914, as soldiers were marching off to World War I. It could be read as an anti-war poem, wishing for a world beyond war, or refusing to step in time to the rhythms of wartime poetry. And because it was written in Sapphic stanzas, it served as an alternative to the ideology of marching meters by introducing more variation into English verse. For example, Edwin Marion Cox concludes his 1916 pamphlet, *Sappho and the Sapphic Metre in English*, with reference to "the latest important Sapphic discovery" as an invitation to modern poets to "expand this fragment into nearly the whole of a poem."[28] Although Cox acknowledges that "the transfer of perfection in one language into another is not within the bounds of possibility" and "approximation is all that even genius can hope for," he believes that perfecting Sapphic meter in English would be one way to make Sappho whole again, and so perfect English poetry as well.

To take up this invitation, another American Man of Letters named Dr. Marion Mills Miller attempted a metrical translation in "Two New Poems of Sappho," published in *The Independent* (1916). While agreeing with Cox that English versification could only approximate the Greek of Sappho, Miller nevertheless aspires to translate Sappho "in as near an approach to the original 'Sapphic meter' as a language permits in which accent (time and force) is the rhythmic principle, and not so-called classic 'quantity.'"[29] Entitled "To Anactoria," his translation of the fragment compensates for what is lacking in English by introducing rhyme for the amplification of metrical effect:

> Of all that the world holds, some deem the fairest
> A brave show of horsemen; others praise as rarest
> Footmen a-march, or a fleet to battle movéd—
>   I, my belovéd.

In this first stanza, the accentuation of the final syllables in "movéd" and "belovéd" strains the rhyme in order to highlight the final Adonic. And the extra syllable in "footmen a-march" is also an awkward attempt to fit the Sapphic line, suggesting the difficulty of finding the right rhythmic principle to create equivalence to the Greek meter. The marching feet at the start of the poem are transformed in stanza 4, however, by the "soft footfall" of Sapphic meter:

> Whose soft footfall sets my heart a-bounding
> Wider than when the clarions are sounding;
> Whose bright face hath power more to charm me
>   Than Lydia's army.

While we may debate the virtues of "charm me" and "army" as a lighthearted rhyme, it reinforces the lighter rhythm that "sets my heartabounding," making the heart as well as the feet skip a beat in Sapphic meter.

The metrical allegory of marching versus dancing feet in the Sapphic stanza is made explicit by Miller in his Preface to *The Songs of Sappho* (1925):

> The rhythmic units used by Sappho in her characteristic metre are the trochee and dactyl, one a marching and one a dancing foot which combine to express vigorous action and graceful movement.... The following verse reproduces very well the rhythmic effect of the original sapphic line, which is a succession of four trochees with a dactyl intervening in the middle:
>
> *Sappho's trochees march with a dancing dactyl.*
>
> Let the reader see in his mind four Greek soldiers marching in line with a dancing girl in the middle keeping step with her left foot while her right one executes two skips in the time of one steady stride forward by the soldiers.[30]

While this vision draws on Victorian ideas about the Sapphic stanza as "a woman's hexameter," the meter is no longer visualized on the page as dactylic hexameter at all. Rather it is reimagined ("let the reader see in his mind") as four trochees marching in "steady stride" like Greek soldiers, with one dactyl inserting "two skips" like a dancing girl in the middle: Homeric hexameters reversed (and re-versed) in Sapphic meter. And indeed, Miller goes one step further in turning the Sapphic stanza into a pirouette around its own meta-metrical performance:

> Stamp in trochees two to a gliding dactyl;
> Two more trochees trip to the turn; go back till
> Verses three are trod. With the two feet blended
>   Strophe is ended.

Thus poets in the early twentieth century turned to Sapphic stanzas to dance around the tread of metrical feet, not only as a variation on epic hexameter but also as a way to "break the back of the iambic pentameter!"— Ezra Pound's imperative, passed along to young modernist poets like Mary Barnard, who was urged by Pound to "write Sapphics until they come out of your ears."[31]

But imitating Sapphic stanzas to suit the English ear is easier said than done, as John Trantner ironically proclaims in "Writing in the Manner of Sappho" (1997):[32]

> Writing Sapphics well is a tricky business
> Lines begin and end with a pair of trochees;
> in between them dozes a dactyl, rhythm
>   rising and falling,
>
> like a drunk asleep at a party. Ancient
> Greek—the language seemed to be made for Sapphics,
> not a worry: anyone used to English
>   finds it a bastard.

Writing in the manner of Sappho is like hosting a bad-mannered guest, a bastard in the colloquial sense (unruly and difficult) and in the figurative sense (born from the illegitimate union of ancient Greek and modern English). In contrast with the "dancing dactyl" imagined by Marion Mills Miller to introduce "graceful movement" into English verse, the "dozing dactyl" in Trantner's poem rudely interrupts the line in "rhythm / rising and falling, / like a drunk asleep at a party." This rhythmic snoring is an interruption (emphasized in the enjambment after "rhythm" and the stanzaic enjambment after "falling") that nevertheless awakens the English language to other rhythms. Trantner delights in such irregularities, as John Kinsella points out about this poem: "This seems like a solid argument for metrical consistency, for respecting the rhythms of 'accepted English.' It is not." Rather, he accentuates the interplay of Australian and American rhythms: "Tranter plays with metrics and destabilizes a canonical reading by doing so. These are meta-metrics," Kinsella concludes.[33] By diversifying the rhythms of English in pseudo-classical versification, Tranter discovers new tricks at the end of the twentieth century, turning the "tricky business" of the Sapphic stanza into a postmodern meta-metrical performance.

Bracketing Rhythm

Following the steps of Anactoria in the measures of Sappho, I have been reading Fragment 16 meta-metrically to suggest how twentieth-century poets used the Sapphic stanza to reimagine the relation between rhythm and meter, sometimes performing meter to produce allegories of rhythm and other times performing rhythm to produce allegories of meter. At the turn of the twenty-first century, Anglo-American poetics revolve less around the movement of metrical feet, but the Sapphic stanza persists as a metrical imaginary. I conclude with two recent translations of Fragment 16 by Jim Powell and Anne Carson, who experiment with different ways to see and hear the poems of Sappho, not only in print but also in sound recording and multi-media performance, mediating between what Hollander calls "the poem in the ear" and "the poem in the eye" to perform new forms of Sapphic rhythm.[34]

In *Sappho: A Garland* (1993) Jim Powell arranges his translation of Sapphic fragments into "an integrated collage or mosaic, playing off modernist techniques of poetics sequence, fragmentary montage, and stream of consciousness to create a cumulative movement that points to the integrity of her art," and in doing so he re-creates and re-integrates an idea of Greek metrics in American verse that moves beyond the foot to the measure of the line.[35] As he explains in the section of his translator's *Afterword* entitled "Sappho's Measures," the metrical virtuosity of Sappho has "exerted a marked influence on later poetry," because "Aeolic metrics envisions the poetic line not as a composite entity formed by the repetition of a given number of identical 'feet' but as an integrated whole" (38). While taking up the measure of the Sapphic stanza is a challenge for all poets—"none succeeds in matching her fluidity, ease, grace, and melodic variety" (39)—his goal in translating the Sapphic fragments is not only to "preserve Sappho's rhythms, replacing quantity with stress, wherever doing so creates a comparable effect in English" (40), but to recreate a longer sense of the line as a comparable rhythmic effect.

Powell therefore translates Fragment 16 with strategic placement of punctuation for rhythmic effect, and numerous enjambments across lines and stanzas:

> Some say thronging cavalry, some say foot soldiers,
> others call a fleet the most beautiful of

sights the dark earth offers, but I say it's what-
    ever you love best.

And it's easy to make this understood by
everyone, for she who surpassed all human
kind in beauty, Helen, abandoning her
    husband (that best of

men) went sailing off to the shores of Troy and
never spent a thought on her child or loving
parents: when the goddess seduced her wits and
    left her to wander,

she forgot them all, she could not remember
anything but longing, and lightly straying
aside, lost her way. But that reminds me
    now: Anactoria,

she's not here, and I'd rather see her lovely
step, her sparkling glance and her face than gaze on
all the troops in Lydia in their chariots and
    glittering armor.

According to Powell, "Sappho's secret consists largely in keeping her caesura moving: in her sapphics the caesura (a pause in mid-verse) seldom falls in the same place in two consecutive lines" (39). Likewise, in order to reimagine the movement of the Sapphic stanza, the secret of his translation is to insert punctuation into the middle of lines (such as the parenthesis around "best of men," the colon after "parents" and in "now: Anactoria," the period after "lost her way") and to create enjambments at the ends of lines, through a series of conjunctions ("and / never") and suspended prepositions ("the most beautiful of / sights" and "that best of / men") and other grammatical suspensions ("she could not remember / anything" and "I'd rather see her lovely / step"). The effect of these enjambments is to amplify the rhythmic effect of caesura that Powell admires in Sappho's poetry: it makes the poem move, and moving to the reader.

A caesura cuts both ways, however. Do such breaks enhance or interrupt the rhythm of the lines? Powell's own reading of his translation is featured in a sound recording on the Academy of American Poets website, where he moves rapidly through the enjambments as if they are not marked on the page, making the poem flow in a more colloquial cadence.[36] Indeed, the meter of the Sapphic stanza can barely be heard. Although Powell takes pains to demonstrate in his translator's "Afterword" how the Sapphic stanza "can be graphed" in metrical notation (38), his primary interest is to make the poems of Sappho sound, or resound, in the rhythmic flow of the speaking voice: "I am instead to re-create the feel of her poetry in contemporary American English," he writes (45), so "we might have the chance to hear at least an echo of Sappho's voice" (48). And yet this echo is less audible than visible, as the Sapphic stanza can only be glimpsed as a metrical counterpoint to the rhythm of his reading: the poem in the ear and the poem in the eye may point to each other, but cannot be read at the same point in time.

Anne Carson gives us another way to read the rhythm of the Sapphic stanza, contrapuntally. Through the juxtaposition of Greek texts and her English translations of Sappho in *If Not, Winter* (2002) she insists on the fragmentation of Sappho, in contrast to Powell's insistence on a process of reintegration. In a section of her translator's introduction entitled "Marks and Lacks," Carson explains:

> When translating texts from papyri, I have used a single square bracket to give an impression of missing matter, so that] or [indicates destroyed papyrus or the presence of letters not quite legible somewhere in the line. It is not the case that every gap or illegibility is specifically indicated: this would render the page a blizzard of marks and inhibit reading. Brackets are an aesthetic gesture toward the papyrological event rather than an accurate record of it.[37]

It is a paradox that the brackets do not "literally" mark missing letters from the Sapphic fragments, as this would "inhibit reading." Rather we are invited to read the brackets figuratively, as an "aesthetic gesture" helping us to imagine the tattered Greek papyrus first presented to the reading public by Grenfell and Hunt, and then prompting us to see that illegibility as part of our own reading experience.

Thus Carson's translation of Fragment 16 closely follows the Greek text line by line, gradually disintegrating into a column of brackets at the bottom, pointing to the lines that are missing:

> Some men say an army of horse and some men say an army on foot
> and some men say an army of ships is the most beautiful thing
> on the black earth. But I say it is
>   what you love.
>
> Easy to make this understood by all.
> For she who overcame everyone
> in beauty (Helen)
>   left her fine husband

behind and went sailing to Troy.
Not for her children nor her dear parents
had she thought, no—
    ]led her astray

        ]for
        ]lightly
    ]reminded me now of Anaktoria
    who is gone.

I would rather see her lovely step
and the motion of light on her face
than chariots of Lydians or ranks
    of footsoldiers in arms.

    ]not possible to happen
    ]to pray for a share
    ]
    ]
    ]
    ]
    ]
    toward [

    ]
    ]
    ]
    out of the unexpected.

While the first three stanzas do not attempt a metrical translation, they preserve the lineation of the Sapphic stanza (including a short fourth line as representation of the Adonic line). And the fifth stanza, still intact, could invite the possibility of a meta-metrical reading, as it contrasts "ranks of footsoldiers" with the "lovely step" of Anactoria. But in contrast to various metrical theories we have surveyed that try to mark the meter of the Sapphic stanza, presenting it in visible form to make it present to the reader, Carson's brackets mark its absence. Instead of creating an image of sound, those marks only show us the traces of Anactoria's disappearance. And yet this too could be another way to imagine the Sapphic stanza. If we look again at the word "toward [" (followed by the only open bracket facing right), we might see it opening toward what emerges "out of the unexpected" in the final line of this translation: a visual prosody produced by the typographical play of brackets in a spatialized rhythm on the page.

Carson's translations of Sappho produce surprising metrical effects precisely because of their fragmentation, as John Melillo observes:

> Even in the most rebarbative fragments, meter matters. Just as the traditional function of meter is to sequence and measure time, the preserved blips and blops of mouthsound work like some broken beat machine. But Carson also places those rhythms and sounds into a new listening context, a new ambience.... The poem is not an incomplete metrical form waiting to be dutifully filled in but rather a construction of fundamentally isolated particles—as if each word functioned as an individual sound event, combining and recombining endlessly to form new networks or constellations of sound.[38]

The spacing of phrases, words, brackets, and other punctuation marks makes room for a rhythmic reading of Carson's text, appealing simultaneously to the eye and to the ear to produce "a new listening context," delineating new combinations of sight and sound.

Carson further expands this new listening context in a performance piece that is based on reading her translations of Sappho out loud, including the brackets. Entitled "Bracko"—a conflation of "bracket" and "Sappho"— this performance turns the papyrological event into a multi-media event, with a video projection of brackets as a visual background for a polyvocal reading by Carson and her collaborators. In the performance, as some voices read randomly selected Sappho translations, other voices read passages from Carson's footnotes at carefully clocked intervals or simply pronounce the word "bracket" whenever it appears in the text. These overlapping voices, combined with the reiteration of "bracket, bracket, bracket," turn Carson's translations of Sappho into a polyvalent text, producing unpredictable polyrhythms that move in many directions at once.

This multi-directional movement is also embodied in dance, variously incorporated into different performances of "Bracko." In one memorable version from 2008, dancer Rashaun Mitchell performed his own choreography while several friends joined Carson in a reading of her Sappho translations. "Like an avant-garde Greek chorus, their voices overlapped, interrupted and moved alongside one other," wrote one reviewer, describing how "absence and its relation to presence was also felt in the performance's silences, when Carson and her chorus stopped breathing, allowing only the sound of the dancers' movements, as well as their breath and the collective breath of the audience, to be heard."[39] In another version of "Bracko" a group of performers raised their arms in bracket-shapes, slowly waving back and forth in front of the video projection, where white brackets moved like expanding constellations of stars on a black screen.[40] Reversing the image of black marks on a white page, these free-floating brackets were projected like vertical scansion marks onto the bodies visible and audible on stage, as another way to imagine the meter.

It was a visionary answer to the question, Sapphic stanzas: how can we read the rhythm? And it remains a question to repeat, over and over.[41]

Notes

1. Charlotte Higgins, *The Guardian*, January 29, 2014. Obbink went on to describe his discovery in *The Times Literary Supplement*, February 7, 2014, and in "Two New Poems by Sappho," *Zeitschrift fur Papyrologie und Epigraphik* (2014): 32–49.

2. Victoria Woollaston, *The Daily Mail,* January 30, 2014; Konstantinos Menzel, *The Greek Reporter*, January 28, 2014, http://eu.greekreporter.com/2014/01/28/new-poems-of-greek-poetess-sappho-recovered; Laura Swift, *The Conversation*, January 30, 2014, http://theconversation.com/new-sappho-poems-set-classical-world-reeling-22608; Tim Whitmarsh, *The Huffington Post*, January 30, 2014 and updated April 1, 2014, http://www.huffingtonpost.co.uk/tim-whitmarsh/sappho-poetry_b_4691297.html; Tom Payne, *The Telegraph*, January 30, 2014.

3. Daniel Mendelsohn, "Girl, Interrupted," *The New Yorker*, March 16, 2015.

4. On the nineteenth-century lyricization of Sappho, see Yopie Prins, *Victorian Sappho* (Princeton, N.J.: Princeton University Press, 1999). On twentieth-century lyric reading, see Virginia Jackson and Yopie Prins, *The Lyric Theory Reader: A Critical Anthology* (Baltimore: Johns Hopkins University Press, 2014).

5. See e.g., Grace Schulman's survey of Sapphics in *An Exaltation of Forms: Contemporary Poets Celebrate the Diversity of Their Art*, ed. Annie Finch and Kathrine Varnes (Ann Arbor: University of Michigan Press, 2002), 132–40.

6. T. V. F. Brogan, *English Versification 1570–1980: A Reference Guide with Global Appendix* (Baltimore: Johns Hopkins University Press, 1981). Meredith Martin, "Counting Victorian Prosodists: Productive Instability and Nineteenth Century Meter," *Victorians Institute Journal Annex* 38 (2010).

7. *Princeton Prosody Archive*, ed. Meredith Martin, Center for Digital Humanities, Princeton University, https://prosody.princeton.edu.

8. Rachel Wetzsteon, "Marvellous Sapphics," *Crossroads* (Fall 1999). Quoted from the Poetry Society of America, https://www.poetrysociety.org/psa/poetry/crossroads/on_poetry/poets_on_form_rachel_wetzsteon

9. John Hollander, *Rhyme's Reason: A Guide to English Verse* (New Haven, Conn.: Yale University Press, 1981), 17–18.

10. Alfred Corn, *The Poem's Heartbeat: A Manual of Prosody* (Ashland, Oreg.: Story Line Press, 1997), 14–16.

11. Ibid., 18.

12. Amittai Aviram, *Telling Rhythm: Body and Meaning in Poetry* (Ann Arbor: University of Michigan Press, 1994), 19.

13. Thomas Foster Barham, "On Metrical Time, or, the Rhythm of Verse, Ancient and Modern," *Transactions of the Philological Society* 1 (1860): 62.

14. Henry Thornton Wharton, *Sappho: Memoir, Text, Selected Renderings, and a Literal Translation* (London: David Stott, 1885).

15. John Frederick Rowbotham, *A History of Music*, vol. 2 (London: Trubner, 1885–86), 127.

16. Ibid., 91–92.

17. Ibid., 111.

18. Joseph Salathiel Tunison, *The Sapphic Stanza: A Tentative Study in Greek Metrical, Tonal and Dancing Art* (Granville, Ohio: The University Press, 1896), 40.

19. Ibid., 35.

20. Ibid., 41.

21. John Williams White, "The Origin and Form of Aeolic Verse," *The Classical Quarterly* 3, no. 4 (October 1909): 291.

22. Ibid., 292.

23. Otto Schroeder, "The New Metric," *Classical Philology* 7, no. 2 (April 1912): 175.

24. William Ross Hardie, *Res Metrica: An Introduction to the Study of Greek and Roman Versification* (Oxford: Oxford University Press, 1920), 128.

25. Ibid., 136.

26. Ibid., 137–38.

27. Bernard P. Grenfell and Arthur S. Hunt, *The Oxyrhynchus Papyri Part X* (Oxford: Oxford University Press, 1914), 40.

28. Edwin Marion Cox, *Sappho and the Sapphic Metre in English, with Bibliographical Notes* (London: Chiswick Press, 1916), 23–24.

29. Marion Mills Miller, "Sappho's Songs of Exile," *The Independent*, September 4, 1916, 344–46.

30. Marion Mills Miller, *The Songs of Sappho, Including the Recent Egyptian Discoveries, Translated into Rimed Verse . . . Greek Texts Prepared and Annotated and Literally Translated in Prose by David Moore Robinson* (New York: Frank-Maurice, 1925).

31. Pound's advice to Mary Barnard is noted by Marilyn Hacker in "A Few Cranky Paragraphs on Form and Content," *Dwelling in Possibility: Women Poets and Critics on Poetry*, ed. Maeera Shreiber and Yopie Prins (Ithaca: Cornell University Press), 196.

32. John Trantner, "Writing in the Manner of Sappho," *Metre* 2 (Spring 1997), 6.

33. John Kinsella, *Disclosed Poetics: Beyond Landscape and Lyricism* (Manchester: Manchester University Press, 2007), 84.

34. John Hollander, *Vision and Resonance: Two Senses of Poetic Form* (New York: Oxford University Press, 1975).

35. Jim Powell, *Sappho, A Garland: The Poems and Fragments of Sappho* (New York: Farrar Straus Giroux, 1993), 37–38. Subsequent references are given parenthetically.

36. Jim Powell, "The Anactoria Poem," Academy of American Poets, https://www.poets.org/poetsorg/poem/anactoria-poem.

37. Anne Carson, *If Not, Winter: Fragments of Sappho* (New York: Knopf, 2002), xi.

38. John Melillo, "Sappho and the Papyrological Event" in *Anne Carson: Ecstatic Lyre*, ed. Joshua Marie Wilkinson (Ann Arbor: University of Michgian Press, 2015), 190–91.

39. Alex Dimitrov, "Anne Carson Makes It New: Postcard from New York City," *Poets and Writers*, December 10, 2008.

40. Anne Carson performs "Bracko" at Cornell University, Cornellcast posted March 6, 2012, http://www.cornell.edu/video/anne-carson-performs-bracko-and-cassandra-float-can.

41. For generous feedback on the question posed by this paper, I am grateful to Ben Glaser and to audiences at Rutgers University, University of Virginia, Northwestern University, University of Washington, University of Tennessee at Knoxville, St. Louis University, University of Arizona, and Princeton University.

Rhythm and Affect in "Christabel"

Ewan Jones

"Christabel" has already represented a crucial transformation for more than one critical history of meter. According to George Saintsbury's *History of English Prosody*, Coleridge's poem almost single-handedly recovered for English verse the expressive variety that neoclassicism had submerged.[1] T. S. Omond, writing in a more temperate register, nonetheless reserved for it no less significance, stating that "[b]y the gradual adoption of [the] principle [of "Christabel"] our verse, and later our theories of prosody, have been revolutionized."[2]

This essay will nonetheless argue that certain elements of "Christabel" have continued to elude criticism, and that these elements usefully supplement—or, where necessary, challenge—prevailing accounts. In order to demonstrate this, I neither undertake a normative scansion of "Christabel," nor seek to identify the optimal metrical method to read it (the poem has been taken both to prove *and* to disprove the objective veracity of "the English foot").[3] I shall read closely Coleridge's verse not to show that it "is" quantitative, accentual, syllabic, or accentual-syllabic, but rather to identify key moments at which its potential vocalization is significantly plural. This plurality is significant, I contend, for the relation it bears to what Coleridge's Preface calls "some transition in the nature of the imagery or passion."[4]

In so doing, I reorient Coleridge's prefatory emphasis on "metre" toward rhythm, by which adjustment I seek to identify several features of our experience of the poem. Firstly, where the Preface to "Christabel" identifies syllabic variation as its fundamental working principle, I propose to focus primarily on the beat that it relegates into comparative insignificance.

Secondly, this apparently simple notion of "beat" is in fact more complex and more various than familiar metrical terms such as accent, ictus, or arsis might suggest. It is well known that Coleridge dragged his feet with "Christabel" rather more than was usual even for him, only publishing the poem in 1815, more than a decade after his composition and series of famously magnetic recitations. Perhaps this unusual publishing history explains why his Preface appears so keen to describe the ensuing poem as a kind of printed script or transparent cue that the reader would only need see in order to know how to scan correctly (to perform as Coleridge himself once had).

But the typographical rendering of "Christabel" fails to corral a wider range of possible rhythmic vocalizations. The question of how or whether we emphasize a beat is at once open and directed: open, given the metrically indeterminate nature of so many significant syllables, directed, given the accumulating experience of rhythm over the course of the poem. This accumulating rhythmic experience goes beyond the sort of foot-based analyses that the Preface might suggest. At the same time, however, it never fully transcends meter; for if "rhythm" is the variety of possible vocalizations that we might choose or feel ourselves compelled to make, some of the most compelling conventions that recur throughout the poem are, precisely, metrical.

This simultaneously open and directed rhythm is precisely what makes "Christabel" significant not only for the history of prosody, but for the relation between verse form and philosophical thought more largely. In the second section of this essay, I will claim that the manner in which we vocalize the poem engenders a historical reflexivity; and that this reflexivity enables us to rethink the category of rhythm, whose recent critical rediscovery has often proceeded on an excessively ahistorical basis. Lastly, I contend that the experience of voice as both constitutive and reactive proves philosophically significant: insofar as Coleridge contributes to the theorization of affect not through the medium of philosophy proper, but by writing verse whose rhythm resists the separation into active and passive states.

Having tiptoed around the Preface in this preamble, it is as well to cite Coleridge's metrical claims in full:

> I have only to add, that the metre of Christabel is not, properly speaking, irregular, though it may seem so from its being founded on a new principle: namely, that of counting in each lines the accents, not the syllables. Though the latter may vary from seven to twelve, yet in each line the accents will be found to be only four. Nevertheless this

occasional variation in number of syllables is not introduced wantonly, or for the mere ends of convenience, but in correspondence with some transition, in the nature of the imagery or passion.[5]

Having been prepared so consciously for what to expect and how to understand it, what then happens at the start of the subsequent Part One? Very little, in narrative terms, but this apparently negligible action responds to and unsettles the Preface's metrical assertions. (The most obvious trespass, as even the earliest readers of "Christabel" noted, is the four-syllable third line; but this does not directly concern me here.) Fresh from Coleridge's assertion of a regularity of accent, we come immediately across a reverberation of sound:

> 'Tis the middle of Night by the Castle Clock,
> And the Owls have awakened the crowing Cock;
> Tu—whit!—Tu—whoo!
> And hark again the crowing Cock,
> How drowsily it crew.
>
> Sir Leoline, the Baron rich,
> Hath a toothless mastiff Bitch;
> From her Kennel beneath the `rock
> She maketh Answer to the Clock,
> Four for the Quarters, and twelve for the hour;
> Ever and aye, by Shine and Shower,
> Sixteen short Howls not over loud;
> Some say, she sees my Lady's Shroud.[6]
>
> (1–13)

The four pledged accents of the Preface and the four invariant howls of the mastiff bitch ("[e]ver and aye, by Shine and Shower") may be coincidental; their proximity, however, makes the reader pause before extending the benefit of the doubt. And the wider passage then begins to suggest a conscious running play on accentual regularity. The clock provides an unyielding temporality, which resonates through the separate forms of nature: the owls in turn wake up the cock, which rhymes almost perfectly with that instigating timepiece, and whose utterance ("Tu—whit!—Tu—whoo!") we feel almost compelled to stress heavily, perhaps exaggeratedly, in concordance with Coleridge's scheme. "Four for the quarters, and twelve for the hour" overtly references the dominant principle; that principle even seeps into the two prepositional homonyms, "for." Four and twelve, meanwhile, map almost perfectly the syllabic range between short

(3) and long (2, 10) lines. All this adds to the sense of a verse line already commenting upon itself in the very moment of its realization.

I say that we feel "almost compelled" to stress the owl's cry shrilly, naturalistically, as a kind of mimic hooting of our own:

/   /   /   /
Tu—whit!—Tu—whoo!

The force of that compulsion comes partly from the contrast with the skipping, almost anapestic second line, which had lengthened its stride only to come to a shuddering halt with these bare four syllables. But despite my claims for the inexorable movement of the passage, neither I nor Coleridge nor his Preface can finally fully compel us to stress the line in accordance with its stated principles. We are not *obliged* to realize four stresses. We can indeed stress lightly a detached utterance like "Tu—," just as we ordinarily would such a soft monosyllable: to voice it not as an owl, but as a human being reporting an owl:

-   /   -   /
Tu—whit!—Tu—whoo!

But, as Omond shrewdly notes, actively disobeying the Preface's claims does not dissolve the more fundamental dilemma it poses: "our perception of rhythmical uniformity persists; persists, even though the syllables transgress instead of enforcing it."[7] Coleridge elsewhere described "Christabel" as depending "for it's beauty always, and often even for it's metrical existence [sic], on the *sense* and *passion*."[8] Yet the smallest accentual decisions that we have to make from the start reveal a more fundamental interdependence, where bare metrical existence itself forms a sense and passion, forms the kind of voice (whether emphatically present, or ironically distanced) that we hear ourselves articulating.

It is curious that such reflections depend upon the question of accent, where Coleridge's Preface had specifically linked the passion and sense to *syllabic* "variation." It may well be that he was sufficiently blinded to the rhythmical novelty of passages such as the above, as to consider his achievement in more conventionally metrical terms: where the number of beats remains constant in number and spacing, the variation of syllables between them can indeed suggest a fluid variation in established metrical feet. (Coleridge was certainly sufficiently interested in such established forms elsewhere: see for instance his schoolboy crib, "Metrical Feet," or, less famously, his attempt to revive the English hexameter.)[9] Indeed, it is noticeable that several readings of "Christabel" approach the relation between poetic form and "passion" in precisely this way—as if a change in the metrical condition of the former led directly (and unilaterally) to an alteration of the latter ("swift anapests" equal exhilaration, or "heavy spondees" equal torpor).

But as the above passages show, the notion of beat is constant in neither number nor spacing; the various potential rhythmical actuations of the line allow us to deviate from the poem's prescribed pattern, while all the time feeling its prescription. Even when we do process a line in adherence to a more conventional metrical principle (and Ada F. Snell is not wrong to see many such lines as resolving themselves into iambic tetrameter), it is a mistake to take it (or the feet that comprise it) in isolation; such moments form part of a series of broader rhythmical contractions or expansions, of which lines 2–3 above offer a clear example. Syllabic quantity proves insufficient to account for affective change in "Christabel": we actuate a certain passion not only when we sound the resounding beat, but also in the manner in which we sound it.

These rhythmical variations therefore offer the reader variant means of voicing the poem, each with a particular affective charge. But the actuation of a line is more than a matter of individual performance choice: it produces a rhythmical pattern to which we are ourselves made subject. Just as our "choice" over which syllables to emphasize produced a particular animate entity (an owl or the report of an owl), so too do the more recognizably human voices that ensue channel and redirect the accumulated rhythmical energy. The first such voice that emerges belongs to none of the recognizable protagonists (Christabel, Geraldine), but rather the unnamed and unannounced narrator. The rhetorical interrogative is its natural mode. "Is the Night chilly and dark?" it asks, before answering its own question, over-fastidiously, "The Night is chilly, but not dark." (14–15). Throughout, this unnamed speaker's torpid reiterations revel in sketching solid form and outline from mere suggestion, only to dissolve it just as rapidly:

> The Night is chill; the Forest bare;
> Is it the Wind that moaneth bleak?
> There is not Wind enough in the Air
> To move away the ringlet Curl
> From the lovely Lady's Cheek—
>
> (43–47)

As Snell observes, the above lines are generally octosyllabic, with slight variations.[10] Yet this does not preclude deeper variations of a different sort. The narrator's question ("[i]s it the Wind that moaneth bleak?")

is not merely rhetorical: it is a question that no reader would dream of answering, given previous other *faux-naïf* suggestions and retractions. But the feel of such passages is determined less by its propositional self-canceling ("[t]here is not Wind enough"), than a series of apparently minor accentual shifts. Unchallenged iambs persist up to and including the narrator's query; yet the following line opens with no real candidates that would preserve the duple measure, where forcing "is" into compliance would sound all the more awry given that the line asserts that which is not. Line 46 reintroduces an iambic progression, only for the ensuing trochaic sequence once again to unsettle it. Scanning such passages accentually, as a consistent recurrence of four beats, is therefore accurate yet insufficient as a measure: such rhythmic variations as we observe above emerge only through periodic departure from a more tightly defined set of accentual-syllabic patternings, which thereby never quite attain the status of laws.

The uncertainty that we feel at such moments is more than a practical anxiety over "correct" scansion: it is an affect in its own right. The constant unsettling of rhythmical patterns offers a sonic counterpart to the doubt that the above passage thematizes; but at the same time, the more radical line variations toy with our doubt, forcing our voice to make sport of our frustrated knowledge. Snell marks five separate instances of four-syllable lines, which can all (as with "Tu—whit!—Tu—whoo!") conceivably be omni-stressed. (As with that earlier moment, the Preface's stipulation vies with our customary—if not necessarily "natural"—inclination to stress the line iambically.) The narrator avails itself of one such moment, asking a further rhetorical question at the significant moment just prior to Geraldine's appearance:

> She folded her Arms beneath her Cloak,
> And stole to the other side of the Oak.
>   What sees She there?
>
> (56–58)

Just as the first tetrasyllable marked the actuation of a particular animate being (the hooting owl), so too does this potentially omni-stressed line sound the knowing narrator most fully. We could well imagine our voice, following another two flurried anapestic lines, congealing so as to intone, as if to a child, 'WHAT . . . SEES . . . SHE . . . THERE?'—the internal rhyme, assonance and provision for caesurae only adding to a gloomy mock-Gothic portentousness. Once again, a wide affective range (is it risking too much to say that even as adults we might feel trepidation at such moments, just as we might find them willfully bathetic?) emerges not through even the thinnest hint of drama or character, but across very concentrated moments of rhythmic variation. The distinction is perhaps too absolute: for this rhythmic variation itself engenders drama and character.

When Christabel and Geraldine do finally make their entrances and speak, as we say, for themselves, their distinct characters and actions emerge only within the terms of this accumulating experience of rhythm. Coleridge, as with his narrator, clearly has a certain amount of fun exploiting this fact from the start. For even the eponymous heroine Christabel's earliest apparition is forcefully controlled in such a manner as to unsettle her singularity. A stanza describing the mysterious Geraldine, seen from a distance, closes with the narrator's emphatic declaration, "Beautiful exceedingly!" (69). The following couplet retains this exclamatory force, in a phrasing that directly recalls the narrator's own "Jesu, Maria, shield her well!" (55); yet Coleridge manipulates the line-break quite overtly:

> Mary mother, save me now!
> (Said Christabel) And who art thou?[11]
>
> (70–71)

The parenthetical diegetic check "(Said Christabel)," which feels willfully unsubtle, arrives too late for us to take it into account. We are already voicing Christabel, before we know that it is she that we are voicing: the manner in which we voice her therefore bears the echoes of even those non-humans or non-characters that have preceded her. We could well imagine that Coleridge, reciting "Christabel" in the years before its publication, shifted his pitch to mimic whatever he imagined Christabel sounded like; but the surmise is inconsequential for the more interesting questions that the printed poem raises. Indeed, typographic features are crucial to, and inseparable from, rhythmic variation: the forced parenthesis encourages us to separate the line into two separate, four-syllable units, a voicing that would be further licensed by the tendency to stress trisyllabic proper names such as Christabel (as also Geraldine, Leoline) firmly; and by the extent to which "And who art thou" resembles the previous, omni-stressed rhetorical questionings of the narrator. The result is a series of abrupt transitions that both mark and call into question who or what is speaking.

Throughout their early exchanges, such marked rhythmic transition is made to compel Christabel and Geraldine's actions, much as it has our own vocalization. The former extends her hand to the latter:

>   She rose: and forth with steps they passed
>   That strove to be, and were not, fast.
>
> (112–13)

Agency here is sieved through prosody. The first of these octosyllabic lines proves emphatically iambic: the comma underscores the rhythm, while the stress falls appropriately on variants of movement ("rose [. . .] forth [. . .] steps [. . .] passed"), each describing the passage of feet (the running pun on metricality runs all the while). This momentum carries naturally over into the following line, where the expectation of propulsion forces itself into the verb "strove," and might, at a push, unusually emphasize even the auxiliary "be"—as if existence precisely were being fought for. The formerly emphatic iambic pattern then further struggles to maintain itself with the same auxiliary, "were," whose conjugation forces the voice to struggle yet further in converting both its softness and pastness into presence.

That faltering rhythm is then brought almost to a decisive halt by the second comma—as if the line could expire into a sigh, finish right there on "not." When, then, following the comma the line does indeed resume, the emphasis is abrupt and redoubled. "[F]ast," standing alone between punctuation and line-ending, receives all the emphasis that had gradually drained from the line, as the softening voice is forced to rouse itself from its pause; compensating, it overcompensates. Where the line has been seen to surrender all momentum, the term falls into its derivative meaning: held fast. We witness the accumulation of a quantum of energy, which seeks a regular outlet only to be frustrated, before finally discharging itself with a belated force; in that process, the disappointment of rhythmic expectation comes to condition even the semantic properties of language.

It is striking that the effect of so many of the above passages depends upon rhythmical variation as it applies to metrically ambiguous monosyllables—the auxiliaries of line 113, or the infantile questionings of the narrator. We earlier saw that such metrical uncertainty produced a distinct (if variable) affect in its own right. The drama proper of "Christabel" further develops the coincidence of rhythmic expectation (the falling of the beat) and significant ambiguity (where or whether the beat falls). Geraldine has collapsed, "belike through pain," at the gate of Christabel's castle; whereupon, "the lady rose again / And moved, as she were not in pain" (133–34). As with more than one of the above examples, we again note the significance of metrically indeterminate particles such as "not." We could well imagine a range of vocalizations of line 134, each with varying degrees of emphasis dispersed across apparently simple connectives: weighting "as" stresses the causal function of the connective (Geraldine really is only feigning pain), while weighting "were" stresses the subjunctive (*as if* she were not pained). It is here significant that the less normative (though still plausible) scansion produces a skeptical threat that cannot be expunged.

Coleridge's Preface thus forms only one part of the rhythmical demand that we feel the verse make upon us at this stage: for, aside from the four-beat rule that we follow or contravene, there exists the pressure of rhythmical patternings that possess varying levels of familiarity (iambic, trochaic, anapestic, or other), whose separate claims are each inseparable from the sense we make of the line. And the sense that we make (or feel is made for us) is always also affective—as the line readily concedes, concerning as it does Geraldine's "pain." However much Coleridge may have believed in his verse's transparent communication of "passion," "Christabel" consistently emphasizes those moments at which feeling is significantly dubitable: from the wind that may or may not "moaneth bleak," to the first animate beings ("what can ail the mastiff bitch?"), to the human figures that never wholly disinvest themselves from such animal life.

If Coleridge's Preface proves incapable of controlling the potential rhythmic variation of "Christabel," so too do the various subsequent editorial presentations of the poem. The several manuscripts of "Christabel" vary considerably; that their variations are as much typographic as lexical may well suggest a well-founded doubt on Coleridge's behalf about how to make the poem clearly performable.[12] (It should by now have become clear that I take what might here have struck Coleridge as a problem as one principal reason for the enduring significance of "Christabel.") But we have equally seen several moments at which Coleridge willfully manipulates the slippage or variability of voice, as in the parenthetical "(Said Christabel)." The vexed issue of intentionality makes the editorial task yet more foreboding; as J. C. C. Mays notes in his introduction to the *Bollingen Series Poetical Works*,

> A line or passage may have the same words in several versions, but its emotional burden may be muted or changed by the other factors I have named. Sound, or tone of voice, often says as much as words. When a comma is added, or other punctuation is made heavier, the notation is altered. When an exclamation is substituted for a question-mark, pitch adjusts to a new direction. Hyphens slow down a line by distributing stress more evenly. A quotation-mark lifts a phrase into another register.[13]

The manuscript versions of Christabel cover practically all these bases, which makes the resultant *Bollingen* text all the more interesting, for its effort to subordinate rhythmic variation to a clearer notion of voice and character. The very first encounter between Christabel and Geraldine represents a case in point. Christabel asks, very reasonably, "[a]nd who art thou?" In recording the response, I list respectively the *Bollingen* version, collated from variant manuscripts and printed versions, and the *Oxford World Classics* edition, which reprises the 1834 *Poetical Works*:

The Lady strange made Answer meet	The lady strange made answer meet,
And her Voice was faint and sweet:	And her voice was faint and sweet:—
"Have Pity on my Sore Distress,	Have pity on my sore distress,
I scarce can speak for Weariness.	I scarce can speak for weariness:
Stretch forth thy Hand, and have no fear—"	Stretch forth thy hand, and have no fear!
Said Christabel, "How cam'st thou here?"	Said Christabel, How camest thou here?
And the Lady, whose Voice was faint and sweet	And the lady, whose voice was faint and sweet,
	Did thus pursue her answer meet:—
	Did thus pursue her answer meet.
(71–78)	(71-78)

In two lexically identical passages, variant spacing, punctuation and elision entirely shift the vocal delivery. The *Bollingen* version re-establishes the line breaks that later printings of "Christabel" omitted, thus marking more clearly the vocal shift from Geraldine (71–75) to Christabel (76–78). But the most obvious effort to mark this shift is, of course, the superposition of speech marks at this stage (a form of punctuation present in none of the manuscript versions of this passage, for all their many different ways to designate speech). The 1834 edition makes it significantly ambiguous (once again with the aid of the enjambed diegetic marker) who is delivering a line such as "Stretch forth thy hand, and have no fear!" As I have been endeavoring to demonstrate throughout this reading, such ambiguity is essential to the effect of "Christabel," however much we would or would not choose to call it intentional.

We need such an ambiguity at this stage not for ambiguity's sake, but because the suggestion that Geraldine might be beginning to possess the voice of Christabel is essential not only to the drama at this point, but also to the manner in which the poem has situated and enacted vocalization more generally. The ensuing drama only pushes home this point more fully. The *Bollingen* edition continues to regularize voice into direct speech, until the climactic moment of Part One, which finds itself as a result denuded of significance. There, Geraldine suddenly speaks with "altered voice," being in some way possessed (we intuit) by the spirit of Christabel's dead mother. "'Off, wandering mother! Peak and pine! / I have power to bid thee flee.'" (204–6), she declares, with every single manuscript version marking speech with inverted commas, where previously there had been none. By regularizing speech so thoroughly throughout, the Bollingen edition conceals the poem's morbid but apposite truth—that only at the moment of possession by another, can voice be heard directly to speak.[14]

This moment of "altered voice" is exceptional within the broader pattern of "Christabel" as a whole, which is less interested in designating voice than the process of vocalization, a process that is, from the earliest lines, impelled by the poem's prosodic organization. Perhaps it is in this respect (rather than its gloomy Gothic décor, or suggestive fragmentariness) that "Christabel" anticipates later verse forms such as the monodrama, which, as A. Dwight Culler has noted, feature a much more supple relation between prosody and character than the term "dramatic monologue" tends to imply.[15] Does this entail that, as Christabel and Geraldine conclude Part One by settling down to sleep, they amount to no more than the slumbering moans with which the poem commenced? Is living character no more than the latest enumeration of a rhythmical pulse that has already invited and foreordained it?

This is not, I think, the principal lesson of "Christabel." It is true that I have attempted to demonstrate the many ways in which that poem's rhythmical variation consistently dictates voice, character, sense, and passion—and how part of that dictation often involves leaving such entities significantly open. But this does not mean that the poetic drama can be reduced to unaccountable shifts in pitch or tempo. Admittedly, the earliest lines produce performance dilemmas of various kinds, whose resolution even the clamorous Preface cannot dictate to us, and which we must decide upon in ignorance of the full scene. We make "sense" in the unpremeditated act of voicing.

Yet those decisions are less free than we might imagine: as "Christabel" develops, its rhythm also generates a series of working assumptions, expectations, and conventions. So those earliest lines do indeed seem to call for the four-beat principle; in turn, the periodicity of those emphases (however varying their allocation across the line) is abstracted into regularity, or intimated as feeling. These, then, are no more than beats; and yet we feel them in a certain way: with foreboding, perhaps, or with humor. We have seen this latter possibility form a significant part of the first "real" voice that meter articulates, that of the narrator who at once absorbs and directs metrical uncertainty. Its mock-Gothic is brought into being concretely through heavy stress ("[w]hat sees She there?"), yet then becomes an active voice, an interpretation of and cue to further stresses, a governing expectation.

"Characters" such as Christabel and Geraldine are no different. They respond to rhythm's call, but the poem subsequently finds itself answering to their movements. As the uncertainty that we are compelled to answer through our voicing, these characters interpret the rhythmic patterns that comprise them. Is Geraldine "belike" in pain? While her affect is as irresolvable as the mastiff bitch's own ailment, we cannot but voice her in such a way as to suggest an answer. Character is one demonstration of the force with which we bestow even the slightest stress with significance and feeling. In reality we are forming such voices all the time. Another term for them is "convention." I said earlier that we approach the earliest lines of the poem as a performance dilemma, but this is only a partial truth. For behind even the first emphasis we place lie a variety of voices, sedimentations of past experience that come to dictate the terms of our current engagement, in the form of generic, societal, or even vocal expectation. As readers we may be unknowing in this, but we are also uninnocent. "Christabel" then attains a critical relation to such voices, through charting their rhythmical emergence.

What broader significance does this close reading of "Christabel" hold for our conceptions of rhythm? It is from the beginning essential to be clear about the ways in which this poem is *not* original. It is certainly not original judged by Coleridge's own precepts. As Brennan O'Donnell notes, his loose yet recognizably accentual-syllabic approach had proven a staple of English verse since Chaucer; while Derek Attridge makes the four-stress line the dominant pattern of English verse.[16] Coleridge's "new principle" would then reinvent the most venerable of all prosodic devices! Omond attempts to gloss such derivation in positive terms, claiming that "Christabel" "vindicated for English verse its natural inalienable birthright."[17]

I, on the other hand, prefer to see in the poem a historical singularity that need claim neither essential novelty, nor rediscovery of putative origin.

For Coleridge's reinvention of the wheel—or more accurately, the reflexive form of reading that "Christabel" forces upon us—alters that wheel, alters the nature of poetic technique. By being told to stress the stress that we would otherwise have unthinkingly applied, "Christabel" foregrounds the affective dimension that all verse bears (and conceals). It is new, then, not in the way it imagines itself to be, but in its historical need to highlight or recover those naturalized habits of reading that comprise tradition. A work such as Walter Scott's *Lay of the Last Minstrel* owes a debt to Coleridge's poem, then, not through its adoption of a common, broadly accentual meter, but in the manner that such structural organization enables a comparable historical reflexivity. The failure of the Preface either to explain or direct his achievement therefore does not simply undermine Coleridge's intentions: it proves his intuition of the relation of passion and verse form true in a more radical manner than he was able to conceive.

By emphasizing the category of rhythm in general, and the four-beat line in particular, I am thereby of course following Derek Attridge, whose work has done more than anyone's to inspire the recent resurgence in the critical treatment of the term, to which this volume hopes to contribute. Yet by speaking of the reflexive manner of reading that "Christabel" forces upon us, I wish to append a sense of historical specificity that some of that recent work has a tendency to overlook. We can readily point to other compositions that, inspired by "Christabel," similarly manipulate the syllabically various but consistently four-beat line—Scott's *Last Lay*, Wordsworth's *White Doe of Rylstone*, Byron's *Oriental Tales*. Such affinities encourage many critics to speak of such a thing as "Christabel meter"; and yet the very notion of a template that could be emulated misrepresents Coleridge's defamiliarization of pre-existing tradition.[18]

For even if there is some "innate" inclination to the four-beat line in English vernacular verse (whether biological or linguistic), it is just as sure that such rhythmic patterns have been internalized and socially entrained in a variety of often incompatible ways. "Christabel," offers a hint of one moment at which such patterns might have meant in a particular manner. A critical history of rhythm does, it is true, present practical difficulties that are more obviously surmountable in the case of specific metrical devices (it is not difficult for us to imagine a critical genealogy of, say, the elegiac distich). By contrast, rhythm appears at once so essential and so irreducibly palpable, that to suggest that even it has a history seems both intuitively and practically difficult.

Perhaps it is our innate resistance to consider rhythm historically, or critically, that has permitted the term to serve a variety of regimes as ideological fodder, as "primal" or "dynamic" animating force. We can readily perceive the danger of such appropriations. And yet, a markedly ahistorical treatment of rhythm endures—and not for want of recent theorizing on the subject. In perhaps the most sustained recent discussion of the concept in Anglophone verse, Richard Cureton and Derek Attridge offer subtle and divergent accounts; yet neither the striking positivism of Cureton's system (a positivism that enables several fine readings of William Carlos Williams among others), nor the social, biological, and linguistic contexts that Attridge treats as potential groundings of rhythm, leave much scope for historical articulation.[19]

Amittai Aviram's *Telling Rhythm: Body and Meaning in Poetry* (1994) goes further, treating the rhythmic impulse as an irreducible somatic force that entirely transcends historical circumstance: "[t]he energy of rhythm exceeds the limits of the limited moment in cultural knowledge reflected in the poem's images and ideas."[20] My reading of "Christabel" may, it is true, seem to share something with Aviram's tendency to read poems as self-referring allegories (as Jonathan Culler notes in his contribution to this volume, a poem does not "mean" anything beyond the rhythm that constitutes it). But this resemblance is deceptive: for "Christabel" teaches us that rhythm is never simply a unitary, somatic, positive force, but rather a complex experience that can both be experienced in different ways (many of which are far from liberating), and which is always subject to various historical conventions.

Caroline Levine's "Rhythms Poetic and Political: the Case of Elizabeth Barrett Browning," by contrast, pledges a much more nuanced account of the relation that might obtain between historical and poetic rhythms. In Barrett Browning's three poems on Queen Victoria, we learn that "poetic meter appears [. . .] not as a reflection or expression of political forms, but as precisely another form, one that itself runs up against other poetic or social forms."[21] Yet we might question what room this welcome expansion of "form" leaves for verse rhythm as such. Levine indeed reads Barrett Browning's practice as a strikingly *a*historical (and thereby rather debatable) matter, as "a rhythmic pattern that is all her own, constraining according to no predictable standard and scarcely indebted to tradition."[22] The portrait of a Victorian society subject to several rhythmic impulses (which encompass verse), "plural and colliding, jumbled and constantly altered, each, thanks to the others, incapable of imposing its own dominant order,"[23] may well prove accurate (although it may also smack of Habermas' more utopian descriptions of the public sphere). But either way: if the social sphere is composed of interweaving but non-subordinating rhythms, why need we go to verse at all, if all it provides is an echo chamber in which the "outside" world sounds?

If Aviram makes rhythm ahistorical, therefore, Levine makes it so socio-historically pervasive that the singularity of the poetic medium (or any relation of causality between it and social "rhythms") proves difficult to discern. If the dedicated consideration of verse rhythm is to justify itself beyond descriptive insight or hermeneutic virtuosity, its results can neither be summarized as the self-legitimating immanence of the artwork, nor be collapsed into the "rhythms" of social experience in so total a way as to evacuate formal specificity. A study of this kind, that is to say, need demonstrate how the qualitative singularity of verse form engages critically and sensuously with other bodies of thought, without being reducible to them.

In the second part of this essay, I suggested that "Christabel" offered one instance of where an apparently familiar verse rhythm takes on particular significance at a given historical juncture. How? In this final section, I will argue that Coleridge's poem does not only reveal the affective dimension that all verse continues to bear. Beyond this generic truth, "Christabel" possesses a more contingent and historical—but no less significant—role. For the poem engages the philosophical discourse on affect that underwent such radical shifts over the course of the eighteenth century; and by engaging it through its peculiar formal repertoire, contributes to that discourse in a manner that propositional language could not.

In making such a claim, I draw upon the rich vein of recent work on the philosophy of affect. Susan James' *Passion and Action: The Emotions in Seventeenth-Century Philosophy* charts the slow unraveling of the scholastic understanding of "passion"—where the opposed notions of passivity and activity both structurally resemble, and sanction, several other binaries that include body and mind—across the successive philosophies of Descartes, Hobbes, and Spinoza.[24] Thomas Dixon's *From Passions to Emotions: The Creation of a Secular Psychological Category*, meanwhile, traces the gradual supplanting of "passion" as a category, by the "emotion" increasingly preferred in the experimental psychologies of Thomas Brown, Thomas Chalmers, and others.[25]

Taking these surveys together, we see a growing tendency to treat affect as a motive force that is both active and constitutive of character.[26] (Shelley would, in "Rosalind and Helen: a Modern Eclogue," enjoy rhyming "emotion" and "motion.") At the same time, even those philosophical texts that do most to reshape our understanding of affect frequently find themselves lapsing into the very scholastic logic that they opposed, with its attendant language of mastery and subordination. So we find Hume's famous dictum that "reason is, and always ought to be, slave to the passions" merely gives the whip hand to what had previously been enslaved.[27] Even the radical treatment of passion in Spinoza's *Ethics*, which as James notes "abandon[s] the distinction between active volitions and passive perceptions,"[28] continues to turn on the extent to which "striving" [*conatus*] is passive (a partial cause of the subject) or active (a total cause of the subject). "[A]n affect," states Spinoza, "*or* passivity of the soul, is a *confused idea*. For we have shown that the mind is acted on, only insofar as it has inadequate, *or* confused, ideas."[29]

William Collins' "The Passions: an Ode for Music" (1750) here proves a revealing document, in offering an early instance of the supple relation between rhythmic variation and voiced character that "Christabel" would so fully exploit.[30] In a brief nod to convention, the thronging passions are subjected in the opening stanza to a barrage of passive verb constructions. Listening to an allegorized Music suggestively play herself, they are variously "Disturb'd, delighted, rais'd, refin'd" (8), and subsequently, "fir'd / fill'd [. . .] rapt, inspir'd" (9–10). Those now-archaic elided participles permit a breathlessness that carries, however, into a significant reversal. For the passions, having "snatch'd her instruments of sound," now become significantly, active. Yet the usurping proper names do not merely sing themselves through their song; they sing themselves *as* song. So timorous Fear and rapid Anger are pinched into two swift quatrains; while Hope dilates into an extended stanza, at the end of which "[s]till would her touch the strain prolong." Melancholy sings in heroic couplets, until the disappointed end-rhyme of "soul," which has to wait three further lines for its answering partner—and a disappointing answer at that, "stole." Joy finally takes this delayed satisfaction of couplets to its extreme, waiting a full seven lines for the almost forgotten "advancing" to be triumphantly answered by "dancing" (88).

As Saintsbury notes, much of Collins' expressive novelty stems from the manner in which "the form abolishes the substance," in such a way that metrical variety places a peculiar pressure upon archaic personification. The "Ode to Liberty" is a case in point: "'Liberty' to write like that, will enable no one to write like it."[31] In such cases—as with the "The Passions: an Ode for Music"—we find a logical paradox: do the various affective states (melancholy, joy, even liberty) shape the metrical form that they inhabit, by the force of their capitalized personification? Or does formal variation itself produce emphatic content? This hedging uncertainty over the extent to which affect is reactive or generative indicates, in this specifically poetical context, a shifting attitude to the formative properties of verse (or the "music" that serves as its loose analogy). But it also provides a structural parallel to the impasse charted above, where despite efforts to cut across scholastic distinctions, philosophical treatments of affect found themselves lapsing back into a vocabulary of (total) passivity and (total) activity.

Such issues arise explicitly in Wordsworth's "Essay, Supplementary to the Preface" (1815):

> Passion, it must be observed, is derived from a word which signifies, *suffering*; but the connection which suffering has with effort, with exertion, and *action*, is immediate and inseparable. How strikingly is this property of human nature exhibited by the fact that, in popular language, to be in a passion is to be angry!—But
>
> 'Anger in hasty *words* or *blows*
> Itself discharges on its foes.'
>
> To be moved, then, by a passion, is to be excited, often to external, and always to internal, effort [. . .].[32]

The philosophical endeavor to convert passion into activity—where even Spinoza's innovation failed to resolve the issue of passivity—here poses comparable problems for poetry. Wordsworth's formulation struggles gamely to imply a necessary relation between "exertion, and *action*," on the one hand, and "*suffering*," on the other, an attempt that remains in danger of lapsing into the binary that it would displace. Where the prose extract above appears to lean on the side of action, several of Wordsworth's verse passages incline the other way. Take, for instance, this central passage from *The Borderers*:

> Action is transitory, a step, a blow—
> The motion of a muscle—this way or that—
> 'Tis done—and in the after vacancy
> We wonder at ourselves like men betray'd
> Suffering is permanent, obscure and dark,
> And has the nature of infinity[33]

Lurking beneath an otherwise very familiar Stoic ethic of endurance is, once again, an effort to explore those strangely agential aspects of passive experience, for which a whole host of quintessentially Wordsworthian phrases—"vacancy" (or "after-vacancy"), "torpor," "strenuous indolence"—function as placeholders. "Christabel" extends such considerations through submitting them to the experience and practice of verse in a far more concerted manner than the passage above, where Wordsworth's abrupt caesurae ("'Tis done—") suggest a merely spasmodic agency. Coleridge's poem, that is to say, actuates feeling as the process that Wordsworth calls "excited [. . .] to effort," whereby the compelled voice nonetheless recognizes and actuates itself as such.

To say that "Christabel" proved Coleridge's most significant contribution to the philosophy of affect may well have discomfited Coleridge himself, who often overlooked his more distinctive achievements in favor of grander aims. One such of these aims—though of lesser repute than his lifelong engagement with German idealism—is the late treatment of the Cartesian theory of affect, which emerges most fully in his late essay "On the Passions" (1828). The immediate occasion of the essay is a reading of Descartes' *Passions of the Soul*, which Coleridge took to represent only a partial advance upon scholasticism:

> Action and Passion are, says Des Cartes, are the same thing contemplated as existing in two reciprocally opposed opposite yet corresponding Subjects: and derive their difference from the different relations of the Subjects. An Action in the mind is a Passion in the Body: and Actions of the Body are reflected as Passions in the mind. This, however, is a mere logical antithesis of our *Thoughts*—or scarcely so much lower still—a grammatical antithesis of the Terms, Action and Passion, substituted for a real definition of the Things themselves.[34]

In order to move beyond this mere "grammatical antithesis," Coleridge elaborates a bio-affective design—drawing heavily from his previous *Theory of Life*—that is predictably idiosyncratic and fragmentary, yet which provides a more dynamic account of "organic form" than is often attributed to his work. In this scheme, a "Principium Individuii," or self-individuating impulse, manifests itself at ascending scales of organic complexity: a Leibnizian borrowing that Coleridge inflects by making expressly affective. Passion, then, becomes both the means by which simple organisms refine themselves into complex wholes, and the characteristic form of expression that those organisms possess. Simple appetites such as hunger and thirst give rise naturally to a more complex series of phenomena, which he describes through the neologism "impetites"—from the Latin "*impeto*"—motive forces that are still to some degree spontaneous or reactive, yet which also imply a certain intentionality. Such a scheme attempts to move toward what Coleridge summarizes, at the midpoint of his essay, as "Act and Passion—Life being [the identity of acting and suffering]."[35]

Coleridge understandably struggled to express this "self-individuating" impulse in the form of a discursive treatise. Such a notion does not only provide a structural counterpart to the prosodic organization that we have observed in "Christabel": it requires a form of expression such as verse for its very realization. Where Coleridge's "On the Passions" struggles gamely to explain the formation of organic life by virtue of affective diversification, so too have we witnessed the bare sounding of the verse line give rise to voices (animate, animal, human) of increasing complexity, in a process that is similarly, irreducibly affective. The voicing of which we are made self-conscious precisely is the identity of acting and suffering.

Yet the rhythmic unfolding of "Christabel" perhaps also helps account for the subsequent failure of Coleridge's attempted systematic philosophy of affect. His "impetites" were all along intended to provide a bridge to the third and most complex stage of affective development, the distinctively human passions. But the apparently baser, transitional organic forms already seem to have achieved a remarkable level of affective complexity: indeed, Coleridge locates in them "the Incident of the highest Form of Life."[36] Coleridge calls this self-reflexive moment variously "*Sehnsucht*," "*desiderium*," "*taedium vitae*," and "Storgè"—the exoticism of these importations betraying the difficulty of definition. In what they have in common (a sense of want, lack, or longing), we can note the clear influence of Spinoza's own account of the passions, which proceed through "striving"; interestingly, however, Coleridge's *taedium vitae* suggests a passivity that Spinoza is keen to excise.

At the very point that Coleridge seems capable of an interestingly modified Spinozistic materialism, however, his precarious table of feeling breaks down—to become, in his own words, "a *Miss*." For if the lower level of organic life implied by the "impetites" already possesses *Sehnsucht*, possesses an "incompleteness [that] in itself may pass into a sense [. . .] a dim semi-sense of itself,"[37] what makes the human passions qualitatively distinct? With bare longing, life has already begun, as Coleridge himself hesitatingly concedes: "Life has an analogon of reflection. Life quodam modo [in a certain way] reflects on itself."[38]

Here too, "Christabel" had foreknown the philosophical problems that Coleridge posed himself toward the end of his life. Where "On the Passions" breaks off at the very moment that it was supposed to enumerate distinctively human affect, so Coleridge's poem had promised to communicate a form of "passion" that would be both transparent and readily communicable. The material form that transmitted the message, verse, was on this account to be no more than a transmitter, of a "transition" of feeling that somehow occurred before or beyond it. But "Christabel," too, had already demonstrated a material world of far greater complexity, where the beating clock, moaning wind and echoing bitches did more than merely anticipate the distinctively human voices that emerge. The rhythm of "Christabel" is irreducibly various, and part of that variety concerns the manner in which it actively forms, in addition to being formed by, passion. In this respect, Coleridge's poem enacts what philosophies of affect—including his own—struggle to articulate in propositional terms. In responding to that historical need, it offers a compelling instance of critical rhythm.

Notes

1. George Saintsbury, *History of English Prosody: From the Twelfth Century to the Present Day*, 3 vols. (London: Macmillan, 1906), 3:74–83.

2. T. S. Omond, *English Metrists* (Oxford: Clarendon, 1921), 115.

3. Both Saintsbury and Omond take "Christabel" to explode the lingering belief in foot-based, quantitative modes of metrical analysis; by contrast, Ada F. Snell's paper on "Christabel" (the one extensive scansion of the poem, to which I will subsequently refer) holds that, despite Coleridge's bluster, the overwhelming majority of "Christabel" resolves itself into iambic lines, with occasional anapaestic substitutions. Snell's *Pause: A Study of its Nature and its Rhythmical Function in Verse, Especially Blank Verse* (Ann Arbor, Mich.: Ann Arbor Press, 1918) develops such a view, asserting that the English foot is an "objective" truth.

4. Samuel Taylor Coleridge, *Poetical Works*, ed. J. C. C Mays, 2 vols., each in two parts (Princeton, N.J.: Princeton University Press, 2001) 1, pt. 1, 483; hereafter PW.

5. Coleridge, *PW*, 482–83 .

6. Except where stated, I quote from the Bollingen *Poetic Works* text. In this above extract, I substitute the more commonly printed line 3 ("Tu—whit!—Tu—whoo!"), which has the advantage of engaging more directly the questions of vocal stress, and the subsequent critical debates around it.

7. Omond, *English Metrists*, 117. Omond extrapolates from such examples that Coleridge's poem—unlike the overwhelming majority of prosodic theory from the previous century—apprehends "time," rather than quantity or accent. I depart from Omond by stressing those moments where the question whether or not we accent a syllable (and hence, the temporal structure) is more indeterminate, and what the apprehension of that indeterminacy means for the affective experience of the poem.

8. *The Collected Letters of Samuel Taylor Coleridge*, ed. Earl Leslie Griggs, 6 vols. (Oxford: Clarendon Press, 1956–71), 3:112. Having promised to write two unforthcoming explanatory essays on "Christabel" ("on the Praeternatural—and on Metre"), such tentative formulations were common. A brief, inconclusive fragment on the metre of "Christabel" does exist, in *Shorter Works and Fragments*, ed. H. J. Jackson and J. R. de J. Jackson, 2 vols. (Princeton, N.J.: Princeton University Press, 1995), 1:441–42; hereafter SW&F.

9. See, respectively, Coleridge, *PW* 1, pt. 2, 807–8; *PW* 1, pt. 1, 527–30.

10. Ada F. Snell, "The Metre of *Christabel*," *The Fred Newton Scott anniversary papers, contributed by former students and colleagues of Professor Scott and presented to him in celebration of his thirty-eighth year of distinguished service in the University of Michigan, 1888–1926* (Chicago: The University of Chicago Press, 1929), 93–115.

11. Here, for reasons that will become apparent in my later discussion of the variant manuscript versions and the marking (or not) of speech, I am reproducing the 1834 edition rather than the Bollingen composite text.

12. This claim need not exclude a certain carelessness on Coleridge's part; as J. C. C. Mays notes, "[t]hough one would have expected Coleridge to take special care with the punctuation and capitals of *Christabel*, he appears to have submitted the tidiest manuscript (to impress Byron) instead of the manuscript which incorporated his revisions" (*PW* 1, pt. 1, cxiii–cxiv).

13. Mays, introduction to Coleridge, *PW* 1, pt. 1, lxxxiv–lxxxv.

14. The ensuing conclusion to Part One supports this argument: Geraldine returns to a speech that is undesignated by punctuation of any sort, as she casts the spell of ignorance upon her companion (271–78).

15. A. Dwight Culler, "Monodrama and the Dramatic Monologue," *PMLA* 90, no. 3 (May 1975): 366–85.

16. Brennan O'Donnell, "The 'Invention' of a Metre: 'Christabel' Metre as Fact and Fiction," *Journal of English and Germanic Philology*, 100, no. 4 (2001): 511; Attridge develops his argument at length in *The Rhythms of English Poetry* (London; New York: Longman, 1982).

17. Omond, *English Metrists*, 117.

18. See, *inter alia*, O'Donnell; Charles I. Patterson, "An Unidentified Criticism by Coleridge Related to 'Christabel,'" *PMLA* 67 (December 1952): 973–88.

19. The divergence of these positions crystallized in the exchange that followed Attridge's review of *Rhythmic Phrasing in English Verse* (*Poetics Today* 17, no. 1 [Spring, 1996]: 9–27). For Cureton's response, see 29–50 of the same journal; and for Attridge's increasingly exasperated response to that response, see 51–54. For Attridge's reticent treatment of the relation of rhythm to linguistic and biological essentialism, see his "Rhythm in English Poetry," in *New Literary History*, 21, no. 4 (Autumn 1990): 1015–37.

20. Amittai F. Aviram, *Telling Rhythm: Body and Meaning in Poetry* (Ann Arbor: University of Michigan Press, 1994), 10.

21. Caroline Levine, "Rhythms, Poetic and Political: The Case of Elizabeth Bishop Browning," *Victorian Poetry* 49, no. 2 (Summer 2011): 238.

22. Ibid., 248.

23. Ibid., 250.

24. Susan James, *Passion and Action: The Emotions in Seventeenth-Century Philosophy* (Oxford: Oxford University Press, 1997).

25. Thomas Dixon, *From Passions to Emotions: the Creation of a Secular Psychological Category* (Cambridge: Cambridge University Press, 2003).

26. Dixon in fact claims that the transition from scholastic to materialist conceptions makes affect *more* passive: "[w]hile passions and affections had been thought of by faculty psychologists as 'active powers,' Brownian emotions were passive products of the operations of the laws of the physics and chemistry of the mind" (ibid., 134). Yet Wordsworth's attempt to "activate" passion, as we shall see below, challenge such a broad claim; from the position of the experiencing subject (rather than the receptive brain), affect is increasingly an active means of self-expression, rather than a dominating influence (fate, humors, etc.) to which one is subjected.

27. David Hume, *A Treatise of Human Nature* (Oxford: Clarendon, 1967), 415.

28. James, *Passion and Action*, 150.

29. Benedictus de Spinoza, *The Ethics and Other Works*, trans. Edwin M. Curley (Princeton, N.J.: Princeton University Press), 197. One of Spinoza's signal innovations in this section is to introduce a notion of "active affects"—a notion that would be paradoxical from a traditional scholastic, or even Cartesian, perspective. Yet such

a formulation has the effect both of retaining passivity as the (negative) criterion by which affects are to be judged, and rendering certain affects negative as a result. "Sadness," for instance, is a negative affect for Spinoza insofar as it limits man's capacity to act—the action to which it does (somewhat paradoxically) give rise can de directed only to the overcoming of that sadness. Here we might contrast Wordsworth's later interest in the way in which such states ("torpor") can be both absorptive and impulsive.

30. "The Passions: An Ode for Music," *The Works of William Collins*, ed. Richard Wendorf and Charles Ryskamp (Oxford: Oxford University Press, 1979), 49–53.

31. Saintsbury, *A History of English Prosody* 2:515.

32. *The Poetical Works of William Wordsworth*, ed. E. de Selincourt, rev. Helen Darbishire, 5 vols. (Oxford: Clarendon Press, 1952–59), 3:81–82.

33. William Wordsworth, *The Borderers*, ed. Robert Osborn (Ithaca, N.Y.: Cornell University Press, 1982), act 3, v. 60–65.

34. Coleridge, *SW&F*, 2:1419–20.

35. Coleridge, *SW&F* 2:1443. Coleridge writes the phrase in parenthesis in Greek.

36. Coleridge, *SW&F* 2:1434.

37. Coleridge, *SW&F* 2:1438.

38. Coleridge, *SW&F* 2:1427.

Acknowledgments

Like many collective volumes, this has been long in the making and has demanded much of its contributors, who have patiently undertaken revisions over the years. It began life as a three-day seminar on "Rhythm in Lyric, Literary Theory, and Literary History," at the meeting of the American Comparative Literature Association meeting in Vancouver in April, 2011. We thank the authors of the thirteen initial presentations and the participants in three days of lively discussions, which overflowed into mealtimes and convinced us that we had a very promising foundation for an important volume on rhythm. The great editor Helen Tartar, who inspired so many splendid projects in the humanities, was encouraging from the first, and after her tragic death her colleagues at Fordham, especially Tom Lay and his team, have been extraordinarily helpful in bringing this project to fruition. Two anonymous readers for the Press offered a range of pertinent comments that led both to improvements of individual essays and to the expansion of the collection to include powerful contributions by scholars who were not involved in the Vancouver sessions. We are grateful for their participation and for the patience of the original contributors as the project evolved. Haun Saussy, our series editor, advised us and assisted with many of the volume's essays.

The essay by Ewan Jones is reprinted with permission from Cambridge University Press. We also thank Beinecke Library for providing the scan from *The Souls of Black Folk* that appears in Virginia Jackson's essay.

Ben Glaser
Jonathan Culler

Contributors

DEREK ATTRIDGE is the author or editor of twenty-six books on literary theory, poetic form, South African literature, and the writings of James Joyce. His work on poetic form includes *The Experience of Poetry: From Homer's Listeners to Shakespeare's Readers (2019)*, *Moving Words: Forms of English Poetry* (2013), "Rhythm" in the new edition of the *Princeton Encyclopedia of Poetry and Poetics* (2012), *Meter and Meaning* (with Thomas Carper, 2003), *Poetic Rhythm: An Introduction* (1996), and *The Rhythms of English Poetry* (1982).

THOMAS CABLE is Jane Weinert Blumberg Chair Emeritus of English at the University of Texas at Austin. He is the author of *The Meter and Melody of Beowulf* (1974), *The English Alliterative Tradition* (1991), with Albert Baugh, and *A History of the English Language*, 3rd, 4th, and 5th editions (1978-2002). He has also co-edited *The Union of Words and Music in Medieval Poetry* (1991) with R. Baltzer and J. Wimsatt.

JONATHAN CULLER is Class of 1916 Professor of English and Comparative Literature at Cornell University, and an elected member of the American Academy of Arts and Sciences and American Philosophical Society. His books include *Flaubert: The Uses of Uncertainty*, *Structuralist Poetics*, *On Deconstruction*, *The Pursuit of Signs*, *Ferdinand de Saussure*, *Roland Barthes*, *Framing the Sign*, *The Literary in Theory*, *Literary Theory: A Very Short Introduction*, and *Theory of the Lyric*. He has also edited the collections, *The Call of the Phoneme: Puns and the Foundation of Letters, Just Being Difficult: Academic Writing in the Public Arena* (with Kevin Lamb), *Grounds of Comparison: Around the Work of Benedict Anderson* (with

Pheng Cheah), *Structuralism: Critical Concepts*, and *Deconstruction: Critical Concepts*.

NATALIE GERBER is Associate Professor of English at State University of New York, Fredonia. She has recently published the following articles and book chapters: "Getting the Squiggly Tunes Down on the Page: Williams' Triadic-Line Verse and American Intonation," in *Rigor of Beauty: Essays in Commemoration of William Carlos Williams*, "Intonation and the Conventions of Free Verse" (*Style*), "Stress-Based Metrics Revisited" (*Thinking Verse*), and an award winning article in the Wallace Stevens Journal on "Stevens' Mixed-Breed Versifying." She is also the editor of several special issues of the *Wallace Stevens Journal*.

BEN GLASER is Assistant Professor of English at Yale University. Recent articles include "Modernist Scansion: Robert Frost's Loose Iambics" (*ELH*) and "Folk Iambics, Intertextuality, and Sterling Brown's *Outline for the Study of the Poetry of American Negroes*" (*PMLA*). His book project is entitled *Modernism's Metronome: Meter and Twentieth Century Poetics*.

VIRGINIA JACKSON is UCI Endowed Chair in Rhetoric in the Departments of English and Comparative Literature at University of California, Irvine. She is the author of *Dickinson's Misery: A Theory of Lyric Reading*, which won the Christian Gauss Award, and Modern Language Association Prize for a First Book. She is also the editor of *On Periodization: Selected Papers from the English Institute* and *The Lyric Theory Reader* (with Yopie Prins). Her latest book, *Before Modernism: The Invention of American Poetry*, is forthcoming from Princeton University Press.

SIMON JARVIS is an independent writer and critic. He is the author of *Wordsworth's Philosophic Song*, *Adorno: a Critical Introduction* (1998; reprinted, 2003), *Scholars and Gentlemen: Shakespearean Textual Criticism and Representations of Scholarly Labour, 1725-1765* (1995) and the editor of *Theodor W. Adorno: Critical Evaluations in Cultural Theory* (2006), *Rethinking Beauty*, and a special issue of *Diacritics* (Spring 2002).

EWAN JONES is University Lecturer in 19th Century English Literature, at University of Cambridge. He has published *Coleridge and the Philosophy of Poetic Form* (2014) and has several forthcoming articles: "The Sonic Organization of 'Kubla Khan,'" in *Studies in Romanticism*, "Pretty Vacant: Shelley's Metrical Stops," in *Romantic Circles Praxis*, and "Coventry Patmore's Corpus," in *ELH*. He is currently at work on a book on the historical development of the concept of rhythm in the 19th century.

CONTRIBUTORS / 301

ERIN KAPPELER is Assistant Professor of English at Missouri State University. Her articles include "Editing America: Nationalism and the New Poetry" (*Modernism/Modernity*) and "The Georgian Poets and the Genteel Tradition," with Meredith Martin, in the *Wiley-Blackwell Companion to Modernist Poetry*. She is working on a book manuscript entitled *Shaping Free Verse: American Prosody and Poetics 1880-1920* and the NEH-funded project "Everyday Laureates: Community Poetry in New England, 1865-1900."

MEREDITH MARTIN is Associate Professor of English and Director of the Center for Digital Humanities at Princeton University. She also directs the Princeton Prosody Archive, a full-text searchable database of materials about the study of poetry and language. She created and directs the Princeton Prosody Archive, a full-text searchable database of materials about the study of poetry and language. She wrote *The Rise and Fall of Meter, Poetry and English National Culture, 1860-1930*), which won the MLA Prize for a First Book and the Warren Brooks Prize for Literary Criticism. Her current book project is titled *Before We Were Disciplines*.

DAVID NOWELL SMITH is Senior Lecturer in the School of Literature, Creative Writing, and Drama at the University of East Anglia, and editor of the journal *Thinking Verse*. His books include *Sounding/Silence: Martin Heidegger at the Limits of Poetics* (2013) and *On Voice in Poetry: The Work of Animation* (2015).

YOPIE PRINS is Irene Butter Collegiate Professor of English and Comparative Literature at the University of Michigan. She is the author of *Victorian Sappho* (1999) and *Ladies' Greek: Victorian Translations of Tragedy* (2017), and co-editor of *The Lyric Theory Reader: A Critical Anthology* (2014) and *Dwelling in Possibility: Women Poets and Critics on Poetry* (1997). She has another book in progress, *Voice Inverse: Meter and Music in Victorian Poetry*.

HAUN SAUSSY is University Professor in the Department of Comparative Literature at the University of Chicago. He has authored *The Problem of a Chinese Aesthetic* (1993), *Great Walls of Discourse and Other Adventures in Cultural China* (2001), *The Ethnography of Rhythm: Orality and Its Technologies* (2016), and *Translation as Citation: Zhuangzi Inside Out* (2017). Edited works include *Chinese Women Poets, An Anthology of Poetry and Criticism from Ancient Times to 1911* (1999), *Comparative Literature in an Era of Globalization* (2004), *Sinographies: Writing China* (with Steven Yao and Eric Hayot, 2005), *Chinese Walls in Time and Space* (with Roger des Forges, Chiao-mei Liu, and Gao Minglu, 2009), *Partner to the Poor: A Paul Farmer Reader* (2010), and Ferdinand de Saussure's *Course in General Linguistics* (with Perry Meisel, 2011). Together with César Dominguez and Darío Villanueva, he wrote *Introducing Comparative Literature* (2015).

Index

Abraham, Nicolas, 22
absolute rhythm, 90, 99, 120, 240
accentual verse, 9, 121, 159, 209, 253, 275
accentual-syllabic verse, 27, 131, 154, 156, 167, 252, 285
adonic line, 251–53, 262–63
Adorno, Theodor, 62, 91–92, 95
affect: philosophy of, 288–93
African-American poetry, 5, 10, 14
alienation, 56, 112, 144
allegories of rhythm and meter, 32–33, 251–54, 262, 264, 266
American poetics, 87, 93, 97–103, 233–45
American poetry, 22, 87, 129–31, 134–36, 139–42, 144, 213
Anderson, Benedict, 96–97
Aristotle, 44
Armstrong, Isobel, 6
art: distinctiveness of, 68–69; truth content of, 62–63
Attridge, Derek, 3, 4, 7, 12, 23–24, 29, 88–89, 153–73, 181, 183, 186, 285–87
Auden, Wystan, 1–3, 34
Austin, Mary, 129, 140–44
Aviram, Amittai, 31–32, 33, 254, 287–88

Bach, J. S., 180, 191–92
Barham, Thomas, 254–55
Barthes, Roland, 36–37, 45–46
bathybius, 128, 144–45
Baudelaire, Charles, 43
beat, 277–78; complexity of, 274–75, 279; silent, 29–30, 157, 159, 179, 182–84
Benjamin, Walter, 43, 114
Benveniste, Émile, 44–48, 51
Bergson, Henri, 121–22
Beum, Robert, 197–99, 213
birdsong, 238–39
Blake, William: "Nurse's Song," 170–71; "The Sick Rose," 27, 30–31; "The Tyger," 24–27, 31–34
Blanchot, Maurice, 48, 50, 52–53
Blasing, Mutlu, 7, 33–35
Boaz, Franz, 140
body: techniques of, 109–25. *See also* rhythm: as bodily
Borges, Jorge Luis, 176
Bradley, Henry, 202, 203
Braithwaite, Kamau, 14
Bridges, Robert, 13, 199–209, 211–14
Brogan, T. V. F., 27, 175–76, 251

Brooke, Rupert, 118
Brooks, Cleanth, and Robert Penn Warren, 87–88
Brooks, Van Wyck, 139–40, 144
Browning, Elizabeth Barrett, 287
Browning, Robert: *Sordello*, 11, 60–68, 73–82
Buchanan, George, 257–58
Byron, Lord, 81, 188, 286

Cable, Thomas, 10, 13, 174–96
Campbell, Matthew, 79–80
Carson, Anne, 266, 268–71
Cavitch, Max, 89
Chatman, Seymour, 175–76, 245
Chaucer, Geoffrey, 153, 174, 286
Child, Francis, 91
Chinese poetry, 118–22, 203, 211
cinema, 111, 113–15
cinquain, 200, 208–9, 211–13, 215
Clare, John, 225
Clay, E. R., 186
clock in the mind, 184, 188
cognitive science, 13, 177, 184–90
cognitive studies of sound, 223, 237–40
Cohen, Michel, 130
Coleridge, 13–14, 18, 161, 182–84, 223; "Christabel," 274–95
Collins, William, 289
common measure, 30, 183, 188
Corn, Alfred, 15, 253–54
counterpoint, 109, 231, 233, 236
Cowper, William, 251
Cox, Edward, 263
Crapsey, Adelaide, 13, 200, 208–15
critical rhythm, 3–4, 13–14, 42, 61–63, 72, 286, 288, 293
Culler, A. Dwight, 284
Culler, Jonathan, 3, 7, 11, 21–39, 55
cultural identity, 99, 129–30, 135–36, 139–41; as effect of rhythm, 94, 131–32, 136, 142
culture: concept of, 88, 90, 103
Cureton, Richard, 30–31, 35, 38, 56–57, 287

Dallas, E. S., 133
Dante Aligheri, 74–78
De Man, Paul, 114
Deleuze, Gilles, 55; and Felix Guattari, 42, 50
Democritus, 46
Derrida, Jacques, 48–49
Descartes, René, 288, 291
Dickinson, Emily, 30, 182–83, 188
différance, 49
Dixon, Thomas, 288
dolnik, 3, 12, 24, 157–73; differentiated from accentual-syllabic, 167; two varieties of, 163–72
double offbeats, 161, 163–65, 166, 168, 181–82, 184–85
Dreyfus, Hubert, 187, 190
Du Bois, W. E. B., 100–2
duple rhythms, 28, 31, 156, 163–72, 181, 189, 279

Easthope, Anthony, 34
Edwards, Brent, 102
Eliot, T. S., 122, 200
epic and lyric contrasted, 256, 261–62, 264–65
Erkkila, Betsy, 129
ethnopoetics, 146
evolutionary models, 106–9, 130–34, 140, 144–46

Fenollosa, Ernest, 119–20
Fields, James, 77
Figueroa, John, 14
FitzGerald, Edward, 135
foot-prosody: deficiencies of, 23–31
foot-substitution, 31, 38, 184
four-beat rhythm, 12, 23–30, 155–60, 275–86; and collective subject, 34. *See also* dolnik
Fowler, Roger, 65, 76
free verse, 69, 82, 87, 98, 121, 128–32, 138, 140, 142–44, 198, 202–3, 224, 232; and freedom, 134, 136, 203

French stress patterns, 123, 225–26
French versification 121–23, 138, 148–49, 202, 223
Frost, Robert, 13, 24, 223–46; claims about sound, 224–233; compared with Stevens, 226–39; compared with Williams, 229–33; legacy of, 233–37; performance of poems, 232–35, 245
Fry, Stephen, 25
Frye, Northrop, 96–97
Fussell, Paul, 2, 7, 38

Gallagher, Shaun, 187, 190
generative metrics, 27–28, 175–76
George, Stefan, 54
Gerber, Natalie, 7, 9, 13, 27–28, 33, 213, 223–46
Gielgud, Sir John, 170
Goldfarb, Lisa, 223
Golston, Michael, 89
Gosse, Edmund, 128, 144–45
Gower, John, 155
Grenfell, Bernard, and Arthur Hunt, 248, 260–62
Grimm brothers, 92
Guest, Edwin, 17
Gummere, Francis, 10, 12, 87–105, 110, 132–33, 136–37, 141–42, 145, 202, 209

Habermas, Jürgen, 287
habitus, 110
haiku, 36, 212–13
Hall, Jason, 201
Halle, Morris, 175–76
Hardie, W. R., 259–60
Hartman, Geoffrey, 92
Hegel, G. W. F., 41, 99, 112
Heidegger, Martin, 40, 43, 44–48, 50–54
Helmholtz, Hermann von, 43
Herder, Johann Gottfried, 12, 91–92, 96
Herrick, Robert, 225
historical prosody, 6, 15–16, 131, 153, 251, 254–66
Hölderlin, Friedrich, 41, 43, 53

Hollander, John, 6, 8, 9, 215, 253, 266
Holmes, Oliver, Wendell, 15
Homeric hexameters, 118, 256, 261–62, 264
Hopkins, Gerard Manley, 34, 113, 199, 201, 206, 213; "Inversnaid," 159–62, 167–69
Horne, R. H., 64
Hulme, T. E. 121
Hume, David, 288–89
Husserl, Edmund, 186–87, 189–91
Huxley, Thomas, 145

imagined community, 12, 96–102
imagism, 121–22, 140, 198, 203, 211–14, 232
incantation, 26, 65, 169
intonational contours, 13, 31, 35, 65, 77, 227–31, 235–37, 239–40; expressive force of 228, 230, 233, 235–36; opposed to syntax, 231, 236
isoverbal prosody, 197–98

Jackson, Virginia, 5, 10, 12, 87–105, 132
Jaji, Tsitsi, 14,
James, Susan, 288–89
James, William, 116, 186–87, 189
Jarvis, Simon, 11, 60–83
jazz rhythms, 141–42, 180, 184
Johnstone, Maxine, 191
Jones, Ewan, 13–14, 274–95
Jones, P. M., 148

Kant, Immanuel, 11, 42, 63, 68–73, 82; on prosody, 68–69, 72
Kappeler, Erin, 9, 11, 12, 90, 128–50
Keats, John, 67, 74, 79–80, 232
Kenner, Hugh, 215
Keyser, Samuel Jay, 175–76
Kilmer, Joyce, 248–49, 260, 262–63
Kinsella, John, 265
Kittredge, George Lyman, 110
Kristeva, Julia, 49–51

Lacoue-Labarthe, Philippe, 5, 43, 49
Laforgue, Jules, 122

Lanier, Sidney, 200, 233
Leavis, F. R., 81
Leroi-Gourhan, André, 112
Levine, Caroline, 4–5, 287–88
lexical stress, modulation of, 54, 224–26, 228
limericks, 29–30, 34
Lindsay, Vachel, 140, 142, 235
line: overestimation of, 177, 181–82; temporality of, 176, 186–88; and written representations, 176, 182, 190–93, 247
line and design: war between, 68, 79–82
line breaks, 65, 205, 213–14, 236, 283
linguistics and prosody, 6, 8, 27, 175, 201, 209, 212
London, Justin, 180
Longfellow, Henry Wadsworth, 91
loose iambic, 24, 159, 181
Lowell, Amy, 9, 129, 137–44
Luhmann, Niklas, 88
lyric: as social or individualistic, 34, 89, 95–98, 102, 130–33; utopian horizon of, 9, 92, 94–95, 99, 139, 144, 223–24
lyricization, 16, 99

MacDougall, Robert, 116
MacPhail, Scott, 130
Mallarmé, Stéphane, 42, 43, 48, 52–53, 223
marching cadence, 36, 110–13, 118–19, 202, 262–65
Marey, Etienne-Jules, 114–15
Marlowe, Christopher, 76
Martin, Meredith, 11, 13, 98–99, 118, 131, 197–220, 251
Masters, Edgar Lee, 142, 143
Matthiessen, F. O., 140, 145
Mauss, Marcel, 12, 110–13, 116–17
Mays, J. C. C., 282
McGuiness, Andy, 189
measurement, 13, 192–93, 213–14; of movement, 113–15; of perception, 115–16, 188–90, 201, 210–11, 214; of sound, 115, 125, 201

Melillo, John, 270
melodic accent, 227–38
melodics, 76–80
Mendelsohn, Daniel, 247
Meredith, George, 183–84
Merleau-Ponty, Maurice, 187–88, 191
Meschonnic, Henri, 7, 31, 35, 50, 51
meta-metrics, 251–66
meter: abstraction of, 2, 9–10, 33, 71–72, 174; history of, 4, 6, 13, 131, 153–57, 174–75, 197–215, 251, 274, 277; linguistic approaches to, 175–76; relation to rhythm, 2, 3, 6–11, 26–29, 33–35, 42, 44, 71–72, 199, 251
metrical imaginary, 251, 254, 257–59, 266
metrical rhyme, 65
Meynell, Alice, 148, 211
Middleton, Peter, 223–34
military-metrical complex, 11, 98, 118. *See also* marching cadence
Mill, John Stuart, 96, 98, 99, 128, 132–33
Miller, Marion, 263–65
Milton, John, 24, 79, 97, 203, 206, 209–10
modernist poetry, 7, 8, 9, 13, 117, 122, 129, 144–46, 198–99, 202, 223–40, 260, 265, 266
modernist prosody. 198–201
Monroe, Harriet, 90, 199
Moore, Marianne, 197, 200, 213
music: analogies with poetry, 4, 26, 89, 107–9, 157, 179–84, 223, 289; fantasized, 102, 248–49, 256–57; perception of, 176–77, 185–89, 239; and poetic tradition, 5, 36, 42, 157; and rhythm, 5, 28–29, 36, 42, 89, 180, 185–86, 189–92; settings of poetry to, 105–7, 163; study of, 13, 116, 185–92
Myklebust, Nicholas, 189

Nagy, Gregory, 74
Native American poetry, 140–42
Negro folk song, 5, 100–2
neo-Miltonics, 203, 208

neuroscience, 177, 186, 191
New Criticism, 9, 130, 174, 177, 191
New Poets, 140
Newdick, Robert, 232–33
Norton Anthology of Poetry, 23
nursery rhymes, 21, 26, 29–30, 32, 34, 157–59, 163–67, 209

O'Donnell, Brennan, 285–86
Obbink, Dirk, 247
Omond, T. S. 200, 274, 277, 285
ontology, 9–10, 42, 45–46
oral poetry, 10, 130
Overy, Kate, 189

passion: relation to rhythm, 248, 276–78, 282, 286, 288–93
passions: theory of, 288–93
Pater, Walter, 40
Patmore, Coventry, 133, 192, 200–1
Patterson, William, 137–44
Péguy, Charles, 55
phenomenology, 12–13, 112–13, 177, 185–88
Pickford, Mary, 111
Plato, 46, 256
Playfair, Wiliam, 114
pleasure of rhythm, 3, 22, 34, 36–37, 192
Poema Morale, 182
poetry: and race, 12, 14, 87–103, 107–8, 117, 129, 137–44; stories of origin, 44–46, 89–91, 94–95, 106–10, 130, 145, 248–59
Pope, Alexander, 209–10
postcolonial rhythm, 14
Pound, Ezra, 1, 7, 59, 90, 99, 122, 137, 143, 198–200, 203, 208, 265; "Cathay," 118–21
Powell, Jim, 266–68
Princeton Prosody Archive, 16, 251
Prins, Yopie, 5–6, 13, 131, 247–73
Propp, Valdimir, 92
prosodic fantasies, 144–46
prosodic hierarchy, 228
psycholinguistics, 237, 241

punctuation: and rhythm, 77–78; and voicing, 283–84

quantitative verse, 198–203, 250, 251, 253, 259–64; versus syllabics, 200–1

Ramsay, Paul, 213
Rankine, Claudia, 55
rap, 29, 37
religion, 70–71, 124
Reynolds, David, 129
rhythm: and American identity, 95, 97–98, 129–31, 135–44; as bodily, 5, 15, 22, 28, 35, 36, 40, 108–9, 117, 133, 140, 145, 180, 185, 186, 190–92, 211, 253–54; centrality to poetry, 29, 88, 286, 289; as communal, 90–103, 130, 140, 142–44; cultural character of, 110–17, 130–36; definition of, 14, 40–45, 88, 108; determining force of, 22, 178–79; disruption by translation, 118–23; distinguished from meter, 6–11, 26–27, 28, 35, 42, 71–72, 172–73, 184–85, 191, 199, 251, 275; equated with poetry, 87–88, 100; and evolution, 132, 144–46; Greek concept of, 44–46, 49, 50, 53, 55; idealization of, 251; independence from meaning, 28, 33, 72; and interpretation, 26–27, 31–32; and meaning, 7, 31–32, 35, 37, 49, 178–79, 254; memorability of, 11, 21–23, 26, 37; as natural culture, 88–90, 95; ontology of, 9–10, 14, 175–57, 188, 190; politics of its history, 55, 88–92, 97–99, 131–37, 139–46, 288; primitive, 12, 94–95, 108, 140–42, 146, 257, 259; and race, 12, 14, 87–103, 107–8, 117, 129, 137–44; sciences of, 12, 115–16, 138–39
rhythmics, 89–90
Robertson, Lisa, 55
Rosapelly, Charles, 115
Rothenberg, Jerome, 146
Roussel, Raymond, 55

Rousselot, Pierre-Jean, 115
Rowbotham, Frederick, 256–57
Rudy, Jason, 133

Sainte-Beuve, Charles Augustin, 93
Saintsbury, George, 10, 184, 209, 274, 289
Sandburg, Carl, 140, 142, 143
Santayana, George, 149
Sapphics, 247–73; recreated in English, 251–56, 262–69; twentieth-century accounts of, 259–71
Sappho, 6, 13, 247–73; figure for lyric, 248–49; fragment #16, 260–66; Victorian invention of, 250, 254
Saussy, Haun, 12, 13, 106–27
Schopenhauer, Arthur, 41
Schwartz, Elias, 185
Scott, Clive, 28, 57
Scott, Fred, 129, 131–39, 143–44, 146
Scott, Sir Walter, 286
Scripture, E. W., 209
Senghor, Leopold, 14
Shakespeare, William, 28, 180, 183–83, 187, 191, 236
Shelley, Mary, 177, 179
Shelley, Percy, 79, 81, 161, 177–80, 183, 187, 288
Shklovsky, Viktor, 113
short meter, 29–30
Sidney, Sir Philip, 9
Skelton, John, 155–56
Smith, David Nowell, 5, 11, 40–59
Snell, Ada, 278–79
song, 12, 22–24, 26, 34–37, 74, 77, 100–2, 156–57, 238, 253; imagined, 248–50, 255–59; as origin, 92, 108–10
sounds: belief in, 223–33, 239–40; primacy of, 223–24; value beyond the semantic, 223, 226–27, 239–40
spacing, 48–49, 214, 270, 277–78, 283
Spahr, Juliana, 55
Spencer, Herbert, 106–9
Spinoza, Benedictus de, 288–90, 292

sprung rhythm, 206, 213
Stallworthy, John, 23
Steele, Joshua, 200
Steele, Timothy, 6, 198–99, 233, 236
Stein, Gertrude, 131
Stevens, Wallace, 13, 223–29
Stewart, Susan, 130
stressers versus timers, 175–77, 213
Surrey, Henry, Earl of, 154
Swift, Jonathan, 69
Swinburne, Algernon, 66–67, 77, 80, 181–82, 184, 188, 255–56
syllabic verse, 13, 197–215; as escape, 202–3; rhythm of, 199, 205
Symons, Arthur, 101–2
Symthe, Percy, 135
syntax: evolution of 238–39; and intonation, 228, 231, 236; relation to rhythm, 26, 76–77, 82, 213

Tarlinskaja, Marina, 159, 184
teaching of poetry, 37
temporality, 44–52; of poetry, 1, 26, 54–55, 185–88
Tennyson, Alfred Lord, 169–70
Thomas, Dylan, 197
Thompson, John, 7–10
throng: primitive, 12, 91–95, 106, 109–10, 133, 137, 140, 202
timing versus stressing, 175–77, 213
tone: different from intonation, 235–37
Trakl, Georg, 52
Trantner, John, 265–66
triple rhythm, 12, 102, 156, 161–71, 181, 189
Tsur, Reuven, 186
Tucker, Herbert, 80
Tunison, Joseph, 257–58
Turco, Lewis, 197–98

Untermeyer, Louis, 212, 215

Valéry, Paul, 6, 22, 36, 223
Verrier, Paul, 209

vers libre, 120–23, 137–38, 231
verse: self-reflexivity of, 277, 286; specificity of, 63
Vezey, Stuart, 170
Victorian metrical theory, 254–60
virtual beat, 29–30, 157, 159, 179, 182–84
visual form, 212, 215
vocalization, 36, 134, 279–81; plurality of, 274–75, 278, 284
voice: philosophical significance of, 275, 292
Voigt, Ellen, 238

Wagner, Richard, 40, 41–42
Walcott, Derek, 14,
walking bass, 179–180, 184, 192
walking, 180, 185, 191; culturally differentiated, 110–13
Wallaschek, Richard, 116
Weaver, Bennett, 177–79
Webster, Jean, 211–12
Weeks, Mary, 143–44
Welsh, Andrew, 26
West, Cornel, 102
Wetzsteon, Rachel, 252–54
Wharton, Henry, 255–56

White, John Williams, 259
Whitman, Walt, 11, 12, 97–99, 122–23, 128–50; prosodic innovations of, 129, 131–32, 134, 136, 144; failure of, 133, 135, 139, 141–43; Whitman studies, 128–50
Williams, William Carlos, 13, 117, 197–200, 202, 213–15, 223–24, 239–40; compared with Frost, 229–35; "The Red Wheelbarrow," 198, 213–15
Wimsatt, W. K., 8; and Monroe Beardsley, 10, 174–76, 185, 187, 190–93
Winters, Ivor, 199, 207–8
Wolford, John, and Daniel Karlin, 82
Woodworth, R. S., 116
Woolf, Virginia, 119
Wordsworth, William, 7, 10, 77, 176, 223, 286, 290–91
Wright, George T., 154–55
Wyatt, Thomas, 9, 153–57, 159, 167

Yearsley, David, 180
Yeats, W. B., 21, 114, 182

Zhirmunsky, Mikhail, 72

VERBAL ARTS: STUDIES IN POETICS

Lazar Fleishman and Haun Saussy, series editors

Kiene Brillenburg Wurth, *Between Page and Screen: Remaking Literature Through Cinema and Cyberspace*
Jacob Edmond, *A Common Strangeness: Contemporary Poetry, Cross-Cultural Encounter, Comparative Literature*
Christophe Wall-Romana, *Cinepoetry: Imaginary Cinemas in French Poetry*
Marc Shell, *Talking the Walk & Walking the Talk: A Rhetoric of Rhythm*
Ryan Netzley, *Lyric Apocalypse: Milton, Marvell, and the Nature of Events*
Ilya Kliger and Boris Maslov (eds.), *Persistent Forms: Explorations in Historical Poetics*. Foreword by Eric Hayot
Ross Chambers, *An Atmospherics of the City: Baudelaire and the Poetics of Noise*
Haun Saussy, *The Ethnography of Rhythm: Orality and Its Technologies*. Foreword by Olga Solovieva
Andrew Hui, *The Poetics of Ruins in Renaissance Literature*
Peter Szendy, *Of Stigmatology: Punctuation as Experience*. Translated by Jan Plug
Ben Glaser and Jonathan Culler (eds.), *Critical Rhythm: The Poetics of a Literary Life Form*

www.ingramcontent.com/pod-product-compliance
Lightning Source LLC
Chambersburg PA
CBHW030434300426
44112CB00009B/1001